Lecture Notes in Computer Science 15713

Founding Editors

Gerhard Goos
Juris Hartmanis

Series Editors

The series Lecture Notes in Computer Science (LNCS), including its subseries Lecture Notes in Artificial Intelligence (LNAI) and Lecture Notes in Bioinformatics (LNBI), has established itself as a medium for the publication of new developments in computer science and information technology research, teaching, and education.

LNCS enjoys close cooperation with the computer science R & D community, the series counts many renowned academics among its volume editors and paper authors, and collaborates with prestigious societies. Its mission is to serve this international community by providing an invaluable service, mainly focused on the publication of conference and workshop proceedings and postproceedings. LNCS commenced publication in 1973.

Carmen Santoro · Albrecht Schmidt ·
Maristella Matera · Andrea Bellucci
Editors

End-User Development

10th International Symposium, IS-EUD 2025
Munich, Germany, June 16–18, 2025
Proceedings

Springer

Editors
Carmen Santoro
CNR-ISTI
Pisa, Italy

Maristella Matera
Politecnico di Milano
Milan, Italy

Albrecht Schmidt
Ludwig-Maximilians-Universität München
Munich, Germany

Andrea Bellucci
Universidad Carlos III de Madrid
Madrid, Spain

ISSN 0302-9743 ISSN 1611-3349 (electronic)
Lecture Notes in Computer Science
ISBN 978-3-031-95451-1 ISBN 978-3-031-95452-8 (eBook)
https://doi.org/10.1007/978-3-031-95452-8

This Springer imprint is published by the registered company Springer Nature Switzerland AG
The registered company address is: Gewerbestrasse 11, 6330 Cham, Switzerland

Preface

Welcome to the Proceedings of the 10th International Symposium on End-User Development (IS-EUD 2025), organised at the Ludwig-Maximilians-Universität München (Germany) and held during June 16–18, 2025. IS-EUD is a biennial event that gathers researchers interested in extending knowledge about how to design End-User Development (EUD) technologies and provide scientific accounts of phenomena surrounding EUD practices.

EUD aims to empower end-users who are not necessarily experts in software development to create software to address their specific needs. The goal is to foster greater autonomy, creativity, and contextual relevance in software use, especially in domains where users possess deep domain knowledge but lack formal programming expertise. While originally framed around enabling users to engage with software development, EUD as a field has increasingly expanded to include the customization and configuration of complex systems involving artificial intelligence (AI), the Internet of Things (IoT), robotics, and cyber-security. As such, the scope of EUD today reflects a broader vision, one that supports user agency in shaping the behavior of a wide range of intelligent and interactive technologies.

The conference welcomes contributions that describe new, simple, and efficient environments for EUD, propose novel uses of Generative AI (GenAI) to support and enhance EUD practices, explore no-code/low-code paradigms and visual languages that enable users to create software and systems without traditional programming, and describe new processes, methods, and techniques for empowering users to create, modify, and tailor digital artefacts.

IS-EUD 2025 collected research contributions as full papers, short papers, work-in-progress/demos, and doctoral consortium papers that presented topics surrounding:

- Automation, Sustainability, and Smart Environments
- Democratizing AI and Programming
- AI for End-User Empowerment: Personalization and Wellbeing
- EUD Principles, Methodologies, and Participatory Cultures

The Regular and Short Papers track received 25 submissions, all of which underwent a rigorous double-blind review process, with at least three reviewers from the program committee, which eventually led to accepting 13 regular papers and 8 short papers.

The program was opened by the keynote speaker Enkelejda Kasneci, Distinguished Professor for Human-Centered Technologies for Learning at the School of Social Sciences & Technology in München (Germany), who discussed strategies for using large language models for learner-centered EUD, focusing on intuitive design scaffolding, transparent AI interactions, and fostering creative agency. The other invited speaker of the conference was Antonella De Angeli, Professor at the Free University of Bozen-Bolzano (Italy), who discussed how machine speed influences creative EUD, drawing on research with artists to highlight issues of agency, conflict, and ideology.

The program also hosted four workshops: CoPDA 2025 (Cultures of Participation in the Digital Age: Sustainability Perspectives and Frameworks for Making Cultures of Participation Successful), exploring the intersection of sustainability and cultures of participation in diverse contexts; CSE4IA 2025 (Cyber Security Education for Industry and Academia), focusing on major challenges for cybersecurity education due to evolving threats and a shortage of skilled professionals; AI4EUD 2025 (Empowering the End-User — Software Development with LLMs), exploring how GenAI can empower end-user developers to create high-quality software; and A^2ID 2025 (Augmented Artificial Intelligence: a Symbiotic Approach to Enhance Decision-Making), investigating human-AI collaboration in decision-making, aiming to design ethical, trustworthy, and human-centered AI systems that enhance rather than replace human capabilities.

We extend our deepest gratitude to everybody who contributed to the organization of the conference, especially the chairs: Viktorija Paneva and Daniel Tetteroo (Workshop Chairs), Vittoria Frau and Sebastian Feger (Demos and Work in Progress Chairs), Davide Spano, Fabio Paternò, and Stefan Sauer (Doctoral Consortium Chairs), Marco Manca (Proceedings Chair), Evropi Stefanidi (Publicity Chair), and Andrea Esposito (Web Chair).

We finally thank all the authors and reviewers for their commitment and contribution to making the symposium a successful event!

April 2025

Carmen Santoro
Albrecht Schmidt
Andrea Bellucci
Maristella Matera

Organization

General Chairs

Santoro, Carmen	CNR-ISTI, Pisa, Italy
Schmidt, Albrecht	Ludwig Maximilian University of Munich, Germany
Florian Lang	LMU

Program Committee Chairs

Bellucci, Andrea	Carlos III University of Madrid, Spain
Matera, Maristella	Politecnico di Milano, Italy

Program Committee Members

Baez, Marcos	Hochschule Bielefeld University of Applied Sciences and Arts, Germany
Barricelli, Barbara Rita	University of Brescia, Italy
Borsci, Simone	University of Twente, Netherlands
Bottoni, Paolo	Sapienza University of Rome, Italy
Buono, Paolo	University of Bari Aldo Moro, Italy
Chen, Xiaohong	East China Normal University, China
De Russis, Luigi	Politecnico di Torino, Italy
Desolda, Giuseppe	University of Bari Aldo Moro, Italy
Diaz, Paloma	Carlos III University of Madrid, Spain
Esposito, Andrea	University of Bari Aldo Moro, Italy
Feger, Sebastian	Rosenheim Technical University of Applied Sciences, Germany
Fogli, Daniela	University of Brescia, Italy
Frau, Vittoria	University of Aarhus, Denmark
Greco, Francesco	University of Bari Aldo Moro, Italy
Heil, Sebastian	Chemnitz University of Technology, Germany
Kosch, Thomas	Humboldt University of Berlin, Germany
Lanzilotti, Rosa	University of Bari Aldo Moro, Italy
Letondal, Catherine	École Nationale de l'Aviation Civile, France
Locoro, Angela	University of Brescia, Italy

Ludwig, Thomas	University of Hagen, Germany
Maceli, Monica	Pratt Institute, USA
Malizia, Alessio	University of Pisa, Italy
Manca, Marco	CNR-ISTI, Pisa, Italy
Mattioli, Andrea	CNR-ISTI, Pisa, Italy
Monge Roffarello, Alberto	Politecnico di Torino, Italy
Mørch, Anders	University of Oslo, Norway
Onorati, Teresa	Carlos III University of Madrid, Spain
Paternò, Fabio	CNR-ISTI, Pisa, Italy
Piccinno, Antonio	University of Bari Aldo Moro, Italy
Pittarello, Fabio	Ca' Foscari University of Venice, Italy
Ritschel, Nico	University of Illinois Urbana-Champaign, USA
Rossi, Gustavo	National University of La Plata, Argentina
Schenkenfelder, Bernhard	Software Competence Center Hagenberg GmbH, Austria
Spano, Lucio Davide	University of Cagliari, Italy
Stumpf, Simone	University of Glasgow, UK
Tetteroo, Daniel	Eindhoven University of Technology, Netherlands
Turchi, Tommaso	University of Pisa, Italy
Valtolina, Stefano	University of Milan, Italy
Weber, Thomas	Ludwig Maximilian University of Munich, Germany
Winckler, Marco	Côte d'Azur University, France
Yigitbas, Enes	University of Paderborn, Germany

Reviewers

Baez, Marcos	Hochschule Bielefeld University of Applied Sciences and Arts, Germany
Barricelli, Barbara Rita	University of Brescia, Italy
Borsci, Simone	University of Twente, Netherlands
Bottoni, Paolo	Sapienza University of Rome, Italy
Buono, Paolo	University of Bari Aldo Moro, Italy
Chen, Xiaohong	East China Normal University, China
De Russis, Luigi	Politecnico di Torino, Italy
Desolda, Giuseppe	University of Bari Aldo Moro, Italy
Diaz, Paloma	Carlos III University of Madrid, Spain
Esposito, Andrea	University of Bari Aldo Moro, Italy
Feger, Sebastian	Rosenheim Technical University of Applied Sciences, Germany
Figliè, Roberto	University of Pisa, Italy

Fogli, Daniela	University of Brescia, Italy
Frau, Vittoria	University of Aarhus, Denmark
Greco, Francesco	University of Bari Aldo Moro, Italy
Heil, Sebastian	Chemnitz University of Technology, Germany
Kosch, Thomas	Humboldt University of Berlin, Germany
Lanzilotti, Rosa	University of Bari Aldo Moro, Italy
Letondal, Catherine	École Nationale de l'Aviation Civile, France
Locoro, Angela	University of Brescia, Italy
Ludwig, Thomas	University of Hagen, Germany
Maceli, Monica	Pratt Institute, USA
Malizia, Alessio	University of Pisa, Italy
Manca, Marco	CNR-ISTI, Pisa, Italy
Mattioli, Andrea	CNR-ISTI, Pisa, Italy
Melis, Beatrice	University of Pisa, Italy
Mørch, Anders	University of Oslo, Norway
Onorati, Teresa	Carlos III University of Madrid, Spain
Paternò, Fabio	CNR-ISTI, Pisa, Italy
Piccinno, Antonio	University of Bari Aldo Moro, Italy
Pittarello, Fabio	Ca' Foscari University of Venice, Italy
Ritschel, Nico	University of Illinois Urbana-Champaign, USA
Rossi, Gustavo	National University of La Plata, Argentina
Schenkenfelder, Bernhard	Software Competence Center Hagenberg GmbH, Austria
Spano, Lucio Davide	University of Cagliari, Italy
Stumpf, Simone	University of Glasgow, UK
Tetteroo, Daniel	Eindhoven University of Technology, Netherlands
Turchi, Tommaso	University of Pisa, Italy
Valtolina, Stefano	University of Milan, Italy
Weber, Thomas	Ludwig Maximilian University of Munich, Germany
Winckler, Marco	Côte d'Azur University, France
Yigitbas, Enes	University of Paderborn, Germany

Keynotes

Can Learners Design Their Future? Promoting Agency with Large Language Models in Education

Enkelejda Kasneci

Technical University of Munich, Germany
enkelejda.kasneci@tum.de

Extended Abstract

Large language models are disrupting end-user development by empowering non-experts, particularly learners, to design their own digital tools and environments. In education, this change raises a key question: How can learners gain agency as designers of their learning ecosystems and develop tools such as personalized learning aids, collaborative platforms or AI-powered simulations? This talk explores strategies for using large language models for learner-centered end-user development, focusing on intuitive design scaffolding, transparent AI interactions, and fostering creative agency. Drawing on research in educational technology, human-computer interaction, and Generative AI, this talk presents practical examples that illustrate how learners can be empowered while addressing challenges such as digital literacy barriers, AI and algorithmic literacy, and equitable access to technology.

Bio

Enkelejda Kasneci is a Distinguished Professor ("Liesel Beckmann Distinguished Professorship") for Human-Centered Technologies for Learning at the School of Social Sciences & Technology and in her second affiliation at the School of Computation, Information and Technology. She is Director of the TUM Center for Educational Technologies, Core Member of the Munich Data Science Institute and Fellow of the Konrad Zuse School of Excellence in Reliable AI. From December 2019 until July 2022, she was Professor for Human-Computer Interaction at the Department of Computer Science at the University of Tübingen and served in this department as the Dean of Studies. As a Bosch scholar, she received her M.Sc. degree in Computer Science from the University of Stuttgart in 2007. In 2013, she received her PhD in Computer Science from the University of Tübingen. For her PhD research, she was awarded the Research Prize of the Federation Südwestmetall in 2014. From 2013 to 2015, she was a postdoctoral researcher and a Margarete-von-Wrangell Fellow at the University of Tübingen. She established her research and teaching activities at the University of Tübingen from 2015 to 2019 as an assistant professor and head of the Perception Engineering Lab.

Efficiency and Creativity: The Myth of Natural Language Interaction

Antonella De Angeli

Faculty of Engineering, Free University of Bozen-Bolzano, Italy
Antonella.deangeli@unibz.it

Extended Abstract

Speed is a distinctive feature of Generative Artificial Intelligence (GenAI), the latest technology which is expected to rapidly transform human lives [3, 4]. Starting from verbal prompts, the system swiftly produces outputs that are often described as creative [5]. Therefore, GenAI may be the ideal interaction environment for EUD. In this keynote, I inquire into the effect of the machine speed on end-users' creativity considering issues of agency, conflict and ideology.

Until a few years ago, creativity was considered the distinctive feature of human intelligence, a combination of fast and slow thinking. Its standard definition (originality and effectiveness) has been recently updated to differentiate human from artificial creativity, including *authenticity* and *intentionality* [6]. Independent of its origin, creativity is a rare outcome acknowledged by consensual agreement among domain experts [1]. This keynote focuses on artistic creativity for pointing out omissions in EUD research coverage and suggesting possibilities for development.

Agency is relevant to creative EUD from two perspectives. The first one addresses the question of "Who (or what) should judge GenAI creativity?" Consistent with the consensual assessment technique [1], our preliminary findings suggest dramatic differences between human experts and automated scoring systems. Both judges tend to prefer the answer of their own kind, following what resembles a social and cultural bias. Agency also refers to the recognition of authorship [2], which extends beyond the user and the system, including the hidden work of data curation. We found that interaction roles are not fixed but emerge, shape and change in the intra-action between a choreographer and a performer [2]. In this dance of agency, GenAI can be useful in the divergent phase of artistic creativity, especially when it hallucinates and surprises the user [2, 4]. On the other hand, its speed and overproduction overwhelm the user with what is perceived as art commodification.

Another characteristic of GenAI, which is relevant to creativity, is its inability to disagree with the user [4]. Our longitudinal research involving professional playwrights and novelists identified the absence of conflict as a major obstacle to creative writing. Tragedy is all about catharsis; comedy requires irony and satire. Creative writers tend to dislike GenAI, which they define as verbose, politically correct and moralistic. Their expertise exposes the absence of authenticity of a verbose text, where words are not carefully crafted but statistically related. Furthermore, they interpret GenAI as an ideological embodiment of capitalism, which values speed as profit [3]. On the contrary, technology-induced acceleration (always faster, always more) poses a threat to individuals and society. There is an urgent need to synchronise the interaction if we want humans to regain control over their creative outcomes.

We conclude by highlighting the myth of natural language interaction, the naïve belief that by telling somebody/something to do a task, we can efficiently achieve a creative outcome [4]. This misunderstanding is responsible for the growing misalignment between user research and GenAI development. Bringing the user back into the agenda is one of the most urgent challenges EUD research must embrace.

Bio

Antonella De Angeli (PhD Experimental Psychology, University of Trieste) is Professor of Human-Computer Interaction at the Faculty of Engineering of the Free University of Bozen-Bolzano. Her research promotes a theory-led and empirically grounded approach to investigate the cognitive and social consequences of technology on humans. This work has developed across disciplines and countries. Notable institutions include the University of Trieste, Fondazione Bruno Kessler, the Oregon Graduate Institute, NCR Ltd., and the Universities of Manchester, Trento, and Lincoln. She first approached End-User Development in 2007 as the principal investigator for the University of Manchester of the EC-FP7 project ServfFace. She later developed her participatory vision to give end-users a voice in the design of their technological life in several projects, including Smart Campus and the Horizon 2020 Pie-News project.

References

1. Amabile, T.M.: Social psychology of creativity: A consensual assessment technique. J. Pers. Soc. Psychol. **43**(5), 997–1013 (1982). https://doi.org/10.1037/0022-3514.43.5.997
2. Bomba, F., Menéndez-Blanco, M., Grigis, P., Cremaschi, M., De Angeli, A.: The choreographer-performer continuum: a diffraction tool to illuminate authorship in more than human co-performances. ACM Trans. Comput.-Hum. Interact. **31**(6), 75:1–75:23 (2024). https://doi.org/10.1145/3689040
3. Cremaschi, M., Dorfmann, M., De Angeli, A.: A steampunk critique of machine learning acceleration. In: Proceedings of the 2024 ACM Designing Interactive Systems Conference, pp. 246–257, Association for Computing Machinery, New York, NY, USA (2024). https://doi.org/10.1145/3643834.3660688. Accessed 26 Apr 2025

4. Grigis, P., De Angeli, A.: Playwriting with large language models: perceived features, interaction strategies and outcomes. In Proceedings of the 2024 International Conference on Advanced Visual Interfaces (AVI '24), pp. 1–9, Association for Computing Machinery, New York, NY, USA (2024). https://doi.org/10.1145/3656650.3656688
5. Runco, M.A.: AI can only produce artificial creativity. J. Creat. **33**(3), 100063 (2023). https://doi.org/10.1016/j.yjoc.2023.100063
6. Runco, M.A.: Updating the standard definition of creativity to account for the artificial creativity of AI. Creat. Res. J. **37**(1), 1–5 (2025)

Contents

Automation, Sustainability, and Smart Environments

An EUD Approach to Creating Feasible and Energy-Saving Automations for Smart Homes

Barbara Rita Barricelli[1], Daniela Fogli[1], Simone Gallo[2], Davide Guizzardi[1], Sara Maenza[2], Andrea Mattioli[2](✉), and Fabio Paternò[2]

[1] University of Brescia, Brescia, Italy
{barbara.rita.barricelli,daniela.fogli, davide.guizzardi}@unibs.it
[2] CNR-ISTI, Pisa, Italy
{simone.gallo,sara.maenza,andrea.mattioli, fabio.pateno}@isti.cnr.it

Abstract. This paper presents a novel approach to creating automations for smart home environments, which leverages conversational interaction and is able to detect potential issues during automation creation. Issues may concern the possibility of conflicts between automations, when they aim to set appliances in contradictory modes at the same time or of chains of automations that may lead to unexpected smart home behaviours. Other issues considered in the approach are related to the excessive energy consumption of the automations. All the emerging issues and the ways to solve them are explained to the users in natural language during automation creation. The resulting system can thus help users better control their smart home and obtain suggestions about more sustainable behaviours. A first study with a mixed-method evaluation performed with 10 participants demonstrates the feasibility of the approach.

Keywords: Smart home · Automation · Conflict resolution · Sustainability

1 Introduction

The increasing availability of sensors, connected objects, and intelligent services has made it possible to obtain automations involving the dynamic composition of objects, services, and devices in the places where people live, work, and perform their common activities daily. Since each person has specific needs and preferences, which can also vary over time, it is crucial to empower users of such technological settings to directly control such automations, even when they have no programming experience. Existing software development life cycles typically involve only technical people and are slow to respond to the evolving needs of different types of users, also because professional developers often lack the domain knowledge to address user requirements. Thus, a viable way to make applications better comply with users' expectations is to make users capable of 'programming' the intended behaviour through suitable automations.

C. Santoro et al. (Eds.): IS-EUD 2025, LNCS 15713, pp. 3–21, 2025.
https://doi.org/10.1007/978-3-031-95452-8_1

One of the areas where the growing proliferation of the Internet of Things (IoT) has a main impact is the smart home, also because of the growing demand for low-carbon emission and energy-saving-oriented solutions. The global smart home market is expected to grow from USD 99.89 billion in 2021 to USD 380.52 billion in 2028 at a CAGR (Compounded Average Growth Rate)[1]. However, such technological availability risks being unsuccessful if we do not empower users to control the surrounding ecosystems of connected objects, devices, and services to better meet their personal needs. This aspect has become even more significant in recent years, where each of us is called on to contribute to planet sustainability through the reduction of resource consumption and circular economy. The first step in this direction is managing the resources of our own houses with efficiency and effectiveness.

Automations can be helpful in supporting the achievement of various types of goals. In this work, we focus on how to support goals consistent with the principles of a circular economy, such as energy saving. To achieve this goal, we have designed a platform for home environments to analyse their impact on daily life, and actual ability to empower end users in realising their automation needs. They include a conversational tool for creating new automations that better fit users' needs and controlling those active in the home. Such tool is connected with underlying services useful to understand the potential impact of specific automations both for their actual consistency with the other automations and for their impact in terms of energy consumption.

The approach is based on trigger-action programming (TAP), which offers people without programming experience the possibility of tailoring their smart home behaviours through rules in the format "when something happens (trigger), something must be done (action)". This approach to End-User Development (EUD) for smart environments based on IoT has been proposed and assessed in several scientific works (e.g., [15, 17, 18, 26, 31]). Due to its relevance and success, current commercial tools, such as Google Home, Amazon Alexa, Apple Home, SmartThings, and Home Assistant support TAP to create automations (also called routines). However, the tools that have been put forward are limited in terms of their usability and capability to analyse the impact of the created automations. The proposed environments usually are visual and users must interact with long lists of elements corresponding to the various sensors and objects, which sometimes are difficult to identify. They do not provide support to understand possible problems and conflicts among the created automations, and do not provide information regarding the environmental implications of such automations.

In this paper, after discussion of related work, we present a novel solution that allows users to create automations in a conversational manner. In the possible conversations, the user is also informed about two types of potential issues: one concerns the possibility of conflicts or chains of automations that result in unexpected smart home behaviours; the other one provides results of simulation of the energy consumption implications of the created automations. The resulting environment can provide more meaningful information to the users and allow them to better control their smart home. We also report on a first study with a mixed-method evaluation carried out with 10 users, which provided encouraging feedback and indications for further improvements.

[1] https://www.fortunebusinessinsights.com/industry-reports/smart-home-market-101900.

2 Related Work

A literature review that considered publications from 2010 to 2016 highlighted that all tools available for smart homes till that time implemented TAP with visual interfaces allowing users to compose events and/or conditions with actions, using structures like 'if-condition(s)-then-action(s)' or 'when-event(s)-then-action(s)' [8]. Then, a high-level comparison of such tools considering the design principles [16] discovered that most tools were affected by important weaknesses that made them far from successful adoption in real settings. First, user interfaces for smart home control were usually designed for one single user, while, since usually more than one person inhabits a house, a multi-user approach was needed to deal with household collaborative activities and possible conflicts that may occur among preferences of different household members. Second, considering that the home is more than a location, it was observed that the tools should allow users to enter and update information from various locations, with more natural interactions like those offered by conversational interfaces. Additional issues to be taken into consideration during the design of TAP interfaces have been highlighted in [7], such as the need for debugging and simulation features, conflict resolution support, and the importance of mediating between the user's need for control and the lack of programming experience. A further issue that is recently emerging is supporting users to behave sustainably, enhancing awareness about smart home power consumption, and exploiting automations to improve smart home sustainability. The following discussion of literature work considers these three aspects.

2.1 Conflict Detection, Rule Debugging, and Rule Simulation

Recent literature proposals aim to overcome the previous limitations. For example, several studies propose solutions to detect and resolve various types of conflicts that may arise in an environment inhabited by several people where limited resources need to be shared. Strategies for automated conflict resolution have been proposed in [9, 24, 27, 28]: some of these strategies are based on a fair principle, which does not prefer any user, but instead calculates the average value, when possible, of user preferences (e.g., room temperature is calculated as the average value of the temperature values liked by users); other strategies adopt a first-come-first-serve approach, where the first user accessing the service or device has full control of it [9]. More sophisticated strategies exploit user preferences and/or priorities to provide the most appropriate solution to the context [24, 27]. Other approaches involve user participation in conflict resolution [28], favouring an exchange of information and opinions to find a shared solution. A more general approach to conflict detection and resolution is adopted in those works that consider situations where users deploy a multitude of automation rules to solve the different needs that may emerge at different moments. These situations may quickly become hard to manage since trigger-action rules can interfere with each other. For this reason, research scholars have investigated how to develop tools for end-user debugging of rules [25] that help users understand how interactions between rules may occur and simulate execution before rules are deployed in the real installation. Corno and colleagues [11] classify these problems into: loops (automations that continuously activate one another), inconsistencies (when rules execute at the same time contradictory actions, such as switching on and off the same device), and redundancies (when rules have replicated functionalities). More recently, Chen et al. [10] have classified problems into: rule preventions (when one rule unintentionally blocks the triggering of another), rule collisions (which are comparable to the inconsistencies described before), and unexpected rule chains (when the effects of an action can activate another rule). These logical loopholes not only lead to unexpected behaviours of the smart home, but they may also expose the users to serious threats, such as the inadvertent disclosure of private information or the exposure of their smart environment to attackers [6].

2.2 Approaches to TAP Based on Conversational Interaction

Using tools such as chatbots or, more in general virtual assistants accessible through natural language can be a promising approach to breaking down barriers between the user and technology given their potential ease of use, as demonstrated by the recent success of ChatGPT or by the diffusion of widely adopted commercial products such as Amazon Alexa or Google Assistant. A systematic literature review [20] aimed to analyse proposals of conversational interfaces (i.e., chatbots) applied to IoT domains. In terms of intelligent technologies used to build such systems, two main approaches have been identified: i) rule-based systems, which are implementations that do not use machine learning (ML) to classify intents and extract entities; and ii) AI-based systems, often architectural hybrids, using ML for intent classification and entity extraction, but with rule-based dialogue management and response generation. The first category includes, for example, a system [12] that exploits recommendation features to suggest trigger-action rules by recognizing users' intents in the conversation with a virtual assistant (i.e., Google Assistant). Similarly, the ParlAmI system by Stefanidi et al. [29] offers a chatbot that can be used with a smartphone or a NAO humanoid robot. In the second category, we can find the RuleBot++ [19], which is based on a Large Language Model to allow users to create complex automations for smart homes: the user can create automations with multiple triggers and multiple actions, and the chatbot is also able to distinguish between events and conditions. Some tools [3] exploit the NLP features of commercial virtual assistants (Google Assistant and Amazon Alexa) but simplify automation creation through a guided process, also enriched by voice, visual, and touch interaction. A review [20] also underlined that until May 2023, no published studies employed LLMs (e.g., OpenAI ChatGPT) for such settings. Recently, Giudici et al. [22] presented an application for smart home management empowered by GPT 4. This conversational agent, called GreenIFTTT, allows users to create eco-friendly automations, but no attention is paid to possible conflicts between automations. Such system [23] exploits LLMs with chain-of-thought prompting to bridge the gap between the users' implicit goals (e.g., "help me see better") and the explicit actions to accomplish them (e.g., "turn on the light in the living room"). That system proved to be powerful in generating action plans based on users' goals but did not consider possible conflicts between plans.. The chatbot proposed in this paper not only exploits LLMs but also can help users detect and solve possible conflicts among the created automations and issues regarding the energy-related impact of such automations.

2.3 Smart Home Sustainability

Reducing energy consumption and environmental impact is the main focus of studies on how to enhance end users' awareness of environmental sustainability. Most of them, however, discuss how to visualize information about energy consumption (e.g., [13, 30]) or how to persuade users to behave sustainably (e.g., [1, 2, 4]). Few works so far consider the direct engagement of users in smart home management [14, 21, 22]. An exploratory study [21], with seven participants, investigated the potential of integrating conversational agents and smart devices to promote sustainable behaviours in domestic spaces; then, a conceptual framework highlighting the core dimensions of a possible system is proposed. Even though very inspiring, the results of this paper were still preliminary and informed following papers of the same authors [22]. In this area, as mentioned in the previous section, the GreenIFTTT aims to streamline daily routines through LLMs and enhance energy efficiency for more sustainable electric consumption. However, real-time consumption data gathering and management are not discussed in the paper; thus, it is unclear to what extent these data are used to evaluate automation sustainability and suggest modifications that help reduce energy consumption or avoid circuit breaks. The chatbot presented here, instead, is integrated with Home Assistant and a backend processing data for the sake of automation simulation; therefore, its recommendations and suggestions are based on real data and can be executed in real contexts. The work by Cotti et al. [14] presents a deep-learning approach to the recognition of appliances' activation, to estimate their consumption; then it illustrates how this information can be used to suggest better starting times of automations or to warn the users about potential problems that may occur due to the contemporary activation of several energy-consuming appliances. However, the paper does not discuss how automations can be created by end users with the proposed system and does not address conflicts occurring due to access to shared devices, rule chains, and loops, which are aspects addressed in this proposal.

3 The Proposed Approach

This section presents the architecture of the proposed system implementing a novel EUD approach to smart home control and describes its main components.

3.1 Overall System Architecture

The system architecture consists of three main components. The Rule Checker checks whether there may be problematic interactions between the rule the user is creating and those previously created and saved in the system. The Energy Checker checks whether these new automations may create problems from an energy perspective, such as exceeding the power available in the home. The chatbot coordinates the interaction between these components and the user. Through the chatbot, the user can create an automation by receiving dynamic support, proceeding by iterative refinements of the initial automation idea (see Fig. 1).

The interaction begins with the user describing the desired automation in natural language. The chatbot interprets the request, asks clarification questions if needed (e.g., the sensor or object room), then summarises the automation and asks for confirmation. Once an initial definition is established, the chatbot generates the automation in JSON format and initiates a verification phase to ensure the automation does not introduce conflicts within the existing set of rules. The Rule Checker analyses the automation and detects potential conflicts arising from overlapping actions, dependencies, or cascading activations. If conflicts are identified, the Rule Feedback component provides potential resolutions, allowing the user to refine or modify the automation accordingly.

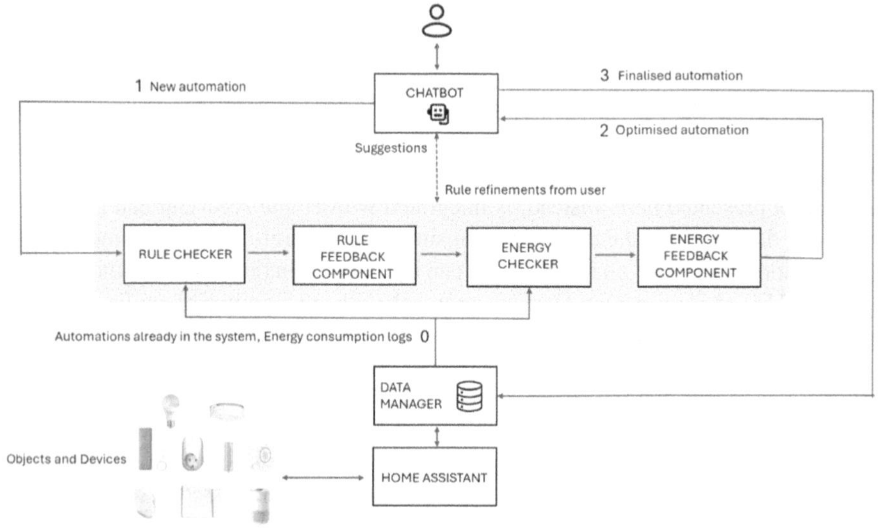

Fig. 1. The architecture of the proposal system.

The resulting modified automation is then evaluated from the energy consumption perspective. This verification step considers whether the new rule may lead to excessive energy usage or suboptimal scheduling of high-power devices. The system queries the Energy Checker, which analyses automation's impact on energy efficiency. If issues are detected, the Energy Feedback component presents the user with alternative scheduling options that may reduce costs or prevent electrical overloads.

Throughout this process, the chatbot autonomously determines which verification steps to invoke, ensuring that all generated automations are compliant with user preferences and system constraints. By offering suggestions rather than enforcing modifications, the system maintains user control over decision-making while providing structured guidance. Once all necessary refinements have been completed, the finalised automation is stored in the system's database and integrated with Home Assistant (HA) for its possible execution.

3.2 Rule Checker

The Rule Checker examines HA automations to identify possible conflicts between actions and activation chains.

In the first case, the system compares the actions of automations to detect pairs that perform conflicting operations on the same device. For example, it might detect a situation where one automation turns on a device while another turns it off, or where two automations set the device to different modes. Once potentially conflicting automations have been identified, the system checks the compatibility of the triggers, excluding pairs with opposite activations (e.g. 'If presence is detected in the kitchen' vs. 'If no presence is detected in the kitchen'). If all conditions are fulfilled, the conflict is reported to the user.

When detecting chains of activations, the Rule Checker analyses the automations for possible cascading activations, distinguishing between direct and indirect chains. Direct chains occur when the action of a first automation directly activates another one, as it corresponds to its trigger. For example, a rule that turns on the air conditioner when the temperature exceeds 22 °C automatically triggers another automation that closes the windows when the air conditioner turns on. Indirect chains, on the other hand, emerge when an action modifies an environmental parameter that could trigger another automation. Although the link between the two is not explicit, the system signals this possible relationship to the user for awareness. For example, an automation that turns on the air conditioner when the temperature exceeds 22 °C could influence a second rule that activates the heating if the temperature drops below 16 °C, since the first action could cause a change in the environmental parameter temperature. The analysis of these interactions is made possible by a set of rules, which associate the actions with the relevant environmental parameters.

When the Rule Checker detects a problem, it connects to a feedback module that proposes possible solutions. This system provides a resolution automation from a list of automation candidates based on the similarity of the user-inserted rule with the others in this list.

3.3 Energy Checker

The Energy Checker relies on historical data to estimate the overall power consumption and duration of each action within the simulated automation. The module periodically extracts data from the underlying HA installation and analyses them, tracking how long each device remains in a particular state and how much energy is consumed. A moving average of the duration and power consumption of each device state is saved into a database and later retrieved during the simulation process. The database information serves as the basis of the construction of the State Matrix. This is a 7×1440 (number of minutes in a week) $\times$ #devices matrix that represents the state of each device for every minute of the week. Initially, the matrix is empty, but it is then populated using both historical data and the automations stored in the system. If an automation, for example, turns on a light at 18:00 on Monday, the system retrieves the average duration for that state and updates the matrix changing the slots between 18:00 and the expected end hour, based on the average duration. This process is repeated sequentially for all automations, ensuring an accurate representation of device behaviour for the entire week.

To identify sustainability conflicts, the system generates seven Cumulative Power Arrays from the data stored in the State Matrix. Each array, representing a day of the week, aggregates the power consumption of all devices in each minute of its corresponding day. Cumulative power arrays allow the system to assess overall energy demand and compare it against the maximum power that the smart home can access at a given moment. If the total power consumption exceeds this threshold at any point, a conflict is detected, and the system records the start and end times of the overload. Additionally, the system looks for solutions that could solve the conflicts at hand. Two solutions are considered: the first is adjusting the start time of the simulated automation to a period where no overload occurs. The second is identifying conflicting automations and suggesting the deactivation of one or more to reduce excessive power demand. Another potential conflict may occur when the automation under creation encompasses appliance activations that together exceed the maximum power threshold. To solve this problem, the system suggests breaking the automation into multiple smaller automations, each consuming less energy in a given time interval to remain within the allowed limits.

Lastly, if no conflicts are detected, the Energy Checker goes a step further and tries to optimize the energy cost of automations. It first calculates the original cost of running the automation based on each action data and energy pricing. Then, it evaluates alternative start times of the automation that could reduce expenses by leveraging lower-cost periods. If a better activation time is found, the system reports the suggestion to the user with its associated savings.

3.4 Chatbot

The chatbot (Fig. 2) is based on previous experiences [19] and is designed to facilitate the creation and refinement of automation rules through natural language interaction. It operates by leveraging a large language model (GPT-4o) as the core dialogue manager, which dynamically determines how to assist users by invoking specific functions through tool-calling mechanisms, allowing the chatbot to use external tools (e.g., Python functions for API calls). The chatbot is integrated with HA for possible automation execution, thus all generated automations are structured in JSON format compatible with HA. The chatbot system supports the following functionalities:

- Retrieving existing automation rules: this allows the system to access automations from the database for modifications or explanations.
- Generating new automations: once the automation is identified and defined, the automation in JSON format for HA is generated with the support of an LLM instance.
- Verifying conflicts and activation chains: this functionality uses the Rule Checker API to verify if the new automation can cause issues (conflicts and/or activation chains) with other automations present in the environment.
- Verifying energy consumption conflicts: this functionality uses the Energy Checker API to verify if the new automation can cause issues related to energy overload and receive energy-related suggestions.
- Saving new automations: storing the final automations in the database.

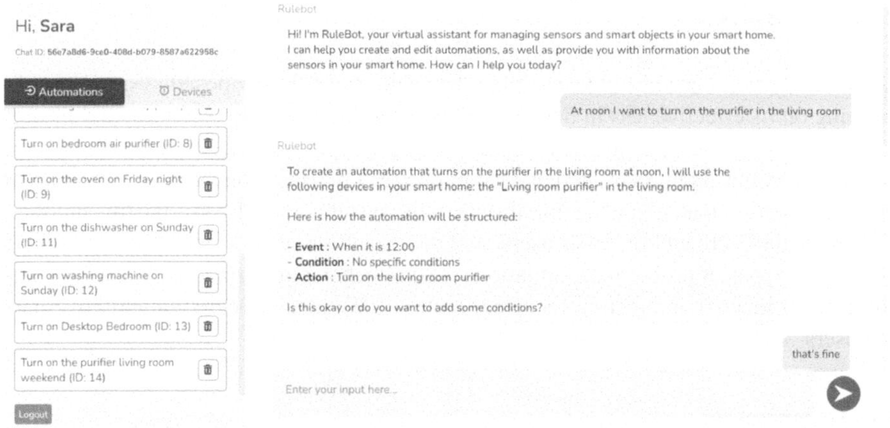

Fig. 2. The chatbot interface. The left tab shows the list of automations and devices. Each element is selectable to show its description.

In an interactive session, after the chatbot's welcome message, the user initiates the interaction by specifying the desired automation (e.g., *"At noon, I want to turn on the air purifier in the living room"*). The system then generates an initial automation proposal, outlining the involved devices and the automation structure, including the trigger event, conditions, and actions. The user is prompted to confirm or modify the proposed configuration. Upon acceptance, the system creates the automation and calls the Rule Checker API to identify potential conflicts or activation chains. If a conflict is detected, an explanation is provided alongside a suggested resolution (e.g., *"A conflict has been identified with another automation [...]. This automation turns off the purifier in the living room when no one is home for 15 min on weekdays (Monday to Friday). To prevent conflicts, I recommend limiting the activation of the new automation to weekends (Saturday and Sunday). Would you like to proceed with this modification?"*). The user may accept, reject, or propose an alternative solution.

Subsequently, the modified automation undergoes verification from an energy consumption perspective via the Energy Checker APIs. If an energy-related conflict is detected, the system informs the user and suggests potential resolutions (*e.g., "An energy conflict has been identified. The automation [...] will exceed the 3000W energy consumption limit on Sunday between 12:00 and 12:36. I recommend adjusting the purifier's activation time to an alternative slot, such as 11:00 or 12:37. Would you like to proceed with one of these adjustments?"*). The user may once again modify the automation, reject the suggestion, or propose an alternative solution. Once all modifications are finalised, the automation is stored in the database, a confirmation message is sent to the user, and the automation list is updated accordingly.

4 User Study

A user study was carried out to evaluate the usability of the proposed system, mainly focusing on its effectiveness in detecting issues during automation creation and in suggesting possible solutions to such issues. Participants involved in the user study were asked to carry out six tasks of increasing complexity. Each task concerned the creation of a new automation that, given the initial state of the system, with already existing automations potentially created by other users, and the execution of previous tasks, could lead to different types of problematic situations. Users' behaviour during task execution was observed to identify interesting recurrent patterns. We also collected quantitative data and users' feedback to inform future improvements.

4.1 Organization

The study sample comprised 10 participants whose ages ranged from 23 to 56 years ($M = 32$, $SD = 9.64$). The gender distribution was equal, with five female and five male respondents. Concerning the level of education of the participants, half of the participants were university degree holders, and the other half had completed secondary education. Regarding programming experience, four respondents answered that they had no experience, whereas one did have general knowledge limited to HTML and CSS. Two respondents stated they had an intermediate degree of knowledge, including familiarity with HTML, CSS, and at least one scripting language, i.e., JavaScript or Python. One respondent also showed advanced knowledge, including comprehensive knowledge of several programming languages. Participants were recruited on a voluntary basis and did not receive any compensation.

Before the experimental phase, each participant was instructed about the test protocol with the aid of a set of preliminary materials composed of a slide deck introducing trigger-action programming, a description of the types of issues that the chatbot can detect, instructions for completing the test, a map of the home environment used in the experiment, and a demo video of the system. The tests were conducted both in person and remotely via video calls with screen sharing. Additionally, participants were asked for consent to record their sessions, allowing for audio data collection in some cases. No dedicated familiarization phase with the tool was included; instead, participants proceeded directly to task execution with the think-aloud method. The choice of the initial state of devices in the home environment and available automations was made to trigger specific chatbot behaviours. The tasks were the following:

***Task 1**: You want all the lights to turn off automatically when you leave the house. Create an automation that turns off all the lights when no presence is detected in the house and resolves any potential issues.*

The system already had an automation that turned on the front door light when no presence was detected in the house. Therefore, the chatbot was supposed to detect a conflict and suggest turning off all lights except the front door light.

***Task 2**: You want to maintain good air quality in your bedroom at all times. Create an automation that turns on the air purifier when air quality becomes poor and resolves any potential issues.*

The system had an automation that turned off the bedroom TV if the noise level in the room exceeded 40dB after 10:30 PM. In this situation, the chatbot should have suggested turning on the air purifier in silent mode after 10:30 PM.

***Task 3**: It's summer, it's Friday, and you want to prepare pizza and bake it as soon as you get home from work. Create an automation that turns on the oven at 7:00 PM and resolves any potential issues.*

To highlight issues related to energy overload, the system had an automation that turned on the air conditioner from Monday to Friday at 6 PM. The chatbot was meant to detect that the maximum energy threshold had been exceeded and suggest turning off the air conditioning while the oven is turned on.

***Task 4**: To take advantage of lower energy costs, you would like the system to start the dishwasher and washing machine every Sunday at 11:00 AM. Create the automation, and if you encounter any issues, remember that the dishwasher should be started before lunch to have clean dishes ready, while the washing machine can wait until the afternoon (e.g., 3:00 or 4:00 PM) so that the laundry can be hung before dinner.*

The system was intended to detect an energy overload and suggest splitting the automation into two sequential automations executed at different times.

***Task 5**: You usually relax after dinner by using the computer in your bedroom. You want it to start automatically at 8:00 PM to avoid waiting for it to turn on. Create the automation and resolve any potential issues.*

The system already had an automation that turned off the desktop when the presence sensor did not detect anyone, which should go on in conflict with the automation under creation. Thus, the chatbot should have provided suggestions on how to solve this conflict. In addition, based on the Energy checker output, the chatbot was expected to propose shifting the automation execution to a more cost-effective time slot.

***Task 6**: You want to have lunch with your family in a space with clean air. Create an automation that turns on the air purifier in the living room every day at 12:00 PM and resolves any potential issues.*

This task aimed to demonstrate how the chatbot would recommend rescheduling the air purifier activation to prevent energy overload issues, given that there was an automation that turns on the oven at 12 PM on every public holiday.

Upon completing the assigned tasks, participants filled out a post-test questionnaire including the Bot Usability Scale (BUS) [5] and four open questions requesting how the system could be useful, aspects that participants liked the most and liked the least, and suggestions for system improvement. Out of the original 11 items included in the BUS, we excluded two: "It was easy to find the chatbot," as the system primarily consists of the chatbot interface, and "I believe the chatbot informs me of any possible privacy issues" since the system is not intended to provide this information.

4.2 Quantitative Results

To evaluate the chatbot's effectiveness, we measured the percentage of user-accepted and rejected suggestions, the number of errors and hallucinations returned by the system, and the modifications users made to system automations during testing.

Analysis of Acceptance of Suggestions. The total number of suggestions is not the same in all tasks because the interaction with users generated a large number of requests and, consequently, a variable number of suggestions, while in some cases the system skipped the energy check. About rule checker suggestions, the data (see Fig. 3) show a balanced distribution between acceptance and rejection: 50% of the suggestions were accepted, and 50% were rejected (M = 3, median = 3.5). The energy-related suggestions, on the other hand, tended slightly towards rejection, with 54.55% of the suggestions rejected (M = 2.5, median = 3) and 45.45% accepted (M = 3, median = 1.5). Looking at the individual tasks, a special case emerges in task 4 in which all the energy-related suggestions were accepted (8 out of 8). In this case, the energy checker suggested splitting the created automation into two separate automations to avoid exceeding the maximum power threshold. In contrast, in tasks 3 and task 5, there is a strong tendency to reject energy-related suggestions. In task 3, 8 users out of 9 rejected the suggestion to change the time in which the desired action (turning on the oven) should be executed, instead preferring to deactivate the already present automation that generates the conflict. In task 5, 7 users out of 8 rejected the optional suggestion to move the starting time of the action to a more cost-effective time. Regarding rule checker suggestions, task 2 stands out for a clear preference in the acceptance of suggestions, with 9 out of 11 suggestions being positively accepted. In these cases, the system suggested resolving the issue by turning on the air purifier in "silence mode" to avoid the activation chain. Finally, task 6 recorded the most rejections (7 out of 10). In this case, the users did not accept the suggestion to limit the activation of the air purifier only on specific days (weekend), prioritizing the environmental air quality over the conflict resolution.

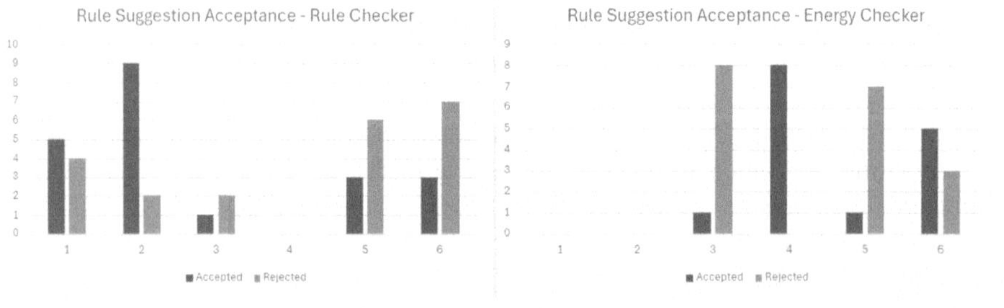

Fig. 3. Comparison of the acceptance rate of the suggestions.

System Errors. An analysis of the errors and hallucinations made by the system (17), including the chatbot, the rule checker and the energy checker, shows a mean of 0.28 errors per task, with a median of 3. Tasks 3 and 4 had the fewest errors (1 each), while task 5 had the most errors (5). Some recurring and interesting criticalities emerge in the user study. The chatbot had a few problems recognising elements of the environment correctly: the external door light, for example, was not identified as part of the house (2 errors), and a non-existent device was inserted without warning (1 error). Another problem area was energy verification, which was occasionally omitted or performed incompletely (e.g., reporting the conflict without the new time suggestions), preventing the correct detection of conflicts (6 errors).

Modified User System Automations. During the test, some participants chose not to accept the suggestions made by the checkers, preferring instead to directly or indirectly modify the actions of the automations in conflict with the one being created. A total of 9 modifications were made to the existing automations to resolve a detected issue (M = 0.5 per task, median = 1.5). Tasks 1, 3, and 6 each recorded three changes, while activities 2, 4, and 5 recorded no changes. In some cases, users extended the automations they were creating to deactivate, even temporarily, a device controlled by a conflicting automation. For example, in task 3, instead of accepting the energy suggestion to postpone the activation of the oven to avoid an overload due to the simultaneous switching on of the air conditioner (managed by another automation), some users preferred to add an action to the automation being created to switch off the air conditioner as long as the oven was on. In other cases, users opted to directly deactivate or eliminate conflicting automations already present in the system, thus resolving the conflict in a more radical way.

4.3 Findings from Direct Observation

All tasks were successfully completed, it was noticed that users freely engaged in the conversations with the chatbot, often requesting additional information or automations that deviated significantly from those designed for the study. As a consequence, various interesting users' behaviours have been observed:

Prioritization of Current Needs. There was an overall tendency to prioritize current needs and automations over past ones. In most cases, when dealing with conflicts, users preferred to alter or delete existing automations rather than modify the one they were currently working on. For example, in Task 6, when users encountered an energy conflict due to the simultaneous activation of the dishwasher (from a saved automation) and the purifier (from the current automation), the system suggested postponing the activation of the purifier. However, the majority of users preferred to change the activation of the dishwasher instead, often justifying their choice with comments like, "I need clean air for lunch.". Even when no conflict emerged, a suggestion to optimize the automation activation to save money was presented in Task 5, but most users chose to reject the recommendation prioritizing the need to use a device at a specific time ("I want to use the desktop at 20 not 21").

Managing Device States with Automations. On several occasions, users expressed a need for control over device states. In particular, they asked the chatbot to create additional automations to disable devices that had been activated by the automation they were creating for the task. Examples of this behaviour can be found in Task 6, where some users felt the need to add an automation to turn off the purifier after a period of time (typically 30/60 min) justifying the choice with comments like "when I finish lunch, I do not need it anymore". Moreover, this observed conduct highlights users' awareness that when an automation sets a device to a specific state, it may remain in that state indefinitely unless a follow-up action is taken.

Expectations About the Chatbot Managing Hazards. There were cases in which users expected the system to automatically suggest follow-up actions. In particular, they trusted the system to handle safety concerns, such as proposing to turn off an oven after it had been on for a long time, and were surprised to see that the chatbot did not warn them about potential hazards. Specifically, when dealing with Task 3 some users commented: "What if I have an accident and cannot be home at 19? I do not want the oven to stay on. It would have been nice if the system automatically created an automation to turn it off after some time".

Expectations About the System's Capabilities. In general, most users had expectations regarding the system's capabilities and felt surprised when it was not able to meet them. Notably, most of the testers, expected the chatbot to know information not strictly related to smart homes. For example, there were several cases in which during Task 3, users wanted to create an automation "for today" but due to the chatbot not knowing the current date they obtained an automation that activated every day of the week. To solve this problem, they had to explicitly specify which day they wanted the automation to activate.

4.4 Questionnaire User Feedback Analysis

As previously mentioned, the post-questionnaire included 9 out of the 11 questions of the BUS [5]. The results are shown in Fig. 4.

Bot Usability Scale. Analysing the results of the BUS questionnaire, some important considerations emerge. Users found the chatbot's functionality easily identifiable, with all responses leaning towards a positive assessment. The perceived clarity was also rated positively, but some users (4) suggested room for improvement. The chatbot's ability to contextualise conversations was generally appreciated: most users (8) gave high marks, but some neutral evaluations (2) indicate that contextual understanding could be improved in certain cases. Regarding ease of understanding, the chatbot is perceived positively, with almost all users (8) finding it clear and easy to use. Perceived usefulness is also high, although a minority (1) expressed a neutral opinion, indicating that effectiveness could vary depending on the user's needs. The information provided by the chatbot was considered adequate and relevant, although some users (2) felt that it could sometimes be too detailed, verbose or not focused enough. Accuracy is rated very positively, with all answers confirming this. Finally, response time is generally considered satisfactory, although some users (3) perceive it as slightly improvable in terms of speed.

As to the additional four open questions of the post-questionnaire, the feedback is reported in the following.

Perceived Usefulness of the Chatbot. All users found the chatbot useful. Many respondents highlighted its ability to facilitate the control of home devices, particularly beneficial for individuals with limited technical knowledge, allowing them to create automation rules without needing to engage in direct programming. One user noted that it "allows the creation of automations without requiring direct system programming," thereby making smart home management more accessible from a non-technical user perspective.

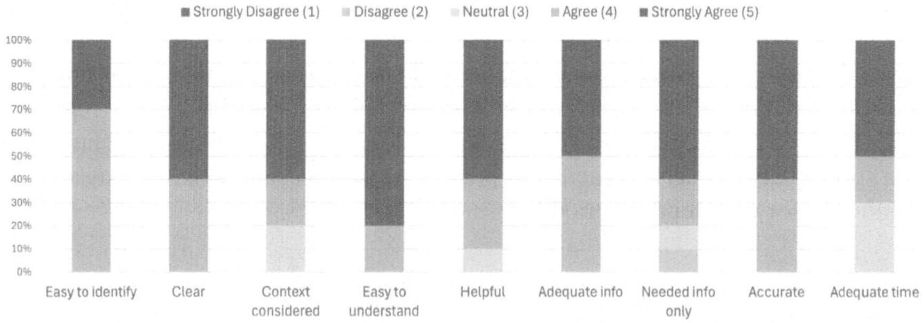

Fig. 4. Results of the Bot Usability Scale considering the 9 relevant items.

Some users appreciated the chatbot's role in reducing energy consumption and optimising automation strategies, and assisting with overall automation management. One user remarked that the chatbot "helps you remember all the functions/automations that are active or that will be activated and adjust them to each other without creating conflicts or problems, while also suggesting possible solutions".

Positive Aspects. Users appreciated its ease of communication, describing it as an intuitive tool that effectively facilitates smart home automation. Many respondents highlighted its conflict detection capabilities, with one stating that they valued "its ability to identify conflicts and provide resolutions". The chatbot's communication clarity was also praised, with users noting its "comprehensible responses and ease of use", "the rapidity and accuracy of responses". These aspects collectively indicate that the chatbot successfully delivers an efficient and user-friendly automation management experience.

Negative Aspects. Despite the positive reception, users identified some limitations. Response times were a notable concern, with multiple respondents mentioning delays in receiving chatbot replies[2]. Additionally, the consistency of confirmation prompts was criticised, with some users finding them incoherent in certain contexts. Some users felt that the chatbot did not always provide sufficiently detailed explanations of detected issues. One user noted that "it failed to specify air quality levels, requiring me to ask for clarification". Lastly, some users expressed a desire for expanded functionality, including the ability to navigate an interactive map displaying all associated smart home devices.

Suggested Improvements. Users proposed various enhancements to improve the chatbot's functionality and usability. One recurring suggestion was the addition of a brief tutorial to guide users through its features and interaction mechanisms. Several users expressed interest in visual representations of automation schedules and conflicts. One user suggested "a graphical timeline displaying activation times and energy consumption," while another recommended "cards highlighting conflicts between automations or a graphical representation of conflicting time slots". Further refinement of the chatbot's conflict resolution capabilities was also suggested. Some users found it challenging

[2] This contrast with some previous positive comments about the interaction speed, unfortunately the interaction speed mainly depends on the LLM API provider traffic in that moment. Some users could have a faster interaction with respect to the others.

to apply conflict resolution suggestions effectively, particularly when modifying overlapping rules. Additionally, integrating real-time data on the current state of the smart home to provide more context-aware recommendations was proposed as an improvement. Another significant concern involved safety mechanisms, particularly regarding device operation durations. A user suggested implementing "a control to monitor how long a specific device has been active to prevent hazardous situations, such as an oven remaining on for an extended period".

5 Conclusions and Future Work

In this paper, we have explored the usefulness and effectiveness of a conversational approach to automation creation, which is able to support users in detecting rule feasibility and energetic sustainability. The approach was generally appreciated by the users, who were able to manage their smart home in a more flexible and conscious manner than with other similar applications. Participants also showed engagement with the chatbot, demonstrating how conversational approaches can be a successful solution to TAP. Indeed, the chatbot behaved quite well and as expected during design in almost all cases. It encountered difficulties in long conversations and with some out-of-scope users' questions. This yielded uncertainty in the users, who were confused by some unexpected answers, due to LLM hallucinations.

On the other hand, users' expectations about the chatbot's capabilities were sometimes too high. For example, the fact that LLMs might not have all the information about a situation (e.g., which day is today) represents a recurrent problem in these systems, which might hinder acceptance and trust in the long run. Furthermore, the non-deterministic nature of such kinds of systems may lead to inconsistent behaviours, while it is well-known that consistency improves usability and user experience. These are important challenges in the design of LLM-based systems targeted at end users who do not know how generative AI works. Mechanisms should be studied to explain the underlying algorithms to users and make them more aware of the systems' capabilities, but these should take into consideration users' skills, backgrounds, and digital literacy.

Another general consideration that could be made when these kinds of systems are applied to the smart home is that users would like to take always control of their home and its devices, often for safety reasons. Indeed, in our case study they tended not to accept uncritically what the intelligent agent suggested but to proactively interact with it to better satisfy their desires. This could be regarded as a positive aspect that contributes to reinforcing the idea that Human-Centered AI is paramount when users' daily lives are affected by technology.

A final interesting lesson learned in this work is that natural language interaction alone is not often enough when the activities to be performed are complex. Graphical interfaces can be useful to complement this kind of interaction, helping users to better understand what is going on and offering alternative action ways. We are already working on a new version of the system that integrates visual and natural language interaction to control a green smart home. Future work will also be dedicated to more extensively validating the approach proposed in longer studies and real homes contexts.

Acknowledgments. This work has been supported by the Italian MUR PRIN 2022 PNRR Project P2022YR9B7, End-User Development of Automations for Explainable Green Smart Homes, funded by European Union – Next Generation EU.

References

1. Alan, A.T., Costanza, E., Ramchurn, S.D., Fischer, J., Rodden, T., Jennings, N.R.: Tariff agent: interacting with a future smart energy system at home. ACM Trans. Comput.-Hum. Interact. **23**(4) (2016). https://doi.org/10.1145/2943770
2. Bang, M., Torstensson, C., Katzeff, C.: The powerhhouse: a persuasive computer game designed to raise awareness of domestic energy consumption. In: IJsselsteijn, W.A., de Kort, Y.A.W., Midden, C., Eggen, B., van den Hoven, E. (eds.) Persuasive Technology, pp. 123–132. Springer, Heidelberg (2006)
3. Barricelli, B.R., Bondioli, A., Fogli, D., Iemmolo, L., Locoro, A.: Creating routines for IoT ecosystems through conversation with smart speakers. Int. J. Hum.-Comput. Interact. **40**(20), 6109–6127 (2024). https://doi.org/10.1080/10447318.2023.2247845
4. Beheshtian, N., Moradi, S., Ahtinen, A., Väänanen, K., Kähkonen, K., Laine, M.: Green-Life: a persuasive social robot to enhance the sustainable behavior in shared living spaces. In: Proceedings of the 11th Nordic Conference on Human-Computer Interaction: Shaping Experiences, Shaping Society (NordiCHI 2020), Article no. 42, pp. 1–12. ACM, New York (2020). https://doi.org/10.1145/3419249.3420143
5. Borsci, S., Prati, E., Malizia, A., Schmettow, M., Chamberlain, A., Federici, S.: Ciao AI: the Italian adaptation and validation of the Chatbot Usability Scale. Pers. Ubiquit. Comput. **27**(6), 2161–2170 (2023)
6. Breve, B., Cimino, G., Deufemia, V.: Identifying security and privacy violation rules in trigger-action IoT platforms with NLP models. IEEE Internet Things J. **10**(6), 5607–5622 (2022)
7. Brich, J., Walch, M., Rietzler, M., Weber, M., Schaub, F.: Exploring end user programming needs in home automation. ACM Trans. Comput.-Hum. Interact. **24**(2) (2017). https://doi.org/10.1145/3057858
8. Caivano, D., Fogli, D., Lanzilotti, R., Piccinno, A., Cassano, F.: Supporting end users to control their smart home: design implications from a literature review and an empirical investigation. J. Syst. Softw. **144**, 295–313 (2018). https://doi.org/10.1016/j.jss.2018.06.035
9. Chaki, D., Bouguettaya, A.: Adaptive priority-based conflict resolution of IoT services. In: Proceedings of the 2021 IEEE International Conference on Web Services (ICWS), pp. 663–668 (2021). https://doi.org/10.1109/ICWS53863.2021.00091
10. Chen, X., Zhang, X., Elliot, M., Wang, X., Wang, F.: Fix the leaking tap: a survey of Trigger-Action Programming (TAP) security issues, detection techniques and solutions. Comput. Secur. **120**, 102812 (2022)
11. Corno, F., De Russis, L., Monge Roffarello, A.: Empowering end users in debugging trigger-action rules. In: Proceedings of the 2019 CHI Conference on Human Factors in Computing Systems, CHI 2019, pp. 1–13. Association for Computing Machinery, New York (2019). https://doi.org/10.1145/3290605.3300618
12. Corno, F., Russis, L., Monge Roffarello, A.: HeyTAP: bridging the gaps between users' needs and technology in IF-THEN rules via conversation. In: Proceedings of the 2020 International Conference on Advanced Visual Interfaces (AVI 2020), Article no. 23, pp. 1–9. . ACM, New York (2020). https://doi.org/10.1145/3399715.3399905
13. Costanza, E., Ramchurn, S.D., Jennings, N.R.: Understanding domestic energy consumption through interactive visualisation: a field study. In: Proceedings of the 2012 ACM Conference on Ubiquitous Computing, UbiComp 2012, pp. 216–225. Association for Computing Machinery, New York (2012). https://doi.org/10.1145/2370216.2370251

14. Cotti, L., Guizzardi, D., Barricelli, B.R., Fogli, D.: Enabling end-user development in smart homes: a machine learning-powered digital twin for energy efficient management. Future Internet **16**(6) (2024). https://doi.org/10.3390/fi16060208
15. Coutaz, J., Crowley, J.L.: A first-person experience with end-user development for smart homes. IEEE Pervasive Comput. **15**(2), 26–39 (2016). https://doi.org/10.1109/MPRV.2016.24
16. Davidoff, S., Lee, M.K., Yiu, C., Zimmerman, J., Dey, A.K.: Principles of smart home control. In: Dourish, P., Friday, A. (eds.) UbiComp 2006: Ubiquitous Computing, pp. 19–34. Springer, Heidelberg (2006). https://doi.org/10.1007/11853565_2
17. Desolda, G., Ardito, C., Matera, M.: Empowering end users to customize their smart environments: model, composition paradigms, and domain-specific tools. ACM Trans. Comput.-Hum. Interact. **24**(2) (2017). https://doi.org/10.1145/3057859
18. Fogli, D., Peroni, M., Stefini, C.: ImAtHome: making trigger-action programming easy and fun. J. Vis. Lang. Comput. **42**, 60–75 (2017). https://doi.org/10.1016/j.jvlc.2017.08.003
19. Gallo, S., Paternò, F., Malizia, A.: A conversational agent for creating automations exploiting large language models. Pers. Ubiquitous Comput. (2024)
20. Gallo, S., Paternò, F., Malizia, A.: Conversational interfaces in IoT ecosystems: where we are, what is still missing. In: Proceedings of the 22nd International Conference on Mobile and Ubiquitous Multimedia (MUM 2023), pp. 279–293. ACM, New York (2023). https://doi.org/10.1145/3626705.3627775
21. Giudici, M., Crovari, P., Garzotto, F.: Candy: a framework to design conversational agents for domestic sustainability. In: Proceedings of the 4th Conference on Conversational User Interfaces, CUI 2022. Association for Computing Machinery, New York (2022). https://doi.org/10.1145/3543829.3544515
22. Giudici, M., Padalino, L., Paolino, G., Paratici, I., Pascu, A.I., Garzotto, F.: Designing home automation routines using an LLM-based chatbot. Designs **8**(3) (2024). https://doi.org/10.3390/designs8030043
23. King, E., Yu, H., Lee, S., Julien, C.: Sasha: creative goal-oriented reasoning in smart homes with large language models. Proc. ACM Interact. Mob. Wearable Ubiquitous Technol. **8**(1), 38, Article no. 12 (2024). https://doi.org/10.1145/3643505
24. Lee, Y.-H., Lin, F. J.: Situation awareness and conflict resolution in smart home with multiple users. In: Proceedings of the 2019 IEEE 5th World Forum on Internet of Things (WF-IoT), pp. 852–857 (2019). https://doi.org/10.1109/WF-IoT.2019.8767178
25. Manca, M., Paternò, F., Santoro, C., Corcella, L.: Supporting end-user debugging of trigger-action rules for IoT applications. Int. J. Hum. Comput. Stud. **123**, 56–69 (2019)
26. Mattioli, A., Paternò, F.: Recommendations for creating trigger-action rules in a block-based environment. Behav. Inf. Technol. **40**(10), 1024–1034 (2021). https://doi.org/10.1080/0144929X.2021.1900396
27. Nurgaliyev, K., Mauro, D.D., Khan, N., Augusto, J.C.: Improved multi-user interaction in a smart environment through a preference-based conflict resolution virtual assistant. In: 2017 International Conference on Intelligent Environments (IE), pp. 100–107 (2017). https://doi.org/10.1109/IE.2017.21
28. Ospan, B., Khan, N., Augusto, J., Quinde, M., Nurgaliyev, K.: Context aware virtual assistant with case-based conflict resolution in multi-user smart home environment. In: Proceedings of the 2018 International Conference on Computing and Network Communications (CoCoNet), pp. 36–44 (2018). https://doi.org/10.1109/CoCoNet.2018.8476898
29. Stefanidi, E., Foukarakis, M., Arampatzis, D., Korozi, M., Leonidis, A., Antona, M.: ParlAm I: a multimodal approach for programming intelligent environments. Technologies **7**(1), 11 (2019). https://doi.org/10.3390/technologies7010011

30. Stogia, M., et al.: A scalable and user-friendly framework integrating IoT and digital twins for home energy management systems. Appl. Sci. **14**(24) (2024). https://doi.org/10.3390/app142411834
31. Ur, B., McManus, E., Pak Yong Ho, M., Littman, M.L.: Practical trigger-action programming in the smart home. In: Proceedings of the SIGCHI Conference on Human Factors in Computing Systems, CHI 2014, pp. 803–812. ACM, New York (2014). https://doi.org/10.1145/2556288.2557420

End-User Customization of Trigger-Action Rules Through Fine-Tuned LLMs

Gaetano Cimino[1,2(✉)] and Vincenzo Deufemia[1]

[1] University of Salerno, Fisciano, Italy
{gcimino,deufemia}@unisa.it
[2] University of British Columbia, Vancouver, Canada
gaetano.cimino@ubc.ca

Abstract. While Trigger-Action Platforms (TAPs) provide an effective solution for end-users to automate interactions between smart devices and online services through customizable rules, their flexibility is often limited by restricted access to source code, confining users to predefined templates and basic configurations, or the need for programming expertise when modifications are allowed. To address this challenge, we propose a methodology using fine-tuned autoregressive Large Language Models (LLMs) that translates natural language descriptions into executable rule code. This approach removes the need for manual coding, reducing the technical barrier and enabling users to express their automation intents more intuitively. To evaluate our approach, we used a dataset of trigger-action rules from the If-This-Then-That (IFTTT) platform along with their natural language descriptions. These descriptions underwent refinement through an LLM-based preprocessing step and were then used to evaluate the performance of eight open-source LLMs in generating syntactically correct and functionally equivalent rule implementations. Among these models, Codestral achieved the best results, obtaining a ROUGE-L score of 63% and a METEOR score of 54%.

Keywords: Trigger-Action Platforms · GenAI · No-code Programming · Rule Customization · User Intent Modeling

1 Introduction

Within the domain of End-User Development (EUD) [2,6,36], Trigger-Action Platforms (TAPs) enable the automation of interactions between smart devices and online services, allowing users—regardless of their programming expertise—to define rules that associate events (triggers) with corresponding actions [16, 24]. These platforms operate based on *trigger-action programming* [23,42], a paradigm structured around an IF-THEN format. In this framework, a *trigger* is defined as an event or condition that occurs within a system, and this event serves to activate the rule. The *action*, in turn, represents the behavior or response that

C. Santoro et al. (Eds.): IS-EUD 2025, LNCS 15713, pp. 22–40, 2025.
https://doi.org/10.1007/978-3-031-95452-8_2

is executed once the trigger is activated. To structure these rules, TAPs rely on an abstract representation of service providers, commonly referred to as *channels* [7,9]. A channel acts as an interface to various services, enabling TAPs to detect triggers and perform the associated actions. Channels are integral in ensuring the interaction between the user's defined rules and the corresponding external services or devices.

A typical IF-THEN rule in a TAP, as illustrated in Fig. 1, could be as follows: **IF** "*the user receives an email*" (with the trigger channel being *Office365*), **THEN** "*post a message to a specific Slack channel*" (with the action channel being *Slack*). This rule automates the process of notifying a designated Slack channel whenever the user receives an email in their Office365 inbox, thus streamlining the communication and task management process. Furthermore, both the trigger and action components may incorporate specific channel-related details, often referred to as *fields* [47], such as the subject of the email for Office365 and the target channel for Slack. Through the use of such trigger-action rules, TAPs provide a flexible and efficient means of automating workflows, allowing users to create meaningful interactions between different devices and services without requiring advanced technical expertise.

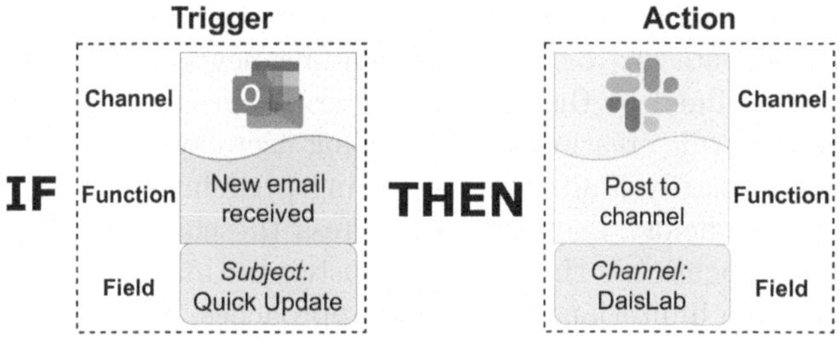

Fig. 1. Example of a trigger-action rule.

TAPs differ in the level of access they provide for rule definition, directly impacting how users can interact with and modify automation processes. Certain platforms, such as Alexa, restrict access to rule source code, making tasks like debugging or verification more challenging. In contrast, others allow users to adjust rule behavior by directly modifying the code. For instance, the If-This-Then-That (IFTTT[1]) platform enables expert users to refine the behavior of a rule through the use of code, commonly referred to as **filter code** [15]. This JavaScript code snippet processes trigger fields to customize action fields or bypass an action event based on specific conditions. For example, if users wish to send a Slack message only when a new email with a subject containing the keyword "IFTTT" is received, they must implement the filter code shown in Fig. 2 [15]. The variable *Office365Mail.newEmail* holds the trigger fields, such as the subject, while *Slack.postToChannel* provides various functions, such as

[1] https://www.ifttt.com/.

setMessage(), to assign values to different action fields. The *skip()* function is used to bypass an action. Writing filter code can be challenging for non-expert users due to its technical complexity and the required programming skills. Consequently, non-expert users are often limited to predefined rule templates or basic configuration options, which constrains their ability to create complex and customized automation behaviors.

```
let str = Office365Mail.newEmail.Subject
if (str.indexOf("IFTTT") === -1) {
    Slack.postToChannel.skip()
} else {
    Slack.postToChannel.setMessage("Email " +
        Office365Mail.newEmail.Subject + " just received!")
}
```

Fig. 2. An example of filter code for the rule shown in Fig. 1.

Research efforts have aimed to simplify the rule definition process by developing methods that convert user intent, expressed in natural language, into structured rule components [22] or by recommending new automation rules based on those already defined by the user [44]. These approaches have proven effective in streamlining rule creation and enhancing user experience. However, their functionality is primarily limited to suggesting predefined values for channels, functionalities, and fields. They do not address the challenge of personalizing trigger-action rule behaviors through code customization.

To overcome the limitations of existing approaches, this paper introduces a novel no-code strategy that leverages Large Language Models (LLMs) to bridge the gap between natural language descriptions and executable rule code. Our goal is to empower end-users, particularly those without programming expertise, to define and customize trigger-action rules without manually writing code. This effort aligns with our main research question:

[redacted]

To answer the research question, we curated a dataset of trigger-action rules from IFTTT, accompanied by their corresponding natural language descriptions. These descriptions were refined using an LLM-based preprocessing step to enhance clarity and consistency before being used to fine-tune eight open-source LLMs. Our methodology employs a transformer-based architecture that incrementally generates source code tokens in a left-to-right sequence, progressively constructing a valid rule implementation based on user-provided descriptions. Model performance was assessed by evaluating the ability to generate syntactically correct and functionally equivalent rule implementations. Among the tested models, `Codestral` achieved the best results, with a METEOR score of 54% and a ROUGE-L score of 63%.

The remainder of this paper is organized as follows. Section 2 reviews related work on natural language processing for automation rule generation and code synthesis. Section 3 formalizes the problem, outlining the challenges of translating natural language descriptions into executable trigger-action rules. Section 4 presents our proposed methodology, detailing the design of our LLM-based approach for rule code generation. Section 5 describes the evaluation framework, including dataset construction, model selection, and assessment metrics. Section 6 reports and discusses the experimental results, comparing the performance of different LLMs in generating rule-based code. Finally, Sect. 7 concludes the paper and outlines directions for future research.

2 Related Work

Several studies have examined methods to enhance the user-friendliness of TAPs. For instance, research in end-user programming [31,32] and visual rule-based systems [17] has focused on simplifying the creation of automation rules. However, these approaches still require manual configuration of rule components, which restricts flexibility and scalability. Recent advancements have explored the application of natural language processing techniques for automation [22,46], aiming to generate rule components from natural language descriptions. While these tools facilitate rule configuration, defining complex behaviors often necessitates writing source code, which remains inaccessible to non-expert users. Furthermore, other studies have investigated methods for recommending modifications to users to debug rule behaviors [18,48,49], with a particular focus on preventing unintended situations. However, these approaches primarily address specific issues in rule configurations rather than enabling users to fully utilize the platform's capabilities. In contrast, our solution facilitates customization by generating specific code, allowing even non-expert users to tailor rule behaviors while ensuring compliance with platform requirements.

The task of code generation from natural language descriptions has been extensively studied in recent years, particularly with the advent of large-scale neural models [30]. Early approaches to code generation relied on template-based methods [27] and rule-based systems [3], which required significant manual effort to define syntactic and semantic rules for mapping natural language to code. With the rise of deep learning, sequence-to-sequence models, initially designed for machine translation, were adapted to generate code from natural language inputs [34,45]. More recently, transformer-based models such as OpenAI Codex [14] and CodeT5 [43] have demonstrated significant improvements in code generation accuracy by leveraging pretraining on large-scale code repositories. Despite these advancements, existing work on code generation has primarily focused on general-purpose programming tasks such as function synthesis, SQL query generation, and API call prediction [14,37,50]. However, no prior research has explicitly addressed the problem of generating code for trigger-action rules.

The present work fills this gap by proposing a methodology that employs fine-tuned LLMs to automatically generate source code for trigger-action rules from natural language descriptions.

3 Problem Formulation

TAPs facilitate task automation by linking trigger events to corresponding action responses. Formally, let $\mathcal{C}$ be the set of available channels, where each channel $c \in \mathcal{C}$ corresponds to an entity responsible for managing services (e.g., Slack for messaging automation). Each channel $c \in \mathcal{C}$ is associated with two distinct sets of functionalities:

- $TF(c)$, denoting the set of **trigger** functionalities provided by the channel,
- $AF(c)$, defining the set of **action** functionalities supported by the channel.

These functionalities determine the conditions a channel can monitor or the operations it can execute, forming the basis for specifying trigger-action rule behaviors. Users configure automation rules by selecting channels and their respective functionalities from a catalog, which lists the available services.

A trigger-action rule can be formally defined as a pair comprising trigger and action components:

$$R = \big(\underbrace{\{(c_i, t_{c_i}, F(t_{c_i}))\}_{i=1}^{m}}_{trigger\ component}, \underbrace{\{(c_j, a_{c_j}, F(a_{c_j}))\}_{j=1}^{n}}_{action\ component} \big)$$

The *trigger component* consists of a set of m triggers, where each trigger is specified by selecting a channel $c_i \in C$ and a functionality $t_{c_i} \in TF(c_i)$, which determines the condition that activates the rule. Additional configuration may be required through a set of fields $F(t_{c_i}) = \{f_{t^1_{c_i}}, \ldots, f_{t^l_{c_i}}\}$, where each $f_{t^k_{c_i}}$ represents a parameter for defining the trigger's behavior. For instance, in the rule depicted in Fig. 1, the trigger channel is *Office365*, and the functionality is "*New email received*". Further configuration is required to define the trigger's behavior, such as specifying the *subject*, *sender*, or *time* fields, which establish the conditions under which the rule is activated.

Similarly, the *action component* consists of a set of n actions, where each action is defined by choosing a channel $c_j \in C$ and a functionality $a_{c_j} \in AF(c_j)$, specifying the system's response when the rule is activated. The action functionality may also require configuration through a set of fields $F(a_{c_j}) = \{f_{a^1_{c_j}}, \ldots, f_{a^u_{c_j}}\}$, where each $f_{a^k_{c_j}}$ is a parameter necessary to define the action's behavior. In the rule depicted in Fig. 1, the action channel is *Slack*, and the functionality is "*Post to Channel*", which triggers the system to post a message to a Slack channel. The fields for this action include *message*, *title*, and *channel*, which define the content of the message, its title, and the target channel in Slack where the message will be posted.

The task addressed in this study involves automatically translating a natural language description d of a trigger-action rule R into a corresponding code snippet $\hat{y}_R$. For example, a possible description for generating the code depicted in

Fig. 2, aimed at personalizing the behavior of the rule shown in Fig. 1, is as follows: "*I would like to send a Slack message only when a new email contains the keyword IFTTT in the subject*". This translation is carried out by a code generation model $\mathcal{M}$, which leverages the intent expressed in d to produce syntactically and semantically meaningful rule implementations.

4 Methodology

The proposed methodology comprises two main steps: (*i*) Data Collection and Preprocessing and (*ii*) Fine-Tuning of the Rule Generation Model, as illustrated in Fig. 3. The first step involves gathering and refining pairs of natural language descriptions of trigger-action rule behaviors along with their corresponding code. The second step involves fine-tuning an autoregressive LLM by optimizing the conditional likelihood of the target code sequence. This process ensures that the model effectively learns to map natural language descriptions to their corresponding executable representations.

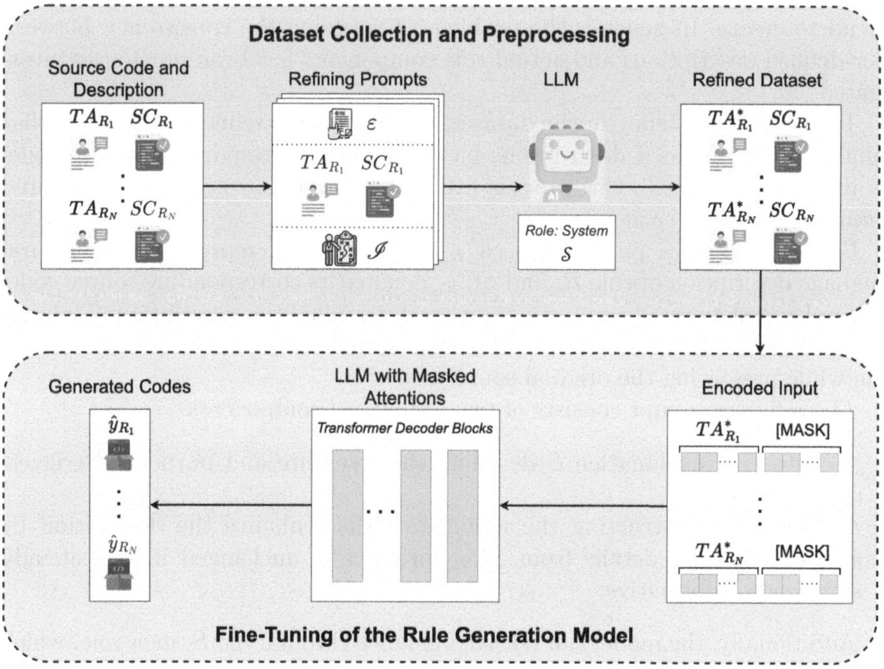

Fig. 3. Overview of the proposed methodology, which includes dataset collection and preprocessing, followed by fine-tuning an LLM for rule code generation.

4.1 Dataset Collection and Preprocessing

For the construction of our dataset, we utilized the IFTTT platform, which offers a key advantage: when defining a rule, users can provide a natural language description of its behavior. This feature serves multiple purposes, enabling users to recall the functionality of their defined rules and allowing others to understand the behavior of a rule created by someone else. Once a rule is established, users have the option to share it within a public catalog, facilitating the activation of predefined rules without requiring manual reconstruction. The catalog can be searched using a description of the desired rule, which is then matched against existing rule descriptions to filter the results. Consequently, these descriptions can be considered as user-expressed intents in natural language, making them particularly valuable for our code generation task.

We collected 615 pairs of natural language descriptions and their corresponding filter codes from IFTTT through the crawler used in [15]. However, as noted in previous studies [8,10,11], user-provided descriptions may be unclear or inconsistent, failing to accurately reflect the defined rule. Since our objective is to obtain a precise source code representation that fully captures the rule's components and fields, we assume that users have complete awareness of the rule they intend to create. In general, the problem of verifying the consistency between user-defined descriptions and actual rule components has been previously investigated [10,11].

To ensure consistency in the dataset, we introduce a refinement process that enhances user-provided descriptions based on their corresponding source code. As illustrated in Fig. 3, this process utilizes an LLM that applies a structured *refining prompt* for each rule.

Formally, given a pair $\langle TA_{R_i}, SC_{R_i} \rangle$, where TA_{R_i} represents the natural language description of rule R_i and SC_{R_i} denotes its corresponding source code, we employ a structured prompting approach to refine the description. The goal is to generate $TA^*_{R_i}$, a version of TA_{R_i} that better captures the semantics of the rule while preserving the original source code.

The refining prompt consists of two structured components:

- A contextual explanation $\mathcal{E}$ detailing the structure and purpose of trigger-action rules.
- A directive $\mathcal{I}$ instructing the model to either enhance the description by adding necessary details from SC_{R_i} or leave it unchanged if it is already sufficiently informative.

Additionally, the model can receive guidance through the *System* role, which specifies domain-specific aspects to emphasize, particularly the refinement of trigger-action rule descriptions. This structured prompting ensures that the generated description is both interpretable and complete.

The exact prompt used for the refinement process is as follows:

Refining Prompt

Context:
A trigger-action rule defines an automation where a specific condition (trigger) leads to an action being executed. These rules can be represented in code, specifying the conditions under which different actions should be performed or skipped.

Given the following code representation of a trigger-action rule:
[Rule Code]
And a description of its functionality:
[Rule Description]

Instruction:
Rewrite the description to fully reflect the logic in the given code, ensuring that it explicitly incorporates the evaluated values of relevant variables in the rule. Do not include the code or variable names in the rewritten description. If the provided description is already complete, return it unchanged.

Instead, the system role was set to emphasize expertise in refining and enhancing descriptions for clarity. The specific instruction given to the model was *"You are an expert in refining and enhancing descriptions of trigger-action rules to ensure clarity"*.

To illustrate the refinement process, consider the following rule description:

Original Description

"This rule will send advisories only during specified times on weekdays."

and the corresponding source code:

```
var Hour = Meta.currentUserTime.hour()
var Day = Meta.currentUserTime.day()

if (Day == 6 || Day == 7) {
  IfNotifications.sendNotification.skip()
}
else if (Hour < 7 || (Hour > 9 && Hour < 17) || Hour > 19) {
  IfNotifications.sendNotification.skip()
}
```

The use of the refining prompt enables the generation of a more detailed and specific version, as demonstrated in the refined description:

Refined Description

"This rule will send an alert for advisories between 7-9 a.m. and 5-7 p.m. on weekdays."

In this case, the model adds specific time frames (7–9 a.m. and 5–7 p.m.) to clarify the conditions under which the rule triggers an alert, enhancing the semantic clarity of the rule description.

4.2 Fine-Tuning of the Rule Generation Model

Fine-tuning an autoregressive LLM for trigger-action rule code generation consists of adapting a pretrained model to a domain-specific task, wherein a natural language description is mapped to an executable rule representation.

Given a dataset of description-code pairs $\mathcal{D} = \{\langle TA^*_{R_i}, SC_{R_i}\rangle\}_{i=1}^{N}$, where $TA^*_{R_i}$ is a refined natural language description of a trigger-action rule and SC_{R_i} is the corresponding source code representing the rule's behavior, the model applies a masking strategy to conceal the source code components SC_{R_i}, as illustrated in Fig. 3. Formally, a masking function Φ is applied to each pair, producing masked training examples:

$$\Phi(TA^*_{R_i}, SC_{R_i}) = (TA^*_{R_i}, \texttt{[MASK]})$$

where `[MASK]` represents the hidden source code that the model must predict. This ensures that the model learns to generate the code solely based on the natural language description.

We employ a transformer-based autoregressive model $\mathcal{M}_\theta$, initialized with pretrained parameters θ_0. Fine-tuning is performed by optimizing the conditional likelihood of the correct code sequence given the natural language description:

$$\theta^* = \arg\max_{\theta} \sum_{i=1}^{N} \log P_{\mathcal{M}_\theta}(\hat{y}_{R_i} \mid TA^*_{R_i})$$

where $P_{\mathcal{M}_\theta}(\hat{y}_{R_i} \mid TA^*_{R_i})$ is the probability assigned by the model to the sequence $\hat{y}_{R_i}$ given $TA^*_{R_i}$.

The model generates source code token-by-token using a left-to-right decoding process. Given a description $TA^*_{R_i}$, the generation follows:

$$P_{\mathcal{M}_\theta}(\hat{y}_{R_i} \mid TA^*_{R_i}) = \prod_{x=1}^{X} P_{\mathcal{M}_\theta}(\hat{y}_{R_{i,x}} \mid \hat{y}_{R_{i,<x}}, TA^*_{R_i})$$

where X is the length of the target code sequence and $\hat{y}_{R_{i,<x}} = (\hat{y}_{R_{i,1}}, \ldots, \hat{y}_{R_{i,x-1}})$ represents the previously generated tokens. Decoding can be performed via greedy search, beam search, or nucleus sampling.

Fine-tuning is conducted using a cross-entropy loss over the token sequences:

$$\mathcal{L}(\theta) = -\sum_{i=1}^{N}\sum_{x=1}^{X_i} \log P_{\mathcal{M}_\theta}(\hat{y}_{R_{i,x}} \mid \hat{y}_{R_{i,<x}}, TA^*_{R_i})$$

Each generated code $\hat{y}_{R_i}$ is compared against the reference implementation $y^*_{R_i}$ to assess the effectiveness of the model.

5 Evaluation Framework

This section outlines the evaluation framework of the proposed methodology. Specifically, it begins by defining the research questions that guide our investigation, followed by a detailed description of the evaluation setup, including model configurations and fine-tuning procedures. Finally, we present the metrics used to assess the performance of the generated code in terms of syntactic correctness and semantic fidelity.

5.1 Assessing Code Quality

To comprehensively answer the main research question, we define two subquestions that guide our investigation:

[redacted]

[redacted]

By addressing these questions, we aim to evaluate whether the generated rule implementations not only adhere to the required syntax but also correctly execute the intended automation logic. This dual perspective is crucial, as syntactic correctness alone does not guarantee that the resulting code aligns with the expected behavior described by users.

5.2 Evaluation Setup

Although proprietary LLMs, such as GPT-4 [1] and Claude 3.7[2], offer advanced capabilities for code generation, their usage is often associated with considerable costs. This poses a potential barrier for certain users, particularly in contexts where TAPs allow the free definition of rules. In such cases, dependence on proprietary models may result in additional expenses that not all users may

[2] https://www.anthropic.com/news/claude-3-7-sonnet.

be willing to pay. To address this limitation, our methodology primarily leverages lightweight, open-source models that are freely available. This choice facilitates broader accessibility and enables deployment even on resource-constrained devices, such as mini PCs equipped with GPUs. Specifically, we fine-tuned four open-source LLMs: `Deepseek-LLM-7B` [20], `Mistral-7B-v0.2` [29], `Qwen2.5-7B` [38], and `Llama-2-7B` [41]. Furthermore, in light of the growing number of LLMs fine-tuned specifically for code generation [30], we also incorporated their corresponding fine-tuned code-generation variants: `Deepseek-Coder-6.7B` [25], `Codestral-7B-v0.1`[3], `Qwen2.5-Coder-7B` [28], and `CodeLlama-7B` [40]. The fine-tuning for all models was conducted with specific configurations to optimize performance while maintaining computational efficiency. During inference, we employed greedy decoding, generating a single code for each natural language description.

To save memory and boost efficiency, we used 4-bit quantization with a normalized floating-point format tailored for transformers. This ensures fast, stable computation with minimal precision loss. We also avoided introducing additional quantization overhead that could destabilize training. To optimize fine-tuning, we used LoRA [26], a memory-efficient method that updates a small parameter subset. We set rank to 16, used a scaling factor of 32, and applied 5% dropout to avoid overfitting. LoRA was adapted for causal language modeling.

For fine-tuning, we configured the training process to span 5 epochs, ensuring sufficient learning while preventing overfitting. The batch size per device was set to 2 to accommodate hardware constraints, and gradient accumulation was employed over 4 steps to simulate a larger batch size without excessive memory usage. A cosine learning rate scheduler was applied, starting with an initial learning rate of $1e-4$ that gradually decayed over time. To prevent excessive weight updates, weight decay regularization was introduced at a rate of 0.01, and gradient clipping was employed with a maximum norm of 1 to maintain stable training dynamics. Mixed precision training was enabled using *bfloat16* to enhance computational efficiency without compromising numerical accuracy.

We refined the natural language descriptions using `DeepSeek-R1` [19], which aided in enhancing the clarity and completeness of the descriptions.

The finalized dataset underwent manual validation and was subsequently partitioned into training, validation, and test sets to ensure robust evaluation. Initially, 80% of the data was allocated to training and 20% to testing. From the training set, an additional 10% was reserved for validation, enabling hyperparameter selection based on performance on unseen samples.

5.3 Evaluation Metrics

To evaluate the effectiveness of the proposed methodology for code generation, we employ a range of widely recognized metrics used in performance assessment:

- **BLEU** [35]: Assesses the precision of n-grams in the generated text by comparing them with reference texts, rewarding greater overlap.

[3] https://mistral.ai/en/news/codestral.

- **ROUGE-L** [33]: Measures the longest common subsequence between the generated and reference text, capturing structural coherence.
- **ROUGE-1** [33]: Calculates unigram recall, quantifying the overlap of individual tokens between the generated and reference code.
- **ROUGE-2** [33]: Computes bigram recall, assessing the overlap of two-token sequences to evaluate structural accuracy.
- **METEOR** [4]: Evaluates the similarity between generated and reference texts by considering factors such as synonymy, stemming, and word order, offering a more flexible approach to handle variations in the output.
- **CodeBERTScore** [51]: Leverages contextual embeddings from CodeBERT [21] to compute the similarity between generated and reference code, capturing semantic equivalence even when exact token matches are absent.
- **CodeBLEU** [39]: Extends BLEU with syntax-aware and data-flow matching techniques to better assess the quality of generated code, ensuring alignment with reference implementations beyond mere token overlap.

6 Results

In the following sections, we compare the strengths and limitations of various LLM models in generating rule implementations. This includes assessing how well the generated code matches the expected structure and syntax of the reference implementations (RQ1) and how effectively it captures the user-intended semantics as described in the natural language input (RQ2). The results from fine-tuned LLMs, based on both syntactic and semantic evaluation metrics, are presented in Table 1. This comparison helps to highlight the most effective models for automating the generation of trigger-action rules and provides insights into the trade-offs between syntactic correctness and semantic fidelity.

6.1 Answering RQ1: Syntactic Quality of Generated Code

To evaluate how well the generated code conforms to the expected syntax, we consider BLEU, ROUGE-L, ROUGE-1, and ROUGE-2. These metrics assess

Table 1. Performance of fine-tuned LLMs for trigger-action rule code generation.

LLM	Metrics						
	BLEU	ROUGE-L	ROUGE-1	ROUGE-2	METEOR	CodeBERTScore	CodeBLEU
`Deepseek-LLM-7B`	0.29	0.56	0.60	0.48	0.46	0.87	0.31
`Deepseek-Coder-6.7B`	0.27	0.53	0.57	0.44	0.41	0.86	0.30
`Mistral-7B-v0.2`	0.36	0.61	0.65	0.55	0.52	0.89	0.35
`Codestral-7B-v0.1`	**0.38**	**0.63**	**0.67**	**0.56**	**0.54**	**0.90**	**0.36**
`Qwen2.5-7B`	0.12	0.26	0.29	0.21	0.36	0.83	0.32
`Qwen2.5-Coder-7B`	0.07	0.22	0.25	0.18	0.34	0.81	0.28
`Llama-2-7B`	0.28	0.55	0.58	0.45	0.43	0.87	0.29
`CodeLlama-7B`	0.25	0.52	0.56	0.44	0.43	0.86	0.32

token-level similarity, measuring how closely the generated code matches reference implementations in terms of structure and sequence accuracy.

Table 1 shows that `Codestral-7B-v0.1` achieves the highest syntactic performance, with BLEU (0.38), ROUGE-L (0.63), ROUGE-1 (0.67), and ROUGE-2 (0.56), demonstrating strong adherence to reference syntax. `Mistral-7B-v0.2` follows closely, attaining a BLEU score of 0.36 and a ROUGE-L score of 0.61, indicating high syntactic fidelity. These models correctly generate rule structures, including conditional checks and function calls, with minimal errors.

`Deepseek-LLM-7B` and `Llama-2-7B` exhibit comparable performance, with BLEU scores of 0.29 and 0.28, respectively, and ROUGE-1 scores of 0.60 and 0.58. While these models effectively capture syntactic patterns, they occasionally produce minor syntax errors. For example, they might generate incorrect assignment operators (`if(Min = 0)` instead of `if(Min == 0)`) or omit necessary closing brackets – e.g., "`var depositAmountString = depositAmount.toString(`".

`Deepseek-Coder-6.7B` performs slightly below these models, with a BLEU score of 0.27 and a ROUGE-1 score of 0.57. This model tends to generate misplaced brackets in rule definitions and omit function calls. `CodeLlama-7B` and `Qwen2.5-7B` display weaker syntactic alignment, with BLEU scores of 0.25 and 0.12, respectively. `CodeLlama-7B` maintains moderate syntactic correctness with a ROUGE-L score of 0.52, but it often generates incorrectly formatted function calls, such as `PhoneCall.callMyPhone.setArgs(''Remaining '' + 10 - Min + '' Minutes'')`, which causes unintended string concatenation errors. `Qwen2.5-7B` struggles significantly, achieving a ROUGE-L score of only 0.26, indicating poor token alignment and structural coherence. Common errors from this model include misplaced parentheses, unterminated string literals, and invalid numeric operations, such as missing operators between numbers and variables, leading to syntax errors. Lastly, `Qwen2.5-Coder-7B` exhibits the lowest syntactic performance among the evaluated models, with a BLEU score of 0.07 and a ROUGE-L score of 0.22, highlighting its limited syntactic fidelity. This model frequently produces syntactically incorrect outputs, such as improper function calls, e.g., `Weather.currentWeatherAtTime_sunriseAt` instead of the correct `Weather.currentWeather[0].SunsetAt`.

In summary, the results achieved allow to answer our first RQ as follow:

> `Codestral-7B-v0.1` achieves the highest syntactic performance among the evaluated models, demonstrating strong alignment with the reference syntax. `Mistral-7B-v0.2` follows closely behind, while `Deepseek-LLM-7B` and `Llama-2-7B` effectively capture syntactic patterns, though they do not outperform `Codestral-7B-v0.1` or `Mistral-7B-v0.2`. In contrast, models such as `CodeLlama-7B` and `Qwen2.5-7B` exhibit weaker syntactic alignment, with `Qwen2.5-Coder-7B` displaying the lowest syntactic fidelity across all models assessed.

6.2 Answering RQ2: Semantic Quality of Generated Code

Beyond syntactic accuracy, it is essential to evaluate whether the generated code correctly implements the intended functionality described in natural language. To assess semantic fidelity, we employ METEOR, CodeBERTScore, and CodeBLEU, which capture both lexical and embedding-based similarity as well as functional correctness.

As presented in Table 1, `Codestral-7B-v0.1` achieves the highest semantic accuracy, with a METEOR score of 0.54, a CodeBERTScore score of 0.90, and a CodeBLEU score of 0.36, indicating its superior ability to capture the intended rule logic. `Mistral-7B-v0.2` follows closely, with a METEOR score of 0.52, a CodeBERTScore score of 0.89, and a CodeBLEU score of 0.35, further confirming its strong semantic alignment.

`Deepseek-LLM-7B` also demonstrates competitive performance, attaining a METEOR score of 0.46, a CodeBERTScore score of 0.87, and a CodeBLEU score of 0.31. This model occasionally generates rules with flawed conditions, such as incorrect time ranges, misplaced conditions, or logical inversions that lead to actions executing at unintended times. For example, one generated rule intended to skip notifications between 22:00 and 08:00 but instead allowed notifications to be sent during this period. In another instance, it generated a rule that misinterpreted the weekday condition, performing an action on weekends instead of weekdays.

Meanwhile, `Llama-2-7B` and `Deepseek-Coder-6.7B` achieve METEOR scores of 0.43 and 0.41, respectively, with corresponding CodeBERTScore scores of 0.87 and 0.86 and CodeBLEU scores of 0.29 and 0.30, reflecting moderate semantic correctness. These models have been seen to introduce errors such as omitting critical conditions or failing to initialize key variables, causing unintended behavior in rule execution. For instance, one rule generated by `Llama-2-7B` attempted to post a message to Slack without specifying the target channel, rendering the action incomplete.

`CodeLlama-7B`, despite exhibiting weaker syntactic performance, attains a CodeBLEU score of 0.32, suggesting that its generated code retains a degree of functional consistency. Interestingly, while `Qwen2.5-7B` also struggles with syntax, its CodeBLEU score of 0.32 indicates that, despite lower token alignment, its outputs still partially preserve the intended functionality. However, its METEOR score of 0.36 and CodeBERTScore score of 0.83 reflect comparatively lower semantic accuracy than most models. Nevertheless, it surpasses `Qwen2.5-Coder-7B`, which exhibits the lowest semantic accuracy. This model has been observed to generate rules with redundant or contradictory conditions, such as skipping an action both during and outside a designated time range, which contradicts the desired behavior. For example, one rule intended to skip light activation at night ended up skipping it both during the night and day. Furthermore, `Qwen2.5-Coder-7B` occasionally generates logic that attempted to modify undefined variables, leading to runtime failures; for example, one rule attempted to adjust a temperature setting using a non-existent variable reference.

In summary, the results achieved allow to answer our second RQ as follow:

> `Codestral-7B-v0.1` leads in semantic accuracy, showing strong functionality alignment. `Mistral-7B-v0.2` closely follows with robust alignment. `Deepseek-LLM-7B` performs well, while `Llama-2-7B` and `Deepseek-Coder-6.7B` show moderate correctness but don't surpass the top models. `CodeLlama-7B`, despite weaker syntax, retains functional consistency. `Qwen2.5-7B`, struggling with syntax, still shows some functionality, though with lower accuracy. `Qwen2.5-Coder-7B` has the weakest semantic performance, struggling to align with the intended rule logic.

6.3 Findings

Our experimental evaluation highlights several key insights regarding the efficacy of LLMs in generating trigger-action rule code from natural language descriptions. The following extended findings provide a deeper analysis of the observed trends and model performance characteristics:

1. **Consistency Across Metrics:** `Codestral-7B-v0.1` consistently outperforms other models across both syntactic and semantic evaluation metrics, establishing itself as the most effective solution for supporting non-expert users in configuring automation rules. Notably, its strong BLEU and ROUGE scores confirm its ability to replicate the structural coherence of reference implementations, while its METEOR, CodeBERTScore, and CodeBLEU results demonstrate superior alignment with user intentions.
2. **Trade-offs Between Syntax and Semantics:** While `Deepseek-LLM-7B` exhibits notable syntactic accuracy, its lower METEOR, CodeBERTScore, and CodeBLEU values indicate occasional misalignment with intended functionality. This suggests that models excelling in token alignment may sacrifice some semantic fidelity. Conversely, `CodeLlama-7B`, despite weaker token-level performance, achieves a comparable CodeBLEU score, underscoring its ability to preserve functional behavior despite reduced syntactic precision.
3. **Performance Variation by Complexity:** An analysis of rule complexity reveals that `Codestral-7B-v0.1` maintains stable performance across simple and complex rules alike. In contrast, models like `Deepseek-Coder-6.7B` and `Qwen2.5-Coder-7B` exhibit pronounced performance degradation for rules featuring multiple conditions, nested logic, or extended parameter configurations. This indicates that robust context modeling and improved sequence dependencies are key strengths of `Codestral-7B-v0.1`.
4. **Performance Discrepancy in Code-Specific Models:** Models fine-tuned specifically for code generation often exhibit lower performance compared to those trained on more diverse datasets. This trend is evident in models such as `Deepseek-Coder-6.7B`, which demonstrates lower semantic fidelity than its general-purpose counterpart, `Deepseek-LLM-7B`. A similar pattern emerges in the comparisons between `CodeLlama-7B` and `Llama-2-7B`, as well

as `Qwen2.5-Coder-7B` and `Qwen2.5-7B`. This discrepancy may arise from the distinctive nature of trigger-action rule code, which integrates domain-specific logic with unconventional syntax patterns. Models trained on a broader range of linguistic structures appear to generalize more effectively to these hybrid patterns. However, the Mistral family presents an exception to this trend. `Codestral-7B-v0.1`, a code-specialized variant, outperforms `Mistral-7B-v0.2` across all metrics. This suggests that while general-purpose models benefit from exposure to diverse linguistic structures, a sufficiently well-trained code-focused model can achieve superior results if it effectively captures both syntactic correctness and the nuanced reasoning required for rule logic. The advantage of `Codestral-7B-v0.1` may stem from its ability to preserve the strong language modeling capabilities of Mistral while incorporating a refined understanding of code structure, thereby facilitating a more effective alignment between textual descriptions and executable rules.

7 Conclusion and Future Work

This paper introduces a methodology that leverages LLMs to enable the no-code configuration of trigger-action rules on TAPs. By enabling end-users to generate rule implementations directly from natural language descriptions, our approach improves accessibility and reduces reliance on programming expertise. Through an extensive evaluation, we demonstrated that LLMs, particularly `Codestral`, achieve high performance in both syntactic correctness and semantic fidelity when generating executable rule code. These findings highlight the potential of LLMs in simplifying EUD and making automation more intuitive and adaptable for non-expert users.

Despite the demonstrated effectiveness of our approach, several limitations remain that warrant further investigation. Although the generated code snippets are structurally coherent and syntactically correct, they do not always fully capture the intended behavior specified by users—particularly in complex scenarios involving intricate conditional logic, interdependent triggers, or multi-step workflows. Additionally, while our refinement process enhances the clarity of rule descriptions, inconsistencies between user-provided inputs and generated outputs may still occur. Future research will explore several directions to address these limitations. First, integrating user feedback mechanisms into the code generation pipeline could improve alignment with user intent, allowing for iterative refinement of generated codes [5]. Second, enhancing the interpretability of generated codes through explainability techniques will be crucial for fostering trust and usability [9,12]. Third, expanding the evaluation to real-world user studies will provide deeper insights into the practical applicability and effectiveness of our approach in diverse automation contexts, such as in understanding and controlling security and privacy threats [13]. Finally, broadening the dataset used to fine-tune the models will be essential for improving generalization and handling a wider variety of user-defined automation scenarios.

References

1. Achiam, J., et al.: GPT-4 technical report. arXiv preprint arXiv:2303.08774 (2023)
2. Alhirabi, N., Rana, O., Perera, C.: Security and privacy requirements for the internet of things: a survey. ACM Trans. Internet Things **2**(1), 1–37 (2021)
3. Bajwa, I.S., Siddique, M.I., Choudhary, M.A.: Rule based production systems for automatic code generation in Java. In: Proceedings of 1st International Conference on Digital Information Management, pp. 300–305 (2006)
4. Banerjee, S., Lavie, A.: Meteor: an automatic metric for MT evaluation with improved correlation with human judgments. In: Proceedings of the ACL Workshop on Intrinsic and Extrinsic Evaluation Measures for Machine Translation and/or Summarization, pp. 65–72 (2005)
5. Bang, Y., et al.: A multitask, multilingual, multimodal evaluation of chatgpt on reasoning, hallucination, and interactivity. arXiv preprint arXiv:2302.04023 (2023)
6. Barricelli, B.R., Cassano, F., Fogli, D., Piccinno, A.: End-user development, end-user programming and end-user software engineering: a systematic mapping study. J. Syst. Softw. **149**, 101–137 (2019)
7. Breve, B., Cimino, G., Desolda, G., Deufemia, V., Elefante, A.: On the user perception of security risks of TAP rules: a user study. In: Proceedings of International Symposium on End User Development (ISEUD 2023). Lecture Notes in Computer Science, vol. 13917, pp. 162–179. Springer, Cham (2023)
8. Breve, B., Cimino, G., Deufemia, V.: Identifying security and privacy violation rules in trigger-action IoT platforms with NLP models. IEEE Internet Things J. **10**(6), 5607–5622 (2022)
9. Breve, B., Cimino, G., Deufemia, V.: Hybrid prompt learning for generating justifications of security risks in automation rules. ACM Trans. Intell. Syst. Technol. **15**(5), 1–26 (2024)
10. Breve, B., Cimino, G., Deufemia, V., Elefante, A.: Unleashing the power of NLP models for semantic consistency checking of automation rules. J. Vis. Lang. Comput. **2023**(2), 1–14 (2023)
11. Breve, B., Cimino, G., Deufemia, V., Elefante, A., et al.: A BERT-based model for semantic consistency checking of automation rules. In: Proceedings of the 29th International Distributed Multimedia Systems Conference on Visualization and Visual Languages, pp. 87–93 (2023)
12. Breve, B., Cimino, G., Deufemia, V., et al.: Towards explainable security for ECA rules. In: Proceedings of the 3rd International Workshop on Empowering People in Dealing with Internet of Things Ecosystems (EMPATHY 20222) co-located with International Conference on Advanced Visual Interfaces (AVI). CEUR Workshop Proceedings, vol. 3172, pp. 26–30 (2022)
13. Breve, B., Desolda, G., Deufemia, V., Greco, F., Matera, M.: An end-user development approach to secure smart environments. In: Fogli, D., Tetteroo, D., Barricelli, B.R., Borsci, S., Markopoulos, P., Papadopoulos, G.A. (eds.) IS-EUD 2021. LNCS, vol. 12724, pp. 36–52. Springer, Cham (2021). https://doi.org/10.1007/978-3-030-79840-6_3
14. Chen, M., et al.: Evaluating large language models trained on code. arXiv preprint arXiv:2107.03374 (2021)
15. Chen, Y., Alhanahnah, M., Sabelfeld, A., Chatterjee, R., Fernandes, E.: Practical data access minimization in trigger-action platforms. In: Proceedings of 31st USENIX Security Symposium, pp. 2929–2945 (2022)

16. Cimino, G., Deufemia, V.: SIGFRID: unsupervised, platform-agnostic interference detection in IoT automation rules. ACM Trans. Internet Things (2025)
17. Corcella, L., Manca, M., Paternò, F., Santoro, C.: A visual tool for analysing IoT trigger/action programming. In: Proceedings of International Working Conference Human-Centered Software Engineering, pp. 189–206. Springer, Cham (2019)
18. Corno, F., De Russis, L., Monge Roffarello, A.: Empowering end users in debugging trigger-action rules. In: Proceedings of the 2019 CHI Conference on Human Factors in Computing Systems, pp. 1–13 (2019)
19. DeepSeek-AI: DeepSeek-R1: Incentivizing reasoning capability in LLMs via reinforcement learning. arXiv preprint arXiv:2501.12948 (2025)
20. DeepSeek-AI, Bi, X., et al.: DeepSeek LLM: scaling open-source language models with longtermism. arXiv preprint arXiv:2401.02954 (2024)
21. Feng, Z., et al.: CodeBERT: a pre-trained model for programming and natural languages. In: Cohn, T., He, Y., Liu, Y. (eds.) Findings of the Association for Computational Linguistics, pp. 1536–1547 (2020)
22. Gao, Y., Xiao, K., Li, F., Xu, W., Huang, J., Dong, W.: ChatIoT: zero-code generation of trigger-action based IoT programs. Proc. ACM Interact. Mob. Wearable Ubiquit. Technol. **8**(3), 1–29 (2024)
23. García-Herranz, M., Haya, P.A., Alamán, X.: Towards a ubiquitous end-user programming system for smart spaces. J. Univers. Comput. Sci. **16**(12), 1633–1649 (2010)
24. Ghiani, G., Manca, M., Paternò, F., Santoro, C.: Personalization of context-dependent applications through trigger-action rules. ACM Trans. Comput.-Hum. Interact. **24**(2), 1–33 (2017)
25. Guo, D., et al.: DeepSeek-coder: when the large language model meets programming–the rise of code intelligence. arXiv preprint arXiv:2401.14196 (2024)
26. Hu, E.J., et al.: LoRa: low-rank adaptation of large language models. arXiv preprint arXiv:2106.09685 (2021)
27. Hu, K., Duan, Z., Wang, J., Gao, L., Shang, L.: Template-based AADL automatic code generation. Front. Comput. Sci. **13**, 698–714 (2019)
28. Hui, B., et al.: Qwen2.5-coder technical report. arXiv preprint arXiv:2409.12186 (2024)
29. Jiang, A.Q., et al.: Mistral 7b. arXiv preprint arXiv:2310.06825 (2023)
30. Jiang, J., Wang, F., Shen, J., Kim, S., Kim, S.: A survey on large language models for code generation. arXiv preprint arXiv:2406.00515 (2024)
31. Krishna, A., Le Pallec, M., Mateescu, R., Salaün, G.: Design and deployment of expressive and correct web of things applications. ACM Trans. Internet Things **3**(1), 1–30 (2021)
32. Lieberman, H., Paternò, F., Klann, M., Wulf, V.: End-user development: an emerging paradigm. In: End User Development, pp. 1–8. Springer, Cham (2006)
33. Lin, C.Y.: ROUGE: a package for automatic evaluation of summaries. In: Text Summarization Branches Out, pp. 74–81. Association for Computational Linguistics (2004)
34. Ling, W., et al.: Latent predictor networks for code generation. In: Erk, K., Smith, N.A. (eds.) Proceedings of the 54th Annual Meeting of the Association for Computational Linguistics (Volume 1: Long Papers), pp. 599–609. Association for Computational Linguistics (2016)
35. Papineni, K., Roukos, S., Ward, T., Zhu, W.J.: BLEU: a method for automatic evaluation of machine translation. In: Proceedings of the 40th annual meeting of the Association for Computational Linguistics, pp. 311–318 (2002)

36. Paternò, F.: End user development: survey of an emerging field for empowering people. Int. Scholarly Res. Not. **2013**(1), 532659 (2013)
37. Phan, H., Sharma, A., Jannesari, A.: Generating context-aware API calls from natural language description using neural embeddings and machine translation. In: Proceedings of 36th IEEE/ACM International Conference on Automated Software Engineering Workshops, pp. 219–226. IEEE (2021)
38. Qwen, Yang, A., et al.: Qwen2.5 technical report. arXiv preprint arXiv:2412.15115 (2025)
39. Ren, S., et al.: CodeBLEU: a method for automatic evaluation of code synthesis. arXiv preprint arXiv:2009.10297 (2020)
40. Roziere, B., et al.: Code Llama: open foundation models for code. arXiv preprint arXiv:2308.12950 (2023)
41. Touvron, H., et al.: Llama 2: open foundation and fine-tuned chat models. arXiv preprint arXiv:2307.09288 (2023)
42. Ur, B., McManus, E., Pak Yong Ho, M., Littman, M.L.: Practical trigger-action programming in the smart home. In: Proceedings of the SIGCHI Conference on Human Factors in Computing Systems, pp. 803–812 (2014)
43. Wang, Y., Wang, W., Joty, S., Hoi, S.C.: CodeT5: identifier-aware unified pre-trained encoder-decoder models for code understanding and generation. In: Moens, M.F., Huang, X., Specia, L., Yih, S.W. (eds.) Proceedings of the 2021 Conference on Empirical Methods in Natural Language Processing, pp. 8696–8708. Association for Computational Linguistics (2021)
44. Yao, Y., Kamani, M.M., Cheng, Z., Chen, L., Joe-Wong, C., Liu, T.: FedRule: federated rule recommendation system with graph neural networks. In: Proceedings of the 8th ACM/IEEE Conference on Internet of Things Design and Implementation, pp. 197–208 (2023)
45. Yin, P., Neubig, G.: A syntactic neural model for general-purpose code generation. arXiv preprint arXiv:1704.01696 (2017)
46. Yusuf, I.N.B., Jamal, D.B.A., Jiang, L., Lo, D.: RecipeGen++: an automated trigger action programs generator. In: Proceedings of the ACM Joint European Software Engineering Conference and Symposium on the Foundations of Software Engineering, pp. 1672–1676 (2022)
47. Yusuf, I.N.B., Jiang, L., Lo, D.: Accurate generation of trigger-action programs with domain-adapted sequence-to-sequence learning. In: Proceedings of the IEEE/ACM International Conference on Program Comprehension, pp. 99–110 (2022)
48. Zhang, L., He, W., Martinez, J., Brackenbury, N., Lu, S., Ur, B.: AutoTap: synthesizing and repairing trigger-action programs using LTL properties. In: Proceedings of IEEE/ACM 41st International Conference on Software Engineering, pp. 281–291. IEEE (2019)
49. Zhang, L., Zhou, C., Littman, M.L., Ur, B., Lu, S.: Helping users debug trigger-action programs. Proc. ACM Interact. Mob. Wearable Ubiquit. Technol. **6**(4), 1–32 (2023)
50. Zhong, V., Xiong, C., Socher, R.: Seq2SQL: generating structured queries from natural language using reinforcement learning. arXiv preprint arXiv:1709.00103 (2017)
51. Zhou, S., Alon, U., Agarwal, S., Neubig, G.: CodeBERTScore: evaluating code generation with pretrained models of code. In: Bouamor, H., Pino, J., Bali, K. (eds.) Proceedings of the 2023 Conference on Empirical Methods in Natural Language Processing, pp. 13921–13937 (2023)

Explaining Problems in Daily Automations with ExplainTAP

Sara Maenza(✉), Andrea Mattioli, and Fabio Paternò

CNR-ISTI, Pisa, Italy
{sara.maenza,andrea.mattioli,fabio.paterno}@isti.cnr.it

Abstract. In smart spaces, multiple connected objects and sensors act in a coordinated manner through automations that are deployed into the environment. A common approach to empowering users to configure the desired automated behaviours is using trigger-action programming (TAP). However, it can be difficult for users to untangle the behaviour of the created rules. In this paper, we propose a novel solution, ExplainTAP, whose objective is to support users in detecting and understanding possible problems between TAP rules (such as conflicts and unexpected direct or indirect rule activations). It also detects inconsistencies between such automations and users' goals. After the analysis, the tool proposes possible improvements. For this purpose, the tool can also simulate and analyse the context in which rules could be activated and provide explanations about possible issues to make the behaviour of the smart space more transparent. The paper also reports on a user test of the tool with 18 participants, which provided overall positive feedback and highlighted its usefulness.

Keywords: End-user development · Internet of things · Trigger-Action rules · Explainability

1 Introduction

The Internet of Things (IoT) has become a pervasive technology and, according to forecasts, will continue to grow in the next years. Together with artificial intelligence, they are changing the ways we live, also in our domestic spaces. Automation allows for the definition of orchestrated behaviours exploiting the network of connected sensors and objects together with associated services. Since the needs of each one can be different, end users should be provided with tools that allow them to create and modify automations to their liking. Several approaches have been proposed to support these operations without needing low-level code, hence aimed at people without programming experience. One relevant approach for this purpose is Trigger-Action Programming (TAP) [29]. It has been studied extensively, and evidence suggests that it is understandable by people without programming experience and flexible enough to meet the users' personalisation needs [30].

In its most basic formulation, a TAP approach activates one action in response to some event, which can be a change detected in the environment or an update from an

C. Santoro et al. (Eds.): IS-EUD 2025, LNCS 15713, pp. 41–58, 2025.
https://doi.org/10.1007/978-3-031-95452-8_3

application or a service. This simple formulation is not powerful enough to express many relevant behaviours [3] since everyday use cases require limiting the activation of an automation to a specific timeframe or as long as certain values are within some boundaries. These cases require defining the trigger with a combination of events and conditions. The user mental model [32] should consider such a distinction to establish a correct vision of the smart space's functioning since the incorrect assimilation of the temporal aspects is often a source of errors in TAP rules [3, 19]. For this purpose, it is important that TAP applications explicitly represent the distinction between these concepts [1]. Another important source of issues can emerge in real situations where multiple automations can be active at the same time, thus making it difficult to understand the resulting behaviours. A way to improve users' control of smart spaces is to provide them with answers to questions concerning the functioning of the active automations, such as "Why does this automation just activate?" or more concretely "Why is the light on since I automated it's turning off?". This additional information provided when needed can improve the overall intelligibility of the system [9].

There is growing attention to how intelligent systems generate their results. All the stakeholders need tools to understand their functioning better and to calibrate their expectations, trust, and level of control required. An analysis in this sense [23] investigated the gap between the algorithmic aspect of eXplainable AI (XAI) and what is needed to address the user needs in real situations, and interpreting explanations as answers to questions, proposed a question bank representing what users may ask about the AI data input and results. Another effort in this sense is XAIR [31], a design framework that addresses when, what, and how to provide explanations in AR.

Intending to make the behaviour of a smart home environment more transparent and intelligible, we investigated how to support users in detecting relations and possible problems in the active rules in their environment and propose a method and an associated tool to ease this task. The results described in this paper are: a description of a method indicating how to support users in detecting and understanding problems in their smart environments, deriving from conflicts or dependencies between automations or between rules and the users' long-term goal; the design and the implementation of a tool prototype to support the intelligibility of a smart environment when multiple automations, represented in trigger-action format, are active at the same time; the feedback obtained in a first user test of the proposed solution.

2 Related Work

2.1 Platform to Analyse Conflicts Between TAP Rules

In terms of supporting platforms, one of the first approaches considering the monitoring of multiple automation is AppsGate [15]. A dependency graph of the state of the entities is used to show users whether an entity state is modified by more than one automation or if one automation refers to an object that is currently missing. However, no direct answers are provided concerning the state of the smart space. An effort to overcome this limitation is ITAD [24], which supports the Interrogative Debugging paradigm [21], exposing the "Why" (highlighting which contextual elements in the automation are verified in the context) and "Why not" (pointing out why a rule does not verify) functionalities.

Furthermore, the tool can detect conflicts between rules and simulate the execution context by allowing users to insert the desired values to test. Another proposed solution is EUDebug [11], which uses a Semantic Colored Petri Net to detect the possible problems between user-created automation rules, simulating the automations activations and their interactions. The prototype shares the same expressiveness limits as the original IFTTT version, only allowing single event-action rules. The same set of problems is detected by Smart Block [2] employing graph analysis. The analysis is static, not allowing the insertion of contextual values to see which automation will activate and how these will affect the environment. A different take on the problem is AutoTap [33], which uses Linear Temporal Logic to formalise user-defined constraints on the automations in the smart space (e.g. raining and windows open should not be possible simultaneously). The application can automatically generate TAP rules that satisfy these properties, or repair previously generated ones. The MenShen tool [6] uses Linear Hybrid Automata to detect problems in one trigger-one action rules. The system can check whether an unwanted system state can be reached and eventually generate a possible fix. In this case, users have to specify which state of the environment should not happen. Coppers and others [9] put forward FORTNIoT, which aims to make the behaviour of smart environments easier to grasp by providing a tool to detect which automations will trigger in the future and what environmental changes they will cause. The system is based on self-sustained predictions and tracks the "why" an action activates. In a subsequent contribution [10], the authors also discuss remediating unintended situations, allowing users to define one-time exceptions to rules. However, the type of visual representation proposed makes it difficult to scale up to address cases with several connected objects.

Overall, it emerges that while some applications can detect some types of issues in TAP rules, the few of them that can also simulate the rules' run-time execution are limited in terms of possible issues they can detect (e.g. only rule conflicts) or by the simplified structure of the automations considered (only one trigger-one action). Furthermore, a tool capable of reasoning and informing users about long-term goals and rules relations is still missing.

2.2 Explainable Smart Homes

A contribution to XAI for smart homes [16] proposed a framework to explain the results of an activity classifier, showing which data led to the classification. Some reflections about XAI also apply to IoT systems, regardless of whether they use deep learning. Such systems can be seen as "boxes" that take as input a set of automations and the state of the context of use and output some actions. The systems' opacity derives from the multiple interactions between automations and the context, which can be difficult to untangle for users. It is crucial to support users in detecting possible conflicts [7, 17] since they can cause an overall decrease in the usefulness of the smart environment [5]. In this case, the goal is not to provide details of the system functioning but rather to provide easy-to-understand explanations concerning why the system is in a certain state, what leads to the activation of some automations, and what other effects this cause. From this perspective, it is useful to consider the relationships between the automations and the users' long-term goals. The functionalities users want to automate are usually linked to some objective they want to improve or optimise in the long term. However, the translation of high-level goals into connections between sensors and actuators can be a hard task. It is also difficult to foresee all the possible effects an automated action can bring when creating it. For instance, a well-thought-out safety automation could still negatively impact energy consumption. Although some studies started to consider the importance of long-term goals in automation rules [18], their relations with the functionalities [14, 26], or how to optimise a single long-term goal [4, 25], to our knowledge, previous work has not sufficiently considered the problems that can emerge between a set of automations and the various (and variable) long-term goals users can prioritise at a time.

3 Design of the Proposed Solution

3.1 Requirements

Based on the literature review, we identified a list of main requirements for the novel solution we propose.

R1: Providing users with easy-to-understand descriptions of the state of the automation system. Understanding which automations are active and the conditions required to execute them is crucial to ensure users' control and understanding of the intelligent environment [27]. Users need access to information that helps them understand the overall functioning of the system, i.e. what effects are caused by the active automations, in order to achieve a balance between human and system control [28]. To this goal, clear information must be provided on the rules and context values that are currently active.

R2: Allowing for the simulation of the execution of automations with user-inserted contextual values. Since many problems only occur during execution [11, 24], users should be able to simulate situations by entering the desired contextual values, answering the question 'What if?' [22]. The rules that would be activated in the specified context should be clearly indicated. Furthermore, the system should automatically deduce subsequent states [10] derived from rule activations, updating the context representation accordingly. To facilitate problem detection, there should be the possibility to save and load presets of common contexts.

R3: Answering questions concerning the functioning of the smart space. The platform aims to make the behaviour of automated IoT systems comprehensible by anticipating users' questions about the system's explicability [23], both on a global level (general understanding of operation) and on a local level (related to a specific system output). Common questions include: 'How', 'Why' or 'Why not' an automation activates [12, 21, 24], 'What if' I change parameters and 'How to be that' (what can be changed to obtain a different result), the 'How to still be this' (what is the allowable range of parameter changes to obtain the same result), and performance information regarding whether an activation is certain or possible. The answers can be implicit (e.g. the question 'What if' can be answered by changing some contextual parameters and seeing in the simulator the effects of these changes) or explicit (triggered by a direct request from the user, such as a 'Why' or 'Why not' an automation is triggered in a context of use).

R4: Detecting rule conflicts. It is crucial to inform users if two actions with incompatible effects on a device (such as 'turn off the light' and 'change the colour of the light to blue') can occur simultaneously [8]. For this purpose, consideration must also be given to the containment relationship between the objects involved (e.g. 'close all windows' and 'open the kitchen window') [24].

R5: Detecting activation chains between automations. The application should detect when the activation of one automation is caused by another. These rule chains [8] can be direct, when a trigger of one rule directly activates another rule, or indirect, when an action acts on an environmental variable 'observed' by a trigger. Although it is not certain that the first rule triggers the second, users must be aware of this. Loops are a special case, where the final action reactivates the first trigger.

R6: Suggesting possible automations optimisations based on a user goal. The execution of a rule in a smart home can have a positive or negative impact on long-term goals. Since it is difficult for the system to understand the long-term intention of the user [18], the application should allow the user to choose the goal to be optimised and inform about the effects of the rules on it. Furthermore, the platform should suggest alternatives that optimise the environment without compromising the chosen goal.

3.2 ExplainTAP: Main Functionalities and User Interactions

Starting from the above requirements, we designed the ExplainTAP tool, a system capable of analysing automation rules in an interactively user-defined context of use. Users select the rules to be examined, enter values related to the context of use (such as device, environment and user status) and start the simulation. Sets of values can be saved and loaded to simplify future evaluations. The control of direct and indirect activation between rules depends on the context values, while identifying conflicts is independent of these (because it is a check on the possibility of overlapping trigger parts and the incompatibility of actions). In goal-based rule optimisation, on the other hand, users must first choose the goal and, possibly, enter their preferences regarding contextual aspects such as temperature and humidity. Moreover, in some cases, these optimisations are linked to the state of a given context of use, which is specified interactively.

To provide a concrete example, a possible user session with the platform is described below. Rachel has installed smart devices in her home to make her family's household routines more comfortable and efficient. She configured a list of rules, including: 1) Turn on the heating if the temperature drops below 18°; 2) Open the windows if the humidity level in the living room reaches 70%; 3) Turn on the coffee machine at 08:00; 4) If no one is in the living room, turn off the TV; 5) Turn on the TV when the coffee machine is on; 6) If the TV is on between 08:00 and 13:00, it must be turned off along with the smartphone; 7) Unlock the front door when a family member is nearby. Rachel uses the "Rule Analysis" service to identify problems, starting up the "Rule Context Simulator" by setting eight o'clock in the morning. She discovers that Rule 3 activates Rule 5, which in turn activates Rule 6. With this information, Rachel immediately makes a change to Rule 6, moving the execution time by half an hour. Next, she changes the humidity value in the simulator to see what happens when it reaches 70%. The instrument informs her that this value will activate Rule 2, which in turn can lead to the activation of Rule 1, as it can cause the temperature to drop. To avoid wasting energy, Rachel adds a condition to Rule 1, preventing it from activating the heating if the windows are open. Finally, she wants to evaluate her rules from a home safety point of view. She selects 'Goal Advisor' in the toolbar and then the 'Security' goal. The system detects some problems in Rules 2 and 7, where open windows and the automatic unlocking of the front door could pose an intrusion risk. It, therefore, decides to delete Rule 7 and modify Rule 2, avoiding activations at night or when no one is at home.

The main user interface (see Fig. 1) is built around two major components: the interactive "Context of Use" on the left, and the "Rules" list on the right. We chose this representation because of the importance of providing a context simulation environment [11, 24]. Displaying the rule list immediately next to it can make evident the link between the considered context values and the rules that they will eventually activate (R1).

We opted for the textual format to provide information to users. Although other approaches employ different visualisations, such as graphs or data streams, to represent the relationships between rules [12, 15], we argue that a textual description, also supported by secondary notations such as colour highlighting, can be compact and easily understood by potential users. Given the large number of objects that may be present in the environment, by default, the "Context of Use" panel shows only the contextual attributes related to the rules selected on the right-hand panel and the environmental variables influenced by the actions of the rules (see Fig. 2, left). These values can be changed to simulate a specific situation (R2) or saved/loaded.

Another main functionality is the rule context simulator, which checks the activation of selected rules against contextual values, changing the background colour to green or

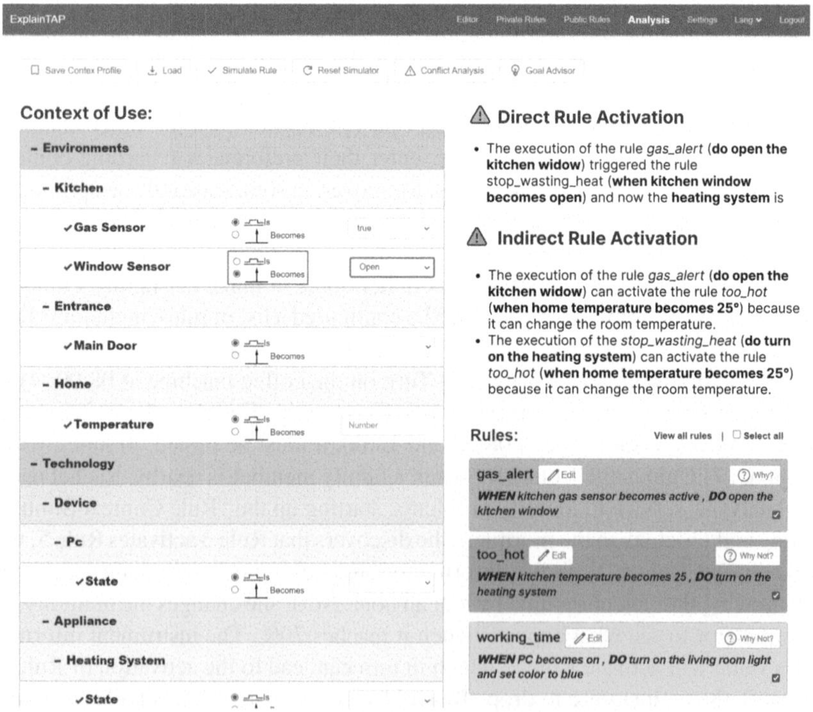

Fig. 1. The ExplainTAP user interface. (Color figure online)

red, depending on whether or not they activate with those values. The rule panels also have the functionality of activating explanations for "Why" or "Why not" questions. The contextual values that determine whether or not that rule is activated are highlighted in the "Context of Use" panel and a textual explanation of these reasons is placed below the rule (R3).

Tied to the rule context simulator is the rule chain analysis functionality (R5). This functionality highlights environmental changes caused by activated rules, highlighting the affected contextual aspects in green in the "Context of Use" panel (see Fig. 1, left/top side). In turn, new rule activations are shown in the "Rules" panel, changing the background colour to green. This process continues until there are no more new activations. Activations that never end (loops) are highlighted in red, while potential rule chains are highlighted with a yellow background, signalling to the user that this is neither an error nor a definite activation. Explanations of these chained activations and their certainty (R3) are located below the rules panel. The conflict analysis (R4) is performed on demand and informs the user of possible situations in which rules predict incompatible states on the same devices, providing a textual description of the situation in which the conflict may occur. Another main functionality is the goal-based rule optimisation (R6). It provides the user with a textual explanation of why (R3) the selected rules might conflict with a selected long-term goal (see Fig. 2). It also provides possible alternative actions that can be used to solve these problems. This is made possible by the semantic module support, described in the following section.

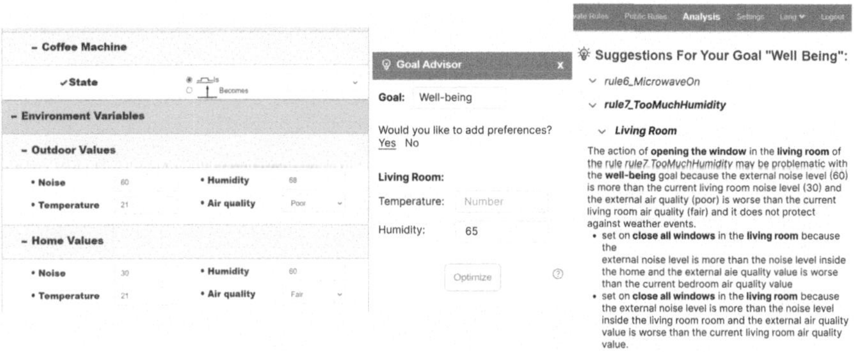

Fig. 2. Goal-Based Rule Optimization with explanations of why rules can be problematic and suggestions for improvements.

3.3 System Architecture

The system architecture exposes and connects the following main functionalities to the front-end: the Rule Context Simulator, the Rule Chain Detection, the Conflict Analysis, the Goal-Based Rules Optimization, and the identified question bank explanations linked to these functionalities (see Fig. 3).

The first steps of the analysis tool are to load the users' automations from the respective repositories, and to build a representation of an interactive context tree that represents the environments and the contained objects that the user can interact with. Then, the different functionalities can be activated. The Rule Context Simulator checks which triggers are satisfied by context data, answering questions such as "How automation activates", "What if" and "How to still be that". The simulator is necessarily intertwined with the Rule Chain Detection functionality: it retrieves the automations selected by the user and if it finds that an automation trigger is verified, it updates the context with the effects of the associated actions, and then checks if new rules are triggered, repeating the process for each rule selected At the end, the interface shows which rules have been activated (directly or by other rules) and why. During the process, if a rule is reactivated due to subsequent updates, the user is notified of a rule loop. Still during this process, another functionality monitors and informs the user whether the activation of a rule may indirectly cause another one to activate, exploiting the Semantic Definitions module. Hence, the Rule Chain functionality also provides performance indicators (whether a trigger is certainly satisfied or not).

The Why/Why Not functionality is also connected to the Simulator. During its execution, the simulator monitors verified and unverified triggers, together with the context-specific elements that led to the trigger activation. This information is then passed to the UI modules that generate a corresponding textual explanation.

The Conflict Analysis functionality is independent of the Rule Context Simulator. It detects rules that act on the same object or on objects in a containment relationship, as in the case of a rule that controls all the lights in a room and another that controls a specific

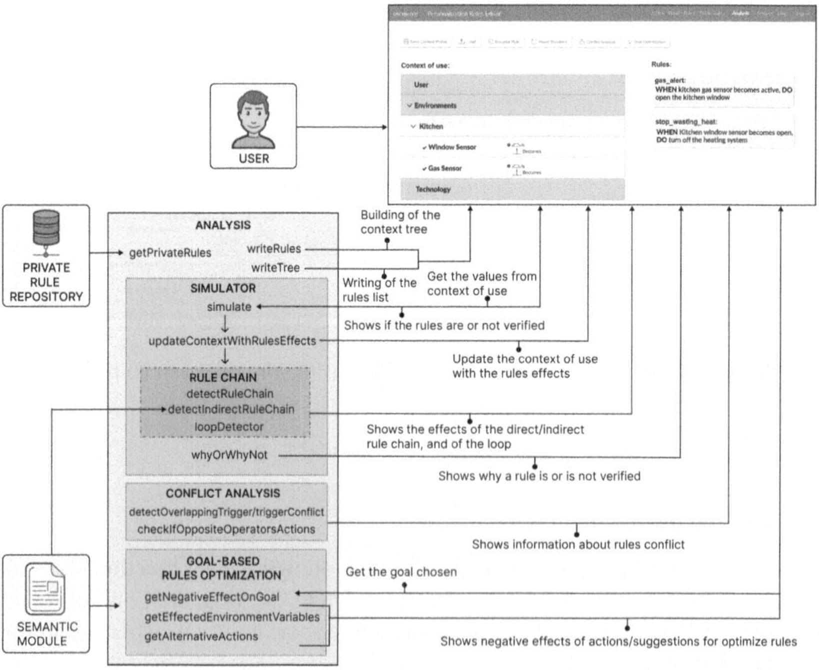

Fig. 3. The architecture of ExplainTAP.

light in the same room. For these rules, it checks whether their effects are incompatible: not only binaries such as On/Off, but also more complex states such as comfort/eco for an air conditioner. Finally, the system analyses the triggers of the conflicting rules for periods of simultaneous activation, notifying the user in case of overlaps.

The last main functionality is the Goal-Based Rule Optimisation. It analyses the selected automations and detects whether they can conflict with the user goal. It relies on the semantic definitions module, which describes the effects of the possible actions in TAP rules. Besides this module, other information is also considered depending on the selected goal. This additional information is the user-preferred values and the context values. For instance, an optimisation related to the "Health" goal can suggest closing or opening windows depending on the inside and outside temperature, humidity, and air quality. Other optimisations depend instead on other active actions: for instance, having windows open and the heater on simultaneously will always conflict with the "Energy-saving" goal, regardless of user preferences. This functionality answers the "How to be that" question by providing suggestions on how to modify an action to obtain a rule that does not conflict with a selected long-term goal.

Figure 4 shows an example of optimisation. The user selects the "Well-being" goal and inserts her preferred temperature and humidity values. Using the Semantic Definitions, the system identifies the rules whose actions can negatively affect variables related to the desired goal. The Optimisation Engine then analyses the Semantic Definitions to select the environmental variables affected by the action in analysis (in the image, "Detect goal - env. variables conflicts") by checking each variable with the indoor and outdoor values and the user preferences if inserted. The variables that pass the check are flagged, and the engine identifies alternative actions that positively influence the selected goal ("Get possible alternative actions"). For instance, if the internal air quality value is better than the outside one, the variable "air quality" is flagged, and the system selects the "turning on the fan" action as a possible solution to solve the "Well-being" problem.

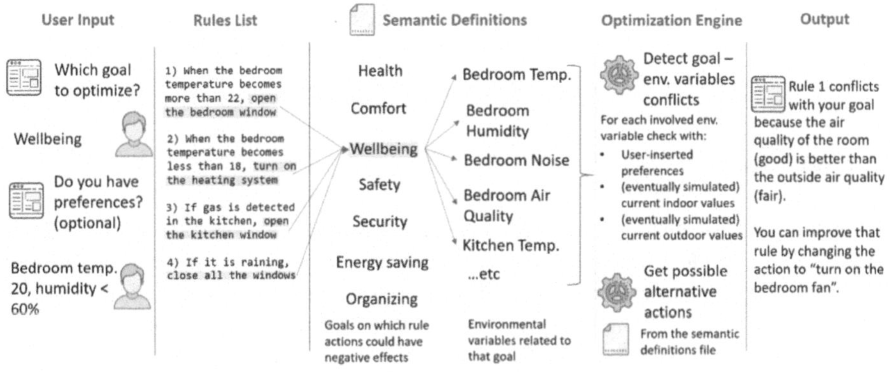

Fig. 4. Schematic functioning of the Goal-Based Rule Optimization.

3.4 The Semantic Definition Module

To support some of the functionalities described so far, the system relies on a structured knowledge base of semantic definitions, represented by the Semantic Module. These definitions explain how objects commonly found in smart home installations can interact with the environment. This knowledge is described in a JSON file and loaded by a module that interfaces with the analysis functionalities. It is organised in objects, also indicating the aspects of their state that can affect the environment: for each object it indicates: ***realName***: the object identification name; ***canActivate***: a list of triggers that can be activated by the object, with a description of the reason (for example, the description of a window actuator contains the variables temperature, humidity, noiseLevel and securityIntrusion, with the associated descriptions); ***possibleValues***: the possible object state values (in the case of the window actuator, open/close).

For each object state value, it also indicates: ***hasPositiveEffectOnGoals***: list of goals on which that specific value can have positive effects (e.g., window open => well-being), including a description of the reason, the environment variables involved (such as air quality), and the eventual other environments' or objects' states that should occur at the same time to cause the effect (outside air quality should be better that a specific value, and better than inside air quality); ***hasNegativeEffectOnGoals***: a similar list but concerning goals that are negatively affected; ***confidentlyIncreaseEnvironmentVariables***: the environment variables the system can confidently indicate that will increase when the device is in a specific state; ***confidentlyDecreaseEnvironmentVariables***: similar but for decreasing variables instead (for the window, these two lists are empty because we do not know for sure the effects on the environment brought by this action); ***canIncreaseEnvironmentVariables***: the environment variables that could increase when the device is in a specific state; ***canDecreaseEnvironmentVariables***: similar, but for decreasing variables instead (in our case, these list contains the noise, temperature, humidity, and air quality values).

These descriptions were devised by analysing solutions in the literature describing the capabilities and effects of IoT objects and devices [13, 20], and introducing the concepts needed for our novel solution, namely the certainty of the effect (confidently or possibly increase/decrease a variable), the connections with the long-term goals, and different functionalities.

4 User Study

A user study was set up to gather direct user feedback about the system's usability (RQ1: is ExplainTAP usable by people who are not programming experts?) and its usefulness in informing users about problems, activations between rules, and possible optimisations of their smart home automations (RQ2: is ExplainTAP useful to potential users?). In detail, the objectives of the test were to assess whether and to what extent the tool can better support users with respect to analysing a list of rules without it in:

- detecting rule chains deriving from direct and indirect activations;
- detecting conflicts between automations;
- detecting issues between their automations and a selected long-term goal;

- providing them with relevant suggestions to improve their automations based on the selected goal.

4.1 Test Organization

Eighteen participants (9 women, 9 men) aged between 24 and 54 years (mean 30.1, std. dev. = 9.06) were recruited via mailing lists or direct contacts. Six of them were younger than 27 years and two between 48 and 54 years. The most frequent age group was 27–34 years (50%). Regarding their background, the sample included a variety of occupations: 10 participants were employed in non-academic sectors, 4 were university students, 2 were currently without occupation, and 1 was a researcher. Thirteen participants stated that they had no programming experience, while three reported limited knowledge of HTML, CSS, JavaScript or other languages. They reported a moderate interest in new technologies (mean of 3.61 on a scale of 1 to 5) and only four of them had already personalised a smart home with Alexa routines.

The study consisted of three phases: familiarisation, task performance and questionnaire. After signing the informed consent, the participants received an introduction to the tasks, a document on TAP rules and the functionality of ExplainTAP, which they then tested with assistance. Afterwards, they analysed a list of 18 rules (see Appendix A1), asking them to imagine that they had IoT devices installed in their homes and that they experienced anomalies in their operation. Finally, they completed the study tasks. Each task described a scenario with a problem or unexpected situation involving some of the automations on the list, providing clues as to the rules involved. Participants had to identify which automations were responsible and explain why. Eight tasks were proposed, divided into two groups of comparable difficulty (same number of rules involved and types of problems): interference with a long-term goal, conflict between automations, direct activation and indirect activation of a rule. There was no time limit, but participants could skip to the next task without completing the current. Participants were divided into two groups, the first performing the first set of tasks without the tool and the second with, and vice versa. It should be noted that commercial platforms such as IFTTT and Home Assistant do not include debugging and simulation capabilities with which to compare ExplainTAP, while research ones do not have public source code. Therefore, we used manual analysis as a baseline. An example of a task (the complete list is in Appendix A2) involved participants receiving a notification at 8:00 a.m. with an invitation to make less noise, without understanding the cause. However, they remembered leaving the bedroom dusty. They therefore had to identify the responsible automations: Rule 4: WHEN the noise level in the bedroom exceeds 40 dB, THEN send a reminder via notification; Rule 9: WHEN the air quality in the bedroom becomes poor, THEN switch on the robot hoover. Dust has worsened the air quality, activating the hoover, whose noise then triggers the notification.

The last study phase involved the completion of a post-survey divided into three sections: demographic information, System Usability Scale (SUS) questionnaire, and specific questions concerning participants' experience with the platform (four binary questions B1-B4, three statements in 5-point Likert scale S1-S3, and three open questions O1-O3).

4.2 Test Results

Figure 5 shows the task performance time. Outliers are present in almost all the cases, but we decided to keep these data in the analysis since they can represent natural variation in the population. The first task was the most challenging and took longer using the tool (Mean = 268.1 s, std. dev. = 133.5 s without tool, M = 298.1 s, std. dev. = 126.4 s with ExplainTAP). The Shapiro-Wilk test indicates that the paired difference between the distributions of times is not normal (W = 0.894, p = 0.045). The Wilcoxon signed-rank test indicates no significant results (W = 27, p = 0.366). The second task was overall quicker (Mean = 130.6 s, std. dev. = 76.6 s without the tool, M = 150.7 s, std. dev = 124.3 s with ExplainTAP). Since the Shapiro-Wilk is significant (W = 0.76, $p < .001$), we used the Wilcoxon signed-rank test, finding no significance (W = 24, p = 0.76). The third task was quicker using the tool (Mean = 184,56 s, std. dev. = 80.48 s without the tool, M = 153.22 s, std. dev. = 85.41 s with ExplainTAP), but the distributions are not normal (W = 0.83, p = 0.004) and the Wilcoxon shows no significance (W = 47, p = 0.053). In the fourth task, not using the tool resulted slightly quicker on average (Mean = 159 s, std. dev. = 120.8 s without the tool, M = 163.6 s, std. dev = 94.45 s with ExplainTAP), but we observed no normal distributions (W = 0.86, p = 0.012) and no significance (W = 23, p = 0.683).

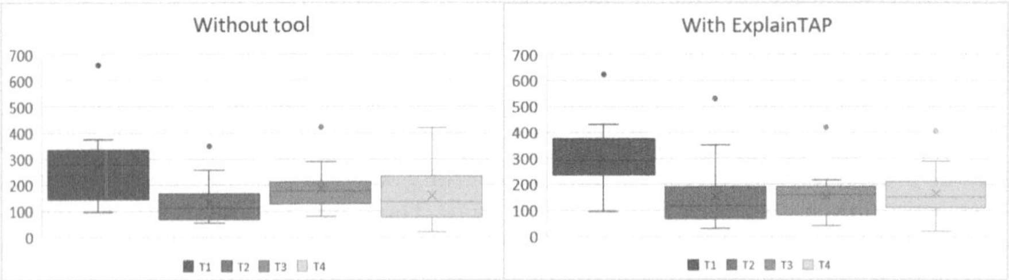

Fig. 5. Comparison of the task completion times.

We computed the success rates (see Fig. 6) by assigning a "success" (1 point) when the participant identified all the rules involved in the issues and the reasons; a "partial success" (0.5) when some rules are detected, or the participant understood the reason for the problem; a "failure" (0) when no correct problematic rule or reason is detected. The summary score is obtained by dividing the partial scores by the number of executions for each task. The first task obtained a success score of 0.42 without the tool, and 0.86 with ExplainTAP. Tasks 2, 3, and 4 obtained 0.69, 0.94 and 0.67 without the tool, and 1 with ExplainTAP. The global success score for all the tasks is 0.68 without the tool and 0.97 with ExplainTAP.

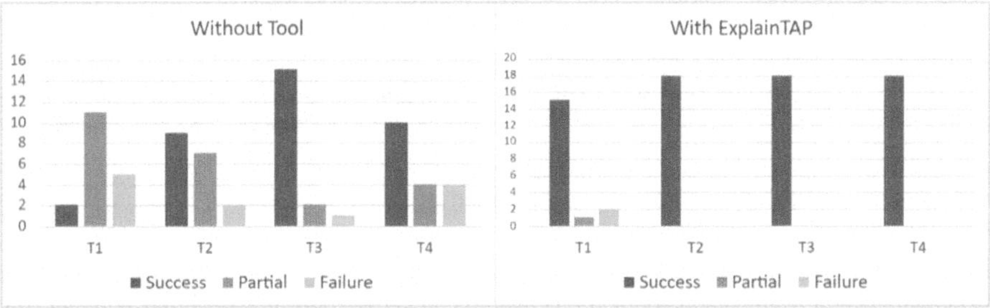

Fig. 6. Success rates in the two conditions.

The average SUS score for ExaplainTAP is 70 (min = 30, max = 92.5, std. dev. = 15.075), meaning acceptable usability. Below are the specific questions and statements concerning the tool. A summary of the responses to B1-B4 and S1-S3 is presented in Fig. 7.

- (B1) Did you encounter difficulties in recognizing automation-related issues with the analysis tool?
- (B2) Did you find it difficult to recognise problems related to automations without the analysis tool?
- (B3) Do you think colour changes in the context of use and text alerts are useful for understanding the effects of your automations?
- (B4) Do you think the tool helped you detect problems between automations?
- (S1) I found the functionality for identifying conflicts between automations useful.
- (S2) I found the functionality for identifying the chains of rule activations useful.
- (S3) I found the suggestion feature for improving the rules useful.
- (O1) What did you like most about the analytics tool?
- (O2) What didn't you like?
- (O3) Do you have suggestions on how we can improve the tool?

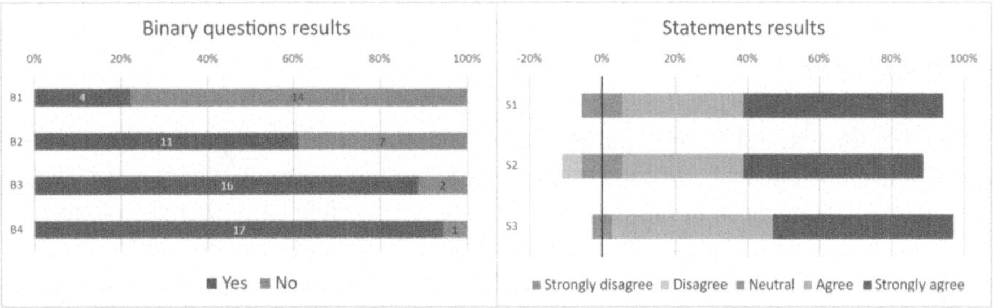

Fig. 7. Questionnaire binary and Likert scale answer.

Participants could elaborate on the responses given to B1-B4 and S1-S3. Concerning the difficulties in detecting problems with and without ExplainTAP, they reported that the analysis functionalities supported them during the tasks, the application's feedback was relatively easy to understand, and the tool can support different people's priorities (e.g., well-being or safety). On the contrary, they generally reported analysing the rule by hand as cumbersome and too difficult. Some participants reported no difficulties completing the tasks without the tool, stating that the hints presented in the scenarios were sufficient to detect the problems. However, they often do not realise they have made mistakes during the tasks. Participants provided positive feedback on the visual signals (e.g., the rules' background colour), stating that they simplify problem detection. They also provide positive feedback concerning the support functionalities, stating that they allow for a quick understanding of the problems. A participant realised that without that tool, she would only be able to detect a conflict when it would happen during the use, and thus found the tool useful in preventing issues. The responses to the open questions are summarised below.

(O1) What did you like most about the analytics tool? The Goal-Based Rules Optimization tool emerged as the most appreciated feature (reported 7 times) because of its capability to highlight issues concerning a specific objective and provide alternative actions. Another appreciated aspect was the clarity of the provided information concerning the various problems between rules (6). Overall, ExplainTAP was described as a useful preventative tool for identifying potential issues.

(O2) What did not you like? The most frequently reported negative aspect concerns the UI of ExpainTAP (8). Some participants found it complex, and the various functionalities and information provided too fragmented. For instance, participants found the visualisation of the "Conflict Analysis" outcome (presented in a modal window) confusing and that the outcome of other functionalities was instead appended at the end of the rule list. They also sometimes forgot to have different functionalities available and focused on only one.

(O3) Do you have suggestions on how we can improve the tool? Participants shared several ideas to improve the application, such as simplifying the "Conflict Analysis" panel and changing the position of its outcome (2); decreasing the scattering of the UI and streamlining the steps to solve a problem (2); automatically filtering rules and information related to conflicts, excluding rules not involved in the simulated rule context (2).

5 Discussion

The goal of the research carried out was to provide users with a support application that expands the possibility of current automations debug tools, introducing new functionalities such as the detection of indirect rule activations, possible issues between long-term goals and automations, and proposing possible solutions. The conducted user study aimed to detect the solution's usability (RQ1) and its usefulness (RQ2). Concerning the first research question, the SUS scores, and the responses to the questionnaire indicate overall sufficient usability, but also some areas of improvement. From an efficiency perspective, the tool generally leads to a similar completion time. However, participants reported that ExplainTAP helped them to better detect the problems. In the test, it emerged that the presentation of the various analysis functionalities and their outcomes in the UI could be further improved. It is unclear whether the possibility to directly access all the control functionalities was always a good choice for novice users. A more usable possibility could be to provide two levels of access: a novice mode, where the accesses to the basic functionalities are grouped and activated through a single interaction, and a standard mode that offers direct control of each of them. Concerning the second research question, the usefulness of the tool has been assessed by analysing the success rate in the tasks (if the tool is able to prevent and explain issues, then it can be useful) and the responses to the questionnaire. From the task success perspective, using the tool reduced the errors in all the tasks. Further attention must be paid to task 1 (issues with a long-term goal), which was the most challenging with ExplainTAP and especially without the tool. Its complexity without tool support is mainly due to participants not fully understanding how the automated actions affected the environment and their lives. This difficulty is reflected by the Goal-Based Rules Optimization being reported as the most useful functionality. Also, using the tool led to a few errors in this case, which suggests that increasing the prediction functionality [9] of the platform considering external data (for example, user behaviour patterns to predict when she will return home automatically) could further improve the ability of the system to provide relevant suggestions. Still concerning the usefulness, it emerged that participants would have also appreciated suggestions to solve conflicts and harmful rule chains. It is, hence, important to research how to generate these repairing patches [33, 34] in a transparent way for users. Concerning the explainability of the solution [23], the tool aims to improve the global understanding of the automated ecosystem, hence answering the "How" question. It also provides information concerning the "Why" and "Why not" an automation is activated, how modifying the environment parameters the outcome changes ("What if" and "How to be still this"), how to change actions to not conflict with a selected long-term goal ("How to be that"), and provides performance information (whether an activation is certain or possible).

Finally, it should be noted that our study is not without limitations. First, the system assumes using another tool to generate automations, which are then passed as input to ExplainTAP. Another limitation concerns the problems identified by ExplainTAP. The case of redundant actions present in the literature is not currently covered. However, it is possible to extend the described approach also for this case, for example, by using the semantic definitions module to identify when two actions have the same effect on the environment. Furthermore, users consider this case less urgent [11]. Lastly, further evaluations of the platform should be carried out for longer periods, also comparing the tool with different approaches to explain automations, or with different interaction paradigms such as conversational or augmented reality.

6 Conclusions and Future Work

In this paper, we have presented ExplainTAP, a platform to detect conflict between automations, direct and indirect activations between them, and to provide explanations to help users analyse how the automations can be inconsistent with their long-term goals, also providing possible solutions. In the user study carried out, these functionalities received clear positive feedback concerning their usefulness, and the platform had an overall encouraging usability score. We have focused on smart home scenarios, but the approach is applicable to any smart space equipped with IoT technologies and associated automations.

We are planning to improve the platform in future work. Since some test participants spent some time analysing the multiple functionalities available, possible improvements can be to provide additional direct activation to the entire set of functionalities, thus avoiding the need to explicitly request access to each of them separately or to also proactively alert users about problems without their intervention.

Acknowledgments. This work has been supported by the Italian MUR PRIN 2022 PNRR Project P2022YR9B7, End-User Development of Automations for Explainable Green Smart Homes, funded by European Union - Next Generation EU. This work is also funded by European Union - Next Generation EU, in the context of The National Recovery and Resilience Plan, Investment 1.5 Ecosystems of Innovation, Project Tuscany Health Ecosystem (THE), CUP: B83C22003920001.

References

1. Andrao, M., Treccani, B., Zancanaro, M.: Language and temporal aspects: a qualitative study on trigger interpretation in trigger-action rules. In: International Symposium on End User Development, pp. 84–103. Springer, Cham (2023)
2. Bak, N.Y., Chang, B., Choi, K.: Smart block: a visual programming environment for Smart-Things. In: 2018 IEEE 42nd Annual Computer Software and Applications Conference (COMPSAC), vol. 2, pp. 32–37. IEEE (2018)
3. Brackenbury, W., et al.: How users interpret bugs in trigger-action programming. In: Proceedings of the CHI Conference on Human Factors in Computing Systems, pp. 1–2 (2019)
4. Breve, B., Cimino, G., Deufemia, V.: Identifying security and privacy violation rules in trigger-action IoT platforms with NLP models. IEEE Internet Things J. **10**(6), 5607–5622 (2022)
5. Brich, J., Walch, M., Rietzler, M., Weber, M., Schaub, F.: Exploring end user programming needs in home automation. ACM Trans. Comput. Hum. Interact. **24**(2), 1–35 (2017)
6. Bu, L., et al.: Systematically ensuring the confidence of real-time home automation IoT systems. ACM Trans. Cyber-Phys. Syst. **2**(3), 1–23 (2018)
7. Caivano, D., Fogli, D., Lanzilotti, R., Piccinno, A., Cassano, F.S.: Supporting end users to control their smart home: design implications from a literature review and an empirical investigation. J. Syst. Softw. **144**, 295–313 (2018)
8. Chen, X., Zhang, X., Elliot, M.G., Wang, X., Wang, F.: Fix the leaking tap: a survey of trigger-action programming (TAP) security issues detection techniques and solutions. Comput. Secur. **120**, 102812 (2022)
9. Coppers, S., Vanacken, D., Luyten, K.: Fortniot: intelligible predictions to improve user understanding of smart home behavior. Proc. ACM Interact. Mob. Wearable Ubiquitous Technol. **4**(4), 1–24 (2020)
10. Coppers, S., Vanacken, D., Luyten, K.: FortClash: predicting and mediating unintended behavior in home automation. Proc. ACM Hum.-Comput. Interact. **6**(EICS), 1–20 (2022)
11. Corno, F., De Russis, L., Roffarello, A.M.: Empowering end users in debugging trigger-action rules. In: Proceedings of the CHI Conference on Human Factors in Computing Systems, pp. 1–13 (2019)
12. Corno, F., De Russis, L., Roffarello, A.M.: My IoT puzzle: debugging IF-THEN rules through the jigsaw metaphor. In: End-User Development, IS-EUD 2019, pp. 18–33. Springer, Cham (2019)

13. Corno, F., De Russis, L., Roffarello, A.M.: A high-level semantic approach to end-user development in the Internet of Things. Int. J. Hum.-Comput. Stud. **125**, 41–54 (2019)
14. Corno, F., De Russis, L., Roffarello, A.M.: From users' intentions to IF-THEN rules in the Internet of Things. ACM Trans. Off. Inf. Syst. **39**(4), 1–33 (2021)
15. Coutaz, J., Crowley, J.L.: A first-person experience with end-user development for smart homes. IEEE Pervasive Comput. **15**(2), 26–39 (2016)
16. Das, D., et al.: Explainable activity recognition for smart home systems. ACM Trans. Interact. Intell. Syst. **13**(2), 1–39 (2023)
17. Desolda, G., Ardito, C., Matera, M.: Empowering end users to customize their smart environments: model, composition paradigms, and domain-specific tools. ACM Trans. Comput. Hum. Interact. **24**(2), 1–52 (2017)
18. Funk, M., Chen, L.L., Yang, S.W., Chen, Y.-K.: Addressing the need to capture scenarios, intentions and preferences: interactive intentional programming in the smart home. Int. J. Des. **12**(1), 53–66 (2018)
19. Huang, J., Çakmak, M.: Supporting mental model accuracy in trigger-action programming. In: Proceedings of the 2015 ACM International Joint Conference on Pervasive and Ubiquitous Computing, pp. 215–225 (2015)
20. Kim, S., Ko, I.-Y.: A conversational approach for modifying service mashups in IoT environments. In: Proceedings of the CHI Conference on Human Factors in Computing Systems, pp. 1–16 (2022)
21. Ko, A.J., Myers, B.A.: Designing the whyline: a debugging interface for asking questions about program behavior. In: Proceedings of the SIGCHI Conference on Human Factors in Computing Systems, pp. 151–158 (2004)
22. Kulesza, T., Burnett, M., Wong, W., Stumpf, S.: Principles of explanatory debugging to personalize interactive machine learning. In: Proceedings of the 20th International Conference on Intelligent User Interfaces, pp. 126–137 (2015)
23. Liao, Q.V., Gruen, D., Miller, S.: Questioning the AI: informing design practices for explainable AI user experiences. In: Proceedings of the 2020 CHI Conference on Human Factors in Computing Systems, pp. 1–15 (2020)
24. Manca, M., Paternò, F., Santoro, C., Corcella, L.: Supporting end-user debugging of trigger-action rules for IoT applications. Int. J. Hum.-Comput. Stud. **123**, 56–69 (2019)
25. Mataloto, B., Ferreira, J.C., Resende, R.: Long term energy savings through user behaviour modeling in smart homes. IEEE Access (2023)
26. Mattioli, A., Paternò, F.: Understanding user needs in smart homes and how to fulfil them. In: International Symposium on End User Development, pp. 125–142. Springer, Cham (2023)
27. Paternò, F., Gallo, S., Manca, M., Mattioli, A., Santoro, C.: Towards understanding the transparency of automations in daily environments. In: CEUR Workshop Proceedings, IUI Workshops 2022, vol. 3124, pp. 187–191 (2022)
28. Shneiderman, B.: Human-centered artificial intelligence: reliable, safe & trustworthy. Int. J. Hum.-Comput. Interact. **36**(6), 495–504 (2020)
29. Ur, B., McManus, E., Pak Yong Ho, M., Littman, M.L.: Practical trigger-action programming in the smart home. In: Proceedings of the SIGCHI Conference on Human Factors in Computing Systems, CHI 2014, pp. 803–812. ACM, New York (2014)
30. Ur, B., et al.: Trigger-action programming in the wild: an analysis of 200,000 IFTTT recipes. In: Proceedings of the 2016 CHI Conference on Human Factors in Computing Systems, pp. 3227–3231 (2016)
31. Xu, X., et al.: XAIR: a framework of explainable AI in augmented reality. In: Proceedings of the CHI Conference on Human Factors in Computing Systems, pp. 1–30 (2023)
32. Zancanaro, M., Gallitto, G., Yem, D., Treccani, B.: Improving mental models in IoT end-user development. Hum. Centric Comput. Inf. Sci. **2** (2022)

33. Zhang, L., He, W., Jesse, M., Brackenbury, N., Lu, S., Blase, U.: AutoTap: synthesizing and repairing trigger-action programs using LTL properties. In: 2019 IEEE/ACM 41st International Conference on Software Engineering (ICSE), pp. 281–291. IEEE (2019)
34. Zhang, L., Zhou, C., Littman, M.L., Ur, B., Lu, S.: Helping users debug trigger-action programs. Proc. ACM Interact. Mob. Wearable Ubiquitous Technol. **6**(4), 1–32 (2022)

Conversational Rule Creation in XR: User's Strategies in VR and AR Automation

Alessandro Carcangiu[1], Marco Manca[2], Jacopo Mereu[1], Carmen Santoro[2], Ludovica Simeoli[2], and Lucio Davide Spano[1(✉)]

[1] Department of Mathematics and Computer Science, University of Cagliari, Via Ospedale 72, 09124 Cagliari, Italy
{alessandro.carcangiu,jacopo.mereu,davide.spano}@unica.it

[2] Human Interfaces in Information Systems (HIIS) Laboratory, ISTI-CNR, Via G. Moruzzi 1, 56124 Pisa, Italy
{marco.manca,carmen.santoro,ludovica.simeoli}@isti.cnr.it

Abstract. Rule-based approaches allow users to customize XR environments. However, the current menu-based interfaces still create barriers for end-user developers. Chatbots based on Large Language Models (LLMs) have the potential to reduce the threshold needed for rule creation, but how users articulate their intentions through conversation remains under-explored. This work investigates how users express event-condition-action automation rules in Virtual Reality (VR) and Augmented Reality (AR) environments. Through two user studies, we show that the dialogues share consistent strategies across the interaction setting (keywords, difficulties in expressing conditions, task success), even if we registered different adaptations for each setting (verbal structure, event vs action first rules). Our findings are relevant for the design and implementation of chatbot-based support for expressing automations in an XR setting.

Keywords: eXtended Reality · End-User Development · Immersive Authoring · Large Language Models · Rules

1 Introduction

Rule-based approaches in End-User Development (EUD) enable users to define and modify system behaviour through configurable rules, allowing for customization and adaptation of dynamic environments to the user's need, especially in scenarios where the requirements rapidly evolve or a fine-grained control over the customization is needed [42]. They are commonly used in home automation [12,16,23,29,50], where user-friendly interfaces enable individuals to create automation rules without needing programming skills. By simplifying technical complexity, these solutions enable users to customize their smart environments, controlling lighting, security, and other devices using rule-based automation.

C. Santoro et al. (Eds.): IS-EUD 2025, LNCS 15713, pp. 59–79, 2025.
https://doi.org/10.1007/978-3-031-95452-8_4

More recently, rule-based approaches have been applied to the development of immersive extended reality experiences [5,8,19,22,51,52]. In these contexts, rules define interactions and dynamic behaviours within virtual spaces, allowing users to create immersive experiences that reflect their preferences. Current authoring tools require users to translate their automation intent into rules by manipulating events, conditions and actions through an interface. This requires abstraction skills that could put a barrier to the users, especially for individuals without any technical background. While most existing approaches rely on visual interfaces for rule composition or enforce structured language patterns (e.g., *if this, then that* [50]), advancements in natural language processing, driven by Large Language Models (LLMs) could introduce a paradigm shift in rule creation. These technologies enable users to define automation logic through natural language conversations with intelligent agents, lowering the technical barrier to rule definition. The conversation with the agent aims to support users in articulating their intent, and to guide them through the rule creation process, ensuring that rules adhere to user intentions. However, we still lack knowledge of the structure and characteristics of such conversations, required to create effective agents. In this paper, we explore the dialogue structure necessary for creating automation rules through conversations. In particular, after discussing related work (Sect. 2), we describe how we initially collected dialogues through a Wizard of Oz study (Sect. 3), whose findings informed the design of a chatbot prototype. The latter was evaluated in a second study (Sect. 4), by applying it to two settings: a virtual reality environment in a museum, and a mobile augmented reality application in a smart home domain. Our findings highlight the common strategies that are consistent in both settings and domains, together with the differences and adaptations providing a useful knowledge base for researchers and practitioners wanting to use LLM-based chatbots to support the automation definition in XR. Lastly, we identify some directions for future work (Sect. 5).

2 Related Work

Rule Format. The use of rule-based customization to lower entry barriers for end-users has been widely studied, particularly through trigger-action programming (TAP), which operates on the principle: 'IF a trigger occurs, THEN an action is executed'. However, in environments with many devices, TAP can lead to user confusion and reasoning errors [4,9,25]. TAP is prevalent in IoT, both in research systems [2,7,21,28,35,39,45,46] and commercial platforms [27,29]. Some studies explore the if-then-else variation of TAP [14,18,32].

Another common methodology is event-condition-action (ECA). Unlike TAP, ECA incorporates optional conditions in the rule, refining when actions are executed. When an event occurs, the system checks conditions, executing the action only if they are met. While ECA can support multiple conditions, many user-friendly languages limit it to a single predicate, simplifying rules [14]. ECA is applied in end-user development across various areas, such as in wellness monitoring systems [6] and tools for debugging TAP rules [38]. Artizzu et al. [5] use

ECA rules in natural language for defining behaviours in VR, and it is also used in home automation [4,15,17,54] and point-and-click game development [8,19].

EUD Authoring Tools for XR. The EUD research for XR mainly focuses in reducing the development barriers to allow people without technical skills to customise or create XR environments. Torres et al. [49] propose an editor to add interactive elements, but limited to 360° videos. Blecic et al. [8,19] created a desktop authoring tool for point-and-click games aimed at unskilled users, using natural language for ECA rules, but it restricts environments to pre-captured media. Immersive authoring tools [1,20,33,34,44,53] are promising in overcoming the "build-test-fix" cycle in desktop tools, which can make it hard for end-users to create applications, but they generally target developers. RUIS [48] allows hobbyists to create VR experiences with building blocks, yet still requires some coding. VR GREP [52] targets end-users in creating VR environments but with limited interactions, and requires technical skills.

Industry and research have proposed various approaches to define EUD systems for IoT home automation, such as IFTTT [50], EFESTO [16], TAREME [23], and ImAtHome [21]. These systems often rely on static visual paradigms, potentially complicating user interaction with rule definitions due to a lack of context. Augmented reality (AR) can enhance user engagement by enabling direct interaction with real objects, allowing for dynamic discovery and modification of automations. AR solutions that use smartphones are particularly useful since they leverage existing devices. Previous work [30] indicates users appreciate on-demand information and enhanced sensory perception from AR in home settings. Reality Editor [24] is one of the first AR contributions to connect IoT object behaviours, allowing users to map graphical elements onto physical interfaces. By linking different object tags, users can manage multi-object functionalities. HoloFlows [43] utilizes a no-code AR approach for configuring IoT workflows, allowing users to connect devices with "virtual wires" though it requires dedicated hardware. MagicHand [47] enables users to control IoT devices with hand gestures using HoloLens, but it primarily focuses on individual device control. HoloHome [37] provides a similar AR framework but also targets basic use cases, limiting its multi-device programming capabilities. In contrast, BricklAyeR [46] uses a 3D building blocks metaphor for unskilled users to define IoT behaviour. Rules are created using virtual blocks as triggers and actions. However, testing with end-users is still limited. The evolution of this concept led to MagiPlay [45], an AR-based game for children to program their surroundings.

Rules Pattern. In the IoT field, some work explored Natural language-based rule formulation. For instance, InstructableCrowd [26] and HeyTAP [13] translate user needs into executable IF-THEN rules. Noura et al. [40] studied how users express their IoT automation goals more naturally through various utterances, noting that, unlike strict commands used in systems like IFTTT, users often use indirect goals (e.g. "it's too cold here"). Chen et al. [11] identified 3 abstraction levels: 1) the *End Users' Intentions*, where users express expectations about their environment without specifying devices, 2) the *Intention Realization*

Plan, including descriptions related to device types without brand specificity, and 3) *Device Scheduling Logic*, requiring specific device instructions. Liu et al. [36] explored combining natural language with multimodal interactions for IoT configurations, revealing challenges like ambiguity and redundancy in user expressions, alongside rule complexity. For instance, 28.3% of complex rules were influenced by user expression, while 62% were affected by rule complexity.

3 Wizard of Oz Study

To explore typical end-user automation intent, we conducted a formative study using the Wizard of Oz (WoZ) method with props to simulate physical devices and virtual content. We created two environments—immersive VR and mobile-based AR—set respectively in a museum and a smart home. One researcher acted as the LLM-based agent, interpreting participants' commands and suggesting automation rules. Participants worked through tasks with a consistent rule structure: T1 focused on familiarization, T2 and T3 involved simple trigger-action automation (a single event and a single action), T4 and T5 required complex rules with conditions, and T6 involved modifying existing automations. We present our findings and qualitative observations from the VR and AR scenarios. Details on the collected data are available in the additional material.

3.1 Virtual Reality Museum

Experiment Setting (Fig. 1-C). We created a physical room resembling a virtual museum, featuring small statues and images on freestanding panels. To ease automation, we included interactive elements like buttons, lamps, and pedestals, each object had an icon and tags were assigned to simulate help tooltips. Users could read these tags or ask chatbot's help during tasks. We combined analogue and digital methods for interactivity: textual information was printed to mimic virtual labels, audio effects played through speakers for auditory feedback, and a tablet provided video playback. This setup enabled participants to engage with the environment as they would in a real virtual museum while allowing the researcher acting as the LLM-based agent to interpret and respond to their inputs in real time.

Session Structure and Tasks. We planned each test session to last about one hour, structured into four phases: demographics interview, test introduction, task execution, and feedback interview. Users provided demographic details, programming experience, and consent to video recording. In the introduction, they watched videos of real VR museum applications to familiarize with interactive exhibitions, then assumed the role of a museum director designing a virtual exhibition for two artefacts: a 19th-century painting and a prehistoric statuette.

During the task phase, users were asked to **T1)** explore the environment, **T2)** display an information panel on pointing to artwork, **T3)** turn on a spotlight when close to an artwork, create automations to **T4)** show additional info on a statue after viewing a painting, **T5)** start audio content when near an artwork and pressing a button, and **T6)** modify an existing automation. The simulated chatbot provided information about the objects' state or interaction capabilities (i.e., the actions supported by each object). The moderator encouraged verbalizing thoughts and uncertainties to better understand the user's intent.

Table 1. Rule groups, with their structure and frequencies in the WoZ and chatbot prototype studies in both AR and VR settings (E=event, C=condition, A=action). The symbols $^+$ and * denote repetition of occurrences (resp.: 1 or more; 0 or more).

Rule Group	Structure	WoZ				Prototype			
		VR		AR		VR		AR	
		#	%	#	%	#	%	#	%
Event-first	E-based (E^+)	0	0.0%	0	0.0%	0	0.0%	1	2.1%
	EA-based (E^+A^+)	62	55.3%	57	35.1%	34	39.5%	11	23.4%
	EAC-based ($EA^+C^+A^*$)	6	5.3%	10	6.1%	7	8.1%	0	0.0%
	ECA-based ($E^+C^+A^*$)	4	3.6%	17	10.4%	6	6.9%	1	2.1%
Action-first	A-based (A^+)	10	8.9%	0	0.0%	3	3.4%	0	0.0%
	AE-based ($A^+E^+A^*$)	18	16.0%	46	28.3%	16	18.6%	17	36.1%
	AEC-based (A^+E^+C)	2	1.8%	12	7.4%	3	3.4%	6	12.7%
	ACE-based (A^+CE^+)	1	0.9%	7	4.3%	3	3.4%	1	2.1%
Condition-first	C-based (C^+)	0	0.0%	0	0.0%	7	8.1%	7	14.8%
	CAE-based (CA^+E^+)	0	0.0%	3	1.8%	3	3.4%	1	2.1%
	CA-based (CA^+)	2	1.8%	0	0.0%	2	2.3%	0	0.0%
	CEA-based (CE^+A^+)	7	6.2%	10	6.1%	2	2.3%	2	4.2%

Participants. The group consisted of 14 participants (5 females, 9 males, with age ranging from 19 to 33 ($\bar{x} = 24, \sigma = 4.09$). Participants were volunteers recruited via convenience sampling and did not receive any form of compensation. Ten participants (71%) had no programming experience, while 4 had basic coding familiarity. None had prior VR development experience. Also, 8 participants (57%) used voice assistants like Siri or Google Home, and 6 (42%) frequently used text-based chatbots like ChatGPT or Gemini. For VR experience, 4 participants (28%) had low familiarity, while the rest had none.

Collected Rules. In the experiment, participants began by exploring the environment, checking the objects' information cards or consulting the moderator acting as the chatbot. We collected 112 rules in total, including 98 new automations and 14 modifications, with 100 meeting structural validity requirements. All users except P3 and P5 completed all tasks; P3 did not define rules in T4 and T5, while P5 did not complete T3. All users except P5 created the required simple rules in T2 and T3, with a total of 37 rules formulated. Three users (P8, P9, and P13) created more rules than requested. In T4 and T5, three participants (P1, P4, and P8) defined complex rules by merging simple ones, resulting in 50 total automations. Eight out of 14 users did not state the triggering subject. T6 involved editing a rule, leading to 14 changes, with most users redefining entire rules instead of only changes, and only 3 provided isolated changes.

The analysis of rule structures indicates a preference for event-first formulations (see Table 1), with simple event-action (EA) sequences occurring 62 times. We registered 16 rules including an event followed by multiple actions (EAA, EAAA, EAAAA). Event-action-condition (EAC) structures appeared less frequently, while event-condition-action (ECA) structures were rare, yet indicating that conditions are placed later in rules. Action-first formulations were also common, especially simple action-event (AE) rules (18 times). More complex structures (e.g. rules with sequences of actions and/or conditions) were less frequent; condition-first structures were the least common. This shows that users conceptualize automation as direct cause-effect relations, preferring event-driven interactions over complex conditional logic. This is further supported by 3 users who split automation requiring conditions into multiple trigger-action rules.

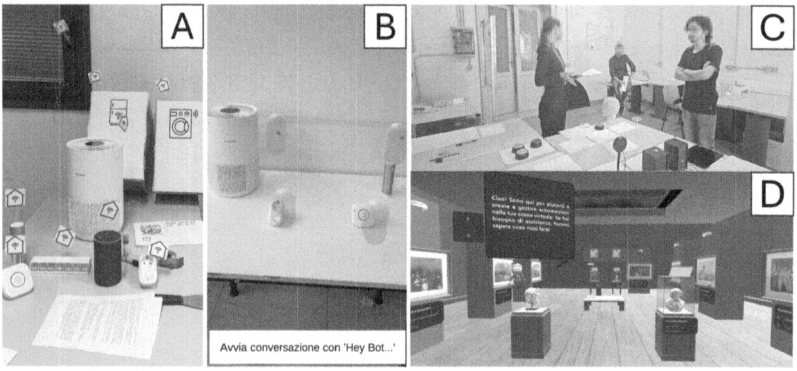

Fig. 1. The environments of the two studies: the AR smart home (WoZ-part A, chatbot prototype- part B) and the VR museum (WoZ- part C, chatbot prototype - part D).

The sentence structure analysis reveals that direct event statements (without any keyword) and implicit formulations (36 and 20 occurrences) are the most common way to define events. The terms "if" (14) and "when" (12) appear but are not dominant, suggesting a flexible approach towards their description. Conditions primarily use "if" (9), alongside temporal expressions ("in the moment that" - 2) and negations ("must not" - 1), reflecting varied constraint structures. Action verbs emphasize media control ("play" - 24, "show" - 16) and interactive commands like "teleport" (7) and "rotate" (5), highlighting engagement with dynamic environments. Verb forms are diverse, with impersonal (60) and first-person (55) being prevalent, while conditional expressions (41) indicate a preference for flexible rule definitions. The presence of spatial references (38) and comparisons (20) further underscores the context-awareness of user actions.

While expressing their rules, participants sometimes used modalities different from speech. The most common was pointing (42 times), often employed to indicate objects or locations relevant to automation. Pantomimes (24) were also frequent, with users acting out the expected effect of automation, such as pressing a button or turning on a light. Body movements (5) were the least common strategy, involving body gestures to simulate interactions (e.g. stepping forward to trigger an event). Such modalities suggest that users relied on a mix of verbal and non-verbal communication to define rules.

3.2 Augmented Reality Smart Home

Experiment Setting (Fig. 1-A). To simulate a smart home, we equipped an office with several devices: most of them were real, and a few were simulated using paper-based artefacts. Over each of them, we placed a card showing the icon of a connected house to indicate that the device could be involved in automation and that it was possible to get additional information about it. In the office, we also provided a 'multi-purpose' panel aimed to support simulated services (e.g. weather, location, time) not associated with a specific device. In our setup, one researcher simulated the AR-based parts of the system by dynamically presenting (using paper-based panels) info about the devices users dynamically framed through a smartphone camera, while exploring the environment. Another researcher impersonated the conversational agent, answering user requests. Users can interact with the system in a multimodal manner: by framing the card of a device (using a smartphone) and then interacting vocally with the agent; or by just speaking with the (simulated) agent, without framing.

Tasks. We designed six tasks. To avoid suggesting rule formulation, each task was described using a *scenario* that the users need to solve through some rules. While the first task (T1, divided into two subtasks: T1.1, T1.2), aimed just to make users familiarise with the experimental setup realised in the lab, in the remaining five tasks (T2-T6), users were presented with specific scenarios, and they had to create suitable automations to solve them. More specifically: in ***T1.1)*** users said 2–3 rules they would like to have in their home; in **T1.2**) they explored the experimental environment; in **T2)** they had to create an automation to enhance kitchen safety by managing smoke and gas -related hazards; in **T3**) they had to ensure that the entrance area is illuminated when arriving home in the evening; in **T4**) users set up a rule to keep the indoor air quality high, by controlling an air purifier based on presence/time; in **T5**) users create a rule to receive notifications when indoor temperatures fall outside an optimal range, to preserve plants; in **T6**) users had to modify an existing rule involving a dryer, to activate it only if outdoor conditions do not allow drying outside.

Participants. Fifteen users (11 women) participated in the study, all Italian, with ages ranging between 40 and 62 years ($\bar{x} = 52, \sigma = 7.3$). Seven users (out of 15: 46.7%) said they did not have prior programming experience, while the remaining eight (53.3%) had only basic knowledge. Also, four participants had never used voice assistants, and the remaining eleven said they had used Siri, Google Home, Alexa, and Google Assistant. Also, five participants had no prior experience with AR, nine had tried AR in contexts such as museums or games.

Only one participant had previously used an open-source AR package before the study. Finally, all did not have prior experience with existing automation platforms. All users were volunteers and did not receive any compensation.

Collected Rules. In the test, we recorded all the rules expressed by users, both those created to solve the scenarios (T2-T6) and those created in the familiarization task (T1). For the analysis, we decided to consider only the final sentences, namely those that, after possible refinements and interactions with the agent, were finally confirmed by the user. Thus, we did not consider the sentences obtained during the intermediate user-agent interactions. During the AR formative test, users created 162 final (non-ambiguous) automation: 64 in Task 1, 98 in T2-T6. The 162 created rules were, in most cases, simple rules composed of one event (E) and one action (A) (84 simple rules: E^+A^+ 57 times, $A^+E^+A^*$ 46 times). Complex rules were defined 78 times by users, and the most frequent structures are those in which the event appears first: $E^+C^+A^*$ (17), $EA^+C^+A^*$ (10), CE^+A^+ (10), A^+CE^+ (7). In Table 1, we show all the structures of rules found, grouped according to the rule element occurring first (between event, condition, or action); the table highlights a clear preference for the Event-first structure (84), followed by the Action-first formulation (65). The percentages were calculated by considering the total number of the final rules collected (162). All users created at least one automation per task; some of them created even more than one automation in some tasks. For instance, in T4 and T5 (where a single complex rule was expected) users sometimes preferred to formulate two distinct rules in each task (or even three rules: this happened with 3 users solving T4). Thus, in T4 and T5, the 15 users created a total of 47 rules (25 simple and 22 complex), instead of the 30 complex ones expected. Thus, it seems that users preferred to break down the complexity associated with single complex automation by creating multiple simpler rules focusing on specific aspects of the task (instead of one complex rule, where to arrange all the elements at once). In T6 (which required to add a condition to a simple rule), we expected that the users would have specified only the rule element they would like to add; instead, they tended to restate the entire, modified rule, sometimes only partially (e.g. they stated again, e.g. only the action of the original rule, while implicitly referring to the event of the original rule, without restating it).

We also analyzed the words used by participants to define events, conditions, and actions of a rule. To introduce an event, users most frequently (34.32% of 169 event occurrences) exploited 'when' and some small variants of it, for example, 'whenever' or 'when not'. However, they also used "if/if not" (16.56%) to introduce events, followed by the indication of a specific time (i.e. "from" <time>, or "at" <time>: 10.05%). They also used expressions such as "in case of" and "only in case" (8.87%). Regarding the condition, users used "if/if not" or "only if" (47.06% out of 68 occurrences of conditions). In addition, other expressions used are "in case" or similar, something related to the seasons, such as "only during the summer" (7.35%) or "from x to y", or "in the time interval from x to y" (5.88%). Users generally introduced the actions using the second person, asking the agent to do something (29.28% out of 181 occurrences of the actions), or using expressions such as "I'd like to" or "I want to" (23.20%); or other third-person forms such as "It must", "It will" (11.60%).

3.3 Discussion

Balancing Simplicity and Complexity in AR and VR Automations. In both the VR and AR experiments, users preferred creating simple automations rather than complex ones. When faced with scenarios requiring multiple triggers, conditions, and actions, they tended to break them down into several simpler rules instead of designing a single intricate automation, a trend already documented in the literature [31]. In AR, we expected that users would create some complex rules in specific tasks, but many of them were broken down into simpler ones. A similar pattern was observed in the VR group, although it was less common.

Dialogue Flow. The dialogue flow observed in the VR setting followed a structured process. Users typically began with vague automation goals, which the assistant helped to translate into actionable triggers and responses. After this, users inquired about interaction possibilities and the properties of devices and objects, to explore options for fulfilling their goals. Next, they clarified conditions and specified rule constraints, with users iteratively adjusting their rules based on system prompts. The final step was to recap the rules before confirming the rule. While most refinements followed a linear flow, some users returned to an exploratory phase to reconsider their options. This suggests that a real chatbot prototype must consider these phases to provide focused support for each one.

Rule Definition Order. Users expressed rules through various patterns. In VR, they typically began with the event before detailing the rule, and also, in AR, there was a strong tendency to start with the event. Starting with conditions was less common and mainly occurred for complex automations, which users aimed to break down into simpler parts. The system should, therefore, support any order for specifying automations. Additionally, users used different terms for events and conditions, often employing "IF" for both. In AR, users favoured first-person verbs ("I'd like to...") to refer to the device, while in VR, commands were directed at the chatbot ("You play the audioguide"). Some users specified the device involved in the action, while others referenced an unrelated entity (e.g., "I'd like that room to be illuminated"). The system should be able to identify the object linked to the specified action.

Familiarity with ICA. We observed a difference between users who were familiar with intelligent assistants and those who were not. The former expressed their ideas more clearly and concisely by formulating precise rules from the outset, while the latter needed several rounds of rephrasing and refining before reaching a final version of their automations. This result suggests that the system should guide users in refining their specifications in a step-by-step manner, progressing from more general and abstract concepts to more precise ones.

Modify Existing Rules. During the modification task, users often repeated the entire new rule rather than specifying just the part they wanted to change.

This could be due to a lack of understanding that only a portion of the original rule needed to be updated. The unfamiliarity with the logical structure of automations—consisting of triggers, actions, events, and conditions may have led users to prefer stating the complete rule rather than isolating the specific change.

Preferred Modality. In AR, users favoured voice interaction over the method based on camera framing, finding it more intuitive to talk with the agent, addressing it either directly while referring to a device or describing the rule outcome. In contrast, VR users created automations by interacting with elements in the environment through different modalities. They often omitted explicit verbal references to objects, relying on the system to infer them from the context. This suggests that contextual info needs to be collected differently in AR and VR.

4 Chatbot Prototype Study

The findings in Sect. 3.3 guided the development of a chatbot prototype we called Tell-XR [10]. It assists users in creating and modifying automations in XR environments, supporting both VR and AR. The chatbot interacts with users through natural language, allowing them to pass through all the identified rule definition phases (define, explore, refine and confirm). It exploits GPT-4o [41] and a custom rule-processing engine to handle automations. It processes speech-to-text (STT) and text-to-speech (TTS) together with the other streams coming from VR and AR devices for multimodal interactions. The system features stateful dialogue management to modify automation rules based on user input and integrates with XR environments via API for automation execution in VR and AR settings. The key features and capabilities of Tell-XR include: 1) *Creating and modifying automations*: Users can interact with the chatbot to create new automation rules. The chatbot follows a structured yet flexible dialogue flow that guides users through the phases described in Sect. 3.3. 2) *Multimodal Interaction*: The chatbot uses voice as the primary interaction mode, but it also receives relevant information coming from other modalities in its context to improve the communication with the user. 3) *Contextual Understanding*: The chatbot can understand the user's context, including the VR/AR environment and current user's actions. This allows to effectively interpret and respond to user's requests by, e.g., suggesting relevant objects/conditions/actions based on the environment and user's prior inputs. 4) *Specific configurations for VR and AR*: In VR, the chatbot helps users interact with virtual objects, while in AR it works with real physical devices. The system provides the chatbot with information about objects and devices that facilitate the suggestions while defining automation.

Though Tell-XR , we repeated an experiment similar to Sect. 3 in a proper VR and AR setting. In the next sections, we detail the experiment and results. The tasks had the same structure and difficulty across AR and VR. **T1** and **T2** required to create a *simple automation* (1 event + 1 action). **T3** asked users to *design an automation* of their choice. **T4** and **T5** requested the creation of a *complex automation*, involving conditions and one or more actions. **T6** asked users to *modify* the (simple) rule got in T2 to make it complex (by adding a condition). Details on the collected data are available in the additional material.

4.1 Virtual Reality Museum

Experiment Setting (Fig. 1-D). The Virtual Museum is a fictional cultural heritage exhibition built in VR, where users take on the role of a museum curator. The museum contains rooms with various artworks, each with multimedia content such as informational panels, videos, or audio narrations the curator can use to enhance the visit. Some artworks include interactive elements like lighting systems or buttons to trigger specific functions. Additionally, the museum contains tables with extra materials that users can arrange freely to personalize the exhibition. Users interact with the environment using VR controllers, enabling object movement, manipulation, and menu navigation.

Participants. Twelve people (6 women) aged 16 to 43 years ($\bar{x} = 26.2, \sigma = 10.0$) participated in the study. Invitations were sent via mailing lists to individuals and groups we collaborate with, excluding those directly involved in the work. We specifically reached out to students from a collaborating high school. All participants were students, professionals in the humanities or people enrolled in courses related to cultural heritage promotion. Before the test, we assessed prior experiences on a 1–5 scale (1 = no familiarity; 5 = high familiarity). Familiarity with voice assistants (e.g., Siri, Alexa) was moderate: 7 participants rated their experience as '3', and 2 rated it as '4'; four users knew Siri, 5 knew Alexa, 1 Cortana, 5 ChatGPT, and 1 Google Assistant. Familiarity with XR applications was low: 8 rated it as '1', 3 as '2', and 1 as '3'. None named a VR application, only headsets. Knowledge of automation systems was limited; only one rated familiarity as '4' (Google Home, Samsung SmartThings), while others rated it as '1'. Programming experience was minimal, with only one user reporting basic HTML knowledge. Participation was voluntary and no compensation was provided. Users received an introduction to the research and a consent form outlining the study's purpose, objectives, and data management. Underage participants required parental consent to participate.

Collected Rules. The VR test took place in either our laboratory or a collaborating high school. Participants used an Oculus Quest 3 or 3S headset to explore the Virtual Museum. The session began with a familiarization phase, where participants watched an instructional video on interacting within the virtual environment. They then explored the museum to understand objects' state and available automations. Next, users received a paper-based description of six tasks, in increasing complexity. Five tasks involved creating new automations, one required modifying an existing one: **T1)** Automate spotlights for a painting when visitors approach (simple rule), **T2)** Display an info panel when a button is pressed (simple rule), **T3)** Create an automation of their choice, **T4)** Unlock hidden information with a related historical object (complex rule), **T5)** Play multimedia content near Beethoven's statue if playback is enabled, **T6)** Modify the simple rule from T2 to create a complex automation.

The analysis of 86 rules collected in this setting (see Table 1) shows a strong preference for event-first formulations, with 26 rules following a simple event-action (EA) pattern. Extended event-action sequences were less common, EAA: 2 times, EAAE: once. Conditions (C) in event-based structures occurred infrequently: EAC appeared four times and ECA five times, thus users generally introduced conditions later in the rule. Action-first rules were more prevalent -15 AE formulations, 3 standalone action (A), 7 condition-based rules. This suggests that some users viewed automation through direct actions or conditions instead of just event-driven triggers. This aligns with previous findings, emphasizing simple cause-and-effect relationships and a tendency to avoid complex logic unless necessary. Unlike the previous study, where participants simplified complex rules with chatbot assistance, our results indicate a broader variety of structures, suggesting LLM-based answers encouraged diverse problem-solving strategies.

We analysed the words used by participants in VR to define events, conditions, and actions, focusing only on their terms. We collected 79 event-related expressions, 35 for conditions, and 97 for actions. Participants primarily used the word "when" (52 occurrences) for events, indicating they view events as temporal triggers. Less common alternatives included direct statements (6), "every"/"once" (5), "if" (5), and conjunctions like "and" (4). For conditions, "when" (8), "and" (7), and "if" (4) were the most frequent, with direct statements (3) and specific constraints appearing. In actions, "play" (17), "turn on" (17), and "activate" (13) were the most common verbs, along with "show" (9) and "start"/"appear" (5 each). This suggests that participants structured automation rules around clear cause-and-effect relationships, emphasising temporal expressions for events and simpler formulations for conditions. Verb structure shows a strong preference for second-person (83) and present-tense (112): thus, participants mainly expressed rules as commands for the chatbot to execute. The frequent use of imperative forms (69) supports this, suggesting that users tend to describe automation clearly and concisely. Also, the presence of modal verbs like "can" (11), "do" (10), "must" (6), and "want" (6) indicates some preference for a more flexible phrasing, introducing variability in rule execution.

Error Types. We identified 132 errors affecting chatbot responses, mainly due to speech recognition failures (62), misinterpretations (26), hallucinations (11), and user mistakes (33). Many errors stemmed from speech recognition issues (11) and ambiguous user input (8). User errors often involve incorrect terminology or misinterpreting automations. In T5, six task failures occurred because users provided incorrect trigger names. T4 errors involved five partially correct rules, primarily due to misinterpreting conditions or actions. On average, users made 2.75 errors, especially in complex tasks (T4, T5). User digressions contributed to inconsistencies but did not affect rule correctness. These findings highlight the need to improve speech recognition and user guidance.

Task Time. Completion times reflect task complexity, with longer durations for open-ended and condition-based tasks. T1 (5 m 21 s, σ=154 s) took some time despite its simplicity, likely due to users' initial learning curve, while T2 (3 m

44 s, σ=89 s) was the fastest, showing quick adaptation. T3 (7 m 25 s, σ=146 s) took the longest time since most participants spent time in setting their specific goals. T4 (6 m 44 s, σ=216 s) also took longer due to complex conditions. T5 (4 m 42 s, σ=189 s) and T6 (4 m 40 s, σ=167 s) were completed faster, suggesting that modifying a rule (T6) was easier than creating a complex one (T4).

4.2 Augmented Reality Smart Home

Experiment Setting (Fig. 1-B). The test was conducted in a lab where we created an environment simulating a smart home with several smart objects, sensors, and devices (e.g., washing machine, smart light, smart plug, gas sensor). Users can move around and (using a Samsung Galaxy S10 smartphone), can anytime interact with the agent either by voice, or by framing a device via the smartphone camera, exploiting AR to receive information about available devices, their state and capabilities, and already defined automations.

Participants. We involved 13 users (10 females), aged between 30 to 64 y.o ($\bar{x} = 48.2, \sigma = 11.1$), recruited via emails in the mailing list of the institute of the authors, and of the larger research area to their institute. As for familiarity of users with smart or conversational agents on a 1 to 5 scale (1= no familiarity; 5= a lot of familiarity), 5 users indicated 1, 3 users indicated 2, 5 indicated 3 ($\bar{x} = 2, \sigma = 0.9$). The agents users are familiar with are Alexa (7 users), ChatGPT (2 users), Siri (2) and Google (1). Still using the same 1–5 scale, almost all (12) were unfamiliar with systems supporting automation, and 1 user had little familiarity with TaDo, a system to remotely manage house heating. Finally, 12 users had no experience at all in programming, only one had low knowledge of HTML (to create websites).

Collected Rules: Structure and Patterns Used. In total, 70 rules were created (32 simple, 38 complex). In 20 cases (10 simple, 10 complex), users accepted the chatbot's proposed rule without modification. This especially happened in T3 (8 cases), followed by T1 (5), T2 (3), T4 (2), and T5 and T6 (1 case each). The higher occurrence in T3 may be due to the open-ended nature of the task. In T6, three users modified only an event parameter of an existing rule. Some tasks did not result in rule creation (8 missing rules) due to inconsistent responses of users when prompted to save the rule or because of chatbot errors. We then analysed the structure of collected rules, also distinguishing between those identified by users and those proposed by the chatbot and then accepted by users. The analysis of rules collected (see Table 1) shows a preference for the action-first pattern (24 rules), indicating that users focus more on the goal they would like to achieve: among them, the most common pattern was $A^+E^+A^*$ (17 rules). Event-first rules were less common (13 rules). The majority followed the E^+A^+ pattern (11 rules). This contrasts with prior findings of the formative study where event-driven formulations were prevalent, suggesting a shift in user preferences when interacting with real automation prototypes in AR. Condition-first rules appeared in 10 cases, with 7 'only-condition' rules (C^+), all referring to T6, where users had to modify an existing rule by adding a condition. In such 7 cases, users only stated the new condition while leaving the event and action implicit (as they were already defined in the original rule). More complex conditional structures, such as CE^+A^+ (2 rules) and CA^+E^+ (1 rules) are less frequent: some users still utilized them to refine automation logic.

We then analysed the words that users exploited to describe events/conditions/actions, counting only the utterances given by them (not those suggested by the chatbot and accepted by them). In total, we got 38 utterances for events, 17 for conditions, 38 for actions. The results confirm some findings of the formative test: to define events, 'when' (24 events) and 'if' (5 events) were used; to express conditions:"only when" (5 conditions), "only", "when", and "during [the weekend]" (2 conditions each).

We also evaluated the meaning of the verbs used for actions, grouping similar ones in the same category: the most used verb was 'to turn' (15 times), likely because it can be employed for many devices. The second most used verb was 'to open' (12): T5 involved 'windows' as devices. Then, 'to notify' and 'to set' occurred both 4 times, followed by the verbs 'to be' and 'to close' (used only once each). Most users used a verbal structure that included the use of want/wish + subjunctive (11 items) and referring to the involved device, e.g. "I would like the purifier to turn on". Instead, nine times users referred directly to the chatbot using phrases like "I would like you to turn on the purifier". In the other 6 cases, users said they wanted an automation that made a certain action or an automation for a specific device. In 9 other cases, users used the infinitive form of the verb: in 2 of such cases the infinitive was alone, while in the other 7 cases it was preceded by "want" or "would" (5 times), or by "of" (2 cases).

Task Time. On average, each user spent 20 m 1 s to fulfil the tasks (max= 31min 37 s, min=12min 9 s). T1 required the highest time, followed by T2, likely due to users' initial lack of familiarity with the system. Many users reported that as they progressed, they felt more in control and completed tasks faster (this was reflected in shorter completion times for T3 and T4). Completion time increased slightly in T5 and T6, however they were still faster than T1.

Error Types. By analyzing the logs of the chatbot-user conversations, we identified different types of errors: those made by the user ('user errors'), those made by the chatbot ('chatbot errors'), and those independent of both of them (voice recognition errors). Among the 102 'user errors' identified, we had 3 error types: i) *inconsistent user response* (the user answer was not coherent with the chatbot's request: 68 occurrences); ii) *incorrect user response* (the user answer led to an error in, e.g. solving the task: 25); iii) *user digressions* (utterances not directly related to the task): 9; Among the total 54 'chatbot errors', we had 2 types: i) *inconsistent/incorrect chatbot response* (42 occurrences); ii) *hallucinations* (plausible but false chatbot response): 12. The 'voice recognition' errors were 24. So, in total, we had 180 errors (on average, 13.84 errors done by each user, max= 25, min= 7). However, they did not necessarily cause severe failures (only in 8 cases no rule was created due to both chatbot and user errors).

We also analyzed errors related to task complexity. In tasks requiring simple rules, we found 36 errors in T1 and 23 in T2. The most common issues were user inconsistencies (11 in T1, 9 in T2), followed by chatbot inconsistencies (10 in T1, 7 in T2) and voice recognition errors (5 in T1, 3 in T2). T2 had fewer total errors, indicating improved user performance with familiarity. In T3 (open goal) we had 27 errors, with user inconsistencies being the most frequent (12). In tasks focusing on complex rules, we had 27 errors in T4 and 29 in T5, with many user issues in both. T6 (modifying simple automation) had the highest error count (38), mainly from inconsistent user responses (18), i.e. one user failed to modify a rule, while another created a new rule instead of modifying an existing one.

Task Success (Correctness of Users' Rules). We analyzed if the created rules correctly fulfilled the scenarios by identifying 6 correctness levels, from completely correct (score=6) to completely incorrect (1). The occurrences were: a) *fully correct rules* (score 6): 34 rules; b) *rules correct compared to the user intent, which in turn is partially correct for the task* (score=5): 10 rules; c) *rules partially correct compared to the user intent, which in turn is correct for the task* (score =4): 12 rules; d) *rules correct compared to user intent, which in turn is incorrect for the task* (score =3): 7 rules; e) *rules correct compared to user intent, which in turn is correct for the task* (2): 1 rule; *fully incorrect rules* (1): 6 rules.

Most (34) of the 70 rules created were fully correct; thus, users achieved their tasks despite some errors. The second most frequent score was '4' (12 times), typically due to minor chatbot omissions, e.g. missing an element, slightly misinterpreting user intent, or chatbot creating a rule involving a non-existing device (hallucination). The '5' score (10 rules) occurred when the chatbot followed the instructions of users, who omitted some elements (e.g. a condition or an action), leading to incomplete rules. A score of '3' occurred (7 rules) when users provided incorrect instructions that the chatbot followed, resulting in technically correct rules, though not fulfilling tasks. The lowest scores, 1 and 2, were less frequent. A score of 1 (fully incorrect rules) was given (6 rules) when both users and the chatbot made multiple errors, often leading to oversimplified rules. The only instance of a '2' score was in T1, when the chatbot referred a non-existent device. The most common issue leading to lower scores was user errors, particularly in T5 and T6 (users either did not include conditions or misunderstood the needed modifications). Chatbot errors, (e.g. hallucinations), also happened, but were less frequent. Thus, user errors were the primary cause of inconsistencies in automation creation, particularly in tasks requiring complex rules or modifications. As users progressed through the tasks, their performance improved (e.g. fewer errors in T2 than in T1, both with simple rules), although tasks requiring complex automation (T5) or rule editing (T6) had an increased error number, thus the chatbot should provide improved guidance in complex tasks.

4.3 Discussion

Approach's Potential for Generalization. The findings from the user studies highlight how users create and modify event-condition-action rules across different XR environments: participants started defining vague goals, then explored the available options and refined their intent, eventually confirming the automation rule. Despite variations in interaction paradigms and devices (HMD vs.

smartphones), the core strategies in rule definition remained consistent in both VR and AR. The studies confirm that rule formulation adapts to the affordances of each setting. Also differences in user goals—ntertainment (museum) vs. utility (smart home)—did not alter the overall strategy to define the automations. These insights suggest that the approach generalizes well across XR applications, potentially extending to Mixed Reality and other domains.

Errors and Task Complexity. A key similarity across both experiments (AR/VR) is the impact of task complexity on error rates: in both cases, users performed better when dealing with simple tasks, while more inconsistencies occurred with complex rules. This trend aligns with prior research [31], indicating that end-user programming becomes more error-prone as rule complexity increases. Additionally, in both cases, users were more likely to accept chatbot-proposed rules in open-ended tasks, suggesting a preference for assistance when the automation goal is not explicitly stated.

Task Success. The comparative analysis of task success in AR and VR reveals both shared patterns and distinct challenges. User errors were the main source of inconsistencies, especially in complex tasks (T5 and T6). In VR, speech recognition failures (62 cases) and misinterpretations (26 cases) notably affected chatbot responses, while in AR, errors were often related to incomplete user intent, with 19 rules scoring 3 or lower due to incorrect instructions. Despite these issues, users were overall able to successfully create correct rules, with a positive trend in both the AR and VR settings, with minor errors. Chatbot hallucinations were observed in both environments.

Keywords. Users in both AR and VR mainly used "when" and "if" for events, and "when", "if", and "only when" for conditions. Even though we registered some domain and setting specific variations, the cause-effect structure remained consistent in both AR and VR. We registered some differences in the verbal structure: VR users favoured the present tense (112 occurrences) and imperative (69), often using 2nd-person commands to instruct the chatbot. AR users adopted a more varied approach, incorporating 1st-person formulations and subjunctive expressions. These findings suggest that chatbots must disambiguate the meaning based on the context, rather than relying solely on specific keywords. This aligns with prior research [3] on adaptive keyword-based interaction, emphasizing the need for a flexible interpretation of natural language.

Rule Structure. Users preferred simple rules in both settings, but VR participants mainly used event-first structures (expressing time), prioritizing *when* an event occurred before specifying its effects. In AR, action-first rules were more common, reflecting a goal-oriented approach: users focused on *what* should happen. Despite these differences, both environments demonstrated that users could successfully create automation rules with chatbot assistance.

Modifying Rules: Woz vs Prototype. The formative study found that, in both AR and VR settings, users often redefined entire automation rules instead of making specific changes, indicating a lack of awareness of rule granularity and difficulties in isolating modifications. In the prototype study, AR users identified the specific components to modify, indicating that the provided guidance was effective in explaining the rule structure. In contrast, VR users still faced challenges in articulating these types of changes, and this led to misunderstandings between users and the chatbot. This highlights the need for improved guidance in rule editing tasks, e.g. in identifying the parts that require updates.

5 Conclusion and Future Work

In this paper we report on the structure and patterns of conversations between end-users and an intelligent chatbot for creating automation rules. We collected data in two user studies, one using the Wizard of Oz and one with a chatbot prototype in two experimental settings: a virtual museum in VR and a smart home in AR. The analysis of such data shows that the dialogues share consistent strategies across the two interaction settings (AR and VR) and domains, such as the use of keywords, difficulties in expressing conditions and task success. In each setting, we also identified different adaptations to the verbal structure and in expressing rules (event vs action-first). Future work will focus on issues in expressing conditions, which require specific support to raise the ceiling of automation and to design specific chatbot guidance to edit rules.

Acknowledgements. Funded by the Italian PRIN 2022 "EUD4XR: End-User Development for eXtended Reality" funded by the Italian MUR and European Union - NextGenerationEU, Mission 4, Component 2, Investment 1.1 (grant F53D23004380006, MUR code 2022Y3CZZT) https://prin.unica.it/eud4xr/.

Jacopo Mereu participated in this research while attending the PhD program in Mathematics and Computer Science at the University of Cagliari (39th cycle), supported by a scholarship funded under D.M. n. 118 (2.3.2023), within the Italian National Recovery and Resilience Plan (PNRR) - funded by the European Union - NextGenerationEU - Mission 4, Component 1, Investment 4.1.

References

1. Adão, T., et al.: A rapid prototyping tool to produce 360 video-based immersive experiences enhanced with virtual/multimedia elements. Procedia Comput. Sci. **138**, 441–453 (2018)
2. Andrao, M., et al.: Enhance gamification design through end-user development: a proposal. In: IS-EUD Workshops (2023)
3. Andrao, M., Treccani, B., Zancanaro, M.: Language and temporal aspects: a qualitative study on trigger interpretation in trigger-action rules. In: Spano, L.D., Schmidt, A., Santoro, C., Stumpf, S. (eds.) End-User Development, pp. 84–103. Springer, Cham (2023)
4. Ariano, R., Manca, M., Paternò, F., Santoro, C.: Smartphone-based augmented reality for end-user creation of home automations. Behav. Inf. Technol. **42**(1), 124–140 (2023)

5. Artizzu, V., et al.: Defining configurable virtual reality templates for end users. Proc. ACM Hum.-Comput. Interact. **6**(EICS) (2022). https://doi.org/10.1145/3534517
6. Barricelli, B.R., Cassano, F., Fogli, D., Piccinno, A.: End-user development, end-user programming and end-user software engineering: a systematic mapping study. J. Syst. Softw. **149**, 101–137 (2019)
7. Bellucci, A., Vianello, A., Florack, Y., Micallef, L., Jacucci, G.: Augmenting objects at home through programmable sensor tokens: a design journey. Int. J. Hum. Comput. Stud. **122**, 211–231 (2019)
8. Blečić, I., et al.: First-person cinematographic videogames: game model, authoring environment, and potential for creating affection for places. J. Comput. Cult. Herit. **14**(2) (2021). https://doi.org/10.1145/3446977
9. Brackenbury, W., et al.: How users interpret bugs in trigger-action programming. In: Proceedings of the 2019 CHI Conference on Human Factors in Computing Systems, pp. 1–12 (2019)
10. Carcangiu, A., Manca, M., Mereu, J., Santoro, C., Simeoli, L., Spano, L.D.: Tell-XR: Conversational End-User Development of XR Automations (2025). https://arxiv.org/abs/2504.09104
11. Chen, X., Chen, S., Jin, Z., Bian, H., Chen, Z., Li, H.: Expressing the needs in smart home: what is the end users' favorite way. ACM Trans. Comput.-Hum. Interact. (2025). https://doi.org/10.1145/3715114
12. Corno, F., De Russis, L., Monge Roffarello, A.: Empowering end users in debugging trigger-action rules. In: Proceedings of the 2019 CHI Conference on Human Factors in Computing Systems, CHI 2019, pp. 1–13. Association for Computing Machinery, New York (2019). https://doi.org/10.1145/3290605.3300618
13. Corno, F., De Russis, L., Monge Roffarello, A.: Heytap: bridging the gaps between users' needs and technology in if-then rules via conversation. In: Proceedings of the 2020 International Conference on Advanced Visual Interfaces, AVI 2020. Association for Computing Machinery, New York (2020). https://doi.org/10.1145/3399715.3399905
14. Coutaz, J., Crowley, J.L.: A first-person experience with end-user development for smart homes. IEEE Pervasive Comput. **15**(2), 26–39 (2016)
15. De Russis, L., Corno, F.: Homerules: a tangible end-user programming interface for smart homes. In: Proceedings of the 33rd Annual ACM Conference Extended Abstracts on Human Factors in Computing Systems, pp. 2109–2114 (2015)
16. Desolda, G., Ardito, C., Matera, M.: Empowering end users to customize their smart environments: model, composition paradigms, and domain-specific tools. ACM Trans. Comput.-Hum. Interact. **24**(2) (2017). https://doi.org/10.1145/3057859
17. Desolda, G., Greco, F., Guarnieri, F., Mariz, N., Zancanaro, M.: Sensation: an authoring tool to support event–state paradigm in end-user development. In: Human-Computer Interaction–INTERACT 2021: 18th IFIP TC 13 International Conference, Bari, Italy, 30 August–3 September 2021, Proceedings, Part II 18, pp. 373–382. Springer, Cham (2021)
18. Dey, A.K., Newberger, A.: Support for context-aware intelligibility and control. In: Proceedings of the SIGCHI Conference on Human Factors in Computing Systems, pp. 859–868 (2009)
19. Fanni, F.A., et al.: PAC-PAC: end user development of immersive point and click games. In: Malizia, A., Valtolina, S., Morch, A., Serrano, A., Stratton, A. (eds.) End-User Development, pp. 225–229. Springer, Cham (2019)

20. Farias, F., De Mattos, D.P., Ghinea, G., Muchaluat-Saade, D.C.: Immersive authoring of 360 degree interactive applications. IEEE Access **10**, 115205–115221 (2022). https://doi.org/10.1109/ACCESS.2022.3217799
21. Fogli, D., Peroni, M., Stefini, C.: Imathome: making trigger-action programming easy and fun. J. Vis. Lang. Comput. **42**, 60–75 (2017)
22. Frau, V., Spano, L.D., Artizzu, V., Nebeling, M.: Xrspotlight: example-based programming of XR interactions using a rule-based approach. Proc. ACM Hum.-Comput. Interact. **7**(EICS) (2023). https://doi.org/10.1145/3593237
23. Ghiani, G., Manca, M., Paternò, F., Santoro, C.: Personalization of context-dependent applications through trigger-action rules. ACM Trans. Comput.-Hum. Interact. **24**(2) (2017). https://doi.org/10.1145/3057861
24. Heun, V., Hobin, J., Maes, P.: Reality editor: programming smarter objects. In: Proceedings of the 2013 ACM Conference on Pervasive and Ubiquitous Computing Adjunct Publication, pp. 307–310 (2013)
25. Huang, J., Cakmak, M.: Supporting mental model accuracy in trigger-action programming. In: Proceedings of the 2015 ACM International Joint Conference on Pervasive and Ubiquitous Computing, pp. 215–225 (2015)
26. Huang, T.H.K., Azaria, A., Romero, O.J., Bigham, J.P.: Instructablecrowd: creating if-then rules for smartphones via conversations with the crowd. Hum. Comput. **6**(1), 113–146 (2019). https://doi.org/10.15346/hc.v6i1.7. https://hcjournal.org/index.php/jhc/article/view/104
27. IFTTT: IFTTT: Connect your apps and devices. https://ifttt.com/. Accessed: [Inserisci la data di accesso]
28. Ikeda, B., Szafir, D.: Programar: augmented reality end-user robot programming. J. Hum.-Robot Interact. **13**(1) (2024). https://doi.org/10.1145/3640008
29. Zapier Inc.: Zapier (2022). https://zapier.com. Accessed 17 Feb 2022
30. Knierim, P., Woźniak, P.W., Abdelrahman, Y., Schmidt, A.: Exploring the potential of augmented reality in domestic environments. In: Proceedings of the 21st International Conference on Human-Computer Interaction with Mobile Devices and Services, MobileHCI 2019. Association for Computing Machinery, New York (2019). https://doi.org/10.1145/3338286.3340142
31. Ko, A.J., Myers, B.A., Aung, H.H.: Six learning barriers in end-user programming systems. In: 2004 IEEE Symposium on Visual Languages - Human Centric Computing, pp. 199–206 (2004). https://doi.org/10.1109/VLHCC.2004.47
32. Kubitza, T., Schmidt, A.: Towards a toolkit for the rapid creation of smart environments. In: End-User Development: 5th International Symposium, IS-EUD 2015, Madrid, Spain, 26–29 May 2015. Proceedings 5, pp. 230–235. Springer, Cham (2015)
33. Lee, G.A., Kim, G.J.: Immersive authoring of tangible augmented reality content: a user study. J. Vis. Lang. Comput. **20**(2), 61–79 (2009). https://doi.org/10.1016/j.jvlc.2008.07.001
34. Lee, G.A., Kim, G.J., Billinghurst, M.: Immersive authoring: what you experience is what you get (wyxiwyg). Commun. ACM **48**(7), 76–81 (2005). https://doi.org/10.1145/1070838.1070840
35. Leonardi, N., Manca, M., Paternò, F., Santoro, C.: Trigger-action programming for personalising humanoid robot behaviour. In: Proceedings of the 2019 CHI Conference on Human Factors in Computing Systems, pp. 1–13 (2019)
36. Liu, X., et al.: Understanding in-situ programming for smart home automation. Proc. ACM Interact. Mob. Wearable Ubiquitous Technol. **7**(2) (2023). https://doi.org/10.1145/3596254

37. Mahroo, A., Greci, L., Sacco, M.: HoloHome: an augmented reality framework to manage the smart home. In: De Paolis, L.T., Bourdot, P. (eds.) AVR 2019. LNCS, vol. 11614, pp. 137–145. Springer, Cham (2019). https://doi.org/10.1007/978-3-030-25999-0_12
38. Manca, M., Paternò, F., Santoro, C., Corcella, L.: Supporting end-user debugging of trigger-action rules for IoT applications. Int. J. Hum. Comput. Stud. **123**, 56–69 (2019)
39. Monge Roffarello, A., De Russis, L.: Defining trigger-action rules via voice: a novel approach for end-user development in the IoT. In: International Symposium on End User Development, pp. 65–83. Springer, Cham (2023)
40. Noura, M., Heil, S., Gaedke, M.: Natural language goal understanding for smart home environments. In: Proceedings of the 10th International Conference on the Internet of Things, IoT 2020. Association for Computing Machinery, New York (2020). https://doi.org/10.1145/3410992.3410996
41. OpenAI: GPT-4o system card. arXiv preprint arXiv:2410.21276 (2024)
42. Paternò, F., Santoro, C.: End-user development for personalizing applications, things, and robots. Int. J. Hum. Comput. Stud. **131**, 120–130 (2019)
43. Seiger, R., Gohlke, M., Aßmann, U.: Augmented reality-based process modelling for the internet of things with holoflows. In: Reinhartz-Berger, I., Zdravkovic, J., Gulden, J., Schmidt, R. (eds.) BPMDS/EMMSAD -2019. LNBIP, vol. 352, pp. 115–129. Springer, Cham (2019). https://doi.org/10.1007/978-3-030-20618-5_8
44. Steed, A., Slater, M.: A dataflow representation for defining behaviours within virtual environments. In: Proceedings of the IEEE 1996 Virtual Reality Annual International Symposium, pp. 163–167 (1996). https://doi.org/10.1109/VRAIS.1996.490524
45. Stefanidi, E., Arampatzis, D., Leonidis, A., Korozi, M., Antona, M., Papagiannakis, G.: Magiplay: an augmented reality serious game allowing children to program intelligent environments. Trans. Comput. Sci. XXXVII: Special Issue Comput. Graph. 144–169 (2020)
46. Stefanidi, E., Arampatzis, D., Leonidis, A., Papagiannakis, G.: Bricklayer: a platform for building rules for AMI environments in AR. In: Gavrilova, M., Chang, J., Thalmann, N.M., Hitzer, E., Ishikawa, H. (eds.) Advances in Computer Graphics, pp. 417–423. Springer, Cham (2019)
47. Sun, Y., Armengol-Urpi, A., Reddy Kantareddy, S.N., Siegel, J., Sarma, S.: Magichand: interact with IoT devices in augmented reality environment. In: 2019 IEEE Conference on Virtual Reality and 3D User Interfaces (VR), pp. 1738–1743 (2019). https://doi.org/10.1109/VR.2019.8798053
48. Takala, T.M.: Ruis: a toolkit for developing virtual reality applications with spatial interaction. In: Proceedings of the 2nd ACM Symposium on Spatial User Interaction, SUI 2014, pp. 94–103. Association for Computing Machinery, New York (2014). https://doi.org/10.1145/2659766.2659774
49. Torres, A.B.B., et al.: A 360 video editor framework for interactive training. In: 8th IEEE International Conference on Serious Games and Applications for Health, SeGAH 2020, Vancouver, BC, Canada, 12–14 August 2020, pp. 1–7. IEEE (2020). https://doi.org/10.1109/SeGAH49190.2020.9201707
50. Ur, B., McManus, E., Pak Yong Ho, M., Littman, M.L.: Practical trigger-action programming in the smart home. In: Proceedings of the SIGCHI Conference on Human Factors in Computing Systems, CHI 2014, pp. 803–812. Association for Computing Machinery, New York (2014). https://doi.org/10.1145/2556288.2557420

51. Yigitbas, E., Klauke, J., Gottschalk, S., Engels, G.: End-user development for interactive web-based virtual reality scenes. J. Comput. Lang. **74**, 101187 (2023). https://doi.org/10.1016/j.cola.2022.101187
52. Zarraonandia, T., Díaz, P., Montero, A., Aedo, I.: Exploring the benefits of immersive end user development for virtual reality. In: Ubiquitous Computing and Ambient Intelligence: 10th International Conference, UCAmI 2016, San Bartolomé de Tirajana, Gran Canaria, Spain, 29 November–2 December 2016, Proceedings, Part I 10, pp. 450–462. Springer, Cham (2016)
53. Zhang, L., Oney, S.: Flowmatic: an immersive authoring tool for creating interactive scenes in virtual reality. In: Proceedings of the 33rd Annual ACM Symposium on User Interface Software and Technology, pp. 342–353 (2020)
54. Zhao, V., Zhang, L., Wang, B., Littman, M.L., Lu, S., Ur, B.: Understanding trigger-action programs through novel visualizations of program differences. In: Proceedings of the 2021 CHI Conference on Human Factors in Computing Systems, pp. 1–17 (2021)

From User Needs to Smart Ecosystems Through LLMs: The Smartifier Case Study

Giacomo Caslini[1(✉)], Mattia Gianotti[1], and Franca Garzotto[1,2]

[1] Politecnico di Milano, 20133 Milan, MI, Italy
{giacomo.caslini,mattia.gianotti}@polimi.it
[2] Università degli Studi di Milano-Bicocca, 20126 Milan, MI, Italy
franca.garzotto@unimib.it

Abstract. Smartifier is a conversational platform that leverages Large Language Models (LLMs) to help non-technical users design, implement, and manage smart objects. It addresses persistent challenges in the Internet of Things (IoT) domain, where the "making community" and End-User Development approaches have yet to empower novices fully. The system features two distinct chat interfaces: one dedicated to creating customized devices, and another for generating automation rules. Building on an iterative design model, Smartifier translates high-level, daily-life needs into hardware selections and automatically compiled software, ensuring correct APIs for seamless integration. A technical evaluation compared different ChatGPT-based models and temperature values, revealing an optimal configuration that curbs hallucinations and maximizes reliability. In a user study with 17 participants lacking ICT expertise, Smartifier achieved high correctness (averaging over 91% across all tasks) and high scores regarding usability and user satisfaction. A thematic analysis of conversations revealed insights around user need expression, iterative negotiation, and system feedback. These findings will inform future refinements, especially regarding user experience design and the handling of advanced functionalities in complex real-world settings. While the study's sample size is limited, findings confirm that Smartifier effectively bridges complex technical tasks and everyday needs, reducing cognitive load and streamlining the creation of IoT solutions. These results highlight the potential of LLM-driven platforms to simplify and democratize technology development, suggesting new directions for future research on EUD and software generation for non-expert users.

Keywords: Smart Objects · IoT · Smart Spaces · LLMs · Conversational Agents

1 Introduction

In the contemporary landscape of pervasive computing, the emergence and proliferation of Smart Objects (SOs) marks a paradigmatic shift in the way we interact with and perceive our surroundings, fulfilling Weiser's prediction [40].

C. Santoro et al. (Eds.): IS-EUD 2025, LNCS 15713, pp. 80–98, 2025.
https://doi.org/10.1007/978-3-031-95452-8_5

Kortuem et al. defined Smart Objects as "autonomous physical/digital objects augmented with sensing, processing, and network capabilities" [26]. As these objects become more pervasive, they introduce unprecedented opportunities for innovation and optimization across various sectors of society. *Making approaches*, in this context, refer to the creation, design, and fabrication [36] of SOs to meet user needs. However, such approaches are deemed complex. Even experts face complex iteration processes to refine the design and implementation of a SO [11]. This complexity is even more significant for individuals lacking technical expertise. Making spaces are often perceived as closed communities composed of knowledgeable people [4]; this may be intimidating to inexperienced people, hindering the diffusion of the abilities and concepts necessary to customize IoT systems. End-User Development "can be defined as a set of methods, techniques, and tools that allow users of software systems, who are acting as non-professional software developers, to create, modify, or extend a software artifact" [28]. Desolda et al. called for EUD paradigms supporting smart-object *composition* [12]. They stated that only coordinating the behavior of multiple smart objects can provide added value. Users should be empowered to create networks of objects able to make autonomous decisions, processing information and events without human action [3]. The Trigger-Action Programming (TAP) framework is an effective and common approach to let users define the behavior and the coordination of SOs [12]. The success of IFTTT and Zapier, two publicly available EUD trigger-action engines, is a further confirmation of this trend [39]. In this paper, we introduce Smartifier, a platform based on ChatGPT, designed to empower users to seamlessly create networks of smart objects through an intuitive and user-friendly interface. Smartifier serves as a comprehensive solution, guiding users through a process of 1) identifying high-level needs in their daily lives, 2) designing a SO tailored to those needs, 3) selecting the hardware components, 4) automatically generating the SO's control software for the SO, 5) defining the behavior rules for each SO or among different SOs. The tool aims to bridge the gap between real-world problems and technological solutions, ensuring that users can actively develop smart solutions regardless of their technical expertise. We conducted a technical test to determine the optimal LLM model to support users. Then, we performed a user study involving 17 adults, collecting qualitative impressions from participants and a quantitative analysis of the quality of produced IoT systems. Our study suggests that Smartifier is effective in correctly transforming user needs into system requirements during the creation of SOs (correctness > 93%) and in specifying behavioral rules (correctness > 91%) while imposing a low task load on the user (NASA TLX-SF = 16.65). Additionally, a thematic analysis on conversation logs is presented, providing valuable insights for future refinements and conversational EUD platform design.

2 Related Work

Several strategies have been explored to involve end users without technical skills in the design and implementation of smart objects and technological solutions. Two notable examples are Pineal and IoTgo. Pineal [27] is a design tool to prototype interactive smart devices rapidly. Through a visual interface, it allows users to program the inputs and outputs of a mobile device, which is then embedded into a static 3D-printed object. Subsequently, the system guides users through simplified 3D modeling tasks within the workspace, enabling them to prototype and test various behaviors without the need for advanced skills in 3D modeling, programming, or electronic assembly. IoTgo [18] is a phygital toolkit aimed mainly at simplifying the design and programming of smart things in educational contexts. It employs cards representing various elements, such as user personas, missions, environments, and technological components. Users select cards to define their smart thing's features, and the toolkit generates a base program, which can be later customized in Makecode.

When the research focus is on IoT behavior, instead, Trigger-Action Programming (TAP) or Event-Condition-Action (ECA) rules are the most widely adopted EUD strategy [12]. They allow users without technical expertise to write meaningful rules to automate behavior [1]. On the downside, security concerns have been raised regarding the unexpected results of multiple concurrent rules [9]. Other key issues include users' ability to distinguish between events and conditions on states [24] and to express practically feasible temporal rules [5].

Popular examples of visual rule composition tools include IFTTT [25,30,35, 39] and Node-RED [32,33]. Nevertheless, researchers are investing in more natural interfaces to interact with such systems, such as augmented reality and conversational agents [1]. HeyTAP [10] serves as a multimodal conversational interface that helps users define trigger-action rules based on their abstract needs. This translation leverages an ontology-based model, which abstracts details such as device brands or service names, and factors in user preferences (e.g., security or privacy requirements). However, its functionality is limited to acting as a recommender system, offering suggestions rather than generating new rules.

LLM4TAP [41] delivers TAP rule recommendations by using LLM to interpret a user's immediate objectives and broader motivations from natural language input. It analyzes each user's created rules and textual descriptions to infer deeper goals, and then aligns these inferred demands and intentions with a graph-based representation for more tailored rule suggestions. While it leverages LLMs to interpret user intentions and contextual cues, the automation-creation process follows a relatively linear flow. Users supply instructions, but the system does not explicitly guide them through iterative refinements or explorations. Managing interdependent rules or revisiting partial configurations might prove challenging if the user's needs evolve or new constraints emerge.

Giudici et al. [20] presented GreenIFTTT, a platform that combines GPT-4 with TAP to facilitate energy-aware home automation. The system automatically transforms free-text instructions into actionable rules for domestic IoT devices, thereby reducing the complexity of routine creation and encouraging environmentally sustainable behaviors. ChatIoT [17] is another solution that leverages large language models to automatically generate trigger-action programs. The system incorporates a "compressive prompting" technique to reduce token consumption while maintaining high TAP-generation accuracy.

Another influential example is Rulebot. Its first version [15] uses a rule-based chatbot to link inputs with potential triggers and actions. A second iteration [14] integrates the capabilities of Large Language Models (LLMs). A Rasa-based agent classifies user intent and validates generated rules. The LLM breaks down complex inputs into *triggers* and *actions*, then provides explanations to users and offers broader contextual support for rule creation. The last version [16] uses a fully generative chatbot (GPT-4), enabling the translation of user free text into TAP rules. Although promising results have been reported, the study presents three major limitations: 1) Despite allowing users to express their goals in natural language, participants were pre-instructed on the concepts and semantics of TAP rules before the study. This preconditioning may have limited the extent to which users could apply their own reasoning and mental models. 2) Users were asked to leverage specific devices already present in the space, implying a certain level of IoT literacy is required for hardware selection or creation. 3) Users have variable backgrounds and coding skills, introducing a confounding variable.

On a larger landscape, LLMs (i.e., ChatGPT [34]) have shown their potential in assisting individuals with limited technical expertise in software development [38]. In the context of IoT system development, one study [31] compared the use of machine learning with manual methods for creating a control structure, demonstrating the potential of AI-driven approaches in this domain. However, many commonly used benchmarks for LLM-based code generation focus on function-level tasks. Recent studies have shown that when models are evaluated on class-level code generation, their performance deteriorates significantly [13].

3 Smartifier

Smartifier has been developed to support users in designing and implementing SOs and their (possibly orchestrated) behavior. Unlike other LLM-driven EUD tools, Smartifier allows users to begin by describing a general objective from their daily life. It is then progressively refined through an iterative process, ultimately resulting in a customized SO that seamlessly integrates into the personalized IoT ecosystem. The system retains contextual knowledge, along with each object's purpose and specifications, ensuring these elements are accessible for future refinements. With Smartifier, users can generate functional code for both micro- and macro-level SO management without requiring technical expertise. The system comprises two separate multi-modal chat interfaces: one dedicated to creating smart objects (SOB) and the other focusing on defining automation rules (RB). This separation allows for the decoupling of SO's control software from its behavior, enabling refinement and updates throughout its lifecycle.

3.1 Design Process

We began by delineating an optimal process for designing and implementing SOs. Building on our experience and some significant works from the literature (e.g., [2,11,19]), we formalized a simple, iterative process consisting of: 1) the elicitation of *user needs*, 2) a *design phase* resulting in a structural model (the selected components for the SO) and the behavior rules, and 3) an *implementation phase*, delivering both the software (control software and behavior rules) and the hardware (hardware schema and physical assembly) of the SO. These phases are reflected in the system's conversational strategy but are conducted separately: the SO's structural composition is distinct from its behavior definition.

3.2 User Experience

The user accesses Smartifier via browser, where two options are presented: creating a new smart object (SOB) or defining automations (RB). Upon selecting SOB, the user is presented with a chat interface (Fig. 4) containing a welcome, explanatory message. They can describe their daily life problem or goals. SOB proposes a list of hardware components to meet users' needs through an iterative process of proposals and inquiries, relying on a knowledge base of available hardware. The system allows for user agency by letting them modify the list while also striving to guide them toward an optimal solution through conversation. When the user is satisfied with the proposed solution and has provided the necessary information in the GUI (Wi-Fi credentials and the SO name), they press the "Generate" button. After confirming that the board is connected to the computer, the system compiles the SO's enabling code on the board without further user intervention. We decided not to allow the LLM to generate Arduino/C++ code directly because it would require user understanding and supervision [29]. Instead, Smartifier generates a JSON schema used as input by the *Smartifier Engine* backend, which generates the source code, compiles it, and flashes the IoT software onto a compatible board. Additionally, the Smartifier Engine embeds in the code the APIs for transmitting information and receiving commands, thereby ensuring integration with other devices and applications.

Finally, the user can focus on defining the desired behavior for the SO by selecting the automation creation procedure (RB). Initially, the system promptly proposes suitable automations for newly generated SOs that are consistent with their design purpose. The user can choose whether to follow these suggestions or iteratively discuss with the agent to implement different automations. They do not need to provide the request in a specific format since the LLM can extract the components of the TAP rule (i.e., trigger, action, and additional state conditions) from free natural language. For each rule, the LLM generates a JSON schema, which is synced and kept up to date by the Smartifier Hub. The Hub interfaces with each smart object over the local network via the included APIs.

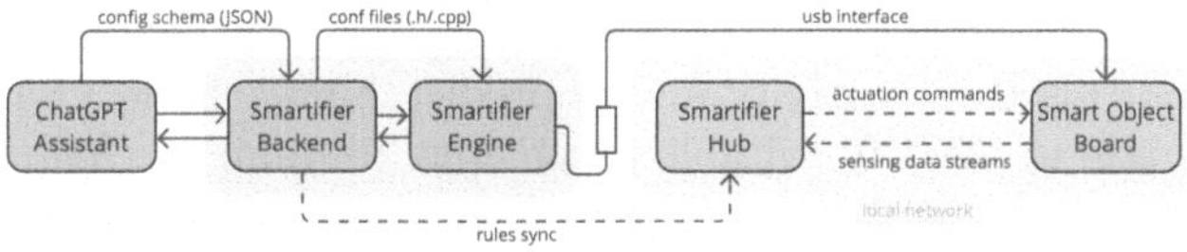

Fig. 1. System Architecture.

3.3 Architecture, Networking, and APIs

Figure 1 illustrates the Smartifier architecture. At its core are two ChatGPT assistants containing the available components [7], supported by a set of functions, implemented with a Python Flask backend, and a database consisting of the specifications for all created smart objects and automation rules. In SOB, functions retrieve the schemas of all previously defined SOs, while RB can also retrieve the already existing rules. The chatbots also use functions to update the side informative panel constantly: SOB renders a component table, while RB shows a subset of relevant rules depending on the conversation's context. Details of the components (sensors, actuators, and the board pinout schema in SOB) are already present as text and files in the ChatGPT assistant [7]. At the end of the SO design phase, a final generation prompt [7] is provided by the backend. SOB verifies the pinout feasibility and provides the backend with a configuration JSON schema (including components and the board connections) by means of a dedicated function.

This configuration is the input for the Smartifier Engine, a custom PlatformIO-based toolchain. During compilation, the platform employs C++ macros to select the specific controllers to include the SO's executable code based on the components indicated in the configuration schema. It also introduces code implementing control APIs, enabling SO integration within the IoT environment. If no errors occur, the operational code is uploaded to the connected board, and the user is notified to disconnect it. The codebase provided by the Smartifier Engine enables each SO to recognize and control sensors and actuators, connect to a Wi-Fi network, and implement the SSDP protocol for automatic SO identification over the local network. Communication is implemented as TCP/HTTP requests for events and actuation commands and UDP streams for states, depending on the component type and request.

RB, more easily, can update, remove or append new rules to the set, so that the Smartifier Hub can autonomously sync the new rule set. It will later use the SO APIs to gather data from each SO, verify sensor input, and command actuators following the defined behavior rules.

4 Technical Testing: LLM Performance Analysis

Scientific literature has shown that Large Language Models (LLMs) can produce hallucinations when generating text [8]. Since our prototype strongly relies on an LLM to interpret user requests—potentially from users who may not recognize such behaviors—we conducted a two-phase evaluation. Phase 1 involved comparing different ChatGPT [34] models (GPT-4-turbo, GPT-4o, and GPT-4o-mini).

Phase 2 focused on determining the optimal value for the *temperature* parameter, which controls the creativity and unpredictability of the LLM's outputs. Our objective was to identify suitable parameters to minimize hallucinations in SO creation and rule identification tasks.

4.1 Phase 1: LLM Model Selection

Having defined a knowledge base of available hardware components and a fictional Smart Space for a generic home automation scenario, we evaluated the LLM's capacity to interpret *making-oriented user prompts* correctly.

Dataset Creation: We created a dataset of prompts that users might employ to describe either a smart object (100 prompts) or behavior rules (100 prompts). Given the lack of guidelines for prompt creation in this specific domain, we built on our previous experience to construct two specialized datasets. Each set comprises 40 *proper prompts* (concise statements containing only essential information), 20 *twisted prompts* (prompts with unnecessarily complex syntax), 20 *truncated prompts* (prompts lacking coherent structure or syntax), and 20 *superfluous prompts* (prompts including irrelevant details). Within each category, only half of the prompts are classified as *feasible*, meaning that the system can provide a correct solution which falls within its current capabilities.

Each of the three ChatGPT models (GPT-4-turbo, GPT-4o, and GPT-4o-mini) was tested on both datasets with the default temperature setting of 1.

Evaluation Metrics: We instructed the LLM to propose solutions for each prompt in both datasets. Since the LLM will be used in multi-stage negotiations with an unexperienced user, we decided not to optimize solely for precision, and to use the F-score as the overall performance metric. In this context, True Positives (TP) are correct solutions to feasible prompts, and False Positives (FP) are either incorrect solutions to feasible prompts or any attempt to provide a solution to an unfeasible prompt. True Negatives (TN) occur when the system correctly declines to solve an unfeasible prompt, and False Negatives (FN) occur when the system refuses to solve a feasible prompt.

Results: The precision and recall scores for each model are illustrated in Fig. 2. In the SO Chatbot (SOB) context, model 4o achieved the highest F-score ($F_1 = 0.76$). For the Rule Chatbot (RB), the best F-score was achieved by the GPT-4-turbo model ($F_1 = 0.69$). Therefore, each best-performing model was chosen for its respective chatbot.

4.2 Phase 2: Temperature Parameter Selection

In Phase 2, we selected the two models identified in Phase 1 and tested them on the same datasets at various temperature settings.

Evaluation Metrics: Evaluation Metrics. We again instructed the LLM to propose solutions for each prompt in both datasets and analyzed the outputs using the same approach as in Phase 1. Precision and recall scores for each temperature setting are reported in Fig. 3, and the corresponding F-score was subsequently calculated.

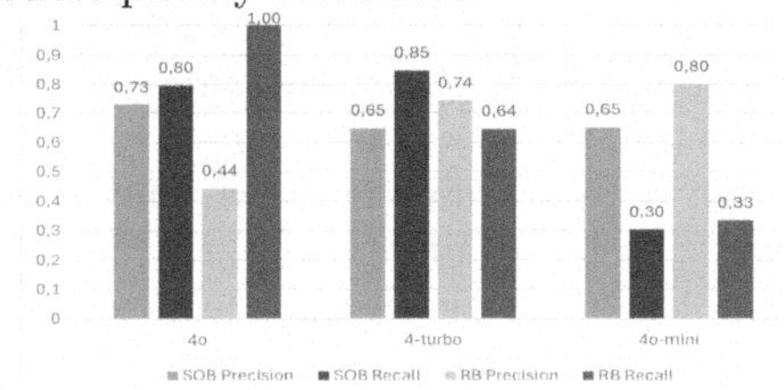

Fig. 2. Scores of precision and recall, by model.

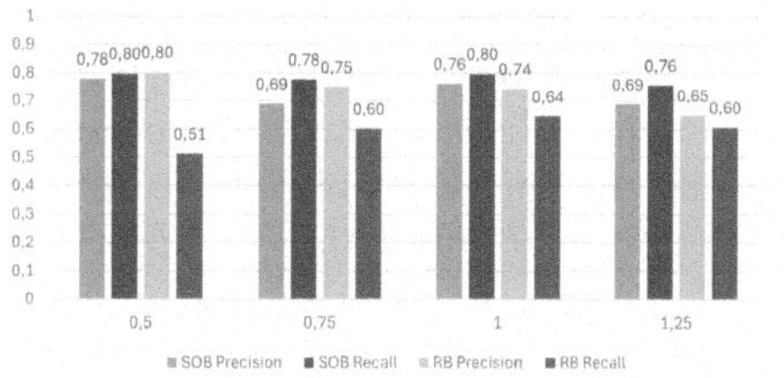

Fig. 3. Scores of precision and recall, by temperature value.

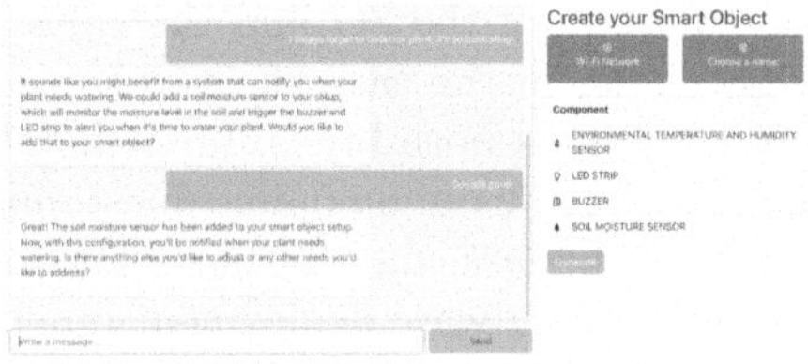

Fig. 4. SOB user interface.

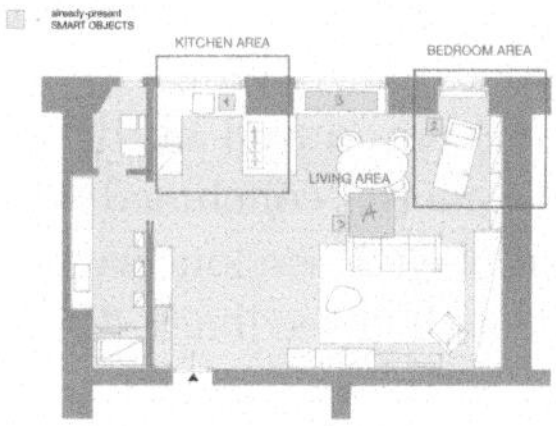

Fig. 5. Map of a fictitious apartment used in the user study.

Results: For the RB, the best F-score was achieved at a temperature of 1 ($F_1 = 0.69$). As for the SOB, the F-score values for $t = 0.5$ and $t = 1$ were similar ($F_{1,t=0.5} = 0.79$, $F_{1,t=1} = 0.78$). We ultimately selected $t = 1$ to allow for greater creative flexibility.

5 User Testing

After identifying the most robust models and temperature parameters to support the task, our objective was to determine whether the LLM-driven solution could effectively assist users in identifying their needs and producing correct specifications for smart objects and automation rules.

5.1 Participants

We decided to test our system with participants who met the following inclusion criteria: 1) young adults (age range 18–40); 2) limited knowledge of ICT topics and no knowledge of IoT or programming; and 3) no opposition to LLM technologies. We recruited 17 participants (5M, 12F) with a mean age of 27.5 years ($\sigma = 6.9$), selected through a convenience sample via personal contacts and word of mouth. All participants took part voluntarily, without compensation, after signing consent forms.

5.2 Experimental Procedures

Each user performed a single test session with our system (average duration = 2034.29 s). One researcher was present to set up the environment, present the tasks, and collect data. After a presentation of the system's general aim (avoiding specific instructions on how to interact with it), each user received, one at a time and in counterbalanced order, two briefs, each containing two tasks. These briefs described: 1) a general daily-life problem the user should try to solve, 2) the high-level goals of the smart objects to be created, 3) some expected behaviors of the new smart object operating alone or in cooperation with other smart objects in the fictitious house, and 4) a map of this house (Fig. 5) showing the placement of the available SOs in the space, indicated as numbered yellow squares. The first project focused on creating a system for plant care, while the second involved creating a smart desk for remote work. A brief was considered concluded when the user completed the creation of the SO and the rules they believed reproduced all desired behaviors listed in the task sheet. The session was considered concluded when the user completed both briefs. Immediately at the end of each session, participants were asked to fill out an online questionnaire to collect their feedback. Each user performed the tasks on a 14-inch laptop with an ESP32 board connected to test the complete software deployment pipeline.

5.3 Research Question and Research Variables

Our research question was: *Does an LLM-driven solution allow people without ICT knowledge to successfully create need-driven SOs and IoT behaviors?* We conducted both qualitative analyses of user perception and quantitative analyses. The evaluation of user production was conducted by the authors.

User Perception Questionnaires: To collect structured feedback from users, we aimed to measure: RQ1) the usability of the system, and RQ2) the task load faced. To address RQ1, participants filled out [RV1] the SUS (System Usability Scale) questionnaire [37], [RV2] the NPS (Net Promoter Score) [21], and, through a dedicated question, [RV3] their satisfaction with the final outcome they created. To measure RQ2, participants completed [RV4] the NASA TLX-SF (NASA Task Load Index Short Form) [22,23] questionnaire.

Performance Evaluation: We were interested in RQ3) user interactions with the LLM and RQ4) the correctness of the final solution obtained in each task. To address RQ3 quantitatively, we measured [RV5] the total time spent to complete the task and [RV6] the predominant content of each message. We separated the measurements between the creation of the Smart Object (RV5.1 and RV6.1) and the creation of the rules (RV5.2 and RV6.2), both to examine the effect of the two different LLM models and because the user's perspective differed for the two tasks. To address RQ4, we relied on expert evaluation, comparing the smart object components and the list of rules generated by each user with a "baseline" smart object and rules set created by an expert to fulfill the same task. We measured RV7) the correctness score, defined as $1 - (\#errors/\#used\_items)$, RV8) the completeness score, defined as (#used_items − #errors)/(#used_items − #errors + #missing_required_items), and RV9) the error balance score, defined as (#errors + #missing_required_items)/(#used_items − #errors). An error was defined as a component or rule which is both superfluous and unrelated to brief tasks. These scores were again separated between the creation of the SO (RV7.1, RV8.1, and RV9.1) and the creation of the rules (RV7.2, RV8.2, and RV9.2).

Thematic Analysis: to further analyze the interplay between users and bots, we performed a thematic analysis on conversation logs to verify RQ5) how humans and bots reached agreements on the design of SOs and rules.

6 Results and Discussion

6.1 Limitations

Before delving into the results and discussion of this study, it is important to acknowledge one limitation. The number of participants in this study is relatively small, and further research is required. Nonetheless, the results are very promising and encouraging, showing an interesting baseline for our future work. While our preliminary results are promising, the external validity of our results is subject to the convenient sample selected, although users have been selected with a large variability of background, and the validation of results is based on a single expert evaluation. Further study needs to be performed.

6.2 Performance Analysis

The time taken by users to complete each Task 1 (independently of the brief) was on average 458.09 seconds (σ = 225.98), with an average of 7.21 messages sent (σ = 2.94). For Task 2, the average was 559.06 seconds (σ = 261.75), with an average of 9.03 messages sent (σ = 4.07). Each complete session lasted, on average, 2034.29 seconds (σ = 713.50). The high variance of the results might be connected to learning effects from reusing SOB and RB twice in a short time.

Task 1. In Task 1A and 1B, the correctness score was very high, respectively [$\mu = 0.93$, $\sigma = 0.10$] and [$\mu = 0.98$, $\sigma = 0.06$]. The completeness score was [$\mu = 0.69$, $\sigma = 0.14$] and [$\mu = 0.89$, $\sigma = 0.11$]. The error balance metric was [$\mu = 0.59$, $\sigma = 0.35$] and [$\mu = 0.15$, $\sigma = 0.15$]. The average frequency of user messages were [$\mu = 0.97$, $\sigma = 0.27$] and [$\mu = 1.17$, $\sigma = 0.48$], respectively.

Task 2. In Task 2A and 2B, the correctness score was comparably high, respectively [$\mu = 0.91$, $\sigma = 0.15$] and [$\mu = 0.93$, $\sigma = 0.12$]. The completeness score was [$\mu = 0.89$, $\sigma = 0.15$] and [$\mu = 0.91$, $\sigma = 0.12$]. The error balance metric was [$\mu = 0.30$, $\sigma = 0.51$] and [$\mu = 0.22$, $\sigma = 0.31$]. The average frequency user messages were [$\mu = 0.98$, $\sigma = 0.34$] and [$\mu = 1.09$, $\sigma = 0.52$], respectively.

The correctness score is uniformly high across all tasks, suggesting that the system is effective in proposing the correct components and rules for the specified use cases. The completeness score for Task 1A was slightly lower, possibly indicating that the chatbot struggled more with extrapolating all the smart object functionalities given the high-level description, which also affected the error balance for that task. This discrepancy in scores may depend on the complexity of the brief itself, but further research is needed to explore the underlying causes.

6.3 Questionnaires Results

We applied the evaluation formulas of the standardized questionnaires. The SUS questionnaire (RV1) reported an average score of 84.26 ($\sigma = 9.63$), which, according to standard metrics, is just below 85, the threshold for excellent usability. The NPS score was 64.71, which is positive and close to the excellence threshold of 70. The NASA TLX-SF score was 16.65 ($\sigma = 5.17$), indicating that our tool requires a relatively low cognitive load from users. We also report that users perceived the tool as useful (4.76 out of 5, $\sigma = 0.94$) and expressive (4.29 out of 5, $\sigma = 0.69$). The high SUS, correctness, and completeness scores support the conclusion that Smartifier was usable and effective in achieving its goal.

Participants noted different response times, attributed to varying model performance between the two chatbots (4o vs. 4-turbo). Notwithstanding these different response times, the frequency of messages is comparable. This might indicate that users either do not feel the need to further question the proposed solution or that RB, despite being slower, effectively conveys all necessary information by leveraging its broader contextual capabilities. The low NASA TLX-SF score, the higher average number of messages exchanged in RB, and the high correctness scores obtained with both SOB and RB seem to support this latter explanation. Considering these findings, we plan to improve user feedback while waiting for the bot's response in a future study to verify our observations.

6.4 Thematic Analysis

We conducted a thematic analysis following Braun and Clarke's six-phase framework [6]. The conversation logs of 17 participants (P1-P17) were extracted.

In the first coding phase, we systematically labeled segments of text that captured meaningful aspects of the interactions. We iteratively refined a code-set, with the labels emerging inductively as we engaged more deeply with the data. Subsequently, codes were grouped into broader themes that encapsulated key interaction patterns. This qualitative approach enabled us to uncover recurring patterns in user-chatbot interactions, highlighting usability challenges and areas for system improvement. Through this iterative process, we identified the following overarching themes: 1) User Needs and System Goals, 2) Explanations, 3) Iteration and Negotiation, 4) User Intervention (Provided or Required), 5) Error Handling and 6) UI and Procedure.

To enhance reliability, the first two authors independently coded the transcripts. Discrepancies were discussed and resolved by consensus, ensuring consistency in theme identification. In the following sections, direct participant quotes were incorporated to illustrate key findings (each tagged with participant number, Px). Given that results differ between brief A or B and the interaction with SOB or RB, quotations are also marked by brief (A or B) and task/chatbot (task 1 for SOB, task 2 for RB)

Theme 1: User Needs and System Goals. Using SOB, participants typically began by stating a problem, often quoting the briefs, and GPT responded by asking basic follow-up questions to prompt users to discuss their needs.

> "***USER:*** *I need an object that takes care of my plant.*" [P1, 1A]

SOB responds to the user by proposing more specific needs that fit with the user request, thus guiding the user from a generic demand to a set of definite and separate needs.

In automation tasks concerning the RB chatbot, it is less simple to discriminate between user needs and system goals, as behavior rules are often guided by previous SO design. However, some relevant examples can be found when the automation rules involved more than one SO.

In Task 1A, users describe a situation in which forgetting to raise the blinds deprives a plant of light. GPT's responses vary depending on how the issue is framed. When a user explains the problem in these terms, GPT interprets this as a need for automation and suggests an actuator to raise the blinds (e.g., an external motor for the blinds, controllable via smart plug). If the user reports to the system that such a device is not available, it adapts by proposing alerts or alternative solutions (for example, using available actuators to provide notifications). Conversely, when the problem is phrased as:

> "***USER:*** *When I am away, the plant does not get enough light because the blinds often remain closed. It needs to receive enough light.*" [P2, 1A]

GPT shifts its approach by suggesting artificial lighting instead, either via an LED strip or an external lamp controlled by a smart plug. The way users articulate their needs directly influences whether GPT prioritizes automation, notifications, or supplementary lighting. While this seems a trend, similar expressions do not always result in identical contextual interpretations by ChatGPT.

Lesson Learned: Influence of Problem Formulation. The way users frame their needs prompts the LLM to propose markedly different solutions. The chatbot should encourage users to provide a precise and comprehensive description of the problem, potentially through targeted questions, to reduce misunderstandings or asymmetries in real-life context identification, which may result in solutions not aligned with user expectations.

Theme 2: Explanations. The "Explanations" theme concerns the description or clarification of components or rules to the user. This process can be initiated either through GPT's proactive explanations or by user inquiries.

In SOB, GPT proactively describes components and their capabilities. For example, when a user asks to adjust the light in Brief B, GPT explained:

> "***GPT:*** *To ensure that your smart desk automatically adjusts lighting based on the environment, we could use a light sensor. This sensor will help us determine how bright the area around the desk is, and then we could use an RGB LED to adjust the lighting accordingly.*" [P1, 1B]

Within SOB, the system also addresses the potential of external appliances that could be controlled via a smart plug component.

> "***GPT:*** *If the irrigation system needs to be connected to power to operate, the water tank by itself cannot activate automatically without electricity. However, our solution allows you to control the irrigation device remotely via the smart plug.*" [P8, 1A]

Using RB, instead, users may proactively ask for information about existing smart objects. This inquiry triggers an explanation from ChatGPT:

> "***USER:*** *What does the smart object that I have in the kitchen do?*
> **GPT:** *The smart object you have in the kitchen* [...] *includes a button for manual inputs, a warning buzzer to emit audible notifications,* [etc.] " [P6, 2B]

Interestingly, RB consistently explains the proposed or newly created rules by integrating them into the real-life context provided by the user. By incorporating situational details, this approach may facilitate users' understanding and help them better anticipate how automation could fit into their daily routines.

> "***GPT:*** *Now, when you press the button on the object in the kitchen after breakfast, the fan near the desk will automatically turn on.*" [P9, 2B]

Analysis shows that RB explanations tend to be more complex and technical than SOB explanations, due to the need to formally define rule triggers and actuation conditions to ensure proper functionality.

> "***GPT:*** *Since the temperature and humidity sensor's conditions can exceed an analog value of 2400 (on a scale from 0 to 4095), I will ensure that the alert is triggered correctly when this occurs.*" [P10 - 2B]

Notice that, while in SOB more informal use-case descriptions can be enough to select the necessary components, RB needs to further elicit specific details to properly create a rule (e.g., numeric values for thresholding on the states).

Lesson Learned: Context of Use and Personalization. Integrating automations into real-life contexts and offering higher-level explanations (e.g., personal routines, preferences) might facilitate understanding of automation rules and increase the perceived usefulness of the system.

Theme 3: Iteration and Negotiation. The interaction logs reveal distinct patterns of iteration and negotiation in both SOB and RB. While both chatbots refine user requests through follow-up questions and rephrasings, their approaches differ based on available system knowledge and the extent of user involvement in shaping the final configuration. SOB, given a lack of prior knowledge about users' intentions, strictly relies on users' inputs. It operates in a design space where users define a vision, later distilled into a functional configuration. The iterative approach investigates various possibilities through proactive proposals, refining user needs and identifying suitable components from these refined requirements, while granting the user the agency to accept, reject, or further refine each proposal. Refinement is performed generally by SOB with questions to clarify ambiguous terms or scenarios. For example, when a user requests improved desk lighting, SOB first seeks clarification rather than suggesting an immediate solution:

> "***GPT:*** *Great idea! [..]. Let's try to better understand what you mean by'good quality light'.*" [P1, 1B]

When the established needs allow for multiple implementing options, SOB engages the user in meaningful choices, without impeding user's agency.

> "***GPT:*** *We can still create a system that notifies you when it's time to raise or lower the blinds based on brightness. We could use a light sensor to detect the amount of light and either a buzzer or an LED strip to provide you with a visual or audible notification. What do you think? Would you prefer to receive a visual notification (with an LED) or an audible one (with a buzzer)?*" [P1, 1A]

RB, instead, knows the structure and objective of the already generated SOs and the rules already defined and active in the space. The chatbot leverages this data, autonomously verifying the feasibility of possible solutions and translating requests into feasible rules. This makes its iteration process more streamlined and less exploratory.

> "***USER:*** *I would like to have a button near the bed to manually control the irrigation in case of need, providing supplementary irrigation myself.*
>
> ***GPT:*** *In "Smart Object 2", which is located near the bed in the bedroom, we have a button that can be used to manually control the irrigation. We can configure this button to activate the smart plug connected to the irrigation on "Smart Object A - Plant". I am configuring this automation now and will let you know as soon as it is ready." [P3, 2A]*

Theme 4: User Intervention: Provided or Required. Other interesting dynamics between users and chatbots emerge when dealing with constraints. Such constraints can be determined by system capabilities (e.g. available sensors and actuators) or by the availability of external devices that can be integrated in the SO (via the smart plug component).

> "***USER:*** *I do not have a motor for the blinds.*

GPT: *I understand, then we will have to focus on a different solution for controlling the blinds. Unfortunately, we do not have motors specifically for blinds in our list of components.*" [P1, 1A]

When the user expresses a constraint impeding the feasibility of a choice, both chatbots react consistently by supporting the user statement. They respond by proposing a possible alternative solution using different elements and, in case of a lack of possibilities, the user can still autonomously express a possible solution to submit to the chatbot. In the first case, the system opts to give agency to the user to select or continue inquiring other alternatives. In the second case, the user may invite the system to use the available components creatively (which could be unfeasible or unrealistic) or propose unsupported components:

> "***USER:*** *Perhaps with a fingerprint sensor or facial recognition, which would be better?*" [P1, 1B]

The system then verifies the feasibility of the proposal and either accepts or explains the reason of the rejection. In case of RB, a similar situation can be achieved by not identifying the specific condition for a rule. For example, when the condition is difficult to interpret or involves abstract measurement. In the following example, the user asked to create a rule to be triggered by darkness, but has no knowledge on how to express "darkness" in mathematical terms.

> "***GPT:*** [...] *Before proceeding, could you confirm if you want the alert to sound when the light falls below a certain level? Additionally, what brightness level do you consider appropriate to define 'dark'?*

USER: *I'm not sure, what is an acceptable level to define as 'dark'?*

GPT: *A light level generally considered 'dark' in indoor environments could be a value below approximately 300. However, this may vary depending on specific preferences or environmental needs. Would you like to set the value at 300, or do you have another preference? If you're unsure, we can start with this value and adjust it later." [P10, 2A]*

Theme 5: Error Handling. This theme summarizes ChatGPT's main mistakes, along with the recurring patterns involved. A frequent example of error in SOB consists in proposing the user to add smart plugs to control devices which were not made available by the user, even though SOB was explicitly instructed to verify that users already possessed the device.

> "***GPT:*** *You can certainly add the smart plug now, so it will be ready when you have the lamp to connect. Even if you do not have a lamp at the moment, having the configuration ready can be useful.*" [P5, 1A]

Another error seldom involving SOB specifically is suggesting operational functionalities that are unachievable with the current system. In this example, it suggests that the selected sensor will allow the SO to log data, a software functionality which cannot be implemented by RB.

> "***GPT:*** *We can use the ambient temperature and humidity sensor [...] to monitor the room's conditions and record this data. This will allow you to track when temperatures and humidity levels exceed the desired limits.*" [P6, 1B]

In two instances, RB did not recognize a user prompt as a request to create an automation rule, even though the prompt was clear. A rephrased request by the users resolved the issue.

Theme 6: UI and Procedure. In this final theme, the focus is on user interface and meta-procedural considerations, particularly in the interactions between users and GPT during both the smart object and rule creation processes.

SOB and RB have different feedback mechanisms to present the user with proposed changes. SOB provides the user with the updated list of selected components in the lateral bar. RB instead uses the lateral bar to display sets of rules depending on the context in the chat (for example, displaying a set of active rules relevant to the discussion with the user), possibly making the feedback for the user more confusing. Instead, RB tends to provide more explicit feedback within the conversation. Nevertheless, users seem to prefer the feedback modality of SOB, as all 10 requests for confirmation and reassurance regarding the creation process occurred within RB. Users also asked the chatbot for help with the procedure and UI, highlighting a need for guidance.

Lesson Learned: Chat-Interface Synergy. The difference in user behavior between the two chatbots, shows that in absence of clear interface feedback, users resort to seeking explicit clarification through natural language.

Another aspect to notice is that, during the iterative phase of SOB, the chatbot repeatedly appended instructions on how to complete the SO design and generation phase at the end of its messages. This persistent repetition might be frustrating and exhausting for the user, especially in case of multiple user needs to express and the resulting number of design iterations. A more balanced communication strategy should be considered for future improvements.

Lesson Learned: Excessive Repetition of Instructions. Repetitions of instructions can become redundant, especially in extended conversations. Mechanisms for more precise control over instruction frequency, potentially through UI notifications and animations, and improved detection of when users are nearing the end of a process phase could reduce user frustration.

7 Conclusion

In recent decades, we have seen the rise and diffusion of smart objects, effectively bringing technology into our everyday physical environments. In this paper, we presented Smartifier, a software tool designed to facilitate the creation and management of smart objects and networks of smart objects. The platform's aim is to enable users with no technical expertise to design and implement smart objects and automations tailored to their needs. Smartifier provides an LLM-driven, comprehensive solution that guides users throughout the design process, assisting them in defining and eliciting daily-life problems. It extracts system requirements from user needs in natural language and implements a technical solution in the form of a smart object. Additionally, it can generate rules and deploy them via a hub. Our user study showed that the tool is usable (SUS = 84.26) and effectively supports users in designing interactive IoT ecosystems. We conducted a thematic analysis on the conversations between user and bots, with useful findings for the use of LLMs in the context of EUD. However, while the results are promising, the scope of the study was limited, and further research with a broader participant base is necessary to validate these findings comprehensively. Smartifier serves as a practical example of how LLMs can be effectively integrated into user-centric applications, demonstrating the potential of LLMs for future developments in this area.

Acknowledgments. This work is partially funded by TIM S.p.A., Innovation Department, and PNNR Project MUSA - Multilayered Urban Sustainability Action-Spoke 6/Task 2.2.

Disclosure of Interests. The authors have no competing interests to declare that are relevant to the content of this article.

References

1. Andrao, Met al.: Understanding concepts, methods and tools for end-user control of automations in ecosystems of smart objects and services. In: Spano, L.D., Schmidt, A., Santoro, C., Stumpf, S. (eds.) IS-EUD 2023. LNCS, vol. 13917, pp. 104–124. Springer, Cham (2023). https://doi.org/10.1007/978-3-031-34433-6_7
2. Ardito, C., Buono, P., Desolda, G., Matera, M.: From smart objects to smart experiences: an end-user development approach. Int. J. Hum. Comput. Stud. **114**, 51–68 (2018)
3. Barricelli, B.R., Valtolina, S.: Designing for end-user development in the internet of things. In: Díaz, P., Pipek, V., Ardito, C., Jensen, C., Aedo, I., Boden, A. (eds.) IS-EUD 2015. LNCS, vol. 9083, pp. 9–24. Springer, Cham (2015). https://doi.org/10.1007/978-3-319-18425-8_2
4. Boden, A., Avram, G., Posch, I., Pipek, V., Fitzpatrick, G.: Workshop on EUD for supporting sustainability in maker communities. In: Dittrich, Y., Burnett, M., Mørch, A., Redmiles, D. (eds.) IS-EUD 2013. LNCS, vol. 7897, pp. 298–303. Springer, Heidelberg (2013). https://doi.org/10.1007/978-3-642-38706-7_30
5. Brackenbury, W., et al.: How users interpret bugs in trigger-action programming. In: Conference on Human Factors in Computing Systems - Proceedings, pp. 12–2019 (2019). https://doi.org/10.1145/3290605.3300782, https://dl.acm.org/doi/10.1145/3290605.3300782
6. Braun, V., Clarke, V.: Using thematic analysis in psychology. Qual. Res. Psychol. **3**(2), 77–101 (2006)
7. Caslini, G.: Smartifier LLM prompts (2025). https://gitlab.com/i3lab/public-materials/smartifier-llm-prompts
8. Chelli, M., et al.: Hallucination rates and reference accuracy of chatGPT and bard for systematic reviews: comparative analysis. J. Med. Internet Res. **26**, e53164 (2024)

9. Chen, X., Zhang, X., Elliot, M., Wang, X., Wang, F.: Fix the leaking tap: a survey of trigger-action programming (tap) security issues, detection techniques and solutions. Comput. Secur. **120**, 102812 (2022). https://doi.org/10.1016/J.COSE.2022.102812
10. Corno, F., Russis, L.D., Roffarello, A.M.: HeyTAP: bridging the gaps between users' needs and technology in if-then rules via conversation. In: ACM International Conference Proceeding Series (2020). https://doi.org/10.1145/3399715.3399905, https://dl.acm.org/doi/10.1145/3399715.3399905
11. Crovari, P., Gianotti, M., Riccardi, F., Garzotto, F.: Designing a smart toy: guidelines from the experience with smart dolphin "SAM". In: Proceedings of the 13th Biannual Conference of the Italian SIGCHI Chapter: Designing the next interaction, pp. 1–10 (2019)
12. Desolda, G., Ardito, C., Bari, U.D., Moro, A., Matera, M., Milano, P.D.: Empowering end users to customize their smart environments. ACM Trans. Comput.-Hum. Interact. (TOCHI) **24** (2017). https://doi.org/10.1145/3057859, https://dl.acm.org/doi/10.1145/3057859
13. Du, X., et al.: Evaluating large language models in class-level code generation. In: Proceedings of the IEEE/ACM 46th International Conference on Software Engineering, pp. 1–13 (2024)
14. Gallo, S., Malizia, A., Paternò, F.: Towards a chatbot for creating trigger-action rules based on chatGPT and Rasa. In: IS-EUD Workshops (2023)
15. Gallo, S., Paterno, F.: A conversational agent for creating flexible daily automation. In: ACM International Conference Proceeding Series (2022). https://doi.org/10.1145/3531073.3531090, https://dl.acm.org/doi/10.1145/3531073.3531090
16. Gallo, S., Paternò, F., Malizia, A.: A conversational agent for creating automations exploiting large language models. Pers. Ubiquit. Comput. 1–16 (2024)
17. Gao, Y., Xiao, K., Li, F., Xu, W., Huang, J., Dong, W.: ChatIoT: Zero-code generation of trigger-action based IoT programs. Proc. ACM Interact. Mob. Wearable Ubiquit. Technol. **8**(3), 1–29 (2024)
18. Gennari, R., Matera, M., Morra, D., Rizvi, M.: A phygital toolkit for rapidly designing smart things at school. In: ACM International Conference Proceeding Series (2022). https://doi.org/10.1145/3531073.3531119, https://dl.acm.org/doi/10.1145/3531073.3531119
19. Gianotti, M., Riccardi, F., Cosentino, G., Garzotto, F., Matera, M.: Modeling interactive smart spaces. In: International Conference on Conceptual Modeling, pp. 403–417. Springer (2020)
20. Giudici, M., Padalino, L., Paolino, G., Paratici, I., Pascu, A.I., Garzotto, F.: Designing home automation routines using an LLM-based chatbot. Designs **8**(3), 43 (2024)
21. Hamilton, D., et al.: Assessing treatment outcomes using a single question: the net promoter score. Bone Joint J. **96**(5), 622–628 (2014)
22. Hancock, P.A., Meshkati, N.: Human Mental Workload, vol. 52. North-Holland Amsterdam (1988)
23. Hart, S.G.: Nasa-task load index (NASA-TLX); 20 years later. In: Proceedings of the Human Factors and Ergonomics Society Annual Meeting, vol. 50, pp. 904–908. Sage Publications, Los Angeles (2006)
24. Huang, J., Cakmak, M.: Supporting mental model accuracy in trigger-action programming. In: UbiComp 2015 - Proceedings of the 2015 ACM International Joint Conference on Pervasive and Ubiquitous Computing, pp. 215–225 (2015). https://doi.org/10.1145/2750858.2805830, https://dl.acm.org/doi/10.1145/2750858.2805830

25. IFTTT Inc.: IFTTT: automation for business and home. https://ifttt.com. Accessed 08 Apr 2025
26. Kortuem, G., Kawsar, F., Sundramoorthy, V., Fitton, D.: Smart objects as building blocks for the internet of things. IEEE Internet Comput. **14**, 44–51 (2010). https://doi.org/10.1109/MIC.2009.143
27. Ledo, D., Anderson, F., Schmidt, R., Oehlberg, L., Greenberg, S., Grossman, T.: Pineal: bringing passive objects to life with embedded mobile devices. Conference on Human Factors in Computing Systems - Proceedings, vol. 2017-May, pp. 2583–2593 (2017). https://doi.org/10.1145/3025453.3025652, https://dl.acm.org/doi/10.1145/3025453.3025652
28. Lieberman, H., Paterno, F., Klann, M., Wulf, V.: End-user development: an emerging paradigm. End User Dev. 1–8 (2006). https://doi.org/10.1007/1-4020-5386-X_1
29. Martins, J., Branco, F., Mamede, H.: Combining low-code development with chatGPT to novel no-code approaches: a focus-group study (2023)
30. Mi, X., Qian, F., Zhang, Y., Wang, X.: An empirical characterization of IFTTT: ecosystem, usage, and performance. In: Proceedings of the 2017 Internet Measurement Conference, pp. 398–404 (2017)
31. Nascimento, N., Alencar, P., Cowan, D., Cheriton, D.R.: Artificial intelligence versus software engineers: an evidence-based assessment focusing on non-functional requirements (2023). https://doi.org/10.21203/RS.3.RS-3126005/V1, https://www.researchsquare.com, https://www.researchsquare.com/article/rs-3126005/v1
32. Node-RED Community: 2023 node-red community survey (2023). https://nodered.org/about/community/survey/2023/. Accessed 08 Apr 2025
33. O'Leary, N., Conway-Jones, D.: Node-red: Low-code programming for event-driven applications (2013). https://nodered.org. Accessed 08 Apr 2025
34. OpenAI: ChatGPT (2024). https://openai.com/blog/chatgpt/. Accessed 16 Jan 2025
35. Ovadia, S.: Automate the internet with "if this then that"(IFTTT). Behav. Soc. Sci. Libr. **33**(4), 208–211 (2014)
36. Peppler, K., Bender, S.: Maker movement spreads innovation one project at a time. **95**, 22–27 (2013). https://doi.org/10.1177/003172171309500306, https://journals.sagepub.com/doi/full/10.1177/003172171309500306
37. Peres, S.C., Pham, T., Phillips, R.: Validation of the system usability scale (SUS) SUS in the wild. In: Proceedings of the Human Factors and Ergonomics Society Annual Meeting, vol. 57, pp. 192–196. Sage Publications, Los Angeles (2013)
38. Stokel-Walker, C., Noorden, R.V.: What chatGPT and generative AI mean for science. Nature **614**, 214–216 (2023). https://doi.org/10.1038/D41586-023-00340-6
39. Ur, B., et al.: Trigger-action programming in the wild: an analysis of 200,000 IFTTT recipes. Conference on Human Factors in Computing Systems - Proceedings, pp. 3227–3231 (2016). https://doi.org/10.1145/2858036.2858556, https://dl.acm.org/doi/10.1145/2858036.2858556
40. Weiser, M.: The computer for the 21st century. Sci. Am. 94–104 (1991)
41. Wu, G., Hu, L., Hu, Y., Xiong, X., Wang, F.: LLM4Tap: LLM-enhanced tap rule recommendation. IEEE Internet Things J. (2025)

Assembly Workers as PLC Programmers: What End Users Need to Understand About Low-Code Development Platforms

Bernhard Schenkenfelder(✉), Raphael Zefferer, Christian Salomon, and Mario Winterer

Software Competence Center Hagenberg GmbH, 4232 Hagenberg, Austria
{bernhard.schenkenfelder,raphael.zefferer,christian.salomon, mario.winterer}@scch.at

Abstract. Low-Code Development (LCD) is a means for domain experts without software engineering training to address their software requirements themselves, bridging the gap between the high demand for software and the low supply of professional developers. By abstracting from traditional textual programming, a Low-Code Development Platform (LCDP) offers tools that are closer to how domain experts think about their problems, such as visual programming. In this paper, we present an LCDP for assembly workers to generate Programmable Logic Controller (PLC) code for the assembly devices they operate. We examine what the assembly workers need to know in order to use the LCPD through three expert interviews. The results indicate that understanding the digital mapping of real-world objects and processes in the LCDP and the underlying technical processes is key for domain experts to create their own software.

Keywords: Low-Code Development Platform (LCDP) · Programmable Logic Controller (PLC) · Assembly Workers · Assembly Devices

1 Introduction

Low-Code Development (LCD) is a human-centered approach to software development that empowers end users with little or no programming training to address their software needs themselves. A Low-Code Development Platform (LCDP) provides users with an abstraction beyond traditional textual programming, such as visual programming or programming by natural language [6,10], to increase productivity and reduce complexity [3]. The key to an intuitive and easy-to-learn platform that optimally supports the way users work is to design an LCDP that reflects users' mental models, or how they think something works

C. Santoro et al. (Eds.): IS-EUD 2025, LNCS 15713, pp. 99–107, 2025.
https://doi.org/10.1007/978-3-031-95452-8_6

in the real world [5]. LCDPs bridge the gap between the growing demand for software and the limited number of professional developers who can write it [2].

As Schenkenfelder et al. point out, End-User Development (EUD) and Low-Code Development (LCD), while having subtle differences, share the goal of empowering domain experts without software engineering training to create their own software using tools with a low barrier to entry [11]. And since the term Low-Code Development was used in the industry-academia collaboration reported on in this paper, we do so in this paper as well. Assembly workers in the context of this paper are considered end users with respect to the software they use, and domain experts with respect to the assembly processes.

The main contribution of this paper is an assessment of what the users of an LCDP need to know in order to use it, as opposed to more traditional definitions that specify only what they do not need to know, namely code-based software engineering. Related work is discussed in Sect. 2, followed by a presentation of the industrial context (Sect. 3). The research methodology is detailed in Sect. 4. Then, *PLC-Flow*, the software this paper reports on, is described (Sect. 5). The results are presented and discussed in Sect. 6. We conclude the paper and outline future work in Sect. 7.

2 Related Work

Carroll and Maher offer recommendations for implementing citizen development programs based on the case of DIY ("do it yourself") software development at Shell, an international energy corporation. While they agree that this approach empowers employees to create their own software, they also point out that "it does require employees to upskill and evlolve their use of various technology capabilities and data sources" [4]. However, they do not disclose any details in this regard.

In an exploratory study of the innovative components of seven LCDPs, Bock and Frank present an approach that promotes the empowerment of non-programmers to develop software, namely by "mirroring their familiar technology" and providing functionality tailored to their tasks. While this suggests that end users are masters of their domain, their study does not elaborate on this question [1].

In the field of digital twins, Michael and Wortmann propose a Low-Code approach for their configuration and reconfiguration by domain experts. They argue that digital twins must be highly adaptable to different system states [8], which requires solid technical background knowledge at a very general level.

Musić et al. present an abstraction layer to handle the ever increasing complexity of automation system–specifically Programmable Logic Controllers (PLCs). While this abstraction layer is supposed to decrease the necessary skills in software engineering by using their own concepts instead of coding, they postulate that this approach is generally applicable to *all* plant and facility automation use cases [9]. However, we follow the reasoning that one-size-fits-all

LCDPs are contradictory in that low complexity and broad scope are conflicting goals; instead, customized LCDPs that reflect the unique skills of domain experts and their different tasks best support them.

Overall, there is a plethora of case studies and research on the potential of Low-Code, its benefits and limitations, on how to evaluate and compare LCDPs, and on their usability. Recently, topics such as AI for Low-Code and Low-Code for AI have become increasingly popular. Building on this, our work contributes to a better understanding of the concepts that an LCDP user needs to know in order to use the platform.

3 Industry Context

This paper reports on the progress and results of an industry-academia collaboration. With a turnover of 1 billion Euro and 1,700 employees, the industry partner is a manufacturer of two-stroke and four-stroke engines for the recreational vehicle industry. To facilitate assembly and quality assurance, some assembly line stations require custom-built assembly devices controlled by PLCs. The shortage of PLC software developers is a pain point; empowering assembly workers to directly program these assembly devices using a Low-Code approach should relieve this bottleneck. This overall context was first identified and described in [12]. In general, production lines are highly dynamic, with approximately 50 such assembly devices to be built and programmed per year. To implement *PLC-Flow*, an LCDP for assembly workers to generate PLC code, the industry partner selected three different use cases representing increasingly complex assembly devices and provided a detailed textual description of each use case, along with bills of materials, CAD drawings, assembly instructions from an ERP system, including time and materials, and signal curves. The following use case description outlines the scope of an assembly device and the corresponding PLC code:

> "Use case 1 consists of four steps and has no higher-level control, meaning that the assembly device is not part of an assembly line and is not controlled by another system. First, the part is placed into the assembly device and after it is detected, there is a one-second delay before a locking mechanism is engaged. This is followed by two control steps, each of which requires a positive signal from a sensor to complete. After the control steps, the locking mechanism is released and the cycle is completed. If the steps are completed successfully, a green light turns on, otherwise a red light turns on and a buzzer sounds for five seconds. In addition, if a cycle step is not completed successfully, a manual reset of the assembly device is required by pressing a button."

4 Methodology

This study follows the guidelines for interviews as outlined in [7]. We formulated the problem and then defined the main research question (Sect. 4.1). After selecting three interviewees (Sect. 4.2), we created an interview guide (Sect. 4.3) that covers the areas of study and conducted in-depth interviews, taking about two hours each. Two interviews were held in person and one via Microsoft Teams. Finally, the information provided was analyzed (Sect. 6).

4.1 Research Question

While it is clear that LCDPs are designed for citizen developers, domain experts, and professional developers, there is still confusion about what is expected of them. Very often, this is expressed in a negative way, such as "no software engineering training required" [6]. In this paper, we try to turn the tables and examine what end users need to know and understand in order to use *PLC-Flow*, which led us to the following research question:

What concepts do assembly workers need to understand in order to use *PLC-Flow* successfully?

Successful use of *PLC-Flow* in this context means that assembly workers can create the PLC programs they need themselves, which is what *PLC-Flow* was designed to do in the first place.

4.2 Interviewee Profiles

Table 1 provides an overview of the three interviewed study participants. Their profiles are described below.

Table 1. Summary of Interviewees

	Interview №		
	1	2	3
Company data			
Products	Two-stroke and four-stroke engines	Injection moulding machines and automation	N/A
Markets	Recreational vehicle manufacturing	Automotive industry	N/A
Turnover	€ 1.0 bn	€ 1.5 bn	N/A
Employees	1,700	7,000	N/A
Role	PLC Programmer	Team Leader	Researcher
Experience	10 years	20 years	10 years

PLC Programmer (№ 1). Interviewee № 1 has been a senior PLC programmer with the industry partner for more than five years. He has 10 years of experience, including his formal education. The original idea of the industry-academia collaboration was to design *PLC-Flow* for less skilled workers to take over his role in a narrow context.

Team Leader (№ 2). Currently working as a the leader of a team of PLC programmers in a global manufacturing company, Interviewee № 2 has been in the field for 20 years and has extensive experience with visual and text-based PLC programming.

Researcher (№ 3). Interviewee № 3 is a postdoctoral researcher at a university and is involved in research and teaching. For 10 years, she has contributed to the development of an open-source Integrated Development Environment (IDE) for distributed industrial control systems.

4.3 Interview Guide

To ensure a systematic and complete interview approach, we created an interview guide that included the following items to explicitly address the research question and related issues:

- What concepts must assembly workers understand to use *PLC-Flow* successfully?
- How long does it take to learn *PLC-Flow*?
- What kinds of tasks is *PLC-Flow* most useful for?
- What kinds of tasks is *PLC-Flow* not useful for?
- What (if anything) would you like to change about *PLC-Flow*?

5 PLC-Flow

This chapter presents *PLC-Flow*[1], an LCDP for assembly workers to create software to control custom-built assembly devices they operate following the Low-Code approach. Figure 1 shows how domain experts can create programs that comprise a number of steps using *PLC-Flow*.

The notion of steps was chosen to reflect the mental model of an assembly worker, i.e., a domain expert's internal representation of reality [5], as the steps in *PLC-Flow* directly relate to the manual tasks to be completed. Each step consists of one or more actions that define what happens in that step (output actuators) and one or more gates. Gates define the conditions that must be fulfilled (input sensors) for the step to complete successfully and for the next step to begin. Both output actuators and input sensors, as well as the corresponding signal type, can be selected from drop-down menus representing variable names, physical addresses, and signal types.

[1] A public version of *PLC-Flow* is available online at https://plcflow.scch.at.

6 Results and Discussion

While assembly workers clearly do not need to read or write Structured Control Language (SCL), a code-based language for PLCs, they do need to understand a few other concepts. The difference between and the order of actions (output actuators) and gates (input sensors) is very important, as is the fact that input and output refer to the PLC's perspective, not that of, for example, a power screwdriver. All in all, the digital mapping of mechatronic systems in *PLC-Flow* is the key to enabling assembly workers to create the programs they need. In the words of Interviewee № 3, "It's much harder to understand what a rising edge is and whether a sensor returns that signal than it is to select the corresponding item from a drop-down menu". One notable detail in this regard is the wiring of sensors and actuators into the PLC and the assignment of their logical addresses.

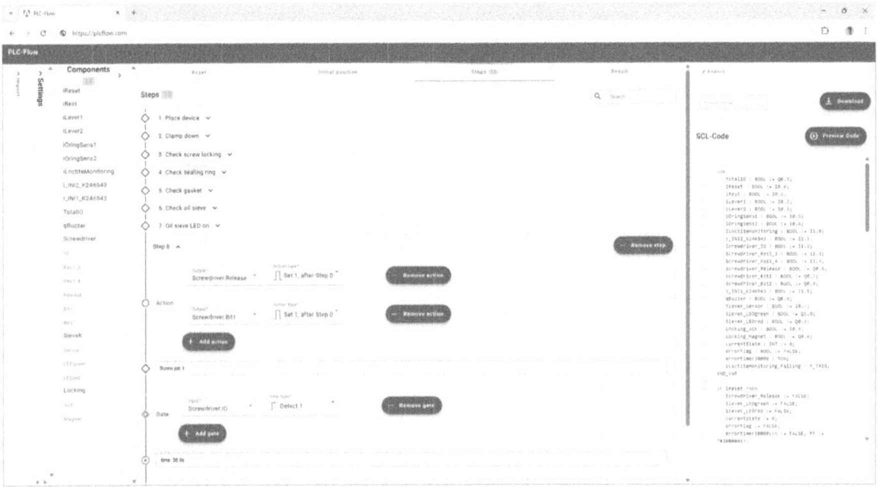

Fig. 1. Programs created with *PLC-Flow* consist of a number of steps (center), which in turn are composed of actions (output actuators) and gates (input sensors). The corresponding PLC code is generated automatically (right).

According to all respondents, *PLC-Flow* is most useful for isolated and engineering projects limited in scope, such as prototyping, small batches, and test labs. Interviewee № 1 added that *PLC-Flow* could be useful for training PLC programmers by automatically converting easy-to-understand engineering steps into SCL code with the correct syntax. Interviewee № 2 noted that the complexity of a PLC program and its visual representation is non-linear in terms of inputs, outputs, parameters, and components, confirming the fact that *PLC-Flow* is best suited for small problems. Regardless of the application area, the experts found it easier to modify than to create a program. It is definitely not a one-size-fits-all solution for visual PLC programming. Regarding the lower barrier to entry for assembly workers to use *PLC-Flow* compared to SCL, Interviewee № 3 pointed out that, in her experience, the responsibility for bugs lies with the suppliers of *PLC-Flow*, as opposed to code, where the responsibility lies with the author.

In terms of how long the experts thought it would take assembly workers to learn how to use *PLC-Flow*, the responses were fairly consistent. Interviewee № 1 estimated a total of one day for assembly workers to independently use *PLC-Flow*, including an introduction, theory, and practical use cases, and given their in-depth engineering knowledge. Similarly, Interviewee № 3 outlined a training phase of about one to two days for assembly workers to familiarize themselves with *PLC-Flow* if they had technical knowledge of the real assembly device. Interviewee № 2, who supervises PLC programmers using the code-based Structured Control Language (SCL), takes only a few hours to introduce them to Sequential Function Charts (SFCs), a visual programming language for PLCs. This observation is consistent with the fact that visual languages are easier to learn than code-based programming languages. In addition, he says, SFCs are much more powerful and versatile than *PLC-Flow*, so a training course of about the same order of magnitude (a few hours for experienced PLC programmers to get used to SFCs vs. a day for domain experts to get used to *PLC-Flow*) seems feasible.

Returning to the research question, the assembly workers need to understand (i) the digital mapping of real-world objects and processes in *PLC-Flow* and (ii) the underlying physical, engineering, mechanical, or electrical processes. In addition, the digital representation is much easier to handle than the actual engineering tasks; the learning curve is clearly in the real world. Considering that assembly workers are experts in the engineering tasks at hand, empowering them to take on the role of PLC programmers is a more than viable solution.

6.1 Limitations and Threats to Validity

The outcome of a publicly funded industry-academia collaboration can only be a working prototype, not a final product in a real-world environment. Therefore, a limitation at this stage is the lack of end-user involvement in this study; once the prototype has evolved into a product, user testing will be conducted. Relying on the individual views of interviewees limits the ability to generalize findings. However, we chose this study design because we are primarily interested in in-depth feedback. Finally, the specific use cases explored in the study may not be directly applicable to other domains, limiting the relevance of the findings outside of the original context.

7 Conclusions and Future Work

This paper presents *PLC-Flow*, a Low-Code Development Platform (LCDP) for assembly workers to generate Programmable Logic Controller (PLC) code using a visual interface for custom-built assembly devices in the engine manufacturing process, reducing the need for professional PLC programmers.

Collaborative reviews throughout the development process have confirmed that the implementation is in line with the original platform vision. Ongoing discussions with assembly workers, its future end users, have provided valuable feedback on the level of abstraction to be used and the overall usability of *PLC-Flow*. Returning to the question posed in the title of this paper, three interviews with highly experienced PLC programmers indicate that end users need to know little about the LCDP they are working with. Instead, understanding the underlying real-world objects and processes from a physical, engineering, mechanical, or electrical perspective and their mapping in the LCDP is paramount.

Future work will focus on activities to mature *PLC-Flow*. First and foremost, the code generated by *PLC-Flow* should be systematically validated against code written by professional PLC programmers to provide feedback to the code generation mechanism of *PLC-Flow*. Second, other data sources such as bills of materials could be integrated to further automate *PLC-Flow* by defining components and processes from this data. Using the CAD drawings of the assembly devices would add another layer of control to configure components and define processes. Finally, *PLC-Flow* could be linked to the Siemens TIA Portal[2] to facilitate automated deployment of the code to PLCs. And when all this is done and *PLC-Flow* is deployed in a production environment, end users should be involved in a subsequent evaluation.

Acknowledgments. The research reported in this paper has been funded by the Federal Ministry for Climate Action, Environment, Energy, Mobility, Innovation and Technology (BMK), the Federal Ministry for Labour and Economy (BMAW), and the State of Upper Austria in the frame of the SCCH competence center INTEGRATE (FFG grant no. 892418) in the COMET - Competence Centers for Excellent Technologies Programme managed by Austrian Research Promotion Agency FFG.

References

1. Bock, A.C., Frank, U.: In search of the essence of low-code: an exploratory study of seven development platforms. In: 2021 ACM/IEEE International Conference on Model Driven Engineering Languages and Systems Companion (MODELS-C), pp. 57–66. IEEE, Fukuoka (2021). https://doi.org/10.1109/MODELS-C53483.2021.00016, https://ieeexplore.ieee.org/document/9643620/
2. Caballar, R.D.: Programming without code: the rise of no-code software development - IEEE spectrum (2020). https://spectrum.ieee.org/programming-without-code-no-code-software-development
3. Cabot, J.: Positioning of the low-code movement within the field of model-driven engineering. In: Proceedings of the 23rd ACM/IEEE International Conference on Model Driven Engineering Languages and Systems: Companion Proceedings, pp. 1–3. ACM, Virtual Event Canada (2020). https://doi.org/10.1145/3417990.3420210, https://dl.acm.org/doi/10.1145/3417990.3420210

[2] https://www.siemens.com/global/en/products/automation/industry-software/automation-software/tia-portal.html.

4. Carroll, N., Maher, M.: How shell fueled digital transformation by establishing diy software development. MIS Q. Execut. 99–127 (2023). https://doi.org/10.17705/2msqe.00076
5. Gentner, D., Stevens, A.L.: Mental Models. Psychology Press, Hove (2014)
6. Hirzel, M.: Low-code programming models. Commun. ACM **66**(10), 76–85 (2023). https://doi.org/10.1145/3587691
7. Lazar, J., Feng, J.H., Hochheiser, H.: Chapter 8 - Interviews and focus groups, pp. 187–228. Morgan Kaufmann, Boston (2017). https://doi.org/10.1016/B978-0-12-805390-4.00008-X, https://www.sciencedirect.com/science/article/pii/B978012805390400008X
8. Thomassey, S., Zeng, X.: FBD_Bmodel digital platform: a web-based application for demand driven fashion supply chain. In: Dolgui, A., Bernard, A., Lemoine, D., von Cieminski, G., Romero, D. (eds.) APMS 2021. IAICT, vol. 630, pp. 21–30. Springer, Cham (2021). https://doi.org/10.1007/978-3-030-85874-2_3
9. Music, G., Heinzl, B., Kastner, W.: AVA: a component-oriented abstraction layer for virtual plug&produce automation systems engineering. J. Ind. Inf. Integr. **26**, 100251 (2022). https://doi.org/10.1016/j.jii.2021.100251
10. Pinho, D., Aguiar, A., Amaral, V.: What about the usability in low-code platforms? a systematic literature review. J. Comput. Lang. **74**, 101185 (2023). https://doi.org/10.1016/j.cola.2022.101185
11. Schenkenfelder, B., Brandstätter, U., Kirchtag, H., Wimmer, M.: Low-code development and end-user development: (how) are they different? In: Tetteroo, D., Feger, S., Fogli, D., Mørch, A., Piccinno, A., Modén, M.U. (eds.) Proceedings of the First International Workshop on Participatory Design & End-User Development - Building Bridges co-located with the International Nordic Conference on Human-Computer Interaction (NordiCHI 2024). No. 3778 in CEUR Workshop Proceedings, Aachen (2024). https://ceur-ws.org/Vol-3778/short5.pdf
12. Schenkenfelder, B., Salomon, C., Buchgeher, G., Schossleitner, R., Kerl, C.: The potential of low-code development in the manufacturing industry. In: 2023 IEEE 28th International Conference on Emerging Technologies and Factory Automation (ETFA), pp. 1–8. IEEE, Sinaia (2023). https://doi.org/10.1109/ETFA54631.2023.10275503, https://ieeexplore.ieee.org/document/10275503/

Democratizing AI and Programming

Fostering Novice Collaboration in ML-Based System Design Through Visual Languages and Touch Interfaces

Serena Versino[1(✉)], Tommaso Turchi[1], Alessio Malizia[1,2], and Giuseppe Riva[3]

[1] Department of Computer Science, University of Pisa, Pisa, Italy
serena.versino@phd.unipi.it, {tommaso.turchi,alessio.malizia}@unipi.it
[2] Molde University College, Molde, Norway
[3] Department of Psychology, Università Cattolica del Sacro Cuore, Milan, Italy
giuseppe.riva@unicatt.it

Abstract. Artificial Intelligence is driving society toward an increasingly algorithmic future, advancing innovation through data-driven predictive analytics. At the core of this transformation lie advanced Machine Learning-based systems, which hold significant societal potential but often remain inaccessible to domain specialists due to their complexity. This reliance on computing experts limits the integration of domain knowledge and raises concerns about transparency and inclusivity. Drawing from research in HCI, Computer-Supported Cooperative Work, and Cognitive Load Theory, this work explores how Visual Programming Languages (VPLs) and touch-based interfaces can support novice collaboration in ML-based system design. We evaluate PyFlowML Touch, a touch-enabled extension of the previously developed PyFlowML system, which enhances node layout and introduces interactive feedback mechanisms tailored to co-located novice collaboration. Designed for domain specialists, PyFlowML guides users through the ML process and incorporates Explainable AI techniques to improve understanding of model behavior [81,82]. In this exploratory study, a multifaceted evaluation combining cognitive walkthrough and heuristic inspection yields promising insights, suggesting that the touch-enabled interface can reduce intrinsic and extraneous cognitive load while promoting schema construction and collective ML understanding through interactive visualizations.

Keywords: Visual Programming Language · Natural User Interface · Cognitive Load · Collaboration · Machine Learning

1 Introduction

Artificial Intelligence (AI) has become pervasive, with applications spanning diverse fields such as language translation, virtual assistants, medical diagnostics, and predictive maintenance [20]. Its integration drives innovation, improves

C. Santoro et al. (Eds.): IS-EUD 2025, LNCS 15713, pp. 111–132, 2025.
https://doi.org/10.1007/978-3-031-95452-8_7

decision making, and improves operational efficiency [8,22,47]. AI technology relies on Machine Learning (ML) models trained on human data, yet their increasing complexity has restricted development to a small group of specialists [31]. Domain experts often lack the computing expertise needed to refine these systems, while computing experts may overlook domain-specific needs. This dynamic limits domain specialists' influence on system design, their understanding and trust in ML decision-making, raises ethical concerns about ML opacity, and ultimately undermines efforts toward AI democratization [62,74].

Moreover, the complexity of ML-based systems poses cognitive challenges on domain specialists, limiting their participation in system design. Cognitive Load Theory (CLT) posits that excessive cognitive demands can overwhelm working memory, reducing motivation and participation [65,79]. Research in Human-Computer Interaction (HCI) suggests that well-designed user interfaces can mitigate cognitive overload by simplifying interactions and contextualizing functionalities [56,70]. Research at the intersection of Computer-Supported Cooperative Work (CSCW) and CLT indicates that collaborative environments can further reduce cognitive load by distributing tasks among group members, fostering collective knowledge-building and enabling domain specialists to actively contribute to complex system design [42,57]. Drawing on Schön's Reflection-In-Action theory, such collaborative settings can integrate action and reflection within domain-specific contexts, encouraging multidisciplinary teams to explore and engage with relevant information spaces [2,67]. However, effective collaboration requires well-designed tools that balance intrinsic (task complexity), extraneous (unnecessary complexity), and germane (effort dedicated to learning) cognitive loads [34,76].

Furthermore, the European Union's General Data Protection Regulation (GDPR) underscores the importance of incorporating interpretability techniques and Explainable AI (XAI) methods into tools accessible to domain specialists [71]. However, XAI techniques are predominantly designed for computing experts, making them less accessible to novices [29]. Research has largely focused on enhancing ML interpretability without adequately considering how domain specialists interact with and comprehend XAI explanations [43]. Recent studies highlight the importance of collaborative efforts in deploying systems with XAI techniques, ensuring that ML-based systems are not only interpretable but also practically useful to domain specialists [16,17,46].

Bridging the gap between domain specialists and computing experts requires well-designed tools that facilitate collaboration. Among the tools that can support such participation and collaboration, research in HCI highlights Visual Programming Language (VPL)-based tools and Natural User Interfaces (NUIs). VPL-based tools are employed to lower coding barriers and simplify programming concepts for novices, as exemplified by Scratch, which enables children to focus on programming principles rather than syntax [13,59,61]. NUIs, such as touch tabletop devices, offer additional means for domain specialists to engage with complex systems [9,73]. These interfaces have shown promising results in promoting collaboration through intuitive interactions [7,27,36].

Despite the growing importance of fostering collaboration between domain specialists and computing experts in designing ML-based systems, the literature on using VPLs and advanced interfaces for this purpose remains sparse [80]. A few emerging studies have started addressing this gap, including work in biology evaluating a tabletop interactive ML-based system aimed at enhancing synchronous collaboration and trust among diverse stakeholders [3]. While results suggest improved interactions and trust in ML models, they do not incorporate XAI methods, underscoring the nascent stage of research in this area. Related applications have explored cognitive assistance [89] and collaborative problem-solving [49], yet lack a focus on tools specifically designed to enable multidisciplinary teams to collaboratively design ML-based systems. Building on this foundation, this work addresses the research question: *How can VPLs facilitate user collaboration in the design of XAI-based systems?*

This research assesses PyFlowML Touch, a version of the previously evaluated PyFlowML prototype optimized for touch interaction. PyFlowML, built on a flow-based language, integrates XAI techniques and interactive features to support domain specialists in designing ML workflows [82]. Building on prior evaluations of usability and cognitive load [81], this study adopts an exploratory approach to investigate how touch interaction influences collaboration in co-located settings. In line with its exploratory nature, the study incorporates the think-aloud protocol and semi-structured interviews. The think-aloud protocol [35,68] is used to investigate cognitive processes during user interactions, providing nuanced insights into how germane and extraneous cognitive loads influence collaboration and guiding tool refinement to align with user needs. To measure collaboration, self-reports on collaborative quality [85] are collected through post-test, semi-structured interviews [52].

This study is organized as follows: Sect. 2 reviews relevant related work on cognitive load, collaboration, interaction design, and visual interfaces. Section 3 introduces PyFlowML Touch. Section 4 outlines the evaluation methodology, followed by Sect. 5, which details the experiment design. Section 6 presents results, with a post-hoc analysis of collaboration and cognitive load in Sect. 7. Section 8 discusses threats to validity, and Sect. 9 concludes with key findings and implications.

2 Related Works

The complexity of ML-based systems can impose cognitive demands that exceed the limits of working memory [65], leading to cognitive overload and reducing user motivation in participatory design processes [79]. Collaborative settings can mitigate this risk by distributing cognitive effort across group members. As shown by Paas and Van Merriënboer, collaboration fosters a collective working memory that enhances task performance [42,57]. Similarly, Yang et al. emphasize the role of participatory design in facilitating collaboration between domain specialists and computing experts during AI development [14]. To support novice participation, tools should minimize memory demands and contextualize functionality [56,70].

2.1 Cognitive Load and Collaborative Design Strategies

Designing ML-based tools for multidisciplinary teams requires balancing cognitive load while supporting collaboration. Cognitive load refers to the mental effort required to process information, solve problems, and learn new concepts [76]. Collaborative Cognitive Load Theory [42] suggests that effective tools should reduce intrinsic load by distributing tasks among users based on expertise, minimize extraneous load through clear instructions and well-designed interfaces, and optimize germane load by fostering transactive processes such as critique, synthesis, and explanation. These principles align with distributed cognition theories, which describe how knowledge, tasks, and tools are distributed across individuals and artifacts in collaborative settings [34]. According to Activity Theory [41], tools mediate action and externalize complexity, enabling coordination and problem-solving. Social Translucence Theory [19] emphasizes the importance of visibility, awareness, and accountability in collaborative systems to build shared understanding and trust. Hutchins' work on distributed cognition further highlights the role of perceptually accessible feedback, modularity, and real-time error detection in supporting novice participation and reducing cognitive load [34].

Collaboration design can also be informed by CSCW frameworks such as Johansen's time-space matrix [39] and Lee and Paine's Model of Coordinated Action (MoCA) [45], which address aspects like synchrony, co-location, role and technology symmetry, group scale, and turnover. Effective collaboration depends on communication [51], coordination [37,48], cooperation [28,64], and regulation [24], and is influenced by group dynamics [32,33]. Touch-based tabletop systems have been shown to facilitate mutual awareness, flexible role division, and collaborative learning through shared artifacts and input modalities [6,10,23,26,63,66].

Together, these frameworks inform the design of tools like PyFlowML Touch, which aims to support novice-expert collaboration in ML prototyping by distributing cognitive effort, scaffolding understanding, and enhancing co-located interaction through visual and touch-based interfaces.

2.2 Touch Interfaces

CSCW research supports Natural User Interfaces (NUIs) in social and collaborative settings to enhance learning and teamwork [83]. Indeed, NUIs can leverage human communicative abilities through touch, voice, gesture, eye gaze, and body movements [86]. Studies highlight touch tabletops as effective tools for collaborative learning [50] and co-design, such as ScratchJr [4]. Touch tabletops foster natural collaboration, enabling direct interaction [69], increasing action visibility, and promoting implicit coordination and awareness among co-located groups [26]. HCI research validates their efficacy in co-located collaborative environments [53]. For example, studies on web search show that collaborators sharing a single display report higher awareness and better group experiences than those using separate screens [1], enhancing visibility and improving teamwork.

Display Size and Orientation. Modern touch tabletops are rooted in decades of technological evolution, evolving from digitally enhanced whiteboards [63] to high-resolution computer-driven displays [18,84]. Display sizes range from small-scale systems that extend beyond the conventional desktop [75] to wall-sized displays enabling multiple users to physically navigate the display space [5,27]. Large, high-resolution displays are valued in workspaces as they allow co-located users to read at different paces and employ diverse analysis strategies. However, these displays present challenges, such as the need for users to stand or sit back at a distance to perceive the entire display. The shift to smaller devices, like tabletops, addresses this issue by guaranteeing users to keep the necessary workspace visible within their cognitive zone [18]. Furthermore, touch displays can be oriented vertically, like wall-sized displays, or horizontally, like tabletops. Research supports the positive correlation between collaboration and co-located interactions around large displays with horizontal orientations [7,27,36]. Studies show that in such conditions, group members effectively share ideas and maintain greater awareness of each other's activities [66]. Furthermore, in horizontal conditions, users can arrange themselves around the display, either face-to-face or side-by-side, facilitating synchronous and co-located interaction. Such configurations ensure that objects on the display, along with any accompanying dialogue and gestures, are oriented toward the entire team, thereby involving all team members.

Building on the advantages of horizontal touch tabletops in co-located collaborative environments, the following Sect. 3 introduces the PyFlowML Touch prototype.

2.3 Interactive Machine Learning

Interactive Machine Learning (IML) is an iterative, human-in-the-loop paradigm in which users actively participate in training, refining, and interpreting ML models through repeated interactions and feedback loops [15,21,38,88]. IML addresses core challenges of traditional ML, such as black-box limitations, resource-intensive computations, and limited involvement of domain specialists [88]. Early implementations demonstrated that iterative, user-driven feedback could simplify ML tasks by allowing domain specialists to visually guide classifiers through examples, rather than explicit coding [21]. Recent research further emphasizes enhancing the trustworthiness, interpretability, and robustness of ML models by engaging novices beyond labeling, involving them in the evaluation of intermediate model behaviors and explanations [38,77,78]. Explanatory IML advances this approach by presenting model explanations interactively, enabling users to validate, critique, and refine the reasoning behind ML outcomes, thus fostering deeper understanding, accountability, and trust [77,78]. Moreover, IML research identifies key interface elements essential for effective workflows, including visualizing the current model state, guiding user input to refine the model, and supporting interactive model revision and inspection [15]. VPL-based tools can address these requirements by visually representing ML workflows, facilitating structured user inputs, and integrating XAI techniques for explaining ML decision-making processes [81,82]. However, current IML literature overlooks the potential benefits of integrating VPLs, XAI techniques, and touch-enabled interfaces to reduce cognitive load and enhance collaborative participation between domain specialists and computing experts. Addressing this gap represents the research objective explored in this study.

3 The PyFlowML Touch Prototype

VPL-based tools reduce coding barriers and simplify programming concepts for novices, as demonstrated by Scratch, enabling children to focus on programming logic rather than syntax [13,59,61]. PyFlowML follows this approach, offering a flow-based visual language tailored to design ML workflows. Flow-based languages employ a data flow paradigm, where computational processes are represented as directed graphs composed of nodes, pins, and arcs. In PyFlowML, nodes encapsulate algorithms and functions, each with defined inputs and outputs. Domain specialists can add, move, and configure nodes via a drag-and-drop interface. Pins or ports appear as color-coded dots, where color indicates data type, ensuring only compatible connections. Arcs define valid data flows between nodes, enforcing type constraints and preventing incorrect linkages. PyFlowML provides an intuitive Graphical User Interface (GUI) that integrates XAI techniques and interactive prompt windows to guide novices in designing ML workflows [81,82]. Its usability was previously assessed using the Cognitive Dimensions framework [82] and the System Usability Scale framework, while cognitive load was measured through NASA-TLX. A comparative analysis with a similar tool [81] yielded promising results, highlighting the potential of VPL-based approaches to support domain specialists in ML prototyping tasks.

PyFlowML Touch extends the PyFlowML platform by optimizing the interface for direct touch interaction and enhancing its suitability for collaborative, co-located settings. The system is implemented in Python using PyQt5 for the GUI and builds upon a customized fork of the PyFlow library to define and manage visual node-based workflows. Touch interaction is enabled through event handling extensions in the canvas class, which map capacitive touch gestures (e.g., tap, drag, multi-touch zoom) to standard GUI operations. To support improved usability, the node layout engine was modified to increase spacing between pins and node edges, facilitating accurate touch input. The canvas was enhanced with scrollable and bounded dimensions to support larger workflows and maintain spatial organization. Moreover, node categories are visually distinguished using a consistent color scheme – green for datasets, blue for ML models, purple for visualizations, and red for XAI components – as illustrated in Fig. 1. The system's architecture maintains separation between the visual interface layer, data processing modules, and explanation rendering components, supporting modular extensibility. While PyFlowML provides the underlying data-flow engine and base interface, PyFlowML Touch introduces novel contributions in gesture-based interaction and multi-touch integration.

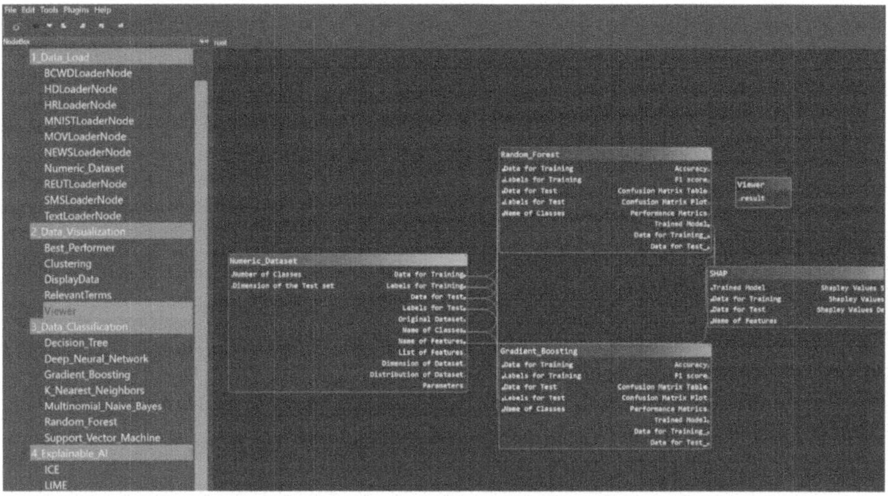

Fig. 1. PyFlowML Touch. (Color figure online)

4 Evaluation

This exploratory study combines cognitive walkthrough, heuristic evaluation, and qualitative feedback to identify strengths, limitations, and interaction patterns in using touch-enabled interfaces and VPLs for novice-oriented ML prototyping, rather than to quantify performance or draw conclusive evidence.

Following Lazar et al. (2017) [44], the evaluation employs established cognitive walkthrough and heuristic approaches [30, 60] to examine user interactions with PyFlowML Touch. A think-aloud protocol [35, 68] and semi-structured interviews [52] offer insight into cognitive processes. Collaborative quality was assessed through self-reported measures [85]. Participants completed a predefined ML task during laboratory sessions, guided by a template outlining subtasks. Video recordings and interview data provided qualitative perspectives on their collaborative experience.

Small-sample evaluations are commonly used in early-stage usability research to uncover key issues [54, 55]. In this study, six participants – specialists in computer science, game design, and engineering – were recruited from the Computer Science Department at Universidad Carlos III de Madrid. This sample size is deemed appropriate to generate both technical and user-centered preliminary insights.

5 Experiment Design

The study was conducted in person with six participants – specialists in computer science, game design, and engineering – working in pairs, randomly assigned. Guided by Nielsen's Theory On Heuristic Evaluations [54], the sessions in this study were structured as follows: approximately 5 min for an instructional video, 35 min for interacting with the PyFlowML Touch prototype and completing the ML task collaboratively, and 20 min for a semi-structured interview. The instructional video introduced the primary features of PyFlowML Touch, focusing on key aspects such as the user interface, operational environment, notation system (i.e., nodes, arcs, and pins), and the available actions within the system. The recruitment scenario was designed to accommodate the diverse professional backgrounds of the participants. To contextualize the task in a collaborative setting, two fictional personas were introduced by the instructional video: one representing a specialist in informatics and the other a specialist in human resources (HR). The personas outlined the task and illustrated their respective roles. Participants engaged with the tool by assuming one of these roles, with the HR specialist interacting directly with the system and the computing specialist supervising the design process, providing guidance on component selection and interpreting results.

5.1 ML Task

During the session, participants collaboratively completed an ML task guided by a step-by-step template. Initially, following the instructional video, one participant interacted with the prototype while the other assisted in decision-making and interpretation of outcomes, with roles deliberately interchanged throughout. The template encompassed key ML analysis tasks, including data loading, supervised classification, result visualization, and interpretability techniques. Colored sticky notes complemented the prompt windows: white notes outlined sequential steps (aligned with the left-to-right unidirectional data flow), yellow notes provided instructions and troubleshooting tips, and light blue notes introduced targeted questions not covered by the prompts. The workflow consisted of four steps: (1) load the data set "IBM HR Analytics Employee Attrition & Performance" dataset [40], (2) select an ML model, fostering discussion and justification based on visualization results, (3) visualize results and (4) apply XAI techniques to interpret ML outputs, as reported in Fig. 2.

The dataset, selected from the recruiting domain as familiar to all participants, included attributes related to employee demographics, income, and work experience, with a binary target variable representing Attrition (Yes/No). At each step, participants responded to questions related to ML outcomes: two focused on data exploration, while the remaining four addressed ML analysis. These six questions are detailed in Table 1. An additional question (**Q_XAI**) targeted a fairness sub-task, prompting participants to interpret the SHAPley Values Summary Plot, identify sensitive attributes in the recruiting domain (e.g., "Age", "Marital Status", and "Gender"), and discuss the potential positive or negative impacts of ML decision-making.

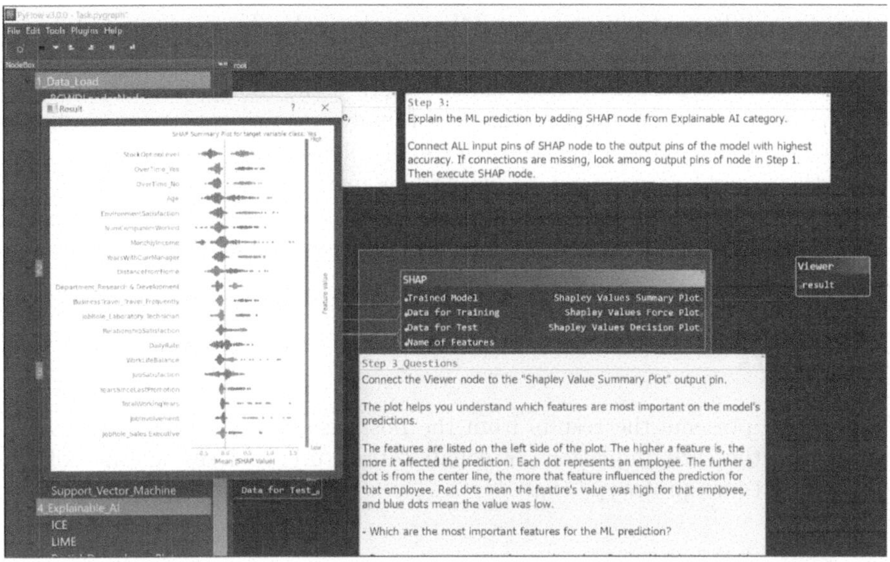

Fig. 2. PyFlowML Touch: Example of SHAPley Values Summary Plot.

Table 1. ML Task: Questions

Question Number	Description
Q1	Identify the target variable
Q2	Determine the number of instances in the test data
Q3	Identify the classes of the target variable and assess if the training set is balanced
Q4	Count the number of true positives and true negatives predicted by the classifier
Q5	Assess the accuracy of the ML models and select one of them
Q6	Determine the most significant features for the prediction in the dataset

5.2 Survey

The post-test semi-structured interview assessed collaboration quality and key PyFlowML Touch features, focusing on five dimensions: **Communication**, **Coordination**, **Cooperation**, **Awareness**, and **Regulation**, identified in CSCW research [12]. The interview captured participants' subjective assessments of how effectively PyFlowML Touch supported collaborative ML prototyping. Questions on **Communication** explored ease of idea exchange, while **Coordination** examined structured task management. **Cooperation** addressed the tool's ability to facilitate joint ML prototype development, and **Awareness** focused on participants' understanding of one another's contributions and project status. **Regulation** investigated whether the tool promoted balanced participation and prevented dominance. Finally, participants were explicitly asked which prototype features most fostered collaboration and what enhancements they would recommend to strengthen team interactions. By centering on these dimensions, the interview provided targeted insights into PyFlowML Touch's effectiveness in supporting collective decision-making and revealed areas for potential improvement.

6 Results

This section presents the results from the post-test semi-structured interview, focusing on the core dimensions of collaboration (6.1) and key features of the PyFlowML Touch prototype (6.2).

6.1 Collaboration

The post-test semi-structured interview provided valuable insights into how participants perceived PyFlowML Touch across key collaborative dimensions. **Communication** was enhanced by the tool, as participants highlighted its role in simplifying idea-sharing and feedback. They valued the data visualizations and the horizontal touch-enabled tabletop in a co-located setting, which facilitated clear and effective communication. **Coordination** was supported through structured task management features, organized into four node categories: data loading, visualization, classification, and XAI. Participants noted that this structured workflow clarified role distribution, distinguishing between those directly interacting with the prototype and those assisting in pipeline-building and result interpretation. **Cooperation** was also reinforced, as the prototype facilitated joint design and seamless interaction throughout the ML process. The touch interface created a concurrent, shared space for collective reasoning, encouraging a unified approach to ML design. **Awareness** was positively influenced by the shared workspace, which improved visibility into individual contributions and overall project progress. However, some participants suggested integrating features to mark nodes or connections, allowing for clearer identification of each team member's contributions. Finally, **Regulation** was perceived as a strength of the tabletop interface, as it promoted balanced participation and prevented any single participant from dominating the process. Nonetheless, participants recommended additional features to better visualize collaboration dynamics and further ensure equitable engagement.

6.2 PyFlowML Touch: Features

This section presents the feedback gathered from the semi-structured interview on the features of PyFlowML Touch that participants identified as influencing collaboration. The feedback highlights both the strengths of the tool in facilitating collaborative efforts and the areas where technical improvements could enhance its effectiveness. They offered suggestions for refining these features to better streamline collaboration and address challenges encountered when designing ML-based systems. A summary of the responses is presented in Table 2.

Table 2. Collaboration: User Feedback on Features

Question	Feature	Feedback
What features of the prototype most fostered collaboration?	Drag-and-Drop	Flexibility in placing nodes within the workspace allows for active participation and collaboration
	Prompt Windows	Notifications regarding unexecuted nodes or errors encourage prompt resolution of these issues
	Display Size	The large tabletop surface combined with simple notation created a clear interface for interaction, which in turn facilitated discussions about the workflow
What improvements would you recommend to enhance collaboration when using the prototype?	Touch Interaction	The touchscreen exhibits poor responsiveness during zooming interactions. Multi-touch functionality would be beneficial
	Execution	Enhance the interface by adding more visual feedback to indicate when a node has been executed would enhance clarity. Additionally, renaming the *'Refresh'* option to *'Execute'* would increase intuitiveness
	Canvas Navigation	Introduce dedicated zoom in/out buttons into the workspace, and adding a button to automatically reposition all nodes, whenever one node is moved, for optimal workspace overview
	Connection	Incorporate intelligent features to streamline the process of connecting the dataset to ML models
	Transparency	Introduce semi-transparency options, such as making nodes visible behind prompt windows displaying results, to enhance workflow tracking
	Data Visualization	Enable the Viewer node to be executed multiple times without the need to redefine connections

7 Post-hoc Analysis and Discussion

This section analyzes and discusses the findings from the post-test semi-structured interview and the oral feedback collected through the think-aloud protocol. The semi-structured interview focused on evaluating the quality of collaboration, while the think-aloud protocol explored the cognitive load experienced by participants in the collaborative environment.

7.1 Coordination

The team operated in a co-located setting with temporally asynchronous interactions, facilitated by the use of a shared horizontal display with single-touch input (technology symmetry). Participants assumed asymmetric roles based on the two personas introduced in the instructional video: one participant interacted directly with the tool, while the other assisted in decision-making tasks such as selecting the ML model and interpreting the ML and XAI outcomes. Following the setup outlined in the video, both team members were spatially arranged side-by-side, oriented toward the horizontal display, with the assisting specialist positioned on the right, as depicted in Fig. 3a. The tabletop interface facilitated real-time interaction, accommodating the physical distribution of participants within the shared workspace.

(a) Side-by-side (b) Face-to-face

Fig. 3. Co-located Setting and Spatial Arrangement of Participants.

Analyzing the results through the dimensions outlined in Lee and Paine's MoCA framework [45], the tabletop's size was reported as suitable to accommodate two participants (Scale dimension), facilitating the exchange of specific knowledge between them (NCoP dimension). The interface also enabled the formation of a newly established collaboration (Nascence dimension) and was valued for its adaptability in supporting both temporary and permanent solutions (Turnover dimension). Participants highlighted the Drag-and-Drop as a key feature to enable flexibility in rearranging components across the workspace, allowing them to focus on specific design stages and accommodate dynamic collaboration needs. For instance, after executing a node, the specialist interacting with the prototype repositioned the Prompt Window displaying results closer to the assisting specialist in order to signal the need for support in interpreting the data. However, the Canvas Navigation feature exhibited poor responsiveness during touch interaction, occasionally hindering the use of the Drag-and-Drop feature. Participants suggested integrating navigation buttons within the workspace to reduce usability challenges and streamline workflows.

In summary, the touch-enabled tabletop interface, integrated with the VPL used by PyFlowML, supported coordination by addressing key dimensions of the MoCa framework, such as co-located asynchronous interactions. Features like Drag-and-Drop for rearranging visual components and Canvas Navigation for dynamically locating elements facilitated efficient task organization and promoted a shared understanding of the workflow in co-located collaboration.

7.2 Communication and Cooperation

The ML task was organized into four steps – Data Loading, Data Visualization, Data Classification, and Explainable AI (XAI) – requiring participants to adjust their physical arrangement as communication needs increased. Tasks such as ML model selection and interpreting XAI outcomes prompted face-to-face interaction, with the assisting specialist moving to the short side of the display, as shown in Fig. 3b. The Data Visualizations in the interactive Prompt Windows, including confusion matrices and SHAPley Value Summary Plots, stimulated dialogue and helped participants collaboratively identify and address potential dataset bias, such as class imbalances in the target variable. Drawing on Activity Theory [41], these visual components externalized complex ML processes, enabling strategies for fairness analysis. The Prompt Windows also supported synchronous cooperation by reporting errors (e.g., missing connections) and facilitated asynchronous collaboration through streamlined workflows. In line with Erickson and Kellogg's Social Translucence theory [19], the prototype provided visibility (real-time system updates), awareness (explicit user actions), and accountability (traceable model decisions). This design aligns with core human-AI interaction principles, improving communication and cooperation in collaborative ML prototyping. Overall, Data Visualization features and interactive Prompt Windows simplified abstract ML concepts, reducing cognitive load and enabling effective negotiation, decision-making, and shared understanding among team members.

7.3 Awareness, Regulation and Group Dynamics

The findings reveal that single-touch interaction enhanced awareness and regulation by enabling flexible role assignment. One specialist directly manipulated the touchscreen while another supervised and provided input. This arrangement was supported by the horizontally oriented display, ensuring equal visibility of the workflow and a left-to-right layout that encouraged natural role shifts. However, during Data Classification and Explainable AI, roles blurred due to the complexity of the SHAPley Value Summary Plot, making participant contributions less distinct. Participants recommended simplifying XAI visualizations to reduce cognitive load. Overall, the interface supported role-switching but highlighted the need for more streamlined plots.

7.4 Collaborative Cognitive Load

Drawing on Kirschner's Collaborative Cognitive Load Theory (CLT) [42], the PyFlowML Touch prototype managed the three types of cognitive load identified by Sweller's CLT [76]: intrinsic, extraneous, and germane. Visual representations reduced intrinsic load – stemming from task complexity – by breaking the ML process into manageable steps. The touch interface and dynamic role assignment enabled participants to fluidly switch between interacting with the tool and assisting with interpretation, integrating diverse expertise. Moreover, extraneous load – caused by poorly designed environments – was minimized through PROMPT WINDOWS providing real-time feedback and interactive error detection. This design, consistent with Hutchins' distributed cognition [34], allowed participants to offload complex reasoning to visual structures and lower barriers to novice participation. The co-located tabletop eliminated split-attention effects [57], ensuring focus on integrated information. Additionally, in line with Schön's Reflection-In-Action theory [67], externalizing complex tasks encouraged both action and reflection. Finally, germane load – reflecting the effort to build and refine schemas – was enhanced through DATA VISUALIZATION features such as confusion matrices and SHAPley Value Summary Plots. These representations translated abstract ML concepts into actionable insights, fostering negotiation, deliberation, and shared knowledge construction, thereby improving participants' comprehension of ML decision-making process.

8 Threats to Validity

Internal validity was addressed by recruiting six participants from diverse fields to preliminarily assess the collaborative benefits of VPLs and touch interfaces in ML-based system design. However, a larger study is needed to validate findings and mitigate isolation effects. Researcher intervention was minimal, reducing experimenter bias, while subject effects were acknowledged due to the study's single-task limitation. In addition, the current implementation of explainability relies primarily on SHAP visualizations. While effective, SHAP alone may not address all user needs. An additional limitation concerns the use of role-play to simulate cross-domain collaboration. While participants were assigned fictional roles (e.g., HR specialists), they primarily came from technical backgrounds. This approach was considered appropriate for early-stage evaluation focused on usability and interaction patterns. Construct validity was ensured through semi-structured interviews on collaboration and cognitive load, with data triangulation via think-aloud feedback enhancing reliability. However, as this study focused on the integrated experience of PyFlowML Touch, it does not isolate the specific effects of the touch interface versus the underlying visual programming environment. External validity is constrained by the single-institution sample; nonetheless, the setting provides a suitable foundation for evaluating collaborative interactions in a controlled environment.

9 Conclusions

Machine Learning (ML)-based systems offer significant societal and economic benefits, often surpassing human performance [20]. As their adoption grows, so does the complexity of human interaction with these systems, revealing a gap between domain-specific needs and ML mechanisms [22]. Domain specialists frequently lack the technical skills to contribute effectively to system design [79], while computing experts may undervalue domain-specific requirements [31], relegating specialists to passive roles [25,87]. This exclusion, compounded by the cognitive demands of ML tasks, discourages participation and raises concerns about transparency. Addressing this divide is central to emerging regulatory frameworks such as the EU "AI Act" [58], which emphasizes transparency, fairness, and accountability. These principles align with the Human-Centered AI (HCAI) framework, which advocates for collaborative system design to ensure trustworthiness and safety [72]. Reducing cognitive load by distributing mental effort across teams has been shown to enhance learning and task performance [57]. Visual Programming Languages (VPLs) and Natural User Interfaces (NUIs), such as touch interfaces, can support novice participation by simplifying logic and enabling co-located collaboration in system design [59,66]. Yet, their role in collaborative ML design remains underexplored.

This exploratory study introduced PyFlowML Touch, an enhanced version of PyFlowML optimized for touch interactions, integrating Explainable AI (XAI) techniques and interactive features to guide novices in ML design. A multifaceted evaluation, combining cognitive walkthrough and heuristic evaluation, was conducted with six domain specialists from diverse fields. Insights into cognitive load and collaboration were derived from video analysis and oral feedback. Post-hoc analysis integrated semi-structured interviews on collaboration quality [52] and think-aloud protocols to assess collective cognitive load [35,68], providing valuable perspectives on ML prototyping dynamics. While not intended to yield generalizable conclusions, the study provides formative insights into user interaction and collaboration dynamics, offering design considerations for future EUD tools in ML contexts and directions for subsequent controlled experimentation.

Collaboration. Analysis based on Computer-Supported Cooperative Work (CSCW) dimensions [11] and Lee and Paine's MoCA framework [45] showed that the touch-enabled tabletop supported coordination in co-located, asynchronous interactions. VPL features like Drag-and-Drop and Canvas Navigation supported shared understanding and task division. Data Visualizations enhanced negotiation and decision-making by translating abstract ML concepts into actionable insights. Drawing on Kaptelinin and Nardi's Activity

Theory [41], these features enabled collective sense-making and fairness exploration (e.g., detecting class imbalance). Interactive PROMPT WINDOWS and visual feedback distributed cognitive load, supporting communication and cooperation. According to Erickson and Kellogg's Social Translucence theory [19], the prototype improved visibility, awareness, and accountability. However, complex XAI visualizations occasionally challenged role clarity, suggesting the need for simplified outputs.

Collaborative Cognitive Load. Following Kirschner's Collaborative Cognitive Load Theory [42] and Sweller's model [76], the prototype helped manage intrinsic, extraneous, and germane load. VPLs structured task division, while touch interaction enabled seamless role adaptation and reduced intrinsic load. Extraneous load was minimized by real-time visual feedback and the co-located setup, which reduced split-attention effects [57]. Germane load was supported by data visualizations, which aided in learning and schema construction. In line with the Hutchins' distributed cognition framework [34] and Schön's Reflection-In-Action theory [67], these representations externalized complexity and enhanced collective reasoning.

Implications for EUD Tool Designers. This study outlines a set of recommendations for designers of ML-based EUD systems supporting user collaboration. Employing familiar visual programming functionalities, such as drag-and-drop interactions and visual indicators, can lower the entry threshold and support intuitive use. These systems should accommodate flexible role configurations to support both symmetric and asymmetric collaboration. Providing real-time feedback through prompts and visual cues can enhance system awareness and task coordination. Additionally, integrating features to mark individual contributions may improve accountability by clarifying each team member's role. XAI outputs should also be simplified to match novices' cognitive needs. Lastly, multi-touch tabletop environments can facilitate co-located interaction and support collaborative dynamics between domain specialists and computing experts.

Overall, this work highlights the potential of VPLs and touch interfaces to foster domain specialists' collaboration in ML-based system design. In line with recent Interactive Machine Learning (IML) literature, future work should explore complementary explanation techniques, such as example-based and counterfactual approaches, and incorporate interactive guidance to help novices interpret internal model processes, including training. Moreover, expanding the participant sample to include domain specialists in real-world settings and conducting comparative studies to isolate the contributions of touch interaction and visual programming will be essential to further validate and generalize the findings of this exploratory study. These results underscore the promise of explainable, touch-enabled VPL tools for supporting meaningful novice participation in ML design, while also pointing to open challenges in refining explanation interfaces and evaluating collaboration across diverse expertise profiles.

Acknowledgments. Research partly funded by PNRR - M4C2 - Investimento 1.3, Partenariato Esteso PE00000013 - "FAIR - Future Artificial Intelligence Research" - Spoke 1 "Human- centered AI", funded by the European Commission under the NextGeneration EU programme. Moreover, the authors acknowledge the support of the Computer Science Department at Universidad Carlos III de Madrid and the DEI Laboratory team for their assistance during the evaluation phase of this study. The provision of the tabletop touch device was instrumental in assessing the prototype.

References

1. Amershi, S., Morris, M.: CoSearch: a system for co-located collaborative web search. In: Proceedings of the SIGCHI Conference on Human Factors in Computing Systems, pp. 1647–1656. ACM, New York (2008). https://doi.org/10.1145/1357054.1357311
2. Arias, E., Eden, H., Fischer, G., Gorman, A., Scharff, E.: Transcending the individual human mind-creating shared understanding through collaborative design. ACM Trans. Comput.-Hum. Interact. **7**(1), 84–113 (2000)
3. Bakogeorge, A., Imtiaz, S., Abu Hantash, N., Manshaei, R., Mazalek, A.: Embodied machine learning. In: Proceedings of the Eighteenth International Conference on Tangible, Embedded, and Embodied Interaction, TEI 2024. Association for Computing Machinery, New York (2024). https://doi.org/10.1145/3623509.3633370
4. Barragán, P., Velasco, M., Urquiza-Fuentes, J., Álvarez, G.D., Anslow, C., Homer, M.: Designing collaborative scratchjr for multi-touch tabletops. In: 2024 International Symposium on Computers in Education (SIIE), pp. 1–6. IEEE (2024). https://doi.org/10.1109/SIIE63180.2024.10604572
5. Beaudouin-Lafon, M., et al.: Multisurface interaction in the wild room. Computer **45**(4), 48–56 (2012). https://doi.org/10.1109/MC.2012.110
6. Birnholtz, J., Grossman, T., Mak, C., Balakrishnan, R.: An exploratory study of input configuration and group process in a negotiation task using a large display. In: Proceedings of the SIGCHI Conference on Human Factors in Computing Systems, pp. 91–100. ACM, New York (2007)
7. Bradel, L., Endert, A., Koch, K., Andrews, C., North, C.: Large high-resolution displays for co-located collaborative sensemaking: display usage and territoriality. Int. J. Hum Comput Stud. **71**(11), 1078–1088 (2013). https://doi.org/10.1016/j.ijhcs.2013.07.004
8. Brynjolfsson, E., McAfee, A.: The Second Machine Age: Work, Progress, and Prosperity in a Time of Brilliant Technologies. WW Norton & Company (2014)
9. Capel, T., Brereton, M.: What is human-centered about human-centered AI? A map of the research landscape. In: Proceedings of the 2023 CHI Conference on Human Factors in Computing Systems, CHI 2023, pp. 1–23 (2023)
10. Cheng, K., Li, J., Müller-Tomfelde, C.: Supporting interaction and collaboration on large displays using tablet devices. In: Proceedings of the International Working Conference on Advanced Visual Interfaces, pp. 774–775 (2012)
11. Cruz, A., Correia, A., Paredes, H., Fonseca, B., Morgado, L., Martins, P.: Towards an overarching classification model of CSCW and groupware: a socio-technical perspective. In: Collaboration and Technology: 18th International Conference, CRIWG 2012 Raesfeld, Germany, 16–19 September 2012 Proceedings, pp. 41–56. Springer (2012)

12. Cruz, A., Paredes, H., Morgado, L., Martins, P.: Non-verbal aspects of collaboration in virtual worlds: a CSCW taxonomy-development proposal integrating the presence dimension. J. Univ. Comput. Sci. **27**, 913–954 (2021). https://doi.org/10.3897/jucs.74166
13. Dasgupta, S., Hill, B.M.: Scratch community blocks: Supporting children as data scientists. In: Proceedings of the 2017 CHI Conference on Human Factors in Computing Systems, Denver, Colorado, USA, CHI 2017, pp. 3620–3631 (2017). https://doi.org/10.1145/3025453.3025847
14. Delgado, F., Yang, S., Madaio, M., Yang, Q.: Stakeholder participation in AI: beyond "add diverse stakeholders and stir". arXiv preprint arXiv:2111.01122 (2021)
15. Dudley, J.J., Kristensson, P.O.: A review of user interface design for interactive machine learning. ACM Trans. Interact. Intell. Syst. (TiiS) **8**(2), 1–37 (2018)
16. Dwivedi, R., et al.: Explainable AI (XAI): Core ideas, techniques, and solutions. ACM Comput. Surv. **55**(9), 1–33 (2023)
17. Díaz-Rodríguez, N., Del Ser, J., Coeckelbergh, M., López de Prado, M., Herrera-Viedma, E., Herrera, F.: Connecting the dots in trustworthy artificial intelligence: from AI principles, ethics, and key requirements to responsible AI systems and regulation. Inf. Fusion **99**, 101896 (2023). https://doi.org/10.1016/j.inffus.2023.101896
18. Endert, A., Bradel, L., Zeitz, J., Andrews, C., North, C.: Designing large high-resolution display workspaces. In: Proceedings of the International Working Conference on Advanced Visual Interfaces, pp. 58–65. ACM, New York (2012). https://doi.org/10.1145/2254556.2254570
19. Erickson, T., Kellogg, W.A.: Social translucence: an approach to designing systems that support social processes. ACM Trans. Comput.-Hum. Interact. (TOCHI) **7**(1), 59–83 (2000)
20. EuropeanCommission: White paper on artificial intelligence. a European approach to excellence and trust (2020). https://eur-lex.europa.eu/legal-content/EN/TXT/HTML/?uri=CELEX:52020DC0065&from=EN
21. Fails, J.A., Olsen, D.R.: Interactive machine learning. In: Proceedings of the 8th International Conference on Intelligent User Interfaces (2003)
22. Feng, K., McDonald, D.: Addressing UX practitioners' challenges in designing ml applications: an interactive machine learning approach. In: Proceedings of the 28th International Conference on Intelligent User Interfaces, pp. 337–352. Association for Computing Machinery (ACM) (2023)
23. Fernaeus, Y., Tholander, J.: Designing for programming as joint performances among groups of children. Interact. Comput. **18**(5), 1012–1031 (2006)
24. Ferraris, C., Martel, C.: Regulation in groupware: the example of a collaborative drawing tool for young children. In: Proceedings of the Sixth International Workshop on Groupware (CRIWG 2000), pp. 119–127. IEEE (2000)
25. Fischer, G.: End-user development: empowering stakeholders with artificial intelligence, meta-design, and cultures of participation. In: Fogli, D., Tetteroo, D., Barricelli, B.R., Borsci, S., Markopoulos, P., Papadopoulos, G.A. (eds.) IS-EUD 2021. LNCS, vol. 12724, pp. 3–16. Springer, Cham (2021). https://doi.org/10.1007/978-3-030-79840-6_1
26. Forlines, C., Wigdor, D., Shen, C., Balakrishnan, R.: Direct-touch vs. mouse input for tabletop displays. In: Proceedings of the SIGCHI Conference on Human Factors in Computing Systems, pp. 647–656. ACM, New York (2007). https://doi.org/10.1145/1240624.1240726

27. Geymayer, T., Schmalstieg, D.: Collaborative distributed cognition using a seamless desktop infrastructure. In: 2016 Workshop on Immersive Analytics (IA), pp. 7–12. IEEE, Greenville (2016). https://doi.org/10.1109/IMMERSIVE.2016.7932375
28. Grudin, J.: Computer-supported cooperative work: history and focus. Computer **27**(5), 19–26 (1994)
29. Gunning, D.: Explainable artificial intelligence (XAI). Defense Advanced Research Projects Agency (DARPA), nd Web **2**(2017), 2 (2017). Add the URL if available
30. Gutwin, C., Greenberg, S.: A descriptive framework of workspace awareness for real-time groupware. Comput. Supported Coop. Work (CSCW) **11**, 411–446 (2002)
31. Harari, Y.N.: Why technology favors tyranny. In: The Atlantic, vol. 322, no. 3, pp. 64–73 (2018)
32. Hare, A.: Groups, Teams, and Social Interaction: Theories and Applications. Praeger Publishers (1992)
33. Hogg, M., Abrams, D.: Social Identifications: A Social Psychology of Intergroup Relations and Group Processes. Taylor & Frances/Routledge (1988)
34. Hollan, J., Hutchins, E., Kirsh, D.: Distributed cognition: toward a new foundation for human-computer interaction research. ACM Trans. Comput.-Hum. Interact. (TOCHI) **7**(2), 174–196 (2000)
35. Hollender, N., Hofmann, C., Deneke, M., Schmitz, B.: Integrating cognitive load theory and concepts of human–computer interaction. Comput. Hum. Behav. **26**(6), 1278–1288 (2010). https://doi.org/10.1016/j.chb.2010.05.031, https://www.sciencedirect.com/science/article/pii/S0747563210001718. Online Interactivity: Role of Technology in Behavior Change
36. Horak, T., Badam, S., Elmqvist, N., Dachselt, R.: When David meets goliath: combining smartwatches with a large vertical display for visual data exploration. In: Proceedings of the 2018 CHI Conference on Human Factors in Computing Systems, pp. 1–13. ACM, New York (2018). https://doi.org/10.1145/3173574.3173593
37. Hornecker, E., Marshall, P., Dalton, N., Rogers, Y.: Collaboration and interference: awareness with mice or touch input. In: Proceedings of the 2008 ACM Conference on Computer Supported Cooperative Work, pp. 167–176. ACM, New York (2008). https://doi.org/10.1145/1460563.1460589
38. Jiang, L., Liu, S., Chen, C.: Recent research advances on interactive machine learning. J. Vis. **22**, 401–417 (2019)
39. Johansen, R.: Groupware: Computer Support for Business Teams. The Free Press, New York (1988)
40. Kaggle: IBM HR analytics employee attrition & performance, predict attrition of your valuable employees (2017). https://www.kaggle.com/datasets/pavansubhasht/ibm-hr-analytics-attrition-dataset. Accessed 29 May 2024
41. Kaptelinin, V., Nardi, B.A.: Activity Theory in HCI: Fundamentals and Reflections, vol. 13. Morgan & Claypool Publishers (2012)
42. Kirschner, P.A., Sweller, J., Kirschner, F., Zambrano R., J.: From cognitive load theory to collaborative cognitive load theory. Int. J. Comput.-Supported Collab. Learn. **13**, 213–233 (2018)
43. Lai, V., Zhang, Y., Chen, C., Liao, Q., Tan, C.: Selective explanations: leveraging human input to align explainable AI. Proc. ACM Hum.-Comput. Interact. **7**(CSCW2), 1–35 (2023)
44. Lazar, J., Feng, J., Hochheiser, H.: Research Methods in Human-Computer Interaction. Morgan Kaufmann (2017)
45. Lee, C.P., Paine, D.: From the matrix to a model of coordinated action (MoCA): a conceptual framework of and for CSCW. In: Proceedings of the 18th ACM Confer-

ence on Computer-Supported Cooperative Work & Social Computing, pp. 179–194 (2015)
46. Liao, Q., Varshney, K.: Human-centered explainable AI (XAI): from algorithms to user experiences. arXiv preprint arXiv:2110.10790 (2021)
47. Makridakis, S.: The forthcoming artificial intelligence (AI) revolution: its impact on society and firms. In: Futures, vol. 90, pp. 46–60 (2017). https://doi.org/10.1016/j.futures.2017.03.006
48. Malone, T., Crowston, K.: The interdisciplinary study of coordination. ACM Comput. Surv. **26**(1), 87–119 (1994). https://doi.org/10.1145/174666.174668
49. Maquil, V., Afkari, H., Arend, B., Heuser, S., Sunnen, P.: Analysis of coordination mechanisms during collaborative problem-solving on an interactive tabletop display. In: Computer Supported Cooperative Work (CSCW), pp. 1–43 (2024)
50. Mateescu, M., Pimmer, C., Zahn, C., Klinkhammer, D., Reiterer, H.: Collaboration on large interactive displays: a systematic review. Hum.-Comput. Interact. **36**(3), 243–277 (2021). https://doi.org/10.1080/07370024.2019.1697697
51. McGrath, J.: Groups: Interaction and Performance. Prentice-Hall, Englewood Cliffs (1984)
52. Morris, M.R., Winograd, T.: Quantifying collaboration on computationally-enhanced tables. In: CSCW 2004 Workshop on Methodologies for Evaluating Collaboration Behaviour in Co-located Environments, pp. 1–4 (2004)
53. Morris, M., Fisher, D., Wigdor, D.: Search on surfaces: exploring the potential of interactive tabletops for collaborative search tasks. Inf. Process. Manage. **46**(6), 703–717 (2010). https://doi.org/10.1016/j.ipm.2009.10.004
54. Nielsen, J.: The theory behind heuristic evaluations. In: Nielsen Norman Group (1994)
55. Nielsen, J.: Usability engineering. In: Morgan Kaufmann (1994)
56. Paas, F., Sweller, J.: Implications of cognitive load theory for multimedia learning. Camb. Handb. Multimed. Learn. **27**, 27–42 (2014)
57. Paas, F., Van Merriënboer, J.: Cognitive-load theory: methods to manage working memory load in the learning of complex tasks. Curr. Dir. Psychol. Sci. **29**(4), 394–398 (2020)
58. Parliament, E., Council: AI act. Official Journal of the European Union (2024). https://eur-lex.europa.eu/legal-content/EN/TXT/?uri=CELEX:32024R1689
59. Paternò, F.: End user development: survey of an emerging field for empowering people. In: International Scholarly Research Notices, vol. 2013. Hindawi (2013)
60. Pinelle, D., Gutwin, C., Greenberg, S.: Task analysis for groupware usability evaluation: modeling shared-workspace tasks with the mechanics of collaboration. ACM Trans. Comput.-Hum. Interact. (TOCHI) **10**(4), 281–311 (2003)
61. Plaza, P., et al.: Promoting computational thinking through visual block programming tools. In: 2021 IEEE Global Engineering Education Conference (EDUCON), pp. 1131–1136 (2021)
62. Ramos, G., et al.: Emerging perspectives in human-centered machine learning. In: Proceedings of CHI Conference on Human Factors in Computing Systems Extended Abstracts (CHI 2019 Extended Abstracts), Glasgow, Scotland, UK, p. 9 (2019). https://doi.org/10.1145/3290607.3299014
63. Rekimoto, J.: A multiple device approach for supporting whiteboard-based interactions. In: Proceedings of the SIGCHI Conference on Human Factors in Computing Systems, pp. 344–351. ACM Press/Addison-Wesley Publishing Co., USA (1998). https://doi.org/10.1145/274644.274692

64. Rodden, T.: A survey of CSCW systems. Interact. Comput. **3**(3), 319–353 (1991). https://doi.org/10.1016/0953-5438(91)90020-3, https://www.sciencedirect.com/science/article/pii/0953543891900203
65. Rogers, Y.: New theoretical approaches for HCI. Ann. Rev. Inf. Sci. Technol. **38**(1), 87–143 (2004)
66. Rogers, Y., Lindley, S.: Collaborating around vertical and horizontal large interactive displays: which way is best? Interact. Comput. **16**(6), 1133–1152 (2004). https://doi.org/10.1016/j.intcom.2004.07.008
67. Schön, D.: From technical rationality to reflection-in-action. In: Boundaries of Adult Learning, pp. 8–31. Routledge (2013)
68. Sharp, H., Rogers, Y., Preece, J.: Interaction Design: Beyond Human-Computer Interaction. Wiley (2007)
69. Shen, C., Everitt, K., Ryall, K.: UbiTable: impromptu face-to-face collaboration on horizontal interactive surfaces. In: International Conference on Ubiquitous Computing, pp. 281–288. Springer (2003)
70. Shneiderman, B.: Designing the User Interface: Strategies for Effective Human-Computer Interaction, 3rd edn. Addison-Wesley Longman Publishing Co., Inc., USA (1997)
71. Shneiderman, B.: Bridging the gap between ethics and practice: guidelines for reliable, safe, and trustworthy human-centered AI systems. ACM Trans. Interact. Intell. Syst. (TiiS) **10**(4), 1–31 (2020)
72. Shneiderman, B.: Human-centered artificial intelligence: reliable, safe & trustworthy. Int. J. Hum.-Comput. Interact. **36**(6), 495–504 (2020)
73. Shneiderman, B.: Human-Centered AI. Oxford University Press (2022)
74. Shneiderman, B., Plaisant, C., Cohen, M., Jacobs, S., Elmqvist, N., Diakopoulos, N.: Grand challenges for HCI researchers. Interactions **23**(5), 24–25 (2016). https://doi.org/10.1145/2977645
75. Starkweather, G.: Dsharp-a wide-screen multi-projector display. J. Opt. A: Pure Appl. Opt. **5**(5), S136 (2003). https://doi.org/10.1088/1464-4258/5/5/354
76. Sweller, J., Ayres, P., Kalyuga, S.: Cognitive Load Theory. Springer, New York (2011)
77. Teso, S., Alkan, Ö., Stammer, W., Daly, E.: Leveraging explanations in interactive machine learning: an overview. Front. Artif. Intell. **6**, 1066049 (2023). Frontiers Media SA
78. Teso, S., Kersting, K.: Explanatory interactive machine learning. In: Proceedings of the 2019 AAAI/ACM Conference on AI, Ethics, and Society (2019)
79. Van Merriënboer, J.J.G., Sweller, J.: Cognitive load theory and complex learning: recent developments and future directions. Educ. Psychol. Rev. **17**(2), 147–177 (2005). https://doi.org/10.1007/s10648-005-3951-0
80. Versino, S., Turchi, T., Malizia, A.: Fostering inexperienced user participation in ml-based systems design: a literature review of visual language tools. In: Proceedings of the 1st International Workshop on Designing and Building Hybrid Human-AI Systems, SYNERGY 2024. Arenzano, Genoa, Italy (2024). https://ceur-ws.org/Vol-3701/paper1.pdf
81. Versino, S., Turchi, T., Malizia, A.: Leveraging visual languages to foster user participation in designing trustworthy machine learning systems: a comparative study. In: Proceedings of the 2024 IEEE Symposium on Visual Languages and Human-Centric Computing (VL/HCC), pp. 24–32. IEEE, New York (2024). https://doi.org/10.1109/VL/HCC60511.2024.00013

82. Versino, S., Turchi, T., Malizia, A.: PyflowML: a visual language framework to foster participation in ML-based decision making. In: International Conference on Human-Computer Interaction, pp. 110–130. Springer (2024)
83. Vetere, F., O'Hara, K., Paay, J., Ploderer, B., Harper, R., Sellen, A.: Social NUI: social perspectives in natural user interfaces. In: Proceedings of the 2014 Companion Publication on Designing Interactive Systems, DIS Companion 2014, pp. 215–218. Association for Computing Machinery, New York (2014). https://doi.org/10.1145/2598784.2598802
84. Vogt, K., Bradel, L., Andrews, C., North, C., Endert, A., Hutchings, D.: Co-located collaborative sensemaking on a large high-resolution display with multiple input devices. In: Campos, P., Graham, N., Jorge, J., Nunes, N., Palanque, P., Winckler, M. (eds.) INTERACT 2011. LNCS, vol. 6947, pp. 589–604. Springer, Heidelberg (2011). https://doi.org/10.1007/978-3-642-23771-3_44
85. Wallace, J.R., Scott, S.D., Stutz, T., Enns, T., Inkpen, K.: Investigating teamwork and taskwork in single-and multi-display groupware systems. Pers. Ubiquit. Comput. **13**, 569–581 (2009)
86. Wigdor, D., Wixon, D.: Brave NUI World: Designing Natural User Interfaces for Touch and Gesture. Elsevier (2011)
87. Winston, P.H.: Artificial intelligence. Addison-Wesley Longman Publishing Co., Inc. (1984)
88. Wondimu, N.A., Buche, C., Visser, U.: Interactive machine learning: a state of the art review. arXiv preprint arXiv:2207.06196 (2022)
89. Zhang, Z., Peng, W., Chen, X., Cao, L., Li, T.: LADICA: a large shared display interface for generative AI cognitive assistance in co-located team collaboration. arXiv preprint arXiv:2409.13968 (2024)

Visual and Textual Language Synchronization for End-User Programming Environments

Anahide Silahli, Jose Pablo De la Rosa Gutierrez, and Thiago Rocha Silva(✉)

The Maersk Mc-Kinney Moller Institute, University of Southern Denmark, Odense, Denmark
{ansil,jode,thiago}@mmmi.sdu.dk

Abstract. End-User Programming (EUP) environments typically offer either a text-based or a visual programming language for end users. Even when both options are provided, they lack real-time synchronization between the two representations. This study explores the integration of the textual and visual representations of a domain-specific language (DSL) for EUP based on Behaviour-Driven Development (BDD) scenarios. By combining a visual editor featuring a block-based language with a textual representation featuring syntax highlighting, error detection, and auto-completion, the platform can enhance accessibility, flexibility, and efficiency in EUP. The primary challenge investigated is achieving real-time, two-way synchronization between the visual and textual editors to maintain consistent code representation, crucial for an optimal user experience. The solution leverages Blockly's custom code generators to translate blocks to text and Abstract Syntax Trees (ASTs) to convert text to blocks. We evaluated our approach in two use cases in the robotics domain, confirming the potential of the dual editor to offer flexible, domain-tailored end-user programming, with potential for broad future applications.

Keywords: End-User Programming · Text-Based Programming · Visual Programming · Block-Based Languages · Language Synchronization · Domain-Specific Languages · Behaviour-Driven Development

1 Introduction

End-User Development (EUD) aims at empowering non-programmers to create, modify, and/or extend software systems [12]. Within EUD, End-User Programming (EUP) focuses on reducing or scaffolding the expertise required from these non-programmers to write programs by e.g., offering high-level domain-specific languages either in textual or visual formats. One of the key challenges of EUP environments, however, is that end users are typically locked into a single programming model, which hinders flexibility in choosing the most appropriate

C. Santoro et al. (Eds.): IS-EUD 2025, LNCS 15713, pp. 133–150, 2025.
https://doi.org/10.1007/978-3-031-95452-8_8

model for a particular context. Even when more than one programming model is provided, such models are not synchronized, requiring end users to pick one or the other in order to program a particular task. These challenges motivated us to investigate the following research questions:

RQ1. How to implement an EUP environment that translates a text-based domain-specific language into a visual representation and vice versa?
RQ2. How to enable the resultant EUP environment to feature real-time synchronization between the textual and visual editors?

As a result, in this paper we propose an EUP environment featuring synchronized visual and textual representations of a high-level domain-specific language (DSL) for end-user programming. The environment implements a DSL based on Behaviour-Driven Development (BDD) [17,18] to allow end users to specify the expected software behavior using natural language (NL)-like scenarios. A web-based editor makes the environment accessible, replacing cumbersome DSL IDEs, while a dual-editor setup allows users to write textual scenarios or build them visually using Blockly blocks [15]. Real-time syncing keeps both editors synchronized, supporting different preferences and boosting usability. This synchronization mechanism ensures consistent bidirectional updates between textual and visual representations.

We evaluated the proposed environment on two use cases in the robotics domain: a collaborative robot (cobot) performing pick-and-place tasks in an industrial setting, and a single-degree-of-freedom rehabilitation robot that allow clinicians to define patient exercises. The evaluation process confirmed the generation of syntactically correct scenarios on both ways across the two cases, demonstrating the tool's capability to support end-user programming in different contexts.

In summary, the main contributions of this paper are:

- A synchronization mechanism to keep both textual and visual representations of a DSL in sync at interaction time.
- A web-based EUP environment to allow end users to program using both representations seamlessly.
- Findings from the evaluation of our approach in two different use cases in the robotics domain.

2 Background

2.1 Behaviour-Driven Development

Behavior-Driven Development (BDD) is a collaborative agile methodology designed to address the communication gap between developers and subject-matter experts [14]. It facilitates communication among developers, testers, and business stakeholders by defining test cases based on user requirements in clear, natural language. BDD extends Test-Driven Development (TDD), which emphasizes writing tests prior to implementing code. BDD builds upon it by utilizing a format that is accessible to non-technical stakeholders, ensuring that software behavior is described through illustrative examples, or "scenarios", following the Gherkin syntax [8].

Gherkin serves as a structured language that organizes scenarios into three primary components: "Given" establishes the initial conditions (e.g., accessing a login page), "When" specifies the action to be performed (e.g., entering a password), and "Then" describes the expected outcome (e.g., reaching the home page). Additional details can be incorporated using "And" allowing for both flexibility and structure. This format, recognized by studies such as [6], enhances shared understanding and mitigates misunderstandings before development begins. Moreover, tools like Behave for Python, and Cucumber for Ruby or Java, enable the conversion of Gherkin scenarios into executable tests, ensuring that the software functions as intended.

As BDD scenarios specify the system's business rules as test cases, previous work has tried BDD scenarios as a programming language for subject-matter experts and other end users in the context of EUP [17,18]. This approach relies on a domain-specific language (DSL) to enforce the Gherkin syntax and guarantee the consistency of the scenarios through a state machine representation. In this representation, "Given" and "Then" statements must always describe initial and resultant states respectively, while "When" statements must always describe transitions on the state machine. The proposal bears some resemblance with Trigger-Action Programming (TAP) [19] but adds the system's expected outcome as a necessary part of the specification, which helps to guarantee the integrity of the state machine.

Studies such as [13] and [11] highlight how DSLs facilitate the involvement of subject-matter experts. High-level DSLs are also the backbone of many EUP approaches. Overall, they help end users by raising the abstraction level of general-purpose programming languages while offering, through their IDEs, key programming features such as syntax highlighting and auto-completion.

2.2 Visual Programming Languages

Visual Programming Languages (VPLs) enhance programming accessibility by employing spatial layouts and graphical representations – such as diagrams, icons, and interactive elements – rather than solely relying on text [3]. While some textual components may be included, VPLs primarily aim to reduce syntactic complexity and improve code expressiveness. By integrating visual semantics, intuitive controls, and real-time feedback, they enhance user interaction and comprehension [3]. Key advantages include accessibility for beginners, improved conceptual visualization, and educational benefits. However, VPLs also have limitations, including restricted hardware control, higher resource consumption, reduced execution speed, and constrained functionality. VPLs can be categorized into flowchart-based systems (e.g., Flowgorithm) and block-based languages (e.g., Scratch, Blockly) in which users assemble visual code blocks.

Block-Based Languages. Block-based languages, a subset of visual programming, utilize modular, interlocking blocks to represent code structures, eliminating syntax errors and improving accessibility. Their clearly labeled constructs and structured design enhance learnability, making them particularly effective in education, robotics, and creative applications. By reducing cognitive load and visually organizing programming concepts, they facilitate understanding and minimize errors [21]. Scratch, developed by MIT, enables users to create interactive projects, fostering algorithmic thinking and problem-solving skills [16]. It has been integrated into introductory programming courses, such as Harvard's CS50, as a gateway to textual programming [1]. Beyond educational contexts, frameworks such as Blockly, OpenBlocks, and Droplets provide customizable block-based coding environments for real-world and domain-specific applications. Notably, Scratch has announced plans to incorporate Blockly to expand its capabilities [1].

Blockly, a web-based library developed by Google [9], enables block-based programming through an intuitive, puzzle-like interface, eliminating syntax concerns. Developers can customize blocks, define relationships, and focus on domain logic while Blockly manages the visual representation, making it particularly suitable for DSLs. Widely used in educational settings and algorithmic training, Blockly empowers domain experts to program with minimal technical expertise. The setup process involves defining custom blocks, creating a toolbox, and configuring a workspace. Toolboxes categorize blocks, enhancing usability and facilitating efficient workflow organization.

3 The Proposed EUP Environment

This section outlines the design and development of an EUP environment that implements the aforementioned BDD-based DSL proposed by Silva [17,18] to leverage the power of both textual and visual representations. Built on the Xtext framework [2] and extended with a web-based interface, the environment combines the benefits of both textual and visual programming to adapt to diverse user needs. Below, we detail the DSL's foundation, its supporting platform, and the synchronization mechanisms that unify its dual interfaces.

3.1 A BDD-Based Domain-Specific Language

In the proposed DSL, BDD scenarios can be written at two abstraction levels: *imperative*, which breaks interactions into detailed, step-by-step instructions, and *declarative*, which uses high-level, domain-specific terms to summarize behavior [7]. Users define system entities – i.e., objects with actions, states, and properties – as shown in Listing 1.1. A model starts with a name and can import other models via a `using` statement. Scenarios follow strict rules: states appear in "Given" and "Then" clauses, while actions reside in "When" clauses. A `which means` keyword connects declarative steps with the imperative scenarios that realize them as illustrated in Listing 1.2.

Listing 1.1. Entity Definition Template in the BDD DSL

```
model <domain model name> using <interactive model name>

entity <domain entity name> {
  actions: <list of supported domain actions>
  states: <list of supported domain states>
  properties: <list of supported domain properties>
}
```

Listing 1.2. Scenario Definition Template in the BDD DSL

```
Scenario: <scenario name>
Given/And <initial domain state>
  which means
    Given/And <initial interactive state>
    When/And <interactive action>
    Then/And <resultant interactive state>
When/And <domain action>
  which means
    Given/And <initial interactive state>
    When/And <interactive action>
    Then/And <resultant interactive state>
Then/And <resultant domain state>
  which means
    Given/And <initial interactive state>
    When/And <interactive action>
    Then/And <resultant interactive state>
```

The DSL's grammar, implemented in Xtext, supports four core constructs: declarative entities (with properties, states, and actions), imperative entities, declarative scenarios, and imperative scenarios.

3.2 Web-Based Platform

To make the DSL accessible beyond Eclipse, a web-based platform was developed using the Xtext Web framework and JavaScript. The resultant environment is shown in Fig. 1. This solution features a browser-based front-end and a back-end server handling API requests, parsing grammar rules, and supplying block definitions. The interface offers two workspaces: a textual editor (shown on the left side of Fig. 1), and a Blockly-based visual editor (shown on the right side of Fig. 1). Both workspaces are kept fully synchronized at runtime, so the end users can work on any of them and see their changes immediately reflected in the other.

The textual workspace, built with Ace.js [5], provides syntax highlighting, error detection, and auto-completion, mirroring modern IDEs (see Fig. 2a). For

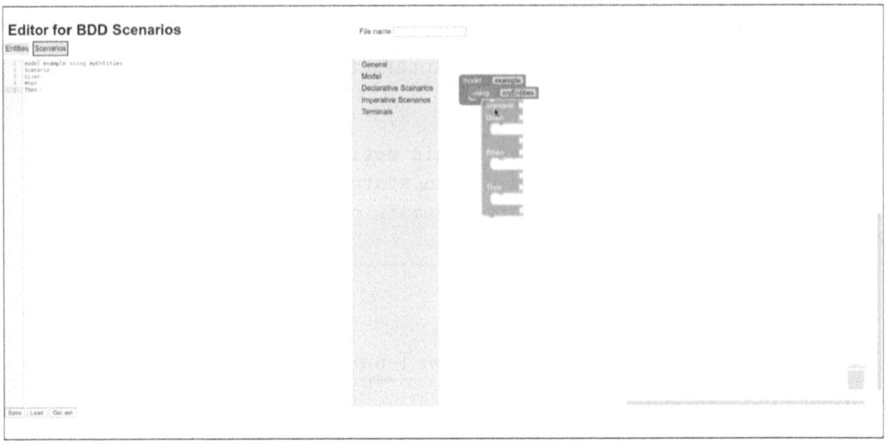

Fig. 1. The Proposed EUP Environment

example, syntax errors are flagged with a red cross, and hovering reveals detailed feedback.

The Blockly workspace offers a drag-and-drop interface with a toolbox of categorized blocks (e.g., `DeclarativeEntityDef`, `Scenario`), dynamically generated from the DSL grammar. In this workspace, the DSL syntax is enforced by the block shapes enriched with text fields and combo boxes to type/select valid inputs for each parameter (see Fig. 2b). A trash can is also offered for discarding unwanted blocks.

Overall, the editor is split into the "Entities" and "Scenarios" tabs, each with tailored workspaces. Within these workspaces, the blocks are organized into the following categories:

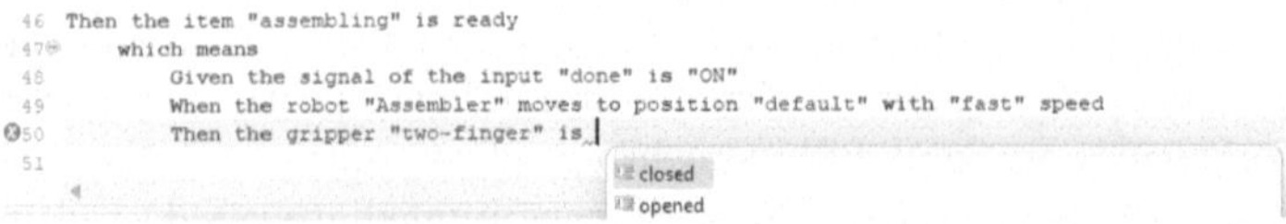

(a) IDE Features in the Textual Workspace

(b) Blocks in the Blocky Workspace

Fig. 2. Elements of the Proposed EUP Environment

- **General:** Blocks used for general purposes in various contexts, that do not fit in a specific category.
- **Model:** Blocks that make it possible to define a model or refer to a model.
- **Declarative Entities:** Blocks that are used for defining declarative entities along with options to define their properties, states, and actions.
- **Imperative Entities:** Blocks that allow defining imperative entities, as well as their properties, states, and actions.
- **Declarative Scenarios:** Blocks that offer users ways to define declarative scenarios, with "Given", "When", and "Then" statements.
- **Imperative Entities:** Blocks that make it possible to define imperative scenarios, with "Given", "When", and "Then" statements.
- **Terminals:** Blocks that correspond to ID and String terminals.

Declarative and Imperative Entities are only shown under the Entities tab. Similarly, Declarative and Imperative Scenarios are only shown under the Scenarios tab. As the scenarios cannot be defined before any entities are defined, end users get a warning message if they try to do so. The Scenarios tab is also disabled by default until the user specifying at least one valid entity either via text or blocks. Finally, the environment also supports saving/loading files to/from local storage and an "Get AST" button to display the Abstract Syntax Tree (AST) in the browser console.

3.3 Dynamic Toolbox and AST Generation

The Blockly toolbox is generated dynamically by parsing Xtext grammar rules via a back-end service. Each non-terminal rule becomes a block (e.g., `Model`), serialized into JSON and rendered in the front-end. Terminal blocks (e.g., String, ID) are hard-coded due to their simplicity. The process ensures the visual interface reflects the DSL's structure accurately.

AST retrieval, triggered by the "Get AST" button, constructs a tree from the textual input using Xtext libraries. Initially limited to the root node (e.g., `Model`), we enhanced it to include all nodes, serialized as JSON, enabling deeper analysis and synchronization.

3.4 Visual and Textual Synchronization

A core feature of the environment is the bidirectional synchronization between the textual and Blockly workspaces, ensuring consistency across interfaces. This is achieved through two processes: generating blocks from text and text from blocks, leveraging the AST and a custom code generator respectively. Figure 3 illustrates the system architecture.

Blocks from Text. Our approach to text-to-block conversion is inspired by Merino et al. [20,21], and relies on the AST as an intermediary. When the text editor changes, the back-end constructs an AST, which `blockGenerator.js`

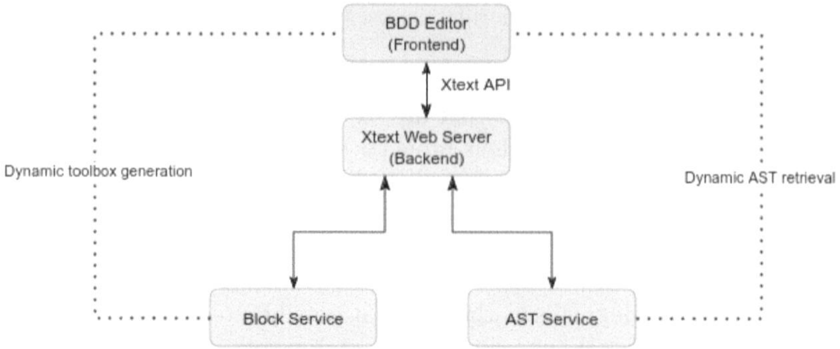

Fig. 3. System Components Diagram

recursively traverses to create corresponding blocks. Each node maps to a block type (e.g., `Model`), with manual mappings for exceptions (e.g., `PropertyDef`). Figure 4 outlines this flow. To avoid overwriting user actions, block generation only occurs if the AST changes meaningfully, and it respects the active tab ("Entities" or "Scenarios").

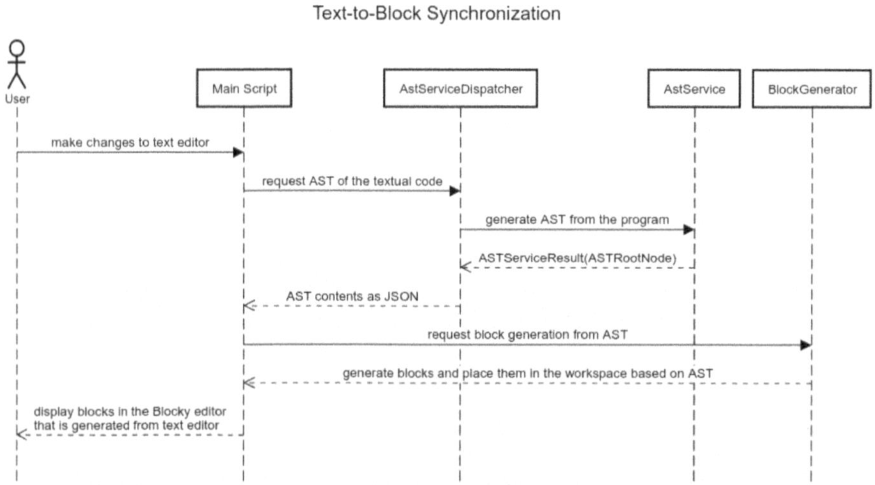

Fig. 4. Text-to-Block Synchronization Sequence Diagram

Text from Blocks. Block-to-text conversion uses a custom `BddGenerator` (in `bddGenerator.js`), initialized with block definitions containing code templates (e.g., `message0`). For each block, the generator replaces placeholders with input values (e.g., `ID`, `statement`) using Blockly's `valueToCode` and `statementToCode` functions. The process, detailed in Fig. 5, triggers on workspace changes, injecting the resulting code into the text editor without overwriting active edits.

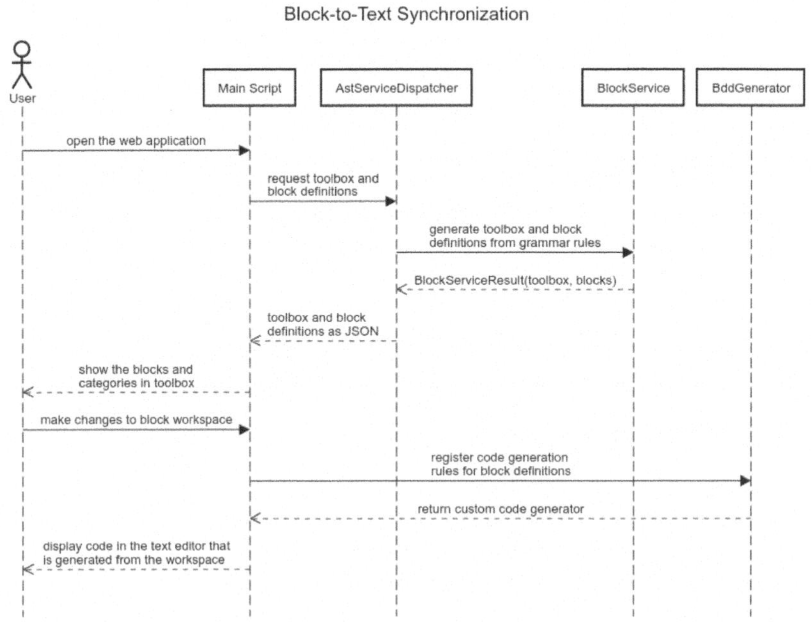

Fig. 5. Block-to-Text Synchronization Sequence Diagram

To prevent disruptions, synchronization respects user context: block edits trigger code generation only, while text edits trigger block generation only. Flags track active interactions (e.g., dragging blocks, typing), ensuring seamless collaboration between interfaces.

4 Evaluation

We evaluated the proposed EUP environment in two use cases in the robotics domain: a Universal Robot (UR) 5 collaborative robot (UR5 cobot), and a physical one Degree Of Freedom (DOF) therapy robot. The objective of the evaluation was to assess the functional integration of the DSL scenarios across both interfaces in different use cases. The evaluation confirmed the platform's ability to generate correct, synced representations and its potential for real-world robot control.

4.1 Case 1: Universal Robots UR5 Cobot

The UR5, a collaborative robot, performs pick-and-place tasks in industrial settings. Traditional programming is time-intensive, requiring manual motion definitions. Our EUP environment simplifies this by enabling users to define trajectories and timing via text or alternatively Blockly blocks. Two scenarios were tested: a trajectory from one position to another and a timed movement. Listing 1.3 shows the entity definition, and Listing 1.4 the second test scenario.

Listing 1.3. UR5 Test Entities

```
model Sample

declarative entity robot { actions: moves, grabs; properties: position }
declarative entity object { states: fixed, placed }
declarative entity trajectory { properties: duration }
```

Listing 1.4. UR5 Second Test Scenario

```
model Scenarios using Sample

Scenario: "Variable duration of trajectory execution"
Given the trajectory "Trajectory" duration is "5 seconds"
And the object "Object" is fixed
When the robot "Robot" moves to position "POS10"
And the robot "Robot" grabs the object "Object"
And the robot "Robot" moves to position "Bucket"
Then the object "Object" is placed
```

We defined entities and scenarios in both editors as seen in Fig. 6. In the text editor, we typed the model and scenarios; in the visual editor, we built them with blocks. Synchronization was tested bidirectionally: text-to-block generated accurate blocks, with occasional order shifts that didn't affect functionality, and block-to-text produced consistent text. Integration with the UR5 succeeded, as shown in Fig. 7, confirming real-time robot control.

4.2 Case 2: Physical Therapy Robot

This case involves a cable-driven robot for shoulder pull-down exercises, requiring precise force and position adjustments across concentric (pulling down) and eccentric (lifting up) phases. Besides the entities (Listing 1.5), six scenarios were defined. Two of them were fully tested and can be seen in Listing 1.6.

Listing 1.5. Therapy Robot Entities

```
model Entities

declarative entity movement { properties: range, phase }
declarative entity hand { actions: moves }
declarative entity robot { states: pulling; properties: force }
```

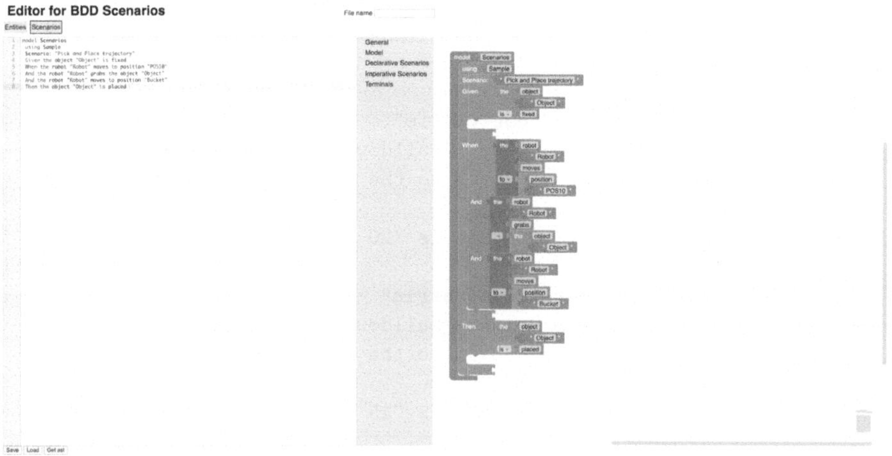

Fig. 6. Block-to-Text Scenario Definition Results for the `Pick and Place trajectory` Scenario

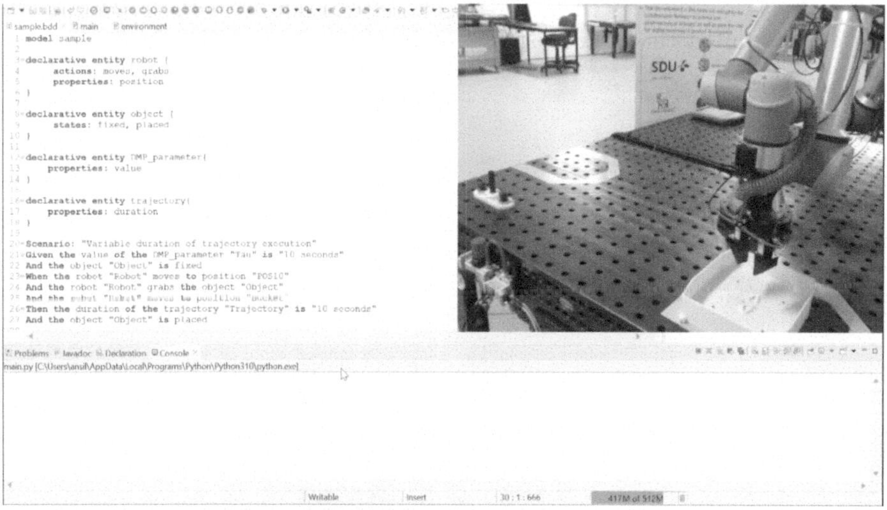

Fig. 7. UR5 Robot Executing a Scenario

Listing 1.6. Therapy Robot Scenarios

```
model Scenarios using Entities

Scenario: "Pulldown upper concentric"
Given the phase of the movement "pulldown" is "concentric"
When the hand "right hand" moves to the range "top" of the movement
     "pulldown"
Then the force of the robot "Rt" is "20 kg"

Scenario: "Pulldown bottom concentric"
Given the phase of the movement "pulldown" is "concentric"
When the hand "right hand" moves to the range "bottom" of the
     movement "pulldown"
Then the force of the robot "Rt" is "15 kg"
```

Entities and scenarios were created in both editors, mirroring the UR5 process. Text-to-block and block-to-text synchronization worked reliably, with minor order variations in blocks that didn't impact outcomes.

The result of the block-to-text synchronization for the *pulldown upper concentric* scenario can be seen in Fig. 8. The integration with the robot, shown in Fig. 9, executed the scenarios accurately after minor DSL adjustments for compatibility.

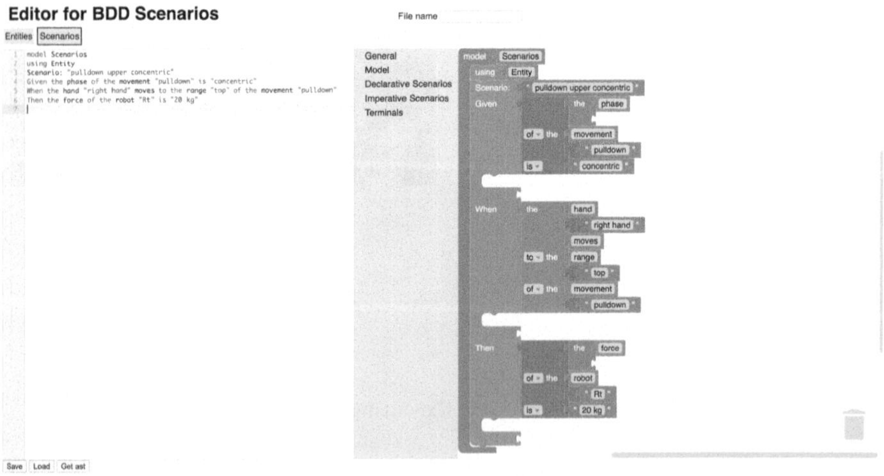

Fig. 8. Block-to-Text Scenario Definition Results for the *pulldown upper concentric* Scenario

Fig. 9. Physical Therapy Robot in Action

4.3 Findings

RQ1. How to implement an EUP environment that translates a text-based domain-specific language into a visual representation and vice versa?

It is necessary to construct an intermediary data format when going from text to blocks. The format was chosen as ASTs, due to the compatibility of this format with the Xtext framework, and the available tools through the Xtext library. There were examples in the existing literature that also showed ASTs as a viable method when going from text-to-blocks [21,22]. Other alternatives, such as parser combinators and string manipulation also exist, which would have added more complexity to the solution as opposed to obtaining the AST of the textual code and mapping the AST nodes to Blockly blocks. Although sometimes this mapping was not straightforward, it proved to be a highly useful method. ASTs expressed the logical structure of the textual program successfully, which could then be translated into the same logical structure in the block format.

RQ2. How to enable the resultant EUP environment to feature real-time synchronization between the textual and visual editors?

The Blockly framework provides a code generation functionality, which can be customized in order to generate custom code from each Blockly block. The custom code generator concept was implemented due to having extensive support from Blockly. Other alternatives such as using an intermediary format from blocks to text (such as JSON or XML) were not considered extensively. Blockly provides the JSON and XML representation of the workspace by serializing the contents. However, this approach would need some kind of custom translator when going from a JSON or XML format to the BDD DSL, which would add more complexity to the final solution. Therefore, Blockly custom generators were preferred over the serialization approach.

5 Discussion and Limitations

Burnett [3] discusses four common strategies when developing VPLs for EUP environments: concreteness, directness, explicitness, and immediate visual feedback. With the proposed EUP environment, we adhered to these strategies in the following ways:

- **Concreteness:** The block based environment allows the user to see the aspects of the BDD language, represented in the form of blocks. The abstractions of the semantics are made clearer and more concrete. The users are then able to verify the textual code equivalent of the blocks that they put together in the workspace.
- **Directness:** The users are able to feel like they are directly manipulating the blocks by dragging and dropping them into the workspace. This kind of feeling is also emphasized when the users make a change to either of the editors and see the equivalent change in the other editor. The feeling of being able to manipulate the objects is important for the user, due to the perceived ease related to achieving specific goals.
- **Explicitness:** In both the visual and the textual environments, inaccurate syntax is presented explicitly to the user. From a broader point of view, the grammar rules are made explicit by showing the users how blocks are allowed to be connected to each other. The relationships between the different components of the language are expressed through the jigsaw-like structure of blocks.
- **Immediate visual feedback:** Whenever the user uses the platform, no matter which editor they use, they almost immediately see both of the representations of the program on their screens. This immediate visual feedback ensures that the state of the program stays consistent. This mechanism can help the users to quickly grasp the scope of the changes they are making to the program, whenever they edit it. The updates to both the text editor and the block-based editor are incremental, and the users are therefore able to observe how every single change to the program reflects on the different representations of code. This can make it clearer for users to see what is actually happening rather than waiting with all the changes and showing them all at once.

In light of these strategies, we categorize and discuss hereafter the findings and limitations identified in our evaluation.

The Environment Can Only Support One Grammar at a Time and is Closely Coupled with the Current BDD DSL Grammar Rules. Because of how Xtext works, the grammar rules need to be defined before compilation time. This means that the grammar rules cannot be changed at runtime and only one version of the grammar can be supported.

The Solution has Limited Support for Imperative Scenarios. While developing the solution, the focus was mostly put on the declarative entities and declarative scenarios. The imperative entity definitions are also supported from text-to-block and block-to-text. However, the imperative scenario definitions are lacking the accurate text-to-block support due to having many edge cases. Code generation from imperative scenarios is not affected though. As the use cases in the evaluation did not make use of imperative entities or imperative scenarios, this feature was not prioritized.

There are Still Two Hard-Coded Blocks. Due to its simplicity, the two blocks representing the terminals category (String and ID blocks) are still hard-coded, instead of being generated dynamically at runtime.

The Block Colors are Randomized. The block colors are generated randomly by setting the seed of the randomizer to the hash value of the type of the block. Using specified colors may be a biased choice as end users might use a culturally sensitive or a non-universal intuitive color scheme. Manually assigning colors to the block types could also be a problem when scaling the system. By randomizing the colors, the users can be introduced to a more objective solution. Random colors can also add a layer of visual diversity and thereby engaging the users more effectively. Even though the block types are unique, there is a possibility of hash values colliding, which would result in different blocks having the same color. This has not been observed during our evaluation though. However, some blocks have very similar colors. If two blocks with different functionalities or purposes have the same color, it would be challenging for the users to differentiate between them [10]. Although randomized color generation may result in hash collisions and thereby confuse users, this can be mitigated through consistent colors. The system is developed in a way that colors are consistent across each program run. This at least provides the users with reliable visual cues which may enhance the usability and UX of the system [10].

Disconnected Blocks Still Generate Code. When a block is dragged into the Blockly workspace, the block generates some code even if it is disconnected from all the other blocks. The disconnected block is technically not a part of the program and should be disregarded. This could confuse the users when adding blocks by mistake. If a user for instance is writing a scenario and by mistake adds a block that has nothing to do with the scenario itself, additional code will be generated in the textual editor. A block can also be hidden by another block, so if this is the case, then the user might not realize where the issue stems from.

The Custom Code Format is Overwritten by the Code Generator. When the user types code into the text editor, they might prefer to do it in a certain style when it comes to spacing and indentations. However, after manually moving the blocks around in the workspace, the code in the text editor is overwritten by the code generator. Therefore, the custom styling and format of the text by the user is also overwritten, which can be confusing for the users.

The Blocks Can be Very Cumbersome. Some blocks, especially the scenario related blocks take up a lot of space vertically in the Blockly workspace. Instead of having the sentences for each step in one line in the Blockly workspace, they are divided into multiple lines. The same occurs when an array of items (e.g., properties, states or actions of an entity) is defined through blocks. Arrays of items are stacked vertically, which takes up space compared to having them together horizontally. Cumbersome blocks can make it harder for the users to define multiple scenarios at once, requiring manual scrolling to see all the defined scenarios. This is, however, a well-known problem in the VPL field [4].

The Text Generated by the Code Generator Does Not Include Blank Spaces. The format in the textual editor does not have empty lines consisting only of white spaces between each phrase that has been added. This could make the generated scenarios less readable for the users. Additionally, correct indentation is also missing in the textual editor, which can affect how the users understand the hierarchy of the code.

The Solution Does Not Generate Blocks in the Correct Order for Some Cases. Sometimes when the blocks are generated from text, the order of the blocks are not correct. This is due to the AST nodes sometimes being processed in the wrong order. When two sibling AST nodes are found, the next and previous statements of the blocks are set, and the sibling blocks are connected to each other. However, these do not always align with the order of the siblings in the text. Sometimes the next and previous statements need to be inverted.

There are Some Transient Errors in the User Interface Due to Scripting Issues. Due to the usage of JavaScript for the developed solution, sometimes the environment behaves unexpectedly, although rare. The causes of the transient issues cannot always be pinpointed. However, the environment behaves normally again after a refresh of the page. An example transient error is that in rare cases, the blocks in the Blockly workspace disappear. However, they reappear when the user performs certain actions such as opening the developer console. When the page is refreshed, the blocks appear as normal. One of the consequences of this issue could be that the user's work is interrupted and their workflow is temporarily affected.

6 Conclusion

This paper introduced an EUP environment that synchronizes text and visual editors, enabling end users to develop programs using a DSL based on BDD. Finding from our evaluation in two use cases in the robotics domain demonstrated that the platform successfully generates correct scenarios, allowing end users to program robot behaviors either textually or visually without requiring programming expertise. Built using Xtext and Blockly, the web-based platform maintains consistency between text and block-based representations, adding significant flexibility to the development environment. The platform, however, is currently constrained to a single DSL grammar, and exhibits limitations in handling BDD imperative scenarios and large programming blocks, reflecting the challenges of tooling and language synchronization [2,22]. This research highlights the feasibility of integrating textual and visual programming in a synchronized web-based environment, with potential for broader applications beyond the robotics domain. Future work include expanding support for additional configurations, refining the user interface, and conducting empirical studies with end users.

Acknowledgments. This work was funded by DIREC (Digital Research Centre Denmark) through the project "Low-Code Programming of Spatial Contexts for Logistic Tasks in Mobile Robotics". It was initiated by Peter Heilbo Ratgen and Joakim Schack Betzer; and further developed by Nida Basaran and Özge Yasayan. We're very thankful for their initial investigation that made this work possible.

References

1. Bau, D., Gray, J., Kelleher, C., Sheldon, J., Turbak, F.: Learnable programming: blocks and beyond. Commun. ACM **60**(6), 72–80 (2017). https://doi.org/10.1145/3015455
2. Bettini, L.: Implementing Domain-Specific Languages with Xtext and Xtend. Packt Publishing Ltd. (2016)
3. Burnett, M.M.: Visual Programming. Wiley (1999). https://doi.org/10.1002/047134608X.W1707
4. Burnett, M., Baker, M., Bohus, C., Carlson, P., Yang, S., Van Zee, P.: Scaling up visual programming languages. Computer **28**(3), 45–54 (1995). https://doi.org/10.1109/2.366157
5. C9: Ace - the high performance code editor for the web (2025). https://ace.c9.io/. Accessed March 2025
6. Chandorkar, A., Patkar, N., Di Sorbo, A., Nierstrasz, O.: An exploratory study on the usage of gherkin features in open-source projects. In: 2022 IEEE International Conference on Software Analysis, Evolution and Reengineering (SANER), pp. 1159–1166. IEEE (2022)
7. Chelimsky, D., Astels, D., Helmkamp, B., North, D., Dennis, Z., Hellesoy, A.: The RSpec Book: Behaviour Driven Development with RSpec, Cucumber, and Friends. Pragmatic Bookshelf (2010)
8. Gherkin: Gherkin syntax (2023). https://cucumber.io/docs/gherkin/. Accessed March 2025
9. Google: Blockly (2025). https://developers.google.com/blockly. Accessed March 2025
10. Harley, A.: Similarity principle in visual design. Nielsen Norman Group (2020). https://www.nngroup.com/articles/gestalt-similarity/. Accessed 16 May 2024
11. Kosar, T., Bohra, S., Mernik, M.: Domain-specific languages: a systematic mapping study. Inf. Softw. Technol. **71**, 77–91 (2016)
12. Lieberman, H., Paternò, F., Klann, M., Wulf, V.: End-user development: an emerging paradigm. In: End User Development, pp. 1–8. Springer (2006)
13. Mernik, M., Heering, J., Sloane, A.M.: When and how to develop domain-specific languages. ACM Comput. Surv. (CSUR) **37**(4), 316–344 (2005)
14. North, D.: Introducing BDD (2006). https://dannorth.net/introducing-bdd/. Accessed 24 Jan 2025
15. Pasternak, E., Fenichel, R., Marshall, A.N.: Tips for creating a block language with blockly. In: 2017 IEEE Blocks and Beyond Workshop (B&B), pp. 21–24. IEEE (2017)

16. Resnick, M., et al.: Scratch: programming for all. Commun. ACM **52**(11), 60–67 (2009). https://doi.org/10.1145/1592761.1592779
17. Silva, T.R.: Towards a domain-specific language to specify interaction scenarios for web-based graphical user interfaces. In: Companion of the 2022 ACM SIGCHI Symposium on Engineering Interactive Computing Systems, EICS 2022. ACM (2022). https://doi.org/10.1145/3531706.3536463
18. Silva, T.R.: Towards a domain-specific language for behaviour-driven development. In: 2023 IEEE Symposium on Visual Languages and Human-Centric Computing (VL/HCC), pp. 283–286 (2023). https://doi.org/10.1109/VL-HCC57772.2023.00054
19. Ur, B., McManus, E., Pak Yong Ho, M., Littman, M.L.: Practical trigger-action programming in the smart home. In: Proceedings of the SIGCHI Conference on Human Factors in Computing Systems, CHI 2014, pp. 803–812. Association for Computing Machinery, New York (2014). https://doi.org/10.1145/2556288.2557420
20. Verano Merino, M., Beckmann, T., van der Storm, T., Hirschfeld, R., Vinju, J.J.: Getting grammars into shape for block-based editors. In: Proceedings of the 14th ACM SIGPLAN International Conference on Software Language Engineering, SLE 2021, pp. 83–98. Association for Computing Machinery, New York (2021). https://doi.org/10.1145/3486608.3486908
21. Verano Merino, M., van der Storm, T.: Block-based syntax from context-free grammars. In: Proceedings of the 13th ACM SIGPLAN International Conference on Software Language Engineering, SLE 2020, pp. 283–295. Association for Computing Machinery, New York (2020). https://doi.org/10.1145/3426425.3426948
22. Wendel, D., Medlock-Walton, P.: Thinking in blocks: implications of using abstract syntax trees as the underlying program model. In: 2015 IEEE Blocks and Beyond Workshop (Blocks and Beyond), pp. 63–66. IEEE (2015)

OMNI: An EUD Tool for Ontological Multisensory Navigation Interface

Attilio Della Greca[1(✉)], Álvaro Montero[2], Ilaria Amaro[1], Ignacio Aedo[2], Paloma Diaz[2], and Teresa Onorati[2]

[1] University of Salerno, Salerno, Italy
{adellagreca,iamaro}@unisa.it
[2] University Carlos III, Madrid, Spain
{ammontes,pdp,tonorati}@inf.uc3m.es, aedo@ia.uc3m.es

Abstract. The representation and exploration of ontologies still present significant challenges, particularly intuitiveness and user interface accessibility. Most approaches are based on textual structures and two-dimensional visualizations that fail to adequately reflect human cognitive and perceptual mechanisms based on multisensory integration. Multisensory interfaces are designed to improve understanding of concept relationships, reduce cognitive load, and improve information retention. To address this limitation, we propose OMNI (Ontological Multisensory Navigation Interface), an innovative tool that facilitates ontology navigation through a multisensory interface integrating visual, auditory, and tactile stimuli. Since multisensory interaction is still unexplored, OMNI has been conceived as an End-User Development (EUD) tool, allowing non-expert users to customize the ontology exploration. The tool enables the association of multisensory stimuli to semantic attributes without requiring programming skills so that experts in the domain of knowledge represented by the ontology can quickly explore different options. This research represents a preliminary step in a more extensive study to identify the most effective sensory codings for ontology representation.

Keywords: Virtual Reality · Ontology · End User Development (EUD) · Multisensory Interface

1 Introduction

An ontology is an explicit and structured representation of concepts, entities, and relations within a domain, designed to provide a simplified view of a reality, usually referred to as knowledge domain [11]. Noy and McGuinness [19] describe ontologies as formal models that identify the classes of a domain, their properties, and the constraints necessary to ensure their coherence. Therefore, an ontology is a knowledge organization model for a specific domain. Although ontologies allow for the effective organization of large volumes of information, designing user interfaces that facilitate efficient navigation in knowledge domains remains

C. Santoro et al. (Eds.): IS-EUD 2025, LNCS 15713, pp. 151–160, 2025.
https://doi.org/10.1007/978-3-031-95452-8_9

an open challenge [31]. This is particularly true considering that these structures are mainly designed for end users as experts in the domain of interest without a strong technical background.

Currently, interfaces for representing and exploring ontologies are mainly based on logical structures and textual annotations that can be complex and difficult to understand intuitively by domain experts unfamiliar with ontological notations. More advanced interfaces often rely on static two-dimensional visualizations or textual search mechanisms to explore the relationships between concepts [24,25]. Although such approaches can be effective in specific contexts, they do not fully reflect the nature of the neural mechanisms involved in multisensory human cognitive and perceptual processes [13]. Furthermore, the use of static stimuli presented in a single modality can generate a cognitive overload for users, limiting their ability to explore and understand the complex relationships represented in ontologies [1,8].

Hence, a key limitation of most approaches lies in exploiting a unique sensory channel (the sight), while humans possess a natural ability to integrate multimodal stimuli to elaborate a holistic representation of the surrounding environment [26,30]. Multisensory perception is expected to improve memory skills, facilitate information storage and retrieval, and consolidate acquired knowledge [16]. This process is particularly relevant in the context of knowledge domain exploration, as a multisensory interface can act as a tool to improve not only the usability and accessibility of the knowledge but also the effectiveness of learning [15]. However, although the multisensory approach might promise benefits, the design of such interfaces requires a deep understanding of how to define an adequate sensorial mapping where stimuli are complementary and easily interpretable to avoid overlaps that may generate effects opposite to those desired, such as confusion or increased cognitive load [17]. Synchronization between sensory stimuli is crucial to ensure an effective user experience. A well-designed multisensory interaction can strengthen the understanding and learning of concepts and relationships within the ontology.

To address some of the challenges related to the multisensory representation and exploration of ontologies, we propose the OMNI (Ontological Multisensory Navigation Interface) tool that helps integrate three primary sensory modalities used in Human-Computer Interaction (HCI), namely sight, hearing, and touch. Since the use of multisensory feedback in knowledge processing is still an emerging research area, OMNI is conceived as an End-User Development tool (EUD), allowing users to explore the multisensory interaction with ontologies in two-dimensional (2D) and three-dimensional (3D) environments. Users can customize and experience sensory mappings for visual, auditory, and tactile stimuli. Adjusting such sensory settings can help reduce cognitive overload, favoring a clearer understanding of the complex relationships that characterize ontologies. The study presented here is the first step in a broader investigation of identifying patterns or heuristics that could help designers fully exploit the advantages of multisensory interaction.

2 Related Work

The topic of ontology visualization and exploration has been widely discussed in the literature to address the challenges related to the representation and interaction with complex and abstract knowledge structures. Marques et al. [14] conducted a systematic review, highlighting the need to identify and adopt ontology visualization tools capable of reducing cognitive load and improving user interaction. In particular, the authors emphasize that most commonly used visualization tools offer limited interaction modes to edit and explore the ontology. Moreover, advanced visualization techniques could be less familiar to users, making operations over the concepts and relations more difficult. For this reason, they suggest making the most of traditional techniques, focusing on exploring how to exploit other characteristics, like textures, colors, or other senses.

In the work of Katifori and Halatsis [12], the authors reviewed several ontology visualization tools and classified them into six categories, including indented lists, node-link diagrams, zoomable, space-filling, focus and context (distortion-based), and 3D information landscapes. Their analysis highlighted the limitations of traditional two-dimensional visualizations, which often do not provide an intuitive understanding of complex relationships. Based on these observations, the authors suggest that adopting more interactive and immersive visualization methods can significantly improve the user experience. Immersive analytics is indeed an emerging research topic that focuses on "the use of engaging, embodied analysis tools to support data understanding and decision making", on the assumption that more immersive experiences facilitate situated analytics, embodied data exploration, multisensory presentation, and more informed and increased engagement with data [9]. Research has highlighted that multisensory stimuli can promote information retention by exploiting the principles of embodied cognition, suggesting that cognitive processes are strongly influenced by sensory and perceptual experiences [3]. In ontology representations, such results have fundamental relevance since combining different sensory modalities can make relations among concepts more understandable and intuitive for users. Although numerous studies have highlighted the importance of integrating multisensory stimuli in user interface design [7,18,27,28], there are still significant challenges in designing adaptive interfaces that align with the nature of human cognitive processes.

The design of effective multisensory interfaces remains a complex task. Ensuring that the representation of ontological concepts is consistent and interpretable across visual, auditory, and tactile stimuli requires a thorough understanding of how stimuli and meanings should be coordinated in efficient sensorial mappings. Determining the appropriate combinations and weightings of different sensory modalities to avoid cognitive overload while maximizing understanding is still critical [29]. Furthermore, cross-cultural factors add further complexity to the design process, as different cultural backgrounds may interpret sensory stimuli differently [4,5]. Previous works of the research team on multisensory immersive analytics demonstrated that people experience sensory stimuli differently.

Therefore, using a unique sensorial mapping could be counterproductive [21,22]. Adaptable interfaces might be required to take into account these variabilities.

Considering the challenges posed by integrating multisensory feedback, more research is needed to understand how to design effective experiences that rely upon adaptive interfaces to optimize user interaction with ontologies. In this context, end-user tools emerge as a feasible approach, enabling non-experts to adapt the ontology visualization. Indeed, EUD tools have already been used to make accessible the refinement of ontological representations to experts in the domain knowledge, who are not very familiar with ontological notations [2,6,23]. In this work, we use EUD to increase such notations with multisensory interactions by integrating three distinct sensory modalities: sight, hearing, and touch. This tool is part of a research project that will include the analysis of a case study with users from different cultural backgrounds. The final goal of this research is to identify the most effective stimuli and the most suitable sensory features to represent an ontology and its attributes, taking into account the variations in sensory perceptions and the influence of cultural factors on their interpretation.

3 OMNI: Enabling End Users to Define Multisensory Interactions with Ontologies

This section details the design and implementation choices that led to the development of OMNI, as shown in Fig. 1, an EUD prototype for multisensory interaction with ontologies.

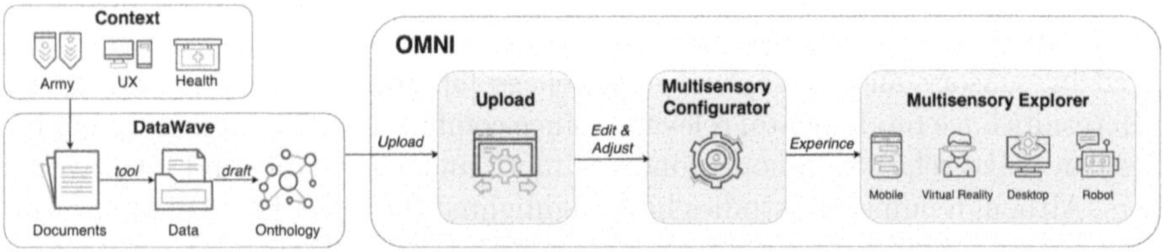

Fig. 1. The proposed architecture of the prototype

3.1 Scenario of Use

To better understand what OMNI can be used for, let us imagine a scenario where Nate, an HCI teacher who has worked with ontologies, has used an ontological representation to help his students explore all the concepts and their underlying relationships in this multi-disciplinary domain. Each concept and relationship has three different attributes: the relevance, assigned by Nate based on his expertise in this domain; popularity, automatically calculated according to the number of concept's visits or relationships activation; and the connectedness that is automatically calculated given the centrality of a concept in the network or the centrality of the connected concepts in a relationship. How can three different attributes be represented without ending up in a messy visualization? Using other senses to deploy information about various attributes might be a good option. However, how does Nate define the proper multisensory codification? Nate is an expert in HCI but implementing a multisensory interaction goes far beyond his technical abilities.

Here is where OMNI can help Nate by providing him with a visual interface to add several multisensory feedbacks to his ontology elements and automatically create an immersive experience that he can test to get feedback on how the codifications he designed work in the real world. Hence, the end-users of OMNI would be ontology editors aiming to add multi-sensorial feedback to immersive experiences of their ontological representations.

3.2 Design Approach

OMNI addresses the limitations of traditional 2D and text-based interfaces by integrating visual, auditory, and tactile sensory channels to support the understanding of complex ontological structures within an immersive 3D environment. As an EUD tool, OMNI allows users like Nate to personalize interaction modalities and dynamically configure sensory attributes tied to ontology elements. It automatically generates immersive VR visualizations using the immersive bubbles technique [20]. The system architecture (Fig. 1) includes:

Dataware: In a previous contribution, we developed DataWave, a tool to collect and process unstructured textual documents and create knowledge graphs [10]. The users can interact with each phase of DataWave, choosing the machine learning model to process the text data and editing the resulting concepts and relations, both textually and visually. The OMNI tool can be integrated into DataWave as the visualization module, designed to support dynamic personalization by enabling the synergistic integration of different sensory channels and laying the foundation for future automatic adaptation mechanisms based on user preferences and interactions.

OMNI: The tool consists of three core modules. The *Upload Module* allows users to import the ontology and edit or enrich attributes. The *Configuration Module* serves as a management and customization interface enabling the definition of the multisensory stimuli associated with the attributes of the elements of the ontology to be represented. The *Multisensory Explorer Module*, Multisensorythe immersive experience, creates and manages real-time dynamic interactions by generating interactive environments that combine visual, auditory, and tactile inputs, enabling users to navigate and manipulate the ontology. These modules communicate through APIs compatible with mobile, desktop, and VR platforms.

3.3 System Architecture

OMNI's architecture is structured in three main modules, which separate functionalities and facilitate the integration of different components.

Upload Module. This module provides an interface for importing existing ontologies in JSON format. During the import process, the module is in charge of automatically checking the format and internal structure of the file to extract concepts and relationships. The aim is to ensure that the imported information's structure and attributes (in our scenario therelevance, popularity and connectedness) are consistent for the subsequent process phases.

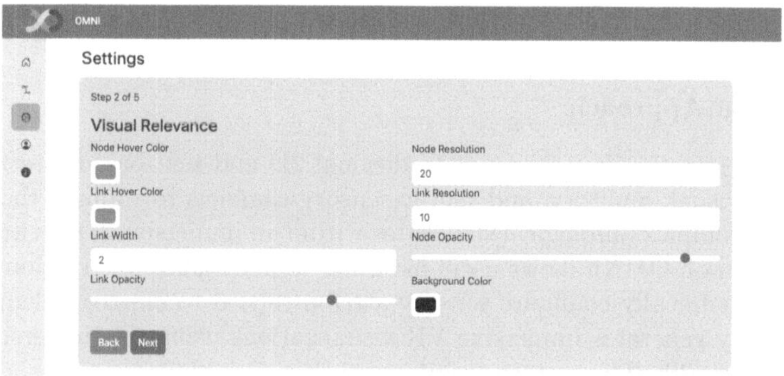

Fig. 2. Visual Relevance configuration panel of the OMNI configurator module.

Configurator Module. This module customises the ontology before transforming it into a multisensory immersive experience. The configuration panel shown in Fig. 2 allows the definition of the multisensory stimuli and the multisensory attributes of the elements of the ontology to be represented. The ontology could include a variety of attributes to help characterize concepts and relations depending on the knowledge domain and the scope. For example, adding the *relevance*, *connectedness* and the *popularity* as in the use scenario to each concept and relation can allow the user to explore the ontology following different strategies.

The configuration panel is an user-friendly wizard divided into six distinct steps, as shown in Fig. 3, divided into:

1. **Instructions:** This introductory step provides clear and concise guidance to users, outlining the configuration process and explaining the purpose of each subsequent step.
2. **Visual Channel Settings:** Users configure visual stimuli associated with ontology attributes. Available visual variables include color, size, and opacity.

Fig. 3. Schema of the configuration wizard divided in six steps to customize the multisensory representation of an ontology.

3. **Auditory Channel Settings:** Users can choose from audio characteristics such as pitch, volume, and type of sound effects to represent different attributes clearly and intuitively.
4. **Tactile Channel Settings:** Users specify tactile feedback if supported by the device e.g. controller or mobile for attribute representation. The module supports multiple tactile stimuli, including vibration intensity, patterns, and durations.
5. **Save Settings:** In this step, users select the preferred saving options and review a comprehensive summary of all sensory mappings configured in previous steps.
6. **Download of the Experience:** Finally, users can download the configured ontology either as an APK file, suitable for use on VR headsets, or directly preview and test the resulting multisensory interactive experience within the Multisensory Explorer Module. This ensures users can immediately verify and experience their customized ontology interactions.

Multisensory Explorer Module. The Multisensory Explorer Module enables users to experience the configured multisensory ontology interactively. It consists of two key features:

Interactive Multisensory Preview - This feature provides a real-time preview environment where users can directly interact with the configured ontology. A dynamic network graph is created where concepts are represented as spheres and relationships as connecting arcs, as shown in Fig. 4 As users navigate, zoom, and select elements within the graph, audio cues and tactile responses are triggered in real time. This dynamic interaction between sensory channels enriches the exploration process by providing immediate and contextual feedback. In this way, users, like Nate, can immediately evaluate the effectiveness and appropriateness of their multisensory settings.

Cross-platform Compatibility - allows users to download the multisensory ontology experiences specifically tailored for VR headsets, Desktop and mobile devices. Additionally, future expansions of OMNI aim to support emerging technologies, including social robots and chatbots, further broadening the potential for diverse user engagement and accessibility.

3.4 Technical and Implementation Details

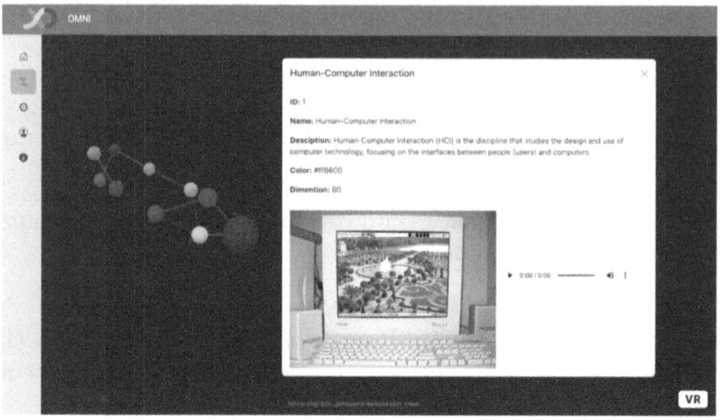

Fig. 4. Example of the Multisensory Explorer module

A modular software architecture based on internal APIs has been implemented to ensure seamless integration and efficient communication among the various modules. The upload and configurator module was prototyped using web technologies, (HTML5, CSS3, and JavaScript) and libraries such as WebXR and 3D Force-Directed Graph, enabling real-time spatial rendering and interactive data visualization. The Multisensory Explorer Module uses web technologies for Desktop and Mobile, while the VR version is developed with Unity, leveraging its capabilities for managing visual, auditory, and haptic feedback. This setup ensures scalable, responsive, and well-coordinated multisensory experiences.

4 Conclusion

This paper introduces OMNI, a multisensory user development tool designed to optimize the exploration of ontologies, providing various sensorial feedback to represent concepts and relations in the ontology in an immersive visualization. OMNI aims to provide a more intuitive and accessible mechanism to define such multi-sensory and immersive experiences non-experts who can easily define and test sensorial codings assigned to specific attributes of the ontology components. The main characteristic of OMNI is giving domain experts the possibility to customize the sensory channels involved in the interaction (i.e., visual, auditory, and tactile stimuli), and automatically create an immersive and multisensory experience that can be used with different devices to test the efficacy of alternative multisensory codings.

In future research, we plan to conduct a user study to identify the visual, tactile, and auditory stimuli most appropriate to represent the ontology attributes. We also plan to evaluate OMNI with students and teachers of a university HCI course to assess its utility and limitations. Possible improvements could be to add pre-defined attributes that can be automatically included in the ontology representation and a fourth module in the architecture to collect data from the interaction of the end users with the visualization. Future research will also provide insights into how multisensory stimuli can improve multisensory interaction with a visual representation of knowledge, such as an ontology.

References

1. Amadori, P.V., Fischer, T., Wang, R., Demiris, Y.: Predicting secondary task performance: a directly actionable metric for cognitive overload detection. IEEE Trans. Cogn. Dev. Syst. **14**(4), 1474–1485 (2021)
2. Barricelli, B.R., Cassano, F., Fogli, D., Piccinno, A.: End-user development, end-user programming and end-user software engineering: a systematic mapping study. J. Syst. Softw. **149**, 101–137 (2019)
3. Barsalou, L.W.: Grounded cognition. Ann. Rev. Psychol. **59**(1), 617–645 (2008)
4. Caballero, R., Paradis, C.: Making sense of sensory perceptions across languages and cultures. Funct. Lang. **22**(1), 1–19 (2015)
5. Cao, L., Gross, J.: Cultural differences in perceiving sounds generated by others: self matters. Front. Psychol. **6**, 1865 (2015)
6. Carrion, B., Onorati, T., Díaz, P., Triga, V.: A taxonomy generation tool for semantic visual analysis of large corpus of documents. Multimedia Tools Appl. **78**(23), 32919–32937 (2019). https://doi.org/10.1007/s11042-019-07880-y
7. Casillo, M., Colace, F., Lorusso, A., Santaniello, D., Valentino, C.: Integrating physical and virtual experiences in cultural tourism: an adaptive multimodal recommender system. IEEE Access (2025)
8. Castro-Alonso, J.C., Sweller, J.: The modality effect of cognitive load theory. In: Karwowski, W., Ahram, T., Nazir, S. (eds.) AHFE 2019. AISC, vol. 963, pp. 75–84. Springer, Cham (2020). https://doi.org/10.1007/978-3-030-20135-7_7
9. Dwyer, T., et al.: Immersive analytics: an introduction. In: Immersive Analytics, pp. 1–23 (2018)
10. Elvira-Martín, L., Onorati, T., Diaz Pérez, P.: Datawave-an interactive and visual tool for creating and exploring large knowledge bases. In: Proceedings of the 2024 International Conference on Advanced Visual Interfaces, pp. 1–3 (2024)
11. Gruber, T.R.: A translation approach to portable ontology specifications. Knowl. Acquis. **5**(2), 199–220 (1993)
12. Katifori, A., Halatsis, C., Lepouras, G., Vassilakis, C., Giannopoulou, E.: Ontology visualization methods-a survey. ACM Comput. Surv. (CSUR) **39**(4), 10–es (2007)
13. Körding, K.P., Beierholm, U., Ma, W.J., Quartz, S., Tenenbaum, J.B., Shams, L.: Causal inference in multisensory perception. PLoS ONE **2**(9), e943 (2007)
14. Marques, E.G., Araújo, C., Henriques, P.R.: Ontology visualization tools: a bibliographic review and a proposal. In: 13th Symposium on Languages, Applications and Technologies (SLATE 2024), pp. 3–1. Schloss Dagstuhl–Leibniz-Zentrum für Informatik (2024)
15. Marucci, M., et al.: The impact of multisensory integration and perceptual load in virtual reality settings on performance, workload and presence. Sci. Rep. **11**(1), 4831 (2021)
16. Matusz, P.J., Wallace, M.T., Murray, M.M.: A multisensory perspective on object memory. Neuropsychologia **105**, 243–252 (2017)

17. McCormack, J., et al.: Multisensory immersive analytics. In: Immersive Analytics, pp. 57–94 (2018)
18. Mishra, A., Shukla, A., Rana, N.P., Dwivedi, Y.K.: From "touch" to a "multisensory" experience: the impact of technology interface and product type on consumer responses. Psychol. Mark. **38**(3), 385–396 (2021)
19. Noy, N.F., McGuinness, D.L., et al.: Ontology development 101: a guide to creating your first ontology (2001)
20. Onorati, T., Muñoz, C.B., Díaz, P., Aedo, I.: Exploring the affordances of immersive visualization spaces: a use case about covid-19. In: International Conference on Ubiquitous Computing and Ambient Intelligence, pp. 252–263. Springer, Heidelberg (2022). https://doi.org/10.1007/978-3-031-21333-5_25
21. Rey, A., Bellucci, A., Díaz, P., Aedo, I.: The effect of teleporting versus room-scale walking for interacting with immersive visualizations. In: IFIP Conference on Human-Computer Interaction, pp. 110–119. Springer, Heidelberg (2023). https://doi.org/10.1007/978-3-031-21333-5_25
22. Rey, A., Bellucci, A., Díaz, P., Aedo, I.: The more the better? Multisensory redundant mappings to convey information in abstract visualizations (2025)
23. Sanctorum, A., et al.: End-user engineering of ontology-based knowledge bases. Behav. Inf. Technol. **41**(9), 1811–1829 (2022)
24. Schulz, S., Stenzhorn, H., Boeker, M., Smith, B.: Strengths and limitations of formal ontologies in the biomedical domain. Revista electronica de comunicacao, informacao & inovacao em saude: RECIIS **3**(1), 31 (2009)
25. Seppälä, S., Schreiber, Y., Ruttenberg, A.: Textual and logical definitions in ontologies. In: Proceedings International Workshop on Definitions in Ontologies, vol. 2 (2014)
26. Sepulcre, J., Sabuncu, M.R., Yeo, T.B., Liu, H., Johnson, K.A.: Stepwise connectivity of the modal cortex reveals the multimodal organization of the human brain. J. Neurosci. **32**(31), 10649–10661 (2012)
27. Spence, C., Ho, C.: Multisensory interface design for drivers: past, present and future. Ergonomics **51**(1), 65–70 (2008)
28. Sutcliffe, A.: Multimedia and Virtual Reality: Designing Multisensory User Interfaces. Psychology Press (2003)
29. Vermeulen, N., Corneille, O., Niedenthal, P.M.: Sensory load incurs conceptual processing costs. Cognition **109**(2), 287–294 (2008)
30. Wallace, M.T., Stevenson, R.A.: The construct of the multisensory temporal binding window and its dysregulation in developmental disabilities. Neuropsychologia **64**, 105–123 (2014)
31. Zhu, M., Yasseri, T., Kertész, J.: Individual differences in knowledge network navigation. Sci. Rep. **14**(1), 8331 (2024)

Explanation-Driven Interventions for Artificial Intelligence Model Customization

Empowering End-Users to Tailor Black-Box AI in Rhinocytology

Andrea Esposito[1(✉)], Miriana Calvano[1], Antonio Curci[1,2], Francesco Greco[1], Rosa Lanzilotti[1], and Antonio Piccinno[1]

[1] Department of Computer Science, University of Bari Aldo Moro, Via E. Orabona 4, 70125 Bari, Italy
{andrea.esposito,miriana.calvano,antonio.curci, francesco.greco,rosa.lanzilotti,antonio.piccinno}@uniba.it
[2] Department of Computer Science, University of Pisa, Largo B. Ponte Corvo, 3, 56127 Pisa, Italy

Abstract. The integration of Artificial Intelligence (AI) in modern society is transforming how individuals perform tasks. In high-risk domains, ensuring human control over AI systems remains a key design challenge. This article presents a novel End-User Development (EUD) approach for black-box AI models, enabling users to edit explanations and influence future predictions through targeted interventions. By combining explainability, user control, and model adaptability, the proposed method advances Human-Centered AI (HCAI), promoting a symbiotic relationship between humans and adaptive, user-tailored AI systems.

Keywords: Customization · Black-box AI · Model Reconfiguration · Explainable AI (XAI) · Human-AI symbiosis

1 Introduction

Artificial Intelligence (AI) has become an integral component of decision-support systems in numerous domains, including healthcare, finance, and law [16]. While AI models could enhance decision-making, their reliance on complex, often opaque, algorithms presents a significant barrier to adoption [16], especially in high-stakes applications such as medical diagnostics [6]. End-users—typically domain experts rather than AI specialists—require mechanisms to refine and adjust AI behavior to better align with their expertise and contextual knowledge.

Most AI systems follow a one-size-fits-all approach, with limited support for post-deployment customization [5]. This lack of adaptability can lead to misaligned recommendations, loss of trust, and decreased usability. End-User Development (EUD) for AI seeks to address this issue by enabling non-technical users to customize AI behavior according to their specific needs [12].

While the integration of EUD for AI has made substantial progress in fields such as the Internet of Things (IoT), education, and business analytics [11,20], AI-based

C. Santoro et al. (Eds.): IS-EUD 2025, LNCS 15713, pp. 161–170, 2025.
https://doi.org/10.1007/978-3-031-95452-8_10

decision-support systems—especially those powered by black-box models—remain challenging for users to modify. Current approaches to AI customization for end-users are (i) *Rule-Based Customization* [11], (ii) *Low-Code/No-Code AI* [20], and (iii) *Human-AI Collaboration Interfaces* [8, 22]. The first one involves the definition from the user of if-this-then-that conditions to influence AI outputs. On the other hand, the platforms that adopt *Low-Code/No-Code AI* allow users to build and deploy AI models without programming (e.g., AutoML tools), but they do not enable real-time intervention on model behavior post-deployment. Lastly, *Human-AI Collaboration Interfaces* enable users to validate and/or override the system's predictions without affecting its future behavior. These approaches do not fully address the need for an interactive and iterative refinement of AI behavior based on human expertise. Using professionals' knowledge and expertise to refine AI reasoning can be a valuable resource to improve the system's performance while building a stronger symbiotic relationship between the two parties [8, 15].

Creating AI-based systems that embody these characteristics can foster collaboration, establishing a symbiotic relationship between humans and AI. Symbiotic Artificial Intelligence (SAI) is a specialization of Human-Centered AI [26] and aims at supporting humans instead of replacing them. This implies creating solutions that reflect humans' needs and preferences by integrating intervention paradigms, transparency, and fairness by design focusing on augmentation rather than automation [8, 17].

This research proposes a novel intervention-based User Interface (UI) within the *Rhino-Cyt* platform, designed to empower rhinocytologists to modify AI-generated classifications and explanations. This proposal aims at embodying the *EUDability* construct [4] by introducing an innovative explanation-driven EUD approach, allowing end-users to adjust AI classifications, edit AI-generated explanations, and indirectly refine and tailor the AI model through the mechanism of *interventions* [24]. This approach goes beyond rule-based or component-based customization, offering a *human-in-the-loop* model refinement paradigm. Thus, Rhino-Cyt involves rhinocytologists as its end-user developers, supporting them in reaching the goal of diagnosing.

The rest of the article is structured as follows. Section 2 discusses prior research in EUD for AI, explainability, and human-AI collaboration, also presenting Rhino-Cyt. Section 3 presents the design of the intervention-based UI, detailing its interaction flow and impact on AI adaptation. Section 4 positions Rhino-Cyt within existing EUD for AI taxonomies and compares it with other customization paradigms. Section 5 concludes this article by summarizing its key contributions and outlining the next steps.

2 Background and Related Work

This section reviews prior research on EUD for AI, explainability as a mechanism for EUD, and human-AI collaboration in decision-support systems.

2.1 End-User Development for AI

EUD encompasses a range of methods, techniques, tools, and socio-technical environments that empower non-professionals to engage in activities usually reserved for professionals in ICT-related areas, including the ability to create, modify, extend, and test digital artifacts without requiring specialized knowledge in conventional software engineering practices [3]. A systematic literature review by Esposito et al. categorized existing EUD for AI approaches into five key paradigms [11]:

1. *Component-Based:* Users assemble predefined AI components through visual programming interfaces.
2. *Rule-Based:* Users are allowed to modify AI behavior through "if-then" rules.
3. *Wizard-Based:* Step-by-step guidance simplifies AI customization, presenting the task as a sequence of operations that guide users throughout the overall activity.
4. *Template-Based:* Users adjust pre-built AI models by modifying parameters.
5. *Workflow and Data Diagrams:* Users define AI processes using flow-based representations.

While these approaches are effective for tasks such as building AI models from scratch or configuring predefined automation rules, they offer limited support for modifying existing black-box AI models. *Explanation-driven interventions* extend EUD for AI by introducing a new paradigm. Instead of requiring users to manipulate AI model components or logic directly, this proposal allows them to edit AI-generated explanations, *indirectly* refining the model's behavior over time.

In this regard, explainability has rarely been explored as an active mechanism for EUD. EXplainable Artificial Intelligence (XAI) seeks to make AI model decisions more interpretable and transparent [16,23]. Through XAI, users can understand AI decisions, deciding whether to rely on its predictions or potentially recognize (and mitigate) biases by assessing its reasoning [16].

In most AI-assisted decision systems, explanations are static, not allowing users to modify them to influence future AI behavior. Our proposal introduces a novel editable explanation mechanism where users can modify explanations associated with AI classifications, provide domain-specific refinements to ensure AI-generated explanations align with expert knowledge, and influence future AI behavior indirectly.

2.2 Human-AI Collaboration in Decision Support Systems

AI-based decision-support systems, especially in medicine, often follow a *human-on-the-loop* paradigm, where users oversee the decision-making process by interacting with AI outputs to merely validate its decisions [8,13,25]. This translates into a validation-based collaboration, where experts review AI predictions but have no direct manipulation mechanism for modifying the AI's reasoning process [8].

Our proposal aims at filling this gap following the model of human–AI interaction proposed by Desolda et al. [7], moving beyond this by enabling direct, explanation-driven interventions, ensuring that AI's decision-making processes evolve alongside domain experts, fostering a symbiosis among humans and AI [8]. Establishing proper collaboration mechanisms between humans and AI is crucial to guarantee that professionals are aware of the processes that lead to outputs.

2.3 Rhino-Cyt: An AI-Based System for Rhinocitology

Our proposal leverages a case study in the context of rhinocytology (a subfield of medical cytology) [9,10]. Currently, the diagnostic process in rhinocytology is mainly based on direct observation under the microscope, which requires a prolonged effort by rhinocytologists [7,14].

Rhino-Cyt is an AI-assisted environment for the classification of nasal cytology samples that supports its end-user developers, i.e., medical professionals, in diagnosing inflammatory and allergic conditions [10]. It employs AI models (namely, a CNN) to automate the cytological examination by segmenting histological samples of the nasal mucosa, identifying and classifying individual cells based on nine cytotypes [10,14]: (i) ciliated, (ii) muciparous, (iii) basal cells, (iv) striated cells, (v) neutrophils, (vi) eosinophils, (vii) mast cells, (viii) lymphocytes, (ix) metaplastic cells.

3 Design of the Intervention-Based User Interface

Rhino-Cyt introduces an innovative intervention-based UI that allows rhinocytologists to refine AI-assisted classifications, presented in Fig. 1. Users can *intervene* modifying decisions and explanations, unlike conventional AI customization methods, which rely on rule-based or low-code paradigms [24].

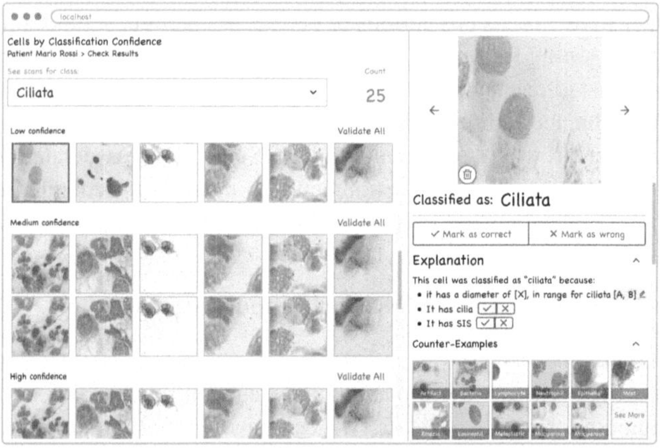

Fig. 1. The user interface for allowing black-box AI model tailoring implemented in Rhino-Cyt

This section details the design principles, UI components, and interaction workflow, demonstrating how the system aligns with EUD for AI by offering an explanation-driven intervention mechanism.

3.1 Design Rationale and Principles

The design of the Rhino-Cyt intervention UI follows three core principles derived from EUD for AI research [11], which emphasize the human intervention that leads to the AI customization while minimizing humans' cognitive load. The referred principles are:

1. *Intervention-Based Interaction.* The system allows logged users to adjust AI classifications and explanations tracking any modifications.
2. *Explainability-Driven Customization.* The system supports it by allowing users to refine AI-generated justifications without requiring them to modify raw model parameters or write explicit rules. Instead, the interface leverages editable explanations as a means of customization, enabling domain experts to adjust and improve AI-generated reasoning based on their medical expertise.
3. *Minimal Cognitive Load for Domain Experts.* The system is designed to minimize the cognitive load for domain experts by providing guided interventions that simplify the interaction process and reduce the need for technical expertise. AI adaptation occurs implicitly through user feedback, allowing the model to refine its reasoning without requiring manual retraining.

3.2 User Interface Components

The elements of Rhino-Cyt's UI (Fig. 1) that allow users to intervene on AI decisions consist of the following key components

1. The *Classification Details and Interventions Panel* presents AI-generated classifications, allowing users to review system decisions. If necessary, users can override AI's decisions by selecting an alternative category which is incorporated into the system, contributing to the continuous adaptation and improvement of the AI's future performance.
2. The *Editable Explanation Area* displays the AI-generated justifications of its classifications, providing transparency into the decision-making process. Users can modify these justifications to guarantee they align more closely with their expertise. Any edits made by users directly influence the AI's reasoning model, refining its approach and shaping future justifications.

3.3 Interaction Workflow: How Users Intervene in AI Decisions

The Rhino-Cyt intervention workflow is structured as a three-step process.

Step 1: Reviewing AI-Generated Classification and Explanation. Upon analyzing a nasal cytology sample, the AI presents a predicted classification and a textual explanation justifying the classification.

Step 2: User Intervention via Adjustment or Explanation Editing. The users have two options for intervention: they can either override the AI classification by selecting an alternative label or modify the AI-generated explanation to reflect expert reasoning more accurately, or both.

Step 3: Model Adaptation and Visualization of Impact. The system logs interventions and updates the AI's explanation model.

This workflow enables AI adaptation to be progressive, ensuring the model evolves alongside experts' knowledge, thus creating a human-in-the-loop customization mechanism for AI-supported decision-making.

3.4 Underlying AI Model Adaptation

Our proposal balances manual user intervention with an automated model refinement process based on users' feedback, thus providing an example of both an *adaptable* and *adaptive* system [12].

The platform continuously logs user interactions, capturing every action performed by users. This includes explicit feedback on the AI model's predictions, where users can either accept the suggested classification or reject it and make modifications. The collected feedback is then leveraged to initiate the retraining of the AI model.

To enhance the adaptivity and adaptability of the AI system, several techniques can be employed, ranging from online learning [1,27] to reinforcement learning from human feedback [18], leveraging detailed explanation obtained either from a gray-box model (as the one presented by Desolda et al. [7]) or through large-language models. Specifically, user feedback on explanations helps refine the AI model in different ways. If there is a direct, one-to-one relationship between an explanation and the model's decision-making process—as seen in decision trees—the model can be updated immediately. In contrast, when using more complex models, such as deep learning, the feedback is transformed into additional data points that contribute to adjusting the model's internal parameters.

4 Positioning Explanation-Driven Interventions as an EUD Tool for AI

The Rhino-Cyt intervention UI introduces a novel approach to EUD for AI, using editable explanations as an AI customization mechanism. This section explores Rhino-Cyt's classification within the current EUD for AI landscape, comparing it with existing AI customization approaches while also examining its impact on human-AI symbiosis. Rhino-Cyt's main features are summarized in Table 1 and described below to highlight the customization aspects of the interaction workflow.

It enables end-users to customize its functionalities through explanation-driven intervention. Based on the information highlighted in the explanation, users can take actions such as marking the explanation as accurate or incorrect or adjusting the feature values used in the reasoning process. This approach puts physicians in control by allowing them to refine the system's outputs and justifications, enhancing its performance, especially in cases involving outliers. In this context, user actions can represent feedback for the system that can adapt its behavior over time.

To classify Rhino-Cyt within the existing EUD for AI landscape, we adopt a recent framework proposed by Esposito et al. [11], which categorizes EUD AI solutions based on the dimensions presented in Table 2.

Table 1. A summary of the main features of Rhino-Cyt's intervention-based UI

Feature	Rhino-Cyt's Intervention UI
Customization Approach	Explanation-driven intervention
User Control	Freeform modifications of AI outputs and justifications
Impact on Model Behavior	Direct, real-time adaptation
Technical Expertise Required	None (domain expertise only)

Table 2. Classification of the intervention-based UI according to [11]

EUD Dimension	Rhino-Cyt Implementation
Composition Paradigm	Explanation-driven, rule-based intervention
Target Users	Domain experts (rhinocytologists)
Technology	AI-assisted medical diagnostics
Usage	Single-user, with potential for collaborative interventions
Customization Level	Tailoring and indirect model refinement
Approach Output	AI model adaptation via explanation modifications

To illustrate the novelty of Rhino-Cyt, we compare it with three common AI customization paradigms: rule-based customization, no-code model building, and collaboration interfaces. The comparison is reported in Table 3.

Table 3. Comparison between the three common customization paradigms and the Rhino-Cyt intervention-based UI.

Approach	Customization Scope	Technical Expertise Required	Impact on AI Model
Rule-Based AI Customization	Predefined rule sets	Moderate	Direct, deterministic changes
No-Code AI Model Building	Component-based visual programming	Low	Configures AI before deployment
Human-AI Collaboration Interfaces	Users validate/override AI outputs	None	No direct AI adaptation
Explanation-Driven Intervention	Editable explanations influence AI reasoning	None	Indirect, adaptive refinements over time

Explanation-Driven Intervention enables users to manipulate the reasoning of the AI model by modifying the explanations. This approach becomes particularly effective in the medical context because no technical expertise is required: professionals can redirect and refine the systems' behavior merely by relying on their knowledge and background in their field. This approach enables adaptive learning ensuring the model evolves in alignment with expert reasoning.

Trust calibration is a major challenge in AI-assisted decision support, particularly in high-stakes domains like medicine [19]. More specifically, AI systems must be created ensuring that users do not simply accept AI recommendations blindly—or, conversely, dismiss them outright [2,6,21]. Our proposal tackles this challenge by allowing users to engage with the AI's reasoning process rather than just its final outputs. Instead of simply overriding a classification, experts can refine the reasoning behind it, fostering a symbiotic relationship in which both the user and the AI system learn in the process [8]. Through explanation-driven interventions, users' refinements gradually steer the AI model toward better, safer, and more reliable predictions. This approach positions AI as a collaborative partner, learning from domain expertise in a way that strengthens both accuracy and user confidence.

5 Conclusions and Future Work

This article proposed *explanation-driven interventions* as an EUD tool for black-box AI systems, illustrated through their adoption in Rhino-Cyt, a system aiding rhinocytologists in cell counting tasks. Unlike traditional AI customization methods that relegate domain experts to passive reviewers, explanation-driven interventions empowers them to directly manipulate AI-generated outputs and explanations, without any programming expertise. This work contributes to ongoing research in human-centered AI and AI-assisted decision supports EUD systems have the potential to bridge the gap between AI automation and expert oversight. Future work includes evaluating the usability and effectiveness of Rhino-Cyt through user studies, identifying improvement areas, and extending support to multi-user collaboration. Better methods for tracking intervention impact and mitigating user errors are also needed. Another key direction is assessing how editable explanations affect model performance, accuracy, and user cognitive load. Structured evaluations could clarify whether this approach enhances trust and understanding more than traditional rule-based customization. Finally, explanation-driven interventions hold promise beyond medicine, with potential in domains like law and finance where professionals must interpret and refine AI reasoning.

Acknowledgments. This research is partially supported by: (i) the co-funding of the European Union - Next Generation EU: NRRP Initiative, Mission 4, Component 2, Investment 1.3 - Partnerships extended to universities, research centers, companies and research D.D. MUR n. 341 del 15.03.2022 - Next Generation EU (PE0000013 - "Future Artificial Intelligence Research - FAIR" - CUP: H97G22000210007); (ii) the Italian Ministry of University and Research (MUR) and by the European Union - NextGenerationEU, Mission 4, Component 2, Investment 1.1, under grant PRIN 2022 PNRR "PROTECT: imPROving ciTizEn inClusiveness Through Conversational AI" (Grant P2022JJPBY) - CUP: H53D23008150001. The research of Andrea Esposito is funded by a Ph.D. fellowship within the framework of the Italian "D.M. n. 352, April 9, 2022"- under the National Recovery and Resilience Plan, Mission 4, Component 2, Investment 3.3 – Ph.D. Project "Human-Centred Artificial Intelligence (HCAI) techniques for supporting end users interacting with AI systems," co-supported by "Eusoft S.r.l." (CUP H91I22000410007). The research of Francesco Greco is funded by a Ph.D. fellowship within the framework of the Italian "D.M. n. 352, April 9, 2022"- under the National Recovery and Resilience Plan, Mission 4, Component 2, Investment 3.3 – Ph.D. Project "Investigating XAI techniques to help user defend from phishing attacks", co-supported by "Auriga S.p.A." (CUP H91I22000410007).

Disclosure of Interests. The authors have no competing interests to declare that are relevant to the content of this article.

References

1. Amari, S.: A theory of adaptive pattern classifiers. IEEE Trans. Electron. Comput. **EC-16**(3), 299–307 (1967). https://doi.org/10.1109/PGEC.1967.264666. http://ieeexplore.ieee.org/document/4039068/
2. Bach, T.A., Khan, A., Hallock, H., Beltrao, G., Sousa, S.: A systematic literature review of user trust in AI-enabled systems: an HCI perspective. Int. J. Hum.–Comput. Interact. **40**(5), 1251–1266 (2024). https://doi.org/10.1080/10447318.2022.2138826. https://www.tandfonline.com/doi/full/10.1080/10447318.2022.2138826
3. Barricelli, B.R., Cassano, F., Fogli, D., Piccinno, A.: End-user development, end-user programming and end-user software engineering: a systematic mapping study. J. Syst. Softw. **149**, 101–137 (2019). https://doi.org/10.1016/j.jss.2018.11.041
4. Barricelli, B.R., Fogli, D., Locoro, A.: EUDability: a new construct at the intersection of end-user development and computational thinking. J. Syst. Softw. **195**, 111516 (2023). https://doi.org/10.1016/j.jss.2022.111516. https://www.sciencedirect.com/science/article/pii/S0164121222001923
5. Chambers, O., Cohen, R., Grossman, M.R., Chen, Q.: Creating a user model to support user-specific explanations of AI systems. In: Adjunct Proceedings of the 30th ACM Conference on User Modeling, Adaptation and Personalization, pp. 163–166. ACM, Barcelona (2022). https://doi.org/10.1145/3511047.3537678
6. Combi, C., et al.: A manifesto on explainability for artificial intelligence in medicine. Artif. Intell. Med. **133**, 102423 (2022). https://doi.org/10.1016/j.artmed.2022.102423. https://www.sciencedirect.com/science/article/pii/S0933365722001750
7. Desolda, G., Dimauro, G., Esposito, A., Lanzilotti, R., Matera, M., Zancanaro, M.: A Human–AI interaction paradigm and its application to rhinocytology. Artif. Intell. Med. **155**, 102933 (2024). https://doi.org/10.1016/j.artmed.2024.102933. https://linkinghub.elsevier.com/retrieve/pii/S0933365724001751
8. Desolda, G., Esposito, A., Lanzilotti, R., Piccinno, A., Costabile, M.F.: From humancentered to symbiotic artificial intelligence: a focus on medical applications. Multimedia Tools Appl. (2024). https://doi.org/10.1007/s11042-024-20414-5. https://rdcu.be/d1RF4
9. Dimauro, G., et al.: Nasal cytology with deep learning techniques. Int. J. Med. Inf. **122**, 13–19 (2019). https://doi.org/10.1016/j.ijmedinf.2018.11.010. https://linkinghub.elsevier.com/retrieve/pii/S1386505618305951
10. Dimauro, G., Girardi, F., Gelardi, M., Bevilacqua, V., Caivano, D.: Rhino-Cyt: a system for supporting the rhinologist in the analysis of nasal cytology. In: Huang, D.-S., Jo, K.-H., Zhang, X.-L. (eds.) ICIC 2018. LNCS, vol. 10955, pp. 619–630. Springer, Cham (2018). https://doi.org/10.1007/978-3-319-95933-7_71
11. Esposito, A., et al.: End-user development for artificial intelligence: a systematic literature review. In: Spano, L.D., Schmidt, A., Santoro, C., Stumpf, S. (eds.) End-User Development, Lecture Notes in Computer Science, vol. 13917, pp. 19–34. Springer, Cham (2023). https://doi.org/10.1007/978-3-031-34433-6_2. https://rdcu.be/dd32o
12. Fischer, G.: Adaptive and adaptable systems: differentiating and integrating AI and EUD. In: Spano, L.D., Schmidt, A., Santoro, C., Stumpf, S. (eds.) End-User Development, vol. 13917, pp. 3–18. Springer, Cham (2023). https://doi.org/10.1007/978-3-031-34433-6_1
13. Fischer, J.E., Greenhalgh, C., Jiang, W., Ramchurn, S.D., Wu, F., Rodden, T.: In-the-loop or on-the-loop? Interactional arrangements to support team coordination with a planning agent.

Concurr. Comput. Pract. Exp. **33**(8), e4082 (2021). https://doi.org/10.1002/cpe.4082, https://onlinelibrary.wiley.com/doi/10.1002/cpe.4082
14. Gelardi, M.: Atlas of Nasal Cytology. Edi.Ermes s.r.l., 14 edn. (2012)
15. Grigsby, S.S.: Artificial intelligence for advanced human-machine symbiosis. In: Schmorrow, D.D., Fidopiastis, C.M. (eds.) AC 2018. LNCS (LNAI), vol. 10915, pp. 255–266. Springer, Cham (2018). https://doi.org/10.1007/978-3-319-91470-1_22
16. Guidotti, R., Monreale, A., Ruggieri, S., Turini, F., Giannotti, F., Pedreschi, D.: A survey of methods for explaining black box models. ACM Comput. Surv. **51**(5), 1–42 (2019). https://doi.org/10.1145/3236009
17. Jarrahi, M.H.: Artificial intelligence and the future of work: human-AI symbiosis in organizational decision making. Bus. Horizons **61**(4), 577–586 (2018). https://doi.org/10.1016/j.bushor.2018.03.007. https://linkinghub.elsevier.com/retrieve/pii/S0007681318300387
18. Kaufmann, T., Weng, P., Bengs, V., Hüllermeier, E.: A Survey of Reinforcement Learning from Human Feedback (2023). https://doi.org/10.48550/ARXIV.2312.14925. https://arxiv.org/abs/2312.14925
19. Kobayashi, K., Takamizawa, Y., Miyake, M., Ito, S., Gu, L., Nakatsuka, T., Akagi, Y., Harada, T., Kanemitsu, Y., Hamamoto, R.: Can physician judgment enhance model trustworthiness? A case study on predicting pathological lymph nodes in rectal cancer. Artif. Intell. Med. **154**, 102929 (2024). https://doi.org/10.1016/j.artmed.2024.102929. https://linkinghub.elsevier.com/retrieve/pii/0933365724001714
20. Li, L., Wu, Z.: How can no/low code platforms help end-users develop ml applications? - A systematic review. In: Chen, J.Y.C., Fragomeni, G., Degen, H., Ntoa, S. (eds.) HCI International 2022 – Late Breaking Papers: Interacting with eXtended Reality and Artificial Intelligence, vol. 13518, pp. 338–356. Springer, Cham (2022). https://doi.org/10.1007/978-3-031-21707-4_25
21. Mehta, V.: Artificial intelligence in medicine: revolutionizing healthcare for improved patient outcomes. J. Med. Res. Innov. **7**(2), e000292 (2023). https://doi.org/10.32892/jmri.292. https://jmrionline.com/jmri/article/view/292
22. Raees, M., Meijerink, I., Lykourentzou, I., Khan, V.J., Papangelis, K.: From explainable to interactive AI: a literature review on current trends in human-AI interaction. Int. J. Hum.-Comput. Stud. **189**, 103301 (2024). https://doi.org/10.1016/j.ijhcs.2024.103301. https://linkinghub.elsevier.com/retrieve/pii/S1071581924000855
23. Sahoh, B., Choksuriwong, A.: The role of explainable Artificial Intelligence in highstakes decision-making systems: a systematic review. J. Ambient Intell. Humanized Comput. **14**(6), 7827–7843 (2023). https://doi.org/10.1007/s12652-023-04594-w
24. Schmidt, A., Herrmann, T.: Intervention user interfaces: a new interaction paradigm for automated systems. Interactions **24**(5), 40–45 (2017). https://doi.org/10.1145/3121357
25. Sherson, J., Rabecq, B., Dellermann, D., Rafner, J.: A multi-dimensional development and deployment framework for hybrid intelligence. In: Lukowicz, P., Mayer, S., Koch, J., Shawe-Taylor, J., Tiddi, I. (eds.) Frontiers in Artificial Intelligence and Applications. IOS Press (2023). https://doi.org/10.3233/FAIA230119. https://ebooks.iospress.nl/doi/10.3233/FAIA230119
26. Shneiderman, B.: Human-Centered AI, 1st edn. Oxford University Press, Oxford (2022)
27. Tallec, C., Ollivier, Y.: Unbiased online recurrent optimization. In: International Conference on Learning Representations (eb 2018). https://openreview.net/forum?id=rJQDjk-0b

Evaluating Visual Prompting Modalities for Generative AI-Assisted UI Design

Tommaso Calò(✉) and Luigi De Russis

Politecnico di Torino, Corso Duca degli Abruzzi 24, 10129 Turin, Italy
{tommaso.calo,luigi.derussis}@polito.it

Abstract. The emergence of Generative AI systems has dramatically transformed design workflows across multiple domains. While text prompting remains the dominant interaction method with these systems, visual prompting—the practice of guiding AI generation through visual or semantic structure—offers designers potentially greater control and expressivity. A critical challenge for design practitioners lies in understanding how different visual prompting modalities integrate into established creative processes and impact design outcomes. This study examines this challenge in the context of UI mockup generation, a domain with well-defined semantic elements and established design methodologies. We evaluate two visual prompting approaches: *free-form visual prompting*, which creates outputs based on hand-drawn sketches, and *semantic-constrained prompting*, which uses predefined visual vocabularies to guide generation. Through experiments with 13 design practitioners, we explore how different prompting modalities impact both designer experience and output quality in the creation of UI artifacts. Results reveal that free-form visual prompting offers superior intuitiveness and expressiveness for ideation, while semantic-constrained prompting produces higher quality and fidelity outputs. Our findings suggest that effective visual prompting strategies should adapt to different stages of the design process, with implications for generative AI applications in design practice. We propose a hybrid approach that leverages the strengths of both modalities throughout the creative workflow, potentially offering design practitioners across domains a more balanced framework for designer-AI collaboration.

Keywords: Visual Guidance · Generative AI · UI Design · User Interfaces · Design Practitioners · Image Generation · Human-AI Collaboration

1 Introduction and Background

User interface designers face daily challenges in creating designs that are effective, usable, and innovative. They often draw inspiration from existing design samples to come up with new ideas [17]. There are two main types of resources that support this process of finding inspiration [19]. The first type are design

C. Santoro et al. (Eds.): IS-EUD 2025, LNCS 15713, pp. 171–181, 2025.
https://doi.org/10.1007/978-3-031-95452-8_11

gallery platforms, such as Dribbble [2] and Behance [1], which allow designers to browse through a collection of designs and find examples that are interesting or useful for their work. The second type are design inspirational tools that suggest examples based on certain types of design input, such as a sketch or an existing design, using algorithms to determine image similarity [4,26,34,37]. While these approaches can be helpful in finding inspiration, they have limitations. Browsing through design galleries can be overwhelming and lead to a shift in design ideas away from the original focus, while relying too much on examples with similar styles can lead to design fixation and hinder the originality of the work [21,28]. Artificial Intelligence has emerged as a potential tool for supporting and enhancing the creative process [36]. AI systems can be trained to generate ideas and outputs based on a set of rules or guidelines, enabling the efficient production of a wide range of options, and providing a variety of applications and systems to support professionals in various visual art fields, such as graphic design [38], UI design [39], webtoon [23], digital art [41], and new media art [33]. Scholars are increasingly studying AI-powered, AI-enhanced, or AI-assisted human creativity [8,10,11,14,29], reporting the application of AI in the creative industry [3] and art industries [9]. Designers and design researchers have also discussed and practiced data-driven design [13,18,22]. Recent advancements in text-to-image (T2I) model capabilities have enabled the generation of realistic images from textual descriptions [5]. These models not only streamline the process of visualizing concepts but may also spark unexpected creative inspirations for users [35]. To find a balance between targeted and serendipitous inspiration, Mozaffari et al. [30] proposed a style-based generative adversarial network (StyleGAN) trained on a large dataset of existing interface designs. It generates a diverse yet focused set of examples based on a preliminary design input. While it can generate a diverse range of interface mockups, the user has no control over the specific layout or design elements of the mockup, which is crucial for a designer to express ideas that are inherently visuo-spatial by nature. Recently, Garg et al. [15] proposed a method to guide design exploration using diffusion models, [42] through different modalities. However, it remains unclear which modality, if any, can work better for specific design tasks and stages of the design process. A growing alternative to text-only prompting is **visual prompting**, which allows users to provide more explicit guidance through sketches, segmentation maps, or semantic labels. This technique is exemplified by ControlNet [43], a deep learning framework that enables fine-grained control over AI-generated outputs by conditioning the model on structured inputs such as edge maps, human poses, or depth maps. By incorporating structured constraints, ControlNet allows designers to generate AI-assisted content that remains consistent with their original composition while still leveraging the generative capabilities of diffusion models. There has been limited focus on comparing different visual prompting modalities for controlling the generation of design artifacts. Our work focuses on evaluating the effectiveness and user experience of two different visual prompting modalities—sketches and semantic-colored drawings—for generating design artifacts. We build upon previous knowledge in several ways: First, the use of sketches as a modality builds upon previous research on the use of visual representations in the design process [25]. Studies have shown that sketches can be used to quickly generate and communicate design ideas, allowing designers to explore a wide range of possibilities in a relatively short amount of time. Additionally, sketches are often used as a way to capture informal, early-stage design ideas, which can then be refined and developed further [24]. Second, the use of semantic-colored drawings [20,44], where each color represents a UI element category, allows for a clear representation of the design elements and their relationships. In this paper, we aim to answer the following research questions: **RQ1:** How do different modalities of UI mockup generation, such as sketches and semantic drawings, compare in terms of their unique strengths, perceived usefulness, and impact on the creative process? **RQ2:** What are the trade-offs between expressiveness, efficiency, and user satisfaction when considering the level of control and abstraction afforded by each modality in UI mockup generation? We answer these questions by exploring two distinct AI-assisted modalities: one based on sketches, and the other based on semantic-colored drawings. Sketch-based mockup generation involves the use of hands-drawn sketches to represent the desired design. Semantic-based mockup generation, instead, involves the use of colored drawings that convey specific design elements. The choice of these two modalities was based on a careful review of the literature, indicating that sketching and semantic drawing are commonly used in the design process due to their ability to balance precision and speed (e.g., [7,27,31]). Sketch-based mockup generation allows for quick exploration of ideas while semantic-colored drawing-based mockup generation provides more accuracy in representing the final product.

2 Study: Evaluating Visual Prompting Modalities

This study aimed to evaluate the sketch-to-mockup and semantic drawing-to-mockup visual prompting modalities in terms of time demand, ease, creative expressivity, and intuitiveness. The study was conducted with 13 human-computer interaction students from the first-year master's program in Computer Engineering. The participants were asked to use both modalities to create a mockup of a mobile application, retrieve the AI-generated mockups, and then rate their experience with each modality and result on various dimensions.

Participants. The study was conducted remotely with 13 participants who gave their explicit and informed consent to participate. All participants in the study had received training in UI design and programming as part of their curriculum (e.g., through a dedicated Human-Computer Interaction course they all passed), indicating that they had some level of experience in this area. The sample consisted of 2 participants who identify themselves as female and 11 people who identify as male, with an age range of 23 to 25 years old.

2.1 Procedure

Participants completed a two-phase task designing a mobile UI through sketching and semantic drawing. The task evaluated time demand, expressiveness,

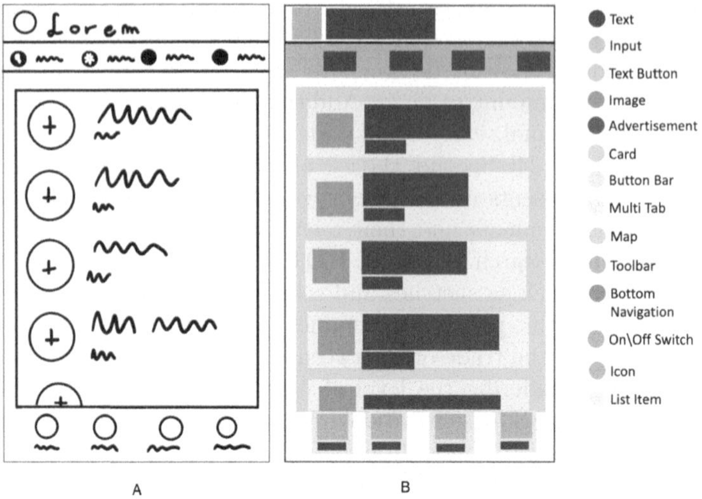

Fig. 1. An example of the same user interface represented in the sketch-based and semantic-based modalities. On the left, we can see a hand-drawn sketch of the user interface (A), with various elements such as buttons, text fields, and icons depicted in a freeform manner. On the right, we can see the same user interface represented in the semantic-based modality (B). These elements are filled with different colors, with each color representing a specific design element such as buttons, text fields, and icons.

intuitiveness, and ease of use in the first phase, followed by assessing the quality and fidelity of generated mockups in the second phase.

In phase one, participants received instructions to design a mobile interface using their preferred digital drawing tools. They first created a sketch, then semantically drew the same interface. This order followed the natural design progression from unstructured ideas to concrete iterations, allowing us to evaluate each modality's strengths in a contextualized design process. Figure 1 shows an example interface in both modalities. After completing this phase, participants rated their experience on a 1–5 Likert scale (5 being most positive) and provided rationales for their ratings.

In phase two, participants' drawings were processed by a network (see "Implementation" section), and the results were shown to them. Participants then evaluated the generated mockups' quality and how well they respected their imagined interface (fidelity), using the same Likert scale. They also had the opportunity to provide additional comments and suggestions at the end of the study.

Implementation. To translate sketches and semantic colored drawings to mockups we finetuned a Pix2Pix [40] model for sketch-based mockup generation and the SPADE [32] model for semantic-based mockup generation, following the same procedure used in [30]. We trained the model on the RICO dataset [12], which uniquely provides both sketches and semantic annotations of the same

UI designs. It is important to acknowledge that the quality of the generated mockups in our study may not be optimal, as the focus of this research is on evaluating the visual prompting modalities rather than the generation results themselves. While the generated mockups may exhibit some artifacts or inconsistencies, the rapid progression of AI technologies suggests that the quality of the generated mockups will likely improve in the future. Nevertheless, our findings and discussions regarding the strengths, weaknesses, and user preferences of the sketch-to-mockup and semantic drawing-to-mockup are expected to hold independently of the specific model performances.

3 Results and Discussion

Table 1. Results of sketch-to-mockup and semantic drawing-to-mockup on intuitiveness, ease of use, perceived time demand, and expressiveness (first phase), as well as the quality and fidelity of the AI-generated mockups (second phase), on a 1 to 5 Likert scale.

	Sketch-to-mockup	Semantic drawing-to-mockup
Intuitiveness	4.54 ± 0.78	3.15 ± 1.28
Ease of use	3.38 ± 1.04	3.69 ± 1.25
Time Demand	3.54 ± 1.13	3.77 ± 1.09
Expressiveness	4.15 ± 0.55	3.38 ± 1.12
Quality	1.50 ± 0.58	2.75 ± 0.50
Fidelity	3.38 ± 2.20	3.60 ± 0.55

The study analyzes the sketch-based and semantic-based visual prompting modalities by gathering participant feedback on their level of intuitiveness, ease of use, and time demand during the generation process, as well as the quality and fidelity of the generated mockups. The results of the questions provide insight into how participants perceive these modalities and their relative strengths and weaknesses. Numerical results are reported in Table 1, and the following sections describe the quantitative and qualitative aspects of those results.

3.1 Intuitiveness

The comparison between modalities revealed a clear preference for the intuitiveness of sketch-based visual prompting. Most participants (11/13) rated the sketch-based modality as fully intuitive (score 5), while only two gave semantic generation a score of 5, and most (8/13) rated it 3 or lower.

Participants favoring the sketch-based approach cited that sketching allowed them to "show others what you have in mind" and "represent at a higher level each part of the layout" (participants 1 and 6). The sketch-based modality made it easier to "imagine the layout" (participant 9) and "pour the idea in mind into drawings" (participant 10).

Some participants found the semantic-based modality challenging, expressing difficulty understanding the "rules about the colors" (participant 4) and finding it "not so clear how it can be useful" (participant 1). However, a few found semantic generation more intuitive, appreciating the "map about element types" (participant 10).

Overall, the sketch-based modality emerged as superior for intuitiveness, facilitating effective communication and translation of mental concepts into visual form, while the semantic-based modality was hindered by its color-coding rules and perceived complexity.

Ease of Use. The comparison between the sketch-based and semantic-based visual prompting modalities for ease of use yielded mixed results, with no statistically significant difference in the mean scores between the two methods. This indicates that both approaches presented challenges and advantages to the participants.

For the sketch-based visual prompting modality, a majority of participants (7 out of 13) rated it as difficult to use, assigning scores of 3 or lower. The primary reasons cited for this difficulty were the need for "drawing skills and tools" (participant 9) and the requirement of "some drawing skills are needed to convey information in a reasonable and clear way" (participant 1). Furthermore, some participants found it "difficult to use the mouse to draw" (participants 3, 4, and 11), while others found it difficult to use because they "had to use different devices to complete the task" (participant 13).

On the other hand, the semantic modality also had its share of ease-of-use concerns. Participant 9 noted that the semantic approach "needs to remember the colors according to the legend," which can be cognitively demanding. However, some participants found the semantic modality easier to use because it "only requires squares and rectangles" (participant 4) and is "just a mechanical exercise" (participant 3). Participant 10 also found the semantic generation easy to use because it is "much more descriptive" and "easier regarding positioning the items" as compared to sketch generation.

The diverse opinions on the ease of use of both visual prompting modalities suggest that individual preferences, skills, and familiarity with the tools play a significant role in determining the perceived difficulty or ease of use. The sketch-based visual prompting modality may be more challenging for those lacking drawing skills or struggling with input devices, while the semantic modality may be seen as cognitively demanding in terms of color association but appreciated for its simplicity and descriptiveness in positioning elements.

Time Demands. The time demand comparison yielded mixed results. Participants had varying opinions on each approach's efficiency.

Some found sketch generation quicker due to its ability to represent layouts at a higher level. Participant 5 mentioned it "only took me some minutes to complete" the sketch, suggesting faster translation of mental concepts. However, others cited challenges affecting efficiency, including "difficulty drawing with a mouse" (participant 10) and "difficulty in getting a decent result" (participant 3).

For semantic generation, some found it less time-demanding. Participant 8 considered it "the quickest one because it's similar to sketch generation but with even fewer details to represent," while participant 3 found it "fairly quick to draw what I was thinking in the semantic way." Conversely, others found it more time-consuming. Participant 1 reported spending "very much time in finding a software to draw colored squares," while participant 12 noted "it can take a long time because there is often a difference between ideas and reality."

Time efficiency ultimately depends on the user's tool familiarity, ability to translate ideas visually, and layout complexity.

Expressivity. The comparison between the visual prompting modalities in terms of expressivity revealed a clear preference for the sketch-based visual prompting modality. Most participants (10 out of 13) rated the sketch generation as highly expressive, assigning it a score of 4 or 5, indicating that they found it to be fully capable of conveying their ideas. In contrast, the majority of participants (7 out of 13) gave the semantic generation a score of 3 or lower, suggesting that they perceived it as less expressive.

Participants who favored the sketch-based visual prompting modality cited several reasons for their preference. They found that sketching "makes it easiest to describe how you want the final result to look like" (participant 3) and "irons out some ambiguity" (participant 5). The ability to "draw almost everything" (participant 5) and express "the alignments and the position of the items" more easily (participant 6) were also highlighted as advantages of the sketch-based visual prompting modality.

On the other hand, some participants found the semantic generation to be less expressive. They felt that it "just conveys information with colored and filled squares that don't reflect very well the actual elements" (participant 1) and is "too restrictive" (participant 4). Participants also encountered difficulties in defining "the role of each component" (participant 7) using the semantic approach.

These findings suggest that while the sketch-based visual prompting modality is generally preferred for its expressivity, the semantic-based modality may still have a role to play in certain contexts or for specific design tasks.

Quality and Fidelity of the Generated Mockups. The evaluation of the generated mockups revealed that the semantic-based modality outperformed the sketch-based modality in terms of both quality and fidelity to the original idea. The mean quality score for the semantic-based modality was 2.75, considerably higher than the 1.50 mean score for the sketch-based modality. This suggests that the mockups generated using the semantic-based approach were generally perceived as being of higher quality compared to those generated using the sketch-based approach.

Similarly, the semantic-based modality scored higher in terms of fidelity to the original idea, with a mean score of 3.60 compared to 3.38 for the sketch-based modality. Although this difference is not as pronounced as the quality score difference, it still shows a significant difference. It indicates that the sketch-based approach was less effective in preserving the designer's original intent and not accurately translating their ideas into the generated mockups.

Additional Comments and Design Implications. The analysis of participant comments reveals diverse opinions regarding the best method for generating mockups. Several participants proposed hybrid solutions integrating elements of both modalities. Participant 7 suggested incorporating color conventions into sketching, combining expressive freedom with semantic clarity. Participant 11 acknowledged each approach's limitations and proposed leveraging their respective strengths. Participant 12 took a context-dependent stance, arguing that method selection should depend on project circumstances.

Our findings indicate that sketch-based approaches are more intuitive and expressive, aligning with research highlighting sketching's importance for design ideation [6,16]. However, this approach requires drawing skills and suitable input devices.

The semantic-based approach, while less intuitive, produced higher quality mockups with better fidelity. Its color-coding and predefined elements contributed to more consistent translations of designers' intentions [32].

These results suggest each approach has unique merits, with selection depending on specific designer needs and project requirements. Future research could focus on developing hybrid tools that integrate both approaches, allowing designers to leverage their respective strengths at different design stages.

4 Conclusions and Future Work

The paper investigated sketch-based and semantic-based visual prompting modalities for AI-assisted mockup generation, evaluating their intuitiveness, ease of use, time demand, expressiveness, quality, and fidelity.

The findings suggest the sketch-based modality is more intuitive and expressive, enabling designers to quickly convey ideas and explore concepts. However, its effectiveness depends on designers' drawing skills and input devices. The semantic-based modality, while less intuitive and expressive, produced higher quality mockups with better fidelity to original designs.

Based on these findings, we conclude that a hybrid approach combining strengths of both modalities offers a promising direction for future research. By integrating sketching and semantic drawing capabilities, AI-assisted tools could provide designers with more flexible, expressive, and accurate means of creating high-quality mockups.

Future work should focus on: (1) larger-scale studies with diverse designer samples to validate findings; (2) developing and evaluating hybrid tools integrating both modalities; (3) conducting longitudinal studies to track how preferences evolve as designers become familiar with AI-assisted tools; (4) exploring integration into existing design workflows; and (5) addressing ethical implications of AI-assisted design tools.

References

1. Behance - search projects: Photos, videos, logos, illustrations and branding (2022). https://www.behance.net
2. Dribbble - discover the world's top designers and creative (2022). https://dribbble.com/
3. Anantrasirichai, N., Bull, D.: Artificial intelligence in the creative industries: a review. Artif. Intell. Rev. **55** (2022). https://doi.org/10.1007/s10462-021-10039-7
4. Behrang, F., Reiss, S.P., Orso, A.: Guifetch: supporting app design and development through gui search. In: Proceedings of the 5th International Conference on Mobile Software Engineering and Systems. MOBILESoft '18, pp. 236–246. Association for Computing Machinery, New York (2018). https://doi.org/10.1145/3197231.3197244
5. Betker, J., et al.: Improving image generation with better captions. Comput. Sci. (2023). https://cdn.openai.com/papers/dall-e-3.pdf
6. Buxton, B.: Sketching user experiences: getting the design right and the right design. Morgan Kaufmann (2010)
7. Calò, T., De Russis, L.: Style-aware sketch-to-code conversion for the web. In: Companion of the 2022 ACM SIGCHI Symposium on Engineering Interactive Computing Systems. EICS '22 Companion, pp. 44–47. Association for Computing Machinery, New York (2022). https://doi.org/10.1145/3531706.3536462
8. Carter, S., Nielsen, M.: Using artificial intelligence to augment human intelligence. Distill (2017). https://doi.org/10.23915/distill.00009, https://distill.pub/2017/aia
9. Chen, W., Shidujaman, M., Xuelin, T.: Aiart: towards artificial intelligence art (2020)
10. Chen, X., Duan, Y., Houthooft, R., Schulman, J., Sutskever, I., Abbeel, P.: Infogan: interpretable representation learning by information maximizing generative adversarial nets. In: Lee, D., Sugiyama, M., Luxburg, U., Guyon, I., Garnett, R. (eds.) Advances in Neural Information Processing Systems. vol. 29. Curran Associates, Inc. (2016). https://proceedings.neurips.cc/paper/2016/file/7c9d0b1f96aebd7b5eca8c3edaa19ebb-Paper.pdf
11. Colton, S., Wiggins, G.: Computational creativity: the final frontier? Front. Artif. Intell. Appl. **242**, 21–26 (2012). https://doi.org/10.3233/978-1-61499-098-7-21
12. Deka, B., et al.: Rico: a mobile app dataset for building data-driven design applications. In: Proceedings of the 30th Annual Symposium on User Interface Software and Technology. UIST '17 (2017)
13. Dove, G.: Codesign with data (2015)
14. Fischer, G., Nakakoji, K.: Amplifying designers' creativity with domain-oriented design environments, pp. 343–364. Springer, Dordrecht (1994). https://doi.org/10.1007/978-94-017-0793-025
15. Garg, A., Jiang, Y., Oulasvirta, A.: Controllable gui exploration. arXiv preprint arXiv:2502.03330 (2025)
16. Goldschmidt, G.: The dialectics of sketching. Creat. Res. J. **4**(2), 123–143 (1991)
17. Gonçalves, M., Cardoso, C., Badke-Schaub, P.: What inspires designers? Preferences on inspirational approaches during idea generation. Des. Stud. **35** (2013). https://doi.org/10.1016/j.destud.2013.09.001

18. Ha, D., Eck, D.: A neural representation of sketch drawings. In: 6th International Conference on Learning Representations, ICLR 2018, Vancouver, BC, Canada, 30 April–3 May 2018, Conference Track Proceedings. OpenReview.net (2018). https://openreview.net/forum?id=Hy6GHpkCW
19. Herring, S.R., Chang, C.C., Krantzler, J., Bailey, B.P.: Getting inspired! understanding how and why examples are used in creative design practice. In: Proceedings of the SIGCHI Conference on Human Factors in Computing Systems, CHI '09, pp. 87–96. Association for Computing Machinery, New York (2009). https://doi.org/10.1145/1518701.1518717
20. Hong, S., Yang, D., Choi, J., Lee, H.: Inferring semantic layout for hierarchical text-to-image synthesis. In: Proceedings of the IEEE Conference on Computer Vision and Pattern Recognition, pp. 7986–7994 (2018)
21. Jansson, D., Smith, S.: Design fixation. Des. Stud. **12** (1991). https://doi.org/10.1016/0142-694X(91)90003-F
22. King, R., Churchill, E.F., Tan, C.: Designing with data: improving the user experience with a/b testing (2017)
23. Ko, H.K., et al.: We-toon: a communication support system between writers and artists in collaborative webtoon sketch revision. In: Proceedings of the 35th Annual ACM Symposium on User Interface Software and Technology, UIST '22. Association for Computing Machinery, New York (2022). https://doi.org/10.1145/3526113.3545612
24. Landay, J., Myers, B.: Sketching interfaces: toward more human interface design. Computer **34**(3), 56–64 (2001). https://doi.org/10.1109/2.910894
25. Landay, J.A., Myers, B.A.: Interactive sketching for the early stages of user interface design. In: Proceedings of the SIGCHI Conference on Human Factors in Computing Systems, CHI '95, pp. 43-50. ACM Press/Addison-Wesley Publishing Co., USA (1995). https://doi.org/10.1145/223904.223910
26. Lee, B., Srivastava, S., Kumar, R., Brafman, R., Klemmer, S.R.: Designing with interactive example galleries. In: Proceedings of the SIGCHI Conference on Human Factors in Computing Systems, pp. 2257–2266. Association for Computing Machinery, New York (2010). https://doi.org/10.1145/1753326.1753667
27. Li, Y., et al.: Gligen: open-set grounded text-to-image generation. In: CVPR (2023)
28. Marsh, R., Landau, J., Hicks, J.: How examples may (and may not) constrain creativity. Memory Cogn. **24**, 669–680 (1996). https://doi.org/10.3758/BF03201091
29. Miller, A.: The Artist in the Machine: The World of AI-Powered Creativity (2019). https://doi.org/10.7551/mitpress/11585.001.0001
30. Mozaffari, M.A., Zhang, X., Cheng, J., Guo, J.L.: Ganspiration: balancing targeted and serendipitous inspiration in user interface design with style-based generative adversarial network. In: Proceedings of the 2022 CHI Conference on Human Factors in Computing Systems. CHI '22. Association for Computing Machinery, New York (2022). https://doi.org/10.1145/3491102.3517511
31. Park, T., Liu, M.Y., Wang, T.C., Zhu, J.Y.: Semantic image synthesis with spatially-adaptive normalization. In: Proceedings of the IEEE Conference on Computer Vision and Pattern Recognition (2019)
32. Park, T., Liu, M.Y., Wang, T.C., Zhu, J.Y.: Semantic image synthesis with spatially-adaptive normalization. In: 2019 IEEE/CVF Conference on Computer Vision and Pattern Recognition (CVPR), pp. 2332–2341 (2019)
33. Qiao, H., Liu, V., Chilton, L.: Initial images: using image prompts to improve subject representation in multimodal ai generated art. In: Creativity and Cognition, pp. 15–28. Association for Computing Machinery, New York (2022). https://doi.org/10.1145/3527927.3532792

34. Ritchie, D., Kejriwal, A.A., Klemmer, S.R.: D.tour: style-based exploration of design example galleries. In: Proceedings of the 24th Annual ACM Symposium on User Interface Software and Technology, pp. 165–174. Association for Computing Machinery, New York (2011). https://doi.org/10.1145/2047196.2047216
35. de Rooij, A., Biskjaer, M.M.: Expecting the unexpected: a review of surprise in design processes. In: Gray, C., Chehade, E.C., Hekkert, P., Forlano, L., Ciuccarelli, P., Lloyd, P. (eds.) DRS2024: Boston, 23-28 June (2024). https://doi.org/10.21606/drs.2024.333
36. Shneiderman, B.: Human-Centered AI. Oxford University Press, Oxford (2022)
37. Swearngin, A., Dontcheva, M., Li, W., Brandt, J., Dixon, M., Ko, A.J.: Rewire: interface design assistance from examples. In: Proceedings of the 2018 CHI Conference on Human Factors in Computing Systems, pp. 1–12. Association for Computing Machinery, New York (2018). https://doi.org/10.1145/3173574.3174078
38. Ueno, M., Satoh, S.: Continuous and gradual style changes of graphic designs with generative model, pp. 280–289. Association for Computing Machinery, New York (2021). https://doi.org/10.1145/3397481.3450666
39. Wang, B., Li, G., Zhou, X., Chen, Z., Grossman, T., Li, Y.: Screen2words: automatic mobile ui summarization with multimodal learning, pp. 498–510 (2021). https://doi.org/10.1145/3472749.3474765
40. Wang, T.C., Liu, M.Y., Zhu, J.Y., Tao, A., Kautz, J., Catanzaro, B.: High-resolution image synthesis and semantic manipulation with conditional gans. In: 2018 IEEE/CVF Conference on Computer Vision and Pattern Recognition, pp. 8798–8807 (2017)
41. Yurman, P., Reddy, A.V.: Drawing conversations mediated by ai. In: Creativity and Cognition, C&C '22, pp. 56–70. Association for Computing Machinery, New York (2022). https://doi.org/10.1145/3527927.3531448
42. Zhang, L., Rao, A., Agrawala, M.: Adding conditional control to text-to-image diffusion models. In: Proceedings of the IEEE/CVF International Conference on Computer Vision, pp. 3836–3847 (2023)
43. Zhang, L., Rao, A., Agrawala, M.: Adding conditional control to text-to-image diffusion models. In: Proceedings of the IEEE/CVF International Conference on Computer Vision (ICCV), pp. 3836–3847. IEEE (2023). https://arxiv.org/abs/2302.05543
44. Zhu, P., Abdal, R., Qin, Y., Wonka, P.: Sean: image synthesis with semantic region-adaptive normalization. In: Proceedings of the IEEE/CVF Conference on Computer Vision and Pattern Recognition, pp. 5104–5113 (2020)

AI for End-User Empowerment: Personalization and Wellbeing

Beyond Usability: Introducing Wellbeing-Driven End-User Development Design

Kevin Krings[1(✉)], Nino S. Bohn[1], Louisa M. Sauter[2], and Thomas Ludwig[1]

[1] University of Hagen, EduTech for Digital Transformation, 58097 Hagen, Germany
{kevin.krings,nino.bohn,thomas.ludwig}@fernuni-hagen.de
[2] University of Siegen, Cyber-Physical Systems, 57072 Siegen, Germany
louisa2.sauter@uni-siegen.de

Abstract. End-User Development (EUD) empowers non-programmers to create, adapt, and extend digital tools according to their needs. Traditional research on EUD has primarily focused on usability and efficiency, often overlooking dimensions of wellbeing and user engagement. While frameworks such as meta-design advocate for transformative potentials beyond mere usability, explicit integration of wellbeing remains insufficiently explored. To address this research gap, this paper proposes a novel conceptual methodology that focuses on wellbeing aspects in EUD components. Drawing from an established wellbeing-driven design philosophy, we emphasize designing tangible interactive artifacts that foster positive user experiences. Building on the novel construct EUDability, we introduce an extended version called xEUDability and demonstrate how it enriches existing methodologies by integrating Design Thinking skills. This extended framework offers a robust foundation for the systematic assessment and improvement of EUD tools, prioritizing sustained positive experiences and meaningful user interactions.

Keywords: End-User Development · Design for Wellbeing · Design Thinking · Socio-technical design · Methodology · EUDability

1 Introduction

End-User Development (EUD) represents a crucial shift toward empowering end users to actively participate in technology creation, adaptation, and extension, democratizing software development beyond traditional professional boundaries [1–4]. Despite significant progress in making EUD tools accessible and user-friendly, existing approaches predominantly emphasize usability and computational thinking (CT) [5, 6], often ignoring critical aspects of wellbeing and engagement [7]. Many current EUD approaches therefore risk designing tools that, while functional and accessible, may not fully capture or sustain user engagement [8]. Fischer et al. [3, 4] extends the understanding of EUD through the meta-design framework, emphasizing that its transformative potential goes beyond mere functionality or usability. However, despite a broader perspective, the explicit incorporation of wellbeing remains underrepresented. Consequently, the question of how to systematically embed principles of wellbeing and engagement into the design and assessment of EUD tools remains a significant research gap.

C. Santoro et al. (Eds.): IS-EUD 2025, LNCS 15713, pp. 185–204, 2025.
https://doi.org/10.1007/978-3-031-95452-8_12

This gap is further highlighted by wellbeing-driven design frameworks, notably by Hassenzahl et al. [7], who emphasize the deliberate and structured design of positive experiences through tangible, interactive artifacts referred to as "stuff." They argue for a systematic approach to experience design, emphasizing that technology should not merely function effectively, but actively facilitate experiences that enhance users' autonomy, competence, relatedness, and stimulation. Such insights invite a reconsideration of existing EUD methodologies, prompting the integration of experience-focused, wellbeing-oriented principles. Furthermore, they highlight the structured process of experience design, which seeks to systematically cultivate such positive interactions. Our paper addresses the research gap by proposing a conceptual framework for *wellbeing-driven EUD design*. We follow the definition of experience provided by [9] which describes it as "*an episode, a chunk of time that one went through—with sights and sounds, feelings and thoughts, motives and actions* [...] *closely knitted together, stored in memory, labeled, relived, and communicated to others. An experience is a story, emerging from the dialogue of a person with her or his world through action.*" By integrating principles of Design Thinking (DT) and systematically incorporating wellbeing into EUD methodologies, we extend existing frameworks such as EUDability [5]. Our approach prioritizes sustained, positive user experiences that support psychological needs [7], such as autonomy, competence, relatedness, and stimulation, thereby enhancing user satisfaction and fostering long-term engagement with EUD tools.

In the following sections, we introduce our extended framework, *xEUDability*, highlighting its theoretical foundation and practical implementation. We discuss how *xEUDability* enhances traditional metrics by incorporating DT skills. Finally, we outline directions for future research, including the need for empirical validation across diverse contexts and the exploration of cooperative and context-sensitive design practices to further refine and advance EUD design methodologies.

2 Background and Related Work

Our study has its roots essentially in two research discourses: Firstly, we considered the field of End-User Development (EUD) and its role in HCI research, as well as a potential EUD assessment strategy. Secondly, we discuss Design for Wellbeing (DfW) and Design Thinking (DT).

2.1 EUD in a Nutshell

The established research discourse on EUD [1, 2, 10–12] focused on the empowerment of end users to adapt technologies to their own practices and vice versa [13]. Specifically, EUD describes the sub-process of adapting new technologies to users' practices and the emergence of new practices in situ [13–15]. Lieberman et al. [1] define EUD as a collection of methods, techniques, and tools that enable non-developers to create, adapt, and extend software, while Ko et al. [16] emphasize that it is predominantly a form of programming whose outcomes are primarily intended for personal rather than public use. In this way, EUD, as a bottom-up approach, contrasts with the discourse on Citizen Development, which also aims to democratize software development but is understood as a top-down approach [17]. Approaches that focus more on user practices [2] refer to EUD when non-developers have to move to a more abstract level to accomplish their specific tasks. End users engage in activities at four different levels of complexity: *"Use," "Parameterization/Customization," "Recomposition/Integration," and "Extension/Altering."* These levels require a wide range of different skills [2, 18]. Activities at the *"Use"* level do not constitute EUD activities in the strict sense of adaptation or tailoring.

In addition to the practice-oriented categorization [2], there have been further attempts to categorize activities performed by non-developers [19, 20]. Typical EUD approaches often operate at the *"Parameterization/Customization"* level, as they typically aim to reduce complexity for non-developers through model-based development [1], wizard-based approaches [21], or simplified abstraction of various functionalities [22]. Examples include flatter hierarchies, limited functionalities, the avoidance of multiple ways to achieve the same function, the use of sliders, drag-and-drop approaches, or Natural User Interfaces (NUI) [11, 22–24]. The transfer of software development methods and techniques to non-developers opens new possibilities for designing development environments and tools [23], and there remains considerable untapped potential to integrate additional practices [25] and strategies [26] into future tool designs. Some approaches focus on understanding and supporting motivational factors influencing non-developers [27, 28], as demonstrated by [24, 29], utilizing the motivational aspects of gamification [30].

A challenge in EUD research lies in assessing the suitability of EUD environments for end users. Traditionally, usability has been the primary construct for evaluating interactive systems, as defined by Nielsen [31], who outlined five dimensions: *learnability, efficiency, memorability, robustness, and satisfaction.* However, usability does not seem to be able to fully capture the complexity and demands of EUD environments [5]. In particular, it lacks the ability to account for the dynamic interplay between user agency, learning processes, and the creative adaptation of tools. This shortcoming has led to the development of new evaluation constructs that extend beyond traditional usability criteria.

2.2 EUDability

Recognizing these limitations, the concept of EUDability has been introduced [5]. EUDability is a novel construct that evaluates the degree to which an EUD environment facilitates user engagement by integrating CT [32] skills with EUD techniques. It builds on previous research highlighting the necessity of aligning tool design with user reasoning habits rather than traditional software engineering logic [5]. This does not mean that people's reasoning is similar to computers, rather it focuses more on problem-solving approaches utilized by computer scientists. CT, as originally defined by Wing [32], encompasses a set of cognitive processes for solving problems using computational methods. These processes include abstraction, decomposition, algorithmic thinking, generalization, and evaluation [33–35]. In the context of EUD, these skills play a crucial role in problem definition, solution implementation, and result analysis, which are operationalized as three key stages: (1) defining the problem (abstraction), (2) solving the problem (decomposition, algorithm design, generalization), and (3) analyzing the solution (evaluation). EUDability is operationalized through five dimensions [5] that align with CT principles [36]:

- Concreteness – the extent to which an EUD system presents concepts and tasks in an intuitive manner, minimizing the need for high abstraction skills.
- Modularity – the system's ability to facilitate decomposition by providing distinct building blocks for structuring solutions.
- Structuredness – the support for organizing steps in a logical, sequential manner to enhance user comprehension.
- Reusability – the potential for repurposing and sharing EUD-created solutions across different scenarios and by other non-developers.
- Testability – the capability of validating and refining the outcome within the EUD environment itself.

Future research on EUDability aims to establish a methodological framework for assessing CT skills in EUD, designing EUD environments based on EUDability heuristics, and developing a comprehensive evaluation methodology that considers both tool difficulty and user expertise [5].

2.3 Design Thinking

DT has evolved from a niche concept within design disciplines to a widely adopted methodology in organizational and educational contexts [37]. The concept has its roots in the "creative engineering" theories developed in the 1950s, which emphasized human-centered design and the role of design in cultural development [38]. DT emphasizes creativity, innovation, and a user-centered perspective, drawing from the practices and cognitive styles focusing on how professional designers know, act and think [39, 40]. There is a common understanding that designers create the frame within design activities take place [39, 41–44]. Many insights into designerly approaches of thinking and acting highlight designers' ability to frame problems and employ strategies to reshape these frames in meaningful ways, a process often referred to as reframing (e.g., Beckman [45]). Various activities, such as user research, material exploration, and the examination of theoretical frameworks and case studies, are directed toward broadening the frame of understanding surrounding the problem [46]. DT is strongly related to design problems [39, 40, 47], while it is defined as *"a goal-oriented, constrained, decision-making, exploration and learning activity which operates within a context which depends on the designer's perception of the context"* [41] and is also described as *"designerly ways of knowing, thinking and acting"* [48] or as *designerly thinking* [49]. DT is conceptualized as the body of knowledge developed regarding the cognitive processes individuals employ when addressing design problems. This conceptualization is grounded in the framework of situated and embodied cognition, which posits that reasoning in design is context-dependent and inherently linked to perceptual and motor experiences [50, 51]. Wicked problems illustrate the kind of challenges that demand DT, as they involve unknown variables and incomplete knowledge [39, 52, 53], e.g. problems that can be found in social planning [52].

DT involves a blend of analytic and creative processes, encouraging experimentation, prototyping, and feedback gathering to refine solutions [54]. The approach is also noted for its emphasis on visualization and creativity, which are crucial for effective DT [54]. Despite its popularity, critics argue that it often relies on a dualism between thinking and knowing, and acting in the world, which can undermine its effectiveness. Additionally, a generalized approach to DT may overlook the diversity of designers' practices and the historical context of design institutions [37]. There is also a need for more rigorous academic anchoring in the management discourse of DT, which tends to be more superficial compared to the designerly discourse [49]. Johansson-Sköldberg et al. [49] explore the evolution of DT within both designerly and management discourses. In the designerly discourse, Kimbell [37] identifies various perspectives on DT, viewing it as a cognitive style, a general design theory, and an organizational resource.

DT has established itself as a valuable approach to innovation and problem-solving across various fields. Its historical development and adoption reflect a broader cultural shift towards integrating design principles into diverse domains. However, ongoing research and refinement are necessary to overcome its challenges and enhance its theoretical and practical applications [37, 49, 55].

2.4 Design for Wellbeing

DfW is an interdisciplinary approach that integrates principles of design with the goal of enhancing individual and collective wellbeing. The concept has its roots in various design disciplines such as HCI, sustainable fashion, and service design, to create environments, products, and services that support psychological and physical health. Within HCI, the focus has been on creating technology that enhances users' subjective wellbeing by addressing psychological needs such as autonomy, relatedness, competence, stimulation, and popularity [7, 56, 57]. These needs, when addressed effectively, foster meaningful, positive user experiences and ultimately happiness [7]. This approach has evolved to a practice-oriented approach to bridge the gap between abstract experiential design objectives and specific products and interactions [56], aiming to create technologies that respect and support psychological health [7, 58]. The shift towards a human-centered vision in designing large-scale ecosystems, such as smart cities, has been significant. It maps wellbeing onto various levels of human needs, allowing for a participatory evaluation of the smartness and wellbeing of these ecosystems [59]. This involves understanding the emotional, psychological, and environmental aspects of wellbeing and integrating them into service improvement strategies [60, 61]. Despite the progress, there remains a gap between theoretical models of wellbeing and their practical application in design. Bridging this gap requires a practice-oriented approach that translates abstract concepts into concrete design solutions [56, 62]. Additionally, the integration of wellbeing into technology development is still in its early stages, with a need for more systematic approaches to ensure technologies genuinely improve psychological health [63].

2.5 EUD and Design for Wellbeing

Upon closer examination, there are more intersections between EUD and DfW, which aims *"to bridge the gap between abstract experiential design objectives and specific products and interactions"* [56] to create positive experiences [7]. While DfW places particular emphasis on psychological factors such as *autonomy* („feeling like you are the cause of your own actions rather than feeling that external forces or pressures are the cause of your actions"), *competence* ("feeling that you are very capable and effective in your actions rather than feeling incompetent or ineffective„), *stimulation* („feeling that you get plenty of enjoyment and pleasure rather than feeling bored and under-stimulated by life") or *security* („feeling safe and in control of your life rather than feeling uncertain and threatened by your circumstances") [7, 56], these aspects also play a crucial role in many EUD approaches. The EUD discourse further highlights the importance of other factors such as *popularity* („feeling that you are liked, respected, and have influence over others rather than feeling like a person whose advice or opinions nobody is interested in"), *relatedness* („feeling that you have regular intimate contact with people who care about you rather than feeling lonely and uncared for") or *physicalness* („feeling that your body is healthy and well taken care of rather than feeling out of shape or unhealthy") [7, 56].

2.6 Research Gap

The literature shows that modern technology design primarily aims to embed competence within materials (e.g. objects, tools and infrastructures) [56], enabling users to fulfil tasks [2, 56]. According to Shove et al. [64] a (social) practice consists of competence (e.g., skill, knowhow and technique), meaning (e.g. symbolic meanings, ideas and aspirations) and the material, while forming a practice is understood as establishing new links between these elements [64]. This is strongly related to the research discourse of EUD [10, 11, 22–24] as it is focused on the technological sphere of appropriation (practices) [13, 15, 65, 66]. Fischer et al. [3, 67] broaden the concept of EUD, through the lens of the meta-design framework, emphasizing that its true impact goes beyond developing new technologies. Instead, it transforms cultures by empowering individuals to actively contribute to personally meaningful activities. Yet, the question of what precisely constitutes meaningful experiences has largely been addressed separately within DfW. The relevance in EUD becomes evident in discussions on cooperative approaches, such as the question of *"how to support cooperative approaches to allow end-user developers to cooperatively climb the gentle slope of complexity"* [2]. Since the process of appropriation inherently involves highly cooperative activities, a key challenge remains how to integrate collaboration and learning among end users into EUD approaches effectively [2]. Despite new concepts such as EUDability, focusing on the systematic evaluation of EUD, the existing frameworks have primarily emphasized computational and interactional suitability, largely overlooking how EUD contributes to users' wellbeing beyond usability. Factors crucial to wellbeing, including autonomy, competence, relatedness, and stimulation, have been neglected. Thus, the integration of *wellbeing-driven* design principles into the efforts around the development of new EUD tools and components remains insufficiently explored. There exists a research gap how EUD can be systematically conceptualized and assessed to foster positive experiences and sustained wellbeing before, during, and after user interaction [7]. Our contribution addresses this gap by proposing a conceptual framework for wellbeing-driven EUD design, extending the concept of EUDability to incorporate explicit activities aimed at enhancing users' long-term wellbeing.

3 A Conceptual Framework for Wellbeing-Driven EUD Design

In the following we introduce the conceptual framework for wellbeing-driven EUD design by extending the work on EUDability [5]. This expansion advances the methodology for the systematic conceptualization of EUD approaches and the assessment of their suitability.

3.1 Extending EUDability by Design Thinking Skills

Barricelli et al. [5] introduced the actionable framework of EUDability to address the duality between tool difficulty and user ability in EUD. However, from our perspective, the existing construct does not fully account for all necessary aspects required to foster positive EUD experiences and ensure user engagement. Furthermore, it fails to consider a UX perspective. Barricelli et al. [5, 6] emphasize the need to evaluate EUD approaches beyond traditional usability and user experience (UX) assessments [6]. In our view, it is essential to integrate both early-stage and post-use evaluation phases. Usability and UX considerations should be addressed early in the design process, as they encompass not only expectations and assumptions prior to use, but also satisfaction, effectiveness, and emotional responses during and after use.

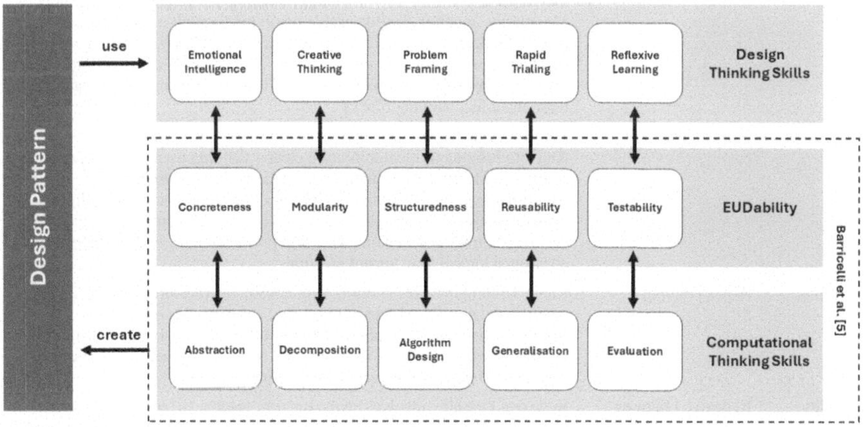

Fig. 1. Extended EUDability construct (oriented towards [5])

Therefore, we propose an extended version of the original concept (see Fig. 1), referred to as *xEUDability* (eXtended EUDability). This extension complements the already integrated CT by incorporating DT and its associated skills, which form the foundation for DfW. Furthermore, the symbiotic relationship between CT and DT in addressing design problems has already been demonstrated by Kelly and Gero [46].

Kelly and Gero [46] argue that DT and CT can be considered as archetypal constructs within a continuum of metacognitive strategies for problem-solving. Within this continuum, the thinker (e.g. the designer) dynamically navigates between the two, adapting their cognitive approach as the problem evolves. In DT, solutions are developed with the primary objective of addressing the specific problem at hand in a coherent and contextually appropriate manner, with minimal consideration for their applicability in other contexts. In contrast, CT emphasizes the development of solutions that extend beyond the immediate problem, striving for generalizability and broader applicability [46].

Each phase of DT requires a unique set of skills that constitute pendants to the CT skills in the EUDability construct and can be mutually related to the EUDability dimensions. The relationship between the dimensions and the DT skills are shown in Table 1:

Table 1. Relationships between EUDability dimensions and DT skills

Dimension	DT Skill	Explanation
Concreteness	Emotional Intelligence	Designers employ emotional intelligence to understand user needs (active listening), connect with their experiences (empathy), and remain open to diverse perspectives (curiosity). This aligns with Concreteness, as emotional intelligence focuses on understanding user needs in a tangible way through direct observation, interviews, and real-world experiences. This helps to translate abstract problems into concrete insights
Modularity	Creative Thinking	Creative Thinking involves idea generation (brainstorming techniques), experimentation (risk-taking and playfulness), and making connections (lateral thinking). Expressing ideas visually (sketching and visual thinking) supports Modularity, enabling flexible problem-solving through combinable and adaptable ideas. Creative Thinking relates to Modularity as it encourages breaking down the problem into multiple possible solutions. Brainstorming often involves modular thinking, where ideas can be combined, separated, or rearranged like building blocks
Structuredness	Problem Framing	Problem Framing involves analytical and synthesizing skills, such as distilling data into insights (critical thinking), clearly defining user-centered problems (framing and structuring), identifying patterns and opportunities (sense-making), and prioritizing challenges (decision-making). It aligns with Structuredness, as it involves synthesizing research findings into a clear and structured problem statement. This step is crucial in organizing insights and ensuring a logical flow toward ideation
Reusability	Rapid Trialing	Rapid Trialing involves building with constraints (resourcefulness), creating quick prototypes (rapid prototyping), and ensuring user relevance (user-centered design). It aligns with Reusability, as it involves creating tangible representations of ideas that can be tested, refined, and sometimes repurposed for other projects or future iterations
Testability	Reflexive Learning	Reflexive Learning involves analyzing user feedback (feedback analysis), evaluating effectiveness (critical reflection), and adapting ideas (resilience). It aligns with Testability, as it involves experimenting with prototypes, gathering feedback, and iterating to refine the solution. This ensures that the design meets user needs and functions correctly

Design patterns encapsulate the core principles of a design solution at a level of abstraction that facilitates the reuse of the underlying conceptual approach [68]. The concept of design patterns has gained prominence across various disciplines, especially UX design and software engineering. While design patterns are predominantly applied within DT, their creation relies on CT [46]. Consequently, within the framework of a dual-process model [46], they must also be considered in the context of xEUDability (see Fig. 1). When assessing the suitability of new EUD tools and components, it is essential to evaluate whether existing design expertise, embodied in established design patterns [4, 27, 28, 69–71], has been incorporated and utilized. If this is not the case, the underlying reasons must be examined to enable the integration of this knowledge into new design patterns through the application of CT skills. This reciprocal process highlights the symbiosis of DT and CT in xEUDability.

3.2 The Practice of Wellbeing-Driven EUD Design

Building upon xEUDability, our methodology emphasizes social practices as the key arena in which positive experiences of end users can actively be fostered through design. Forming or transforming practices involve deliberately shaping the connections among competences (skills, know-how), meanings (symbolic significance, aspirations), and materials (objects, tools, infrastructures), thus enabling or constraining certain actions and experiences.

Today's technological innovations frequently move competences into the domain of materials, with profound implications for how practices evolve. While such shifts offer increased convenience, they may inadvertently undermine essential aspects of wellbeing, such as autonomy, competence, or meaningful engagement. Addressing this, Hassenzahl et al. [7] highlight the critical distinction between universal psychological needs (e.g., relatedness, autonomy, competence) and the concrete, context-specific practices through which these needs are fulfilled. Needs like relatedness, for instance, are universal, but the practices used to satisfy them, such as hugging, handshaking, or verbal interaction, vary greatly depending on context and appropriateness. Recognizing this distinction allows designers to deliberately create practices that fulfill universal psychological needs through context-sensitive, meaningful interactions.

Our proposed wellbeing-driven EUD design methodology (Fig. 2), oriented towards [56] and [6], is structured along 7 phases and operationalizes these insights into a structured yet flexible, iterative design process. Rather than merely addressing functional usability, our approach explicitly targets the hedonic qualities of UX, which Hassenzahl et al. [9] identify as fundamental motivators for sustained user engagement. By integrating these dimensions into the design of EUD environments, we aim not only at empowering users functionally but also at fostering sustained engagement.

In the following, we present each of the seven iterative phases in detail, beginning with the initial delimitation of the design space and culminating in the evaluation of the xEUDability. To illustrate the methodology, we introduce a scenario centered on Ben, a social science researcher who represents a typical end user of tools in academic contexts. He analyzes interview transcripts qualitatively, has limited technical expertise, and no programming background, but frequently engages with digital tools in his research.

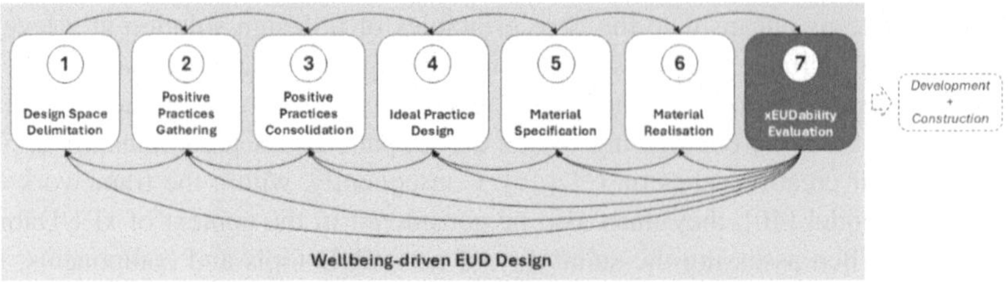

Fig. 2. Overview of the wellbeing-driven EUD design methodology

Step 1 - Design Space Delimitation. When designing EUD techniques and tools, it is essential to define the design space using a top-down design methodology. This approach begins with identifying the positive, meaningful experiences that end users aim to achieve, and only then proceeds to the development of the necessary technological tools. To streamline design efforts, it is beneficial to select a specific theme that targets a clearly defined end-user challenge, such as automating repetitive spreadsheet tasks. While many projects in EUD traditionally adopt a bottom-up approach, relying on pre-existing components, a top-down perspective, which prioritizes understanding user needs and desired outcomes, can lead to more effective technology selection. However, it is crucial to avoid an overly narrow focus. of design practices but also facilitates a manageable exploration of the design space. In our scenario, the researcher observed that Ben often analyzes qualitative data but faces cognitive and technical friction when using conventional software. His desired experience centers around an intuitive way to organize, code, and interpret transcripts without programming or navigating complex user interfaces. This observation informed the delimitation of a design space focused on approachability, visual clarity, and analytical flexibility, specifically tailored to non-technical researchers in academic contexts.

Step 2 - Positive Practices Gathering. A comprehensive understanding of the user context necessitates the systematic gathering of empirical data on workflows and challenges. Collecting authentic insights directly from end users ensures that the design accurately reflects real-world practices. Supplementary research, including feedback from user forums, interviews, case studies, academic literature, and personal programming experiences, further enriches this understanding and contributes to a well-rounded design process. In the context of our scenario, Ben uses a variety of digital and analog tools. Through semi-structured observation and interviews, the researchers found that users like Ben frequently combine Word tables, printed transcripts, highlighters, and handwritten notes to organize and interpret data. Such practices reflect a workaround culture shaped by frustrations with complex or inflexible software environments. In addition, online platforms revealed recurring dissatisfaction with analysis tools, and an interest in lighter-weight, more visual approaches to coding.

Empirical EUD studies focus on identifying usability and accessibility issues, such as difficulties in programming, debugging, or adopting new tools. The predominant design approach aims to address these problems by creating solutions that improve ease of use and efficiency. However, this problem-focused method often results in a "design gap", where the insights gained from studying user challenges do not seamlessly translate into intuitive, empowering design solutions. This gap can hinder the creation of tools that not only solve problems but also actively enhance user experience, creativity, and engagement.

To overcome these limitations, an alternative strategy shifts the focus from problem-solving to understanding successful engagement with EUD tools. Instead of solely analyzing obstacles, the positive practice approach examines "power users" or enthusiastic end-users who effectively and creatively use development environments. Studying these individuals provides valuable insights into how EUD tools can be designed to foster enjoyment, efficiency, and innovation. In Ben's case, one particularly insightful example was identified. A fellow researcher had developed a personal system using Miro boards to visually connect coded segments across multiple transcripts, supporting a more reflective and spatially organized analysis process. This emergent practice served as a key reference point for identifying design patterns that promote autonomy and engagement.

While traditional approaches such as Contextual Inquiry [72] do consider both strengths and weaknesses of user practice, their primary focus often remains on identifying usability issues, inefficiencies, or unmet needs. In contrast, our approach deliberately foregrounds positive experiences within user practices, drawing on wellbeing-centered design paradigms (e.g., [7, 9, 56]).

By identifying and analyzing exceptional examples of successful EUD experiences, this approach helps inform the design of environments that better support non-expert users and encourage productive engagement with development tools. A methodological framework for implementing this approach might be the Positive-Practice Canvas (PPC) [56] as a design-oriented, visual interview guide. In this phase, Ben's practices and those of his colleagues were examined using the PPC to document which tools, techniques, and settings foster moments of emotional satisfaction during the coding process. This included identifying underlying motivations such as personalization, efficiency, or a desire for analytical control, as well as mapping out skill acquisition pathways (e.g., trial and error, peer support, tutorials) and environmental factors like workspace layout or tool accessibility. By analyzing practices step-by-step, he can systematically document key aspects of positive EUD experiences, ensuring that critical elements of user engagement are captured and understood.

It refers to the underlying motivations for engaging in EUD, such as personalization, efficiency, automation, or problem-solving. It seeks to understand why users engage in development activities and what drives their participation, whether it be curiosity, necessity, or professional needs. Furthermore, it focuses on the skills and knowledge required to successfully develop custom tools. This includes understanding how users acquire these skills, whether through trial and error, online tutorials, or community support. The PPC encompasses the tools, platforms, and resources that users rely on, as well as environmental factors such as workplace setup and collaboration, which can influence their success. By tracking how EUD evolves over time, the PPC approach supports iterative improvements, ensuring that EUD tools continue to adapt to user needs. Different motivations shape how users interact with development environments. Competence-driven users are motivated by developing technical skills and exploring more advanced functionalities, whereas socially-driven users are more likely to engage in collaborative customization and knowledge sharing. Clarifying questions such as *"Do you feel empowered when using EUD tools?"* or *"Does it make your work more enjoyable?"* help researchers understand the emotional connections users have with their tools. Identifying these intrinsic motivations aids in refining tool design, optimizing learning curves, and improving user guidance systems to better support diverse user needs.

By implementing this approach, researchers can shift from merely addressing usability problems to fostering a more engaging, empowering, and wellbeing-driven design process in EUD.

Step 3 - Positive Practices Consolidation. While a large collection of observed practices serves as an abundant source of inspiration, it can also become overwhelming. To effectively utilize this diversity, consolidation is necessary to extract key design insights without losing the richness of individual practices. This step corresponds to the third phase of Barricelli et al. [6], with the distinction that it was included due to the *"peculiar nature of EUD"*, as it is an integral part of the wellbeing-driven design process.

Two strategies for consolidating EUD practices can be employed. The first involves selecting the most inspiring and effective practice, one that demonstrates clear usability, efficiency, or innovation, as an anecdotal design reference. The second strategy focuses on grouping similar practices based on the needs they fulfill. Rather than averaging out different approaches, practices are accumulated to enhance understanding, ensuring that the variations contribute to a broader comprehension of the underlying design space. To further refine the consolidation process, it is crucial to identify patterns in EUD practices by analyzing common competencies and materials involved. These may include technical skills such as coding, interaction with drag-and-drop interfaces, or scripting capabilities.

In our scenario, the research team analyzed examples of how Ben and his colleagues structure their data analysis workflows. One particularly creative case was identified in which Ben used a collaborative whiteboard to spatially cluster and code qualitative findings. This practice was selected as an anecdotal anchor due to its balance of simplicity. A practical tool to support such consolidation is an accumulation chart [56], which enables a structured comparison of user practices. This chart organizes practices based on key attributes, such as the specific EUD technique being used (e.g., macro automation, visual scripting), the type of user (e.g., non-programmer, expert), the need being addressed (e.g., efficiency, personalization), the competencies required (e.g., programming logic, interface customization), and the materials involved (e.g., low-code platforms, scripting languages). By structuring practices in this manner, it becomes easier to identify overlaps, distinctions, and emerging patterns that inform more inclusive design decisions.

By consolidating and structuring EUD practices in this way, the design perspective is both broadened and refined. Recognizing the variety of user motivations and methods enables the creation of flexible and inclusive EUD environments. Rather than enforcing a single approach, offering multiple customization pathways ensures adaptability, usability, and accessibility, ultimately making software development more approachable for a wider audience.

Step 4 - Ideal Practice Design. Even well-designed EUD environments do not always guarantee ideal end user experiences. Challenges such as steep learning curves [11], usability issues [8], incomplete functionalities [24], or even missing storytelling [22] can hinder positive experiences. To improve the EUD experience, it is essential to construct a narrative of an ideal end user journey. This process involves envisioning how end users interact with EUD tools or components in ways that fulfill psychological needs [7]. By incorporating real-world user feedback and research findings, designers can ensure authenticity while creating a vision that extends beyond mere summarization of existing data. Anecdotal evidence and success stories serve as valuable foundations, helping to craft narratives that not only describe what users do but also highlight the potential for improved engagement, ease of use, and empowerment. The aim is to make EUD tools more intuitive and engaging, ultimately fostering a sense of accomplishment and satisfaction among users.

Rather than just analyzing how users currently approach EUD, the design effort must focus on constructing a model of a great experience in practice. This vision should depict how non-programmers can successfully create, modify, or extend solutions with minimal friction through well-structured interfaces, intelligent guidance, and automation. The narratives developed from this approach serve as realistic representations of user journeys, shedding light on pain points, critical learning moments, and successful outcomes.

Based on insights gathered in previous phases, the researchers in our scenario formulated an ideal end user journey for individuals like Ben. In this journey, individuals like Ben uploads an interview transcript, highlights meaningful excerpts, and applies visual tags via an intuitive drag-and-drop interface. As the work progresses, the EUD system suggests category names derived from prior coding behavior and automatically maps related themes into a dynamic visual network. This enables individuals like Ben to focus more on the analysis than tool navigation.

An effective EUD narrative should be structured around several key elements. First, context is crucial in establishing the scenario in which users engage with EUD, what was already shown by Nebeling [22] in the area of EUD for Extended Reality (XR). Next, identifying the users themselves provides necessary insights into their backgrounds, technical proficiency, and motivations. Understanding motivation is equally important, as users turn to EUD to solve problems, improve efficiency, or reduce repetitive tasks. Their engagement with EUD tools should fulfill essential psychological needs [7].

The interaction phase of the narrative must detail the step-by-step process that users follow, highlighting critical learning moments, problem-solving experiences, and challenges overcome. To enhance authenticity, real user quotes from research can be integrated into the storytelling. The narrative should culminate in a positive outcome, demonstrating how end-users successfully use EUD tools or components to create, modify and extend their solutions. For the user type represented by Ben, this ideal flow includes selecting a transcript, dragging a quote onto the workspace, linking it to a pre-existing theme, and attaching a reflective note. When uncertainty arises, the system offers helpful prompts such as visual examples or context-aware suggestions ("Did you mean...?"). Maintaining a positive tone throughout the narrative is key to making the story both accessible and engaging for a broad audience, including non-technical users. The format of the narrative can vary based on the intended purpose, with options such as storyboards, UI walkthroughs, explainer videos, or interactive simulations providing alternative ways to communicate the user journey effectively. While videos and animations can illustrate the process in a compelling way, they require significant production effort and may introduce unintended distractions. Written narratives generally allow for more precise control over detail and user focus.

Step 5 - Material Specification. So far, the initial framework of the EUD solution remained flexible to accommodate diverse end user needs and practices. In this step, the "material" for the EUD solution is specified based on the narratives, ensuring that the design process remains grounded in real-world practices and is aligned with EUD principles. The design problem is shaped by the material so that its functionality and interaction naturally support and evoke the intended practice. Ultimately, designers should cultivate empathy for the narratives, enabling them to create material that genuinely resonates with users and supports the EUD approach [56].

Based on the aforementioned end user journey and previously consolidated practices, the core material elements for users like Ben were defined. These included drag-and-drop components for coding, interactive canvases for thematic mapping, and contextual prompts for guidance, which are all intended to support reflective and nonlinear workflows typical of qualitative research. The material specification thus translates abstract user goals into tangible interface features that align with Ben's cognitive strategies and interaction preferences.

Step 6 - Material Realization. The realization of EUD tools requires specialized design skills, including user interface (UI) and user experience (UX) design, programming frameworks, and interaction design. These elements ensure that users can intuitively engage with and modify the material, whether it be software, interfaces, or platforms. The success of EUD depends on the seamless integration of these design principles, making the experience both accessible and effective.

When the EUD tool or component (the material) is used in its intended context, it facilitates achieving a result that closely aligns with the desired ideal in a practice-as-performance scenario [56]. The process can be supported by providing non-developers with additional information about the envisioned practice. In this regard, the ideal practice narrative serves as a valuable reference document [56].

To test material implementation, the researchers in our scenario develop a low-fidelity prototype based on Ben's scenario, including core interaction elements such as transcript upload or quote tagging. A first usability test in a simulated research task revealed that users with similar profiles were able to quickly understand the interface and complete basic analysis steps without training, confirming alignment with the intended user experience.

Step 7 - xEUDability Evaluation. In this final step, we orient our approach towards Barricelli et al. [5], which proposed to proceed with a predictive evaluation for measuring the EUDability of the prototypes. It is an inspective evaluation with HCI and EUD experts. They provide an evaluation checklist that considers CT aspects. For the prototype inspired by Ben's use case, both the original CT-focused criteria and the extended DT dimensions were applied. Experts from the domain of HCI, EUD and/or design research assessed whether the interface supported problem framing, visual ideation, and iterative thinking alongside established measures like modularity and testability. The evaluation confirmed that the tool facilitated not only effective problem-solving but also reflective and creative engagement, aligning with the goals of wellbeing-driven EUD design.

In addition to Barricelli et al. [5] foundational work, we provide an additional checklist that incorporate the newly added DT aspects in Table 2.

Table 2. Checklist for xEUDability evaluation focused on DT aspects

Dimensions	Items to check (Y/N forced choice)
Concreteness	The EUD environment … 1. Demonstrate empathy by actively addressing user experiences and emotions 2. Clearly reflect understanding of user needs through tangible, relatable examples
Modularity	3. Encourage creative thinking through flexible idea generation methods 4. Support visual expression of ideas (e.g., sketching, visual thinking) to facilitate adaptable problem-solving?
Structuredness	5. Help clearly define user-centered problems through systematic framing
Reusability	6. Facilitate identifying and prioritizing design opportunities based on synthesized insights 7. Support rapid prototyping and iterative refinement 8. Prototypes be easily tested, adjusted, and adapted for diverse user scenarios and future uses
Testability	9. Effectively incorporate user feedback analysis and critical reflection into the design cycle 10. Allow for iterative experimentation and resilience in refining solutions

In addition to both checklists, the wellbeing aspect has to be considered. Therefore, we suggest to use established constructs to measure the fulfilment of psychological needs [7], such as the AttrakDiff model [73, 74].

4 Conclusion and Future Work

In this paper, we introduced a novel methodology for *wellbeing-driven EUD design*, addressing the gap identified in existing EUD design methodologies. Our approach significantly extends the existing EUDability construct by integrating principles of DT into the conceptualization, design, and evaluation of EUD tools. By focusing on positive user experiences beyond traditional interactional and usability aspects, our framework facilitates sustained user engagement and is meant to enhance long-term user satisfaction. By grounding EUD designs in meaningful, positive user experiences, we contribute to a deeper understanding of how end users use technology in practice, including appropriation such as creative tool use.

Future research should empirically validate the proposed framework across diverse EUD contexts to refine its components and enhance its applicability in practice. Additionally, in-situ studies employing methods such as the PPC [56], could further enrich our understanding of successful EUD practices, ensuring insights translate directly into actionable design improvements. Investigations into how designers and professional programmers can better anticipate functionalities for future appropriation practices [2, 28] and support infrastructures that evolve through actual use [75, 76] remain critical. Other open questions exist regarding how to integrate cooperative approaches that enable users to cooperatively navigate complexities in EUD environments [2]. Addressing these questions will contribute to establishing a more integrated methodology for designing and evaluating wellbeing-driven EUD systems.

Acknowledgments. In the treacherous wilderness of academic publishing, we encountered mighty reviewers cloaked in anonymity. We are very grateful for their guidance helped us chart a clearer path and avoid falling into the pit trap of vague statements. We are also grateful for the + 2 bonus to Insight granted by the caffeine-enhanced intellect of our writing party.

Disclosure of Interests. The authors have no competing interests to declare that are relevant to the content of this article.

References

1. Lieberman, H., Paternò, F., Klann, M., Wulf, V.: End-user development: an emerging paradigm. In: Lieberman, H., Paternò, F., Wulf, V. (eds.) End User Development. Human-Computer Interaction Series, vol. 9, pp. 1–8. Springer, Dordrecht (2006). https://doi.org/10.1007/1-4020-5386-X_1
2. Ludwig, T., Dax, J., Pipek, V., Wulf, V.: A practice-oriented paradigm for end-user development. In: Paternò, F., Wulf, V. (eds.) New Perspectives in End-User Development, pp. 23–41. Springer, Cham (2017). https://doi.org/10.1007/978-3-319-60291-2_2
3. Fischer, G., Fogli, D., Piccinno, A.: Revisiting and broadening the meta-design framework for end-user development. In: Paternò, F., Wulf, V. (eds.) New Perspectives in End-User Development, pp. 61–97. Springer, Cham (2017). https://doi.org/10.1007/978-3-319-60291-2_4
4. Fischer, G., Nakakoji, K., Ye, Y.: Metadesign: guidelines for supporting domain experts in software development. IEEE Softw. **26**, 37–44 (2009). https://doi.org/10.1109/MS.2009.134
5. Barricelli, B.R., Fogli, D., Locoro, A.: EUDability: a new construct at the intersection of end-user development and computational thinking. J. Syst. Softw. **195**, 111516 (2023). https://doi.org/10.1016/j.jss.2022.111516
6. Barricelli, B.R., Fogli, D., Locoro, A.: Designing for a sustainable digital transformation: the DEA methodology. In: Spano, L.D., Schmidt, A., Santoro, C., Stumpf, S. (eds.) End-User Development. Lecture Notes in Computer Science, vol. 13917, pp. 189–199. Springer, Cham (2023). https://doi.org/10.1007/978-3-031-34433-6_12
7. Hassenzahl, M., Eckoldt, K., Diefenbach, S., Laschke, M., Lenz, E., Kim, J.: Designing moments of meaning and pleasure: experience design and happiness. Int. J. Des. **7**, 21–31 (2013)
8. Vaiani, G., Paternò, F.: End-User development for human-robot interaction: results and trends in an emerging field. Proc. ACM Hum.-Comput. Interact. **8**, 1–40 (2024). https://doi.org/10.1145/3661146

9. Hassenzahl, M., Diefenbach, S., Göritz, A.: Needs, affect, and interactive products-Facets of user experience. Interact. Comput. **22**, 353–362 (2010)
10. Barricelli, B.R., Cassano, F., Fogli, D., Piccinno, A.: End-user development, end-user programming and end-user software engineering: a systematic mapping study. J. Syst. Softw. **149**, 101–137 (2019). https://doi.org/10.1016/j.jss.2018.11.041
11. Paternò, F.: End user development: survey of an emerging field for empowering people. ISRN Softw. Eng. **2013**, 1–11 (2013). https://doi.org/10.1155/2013/532659
12. Paternò, F., Wulf, V. (eds.): New Perspectives in End-User Development. Springer, Cham (2017). https://doi.org/10.1007/978-3-319-60291-2
13. Dourish, P.: The appropriation of interactive technologies: some lessons from placeless documents. Comput. Supp. Cooper. Work (CSCW) **12**, 465–490 (2003). https://doi.org/10.1023/A:1026149119426
14. Ludwig, T., Stickel, O., Boden, A., Pipek, V.: Towards sociable technologies. In: Proceedings of the 2014 Conference on Designing Interactive Systems, pp. 835–844. ACM, New York (2014). https://doi.org/10.1145/2598510.2598528
15. Stevens, G., Pipek, V., Wulf, V.: Appropriation infrastructure: supporting the design of usages. In: Lecture Notes in Computer Science (including subseries Lecture Notes in Artificial Intelligence and Lecture Notes in Bioinformatics), vol. 5435 LNCS, pp. 50–69. Springer, Heidelberg (2009). https://doi.org/10.1007/978-3-642-00427-8_4
16. Ko, A.J., et al.: The state of the art in end-user software engineering. ACM Comput. Surv. **43**, 1–44 (2011). https://doi.org/10.1145/1922649.1922658
17. Binzer, B., Winkler, T.J.: democratizing software development: a systematic multivocal literature review and research agenda on citizen development. In: Carroll, N., Nguyen-Duc, A., Wang, X., Stray, V. (eds.) SOFTWARE BUSINESS. 13th International Conference, ICSOB 2022, Bolzano, Italy, vol. 463, pp. 244–259. Springer, Heidelberg (2023). https://doi.org/10.1007/978-3-031-20706-8_17
18. MacLean, A., Carter, K., Lövstrand, L., Moran, T.: User-tailorable systems: pressing the issues with buttons. In: Chew, J.C., Carrasco, J.C., Carrasco Chew, J. (eds.) Proceedings of the SIGCHI Conference on Human Factors in Computing Systems Empowering People - CHI '90. Human Factors in Computing Systems, pp. 175–182. ACM Press, New York (1990). https://doi.org/10.1145/97243.97271
19. Costabile, M.F., Fogli, D., Mussio, P., Piccinno, A.: End-user development: the software shaping workshop approach. In: Lieberman, H., Paternò, F., Wulf, V. (eds.) End User Development. Human-Computer Interaction Series, vol. 9, pp. 183–205. Springer, Dordrecht (2006). https://doi.org/10.1007/1-4020-5386-X_9
20. Mørch, A.: Three levels of end-user tailoring: customization, integration, and extension. Comput. Des. Cont. **1997**, 61 (1997)
21. Rode, J., Howarth, J., Pérez-Quiñones, M.A., Rosson, M.B.: An end-user development perspective on state-of-the-art web development tools (2005)
22. Nebeling, M.: XR tools and where they are taking us. XRDS **29**, 32–38 (2022). https://doi.org/10.1145/3558192
23. Krings, K., Bohn, N.S., Hille, N.A.L., Ludwig, T.: "What if everyone is able to program?" – exploring the role of software development in science fiction. In: Schmidt, A., Väänänen, K., Goyal, T., Kristensson, P.O., Peters, A., Mueller, S., Williamson, J.R., Wilson, M.L. (eds.) Proceedings of the 2023 CHI Conference on Human Factors in Computing Systems, pp. 1–13. ACM, New York (2023). https://doi.org/10.1145/3544548.3581436
24. Krings, K., Weber, P., Jasche, F., Ludwig, T.: FADER: an authoring tool for creating augmented reality-based avatars from an end-user perspective. In: Mensch und Computer 2022, pp. 52–65. ACM, New York (2022). https://doi.org/10.1145/3543758.3543778

25. Krauß, V., Boden, A., Oppermann, L., Reiners, R.: Current practices, challenges, and design implications for collaborative AR/VR application development. In: Proceedings of the 2021 CHI Conference on Human Factors in Computing Systems, pp. 1–15. ACM, New York (2021). https://doi.org/10.1145/3411764.3445335
26. Falkner, K., Szabo, C., Vivian, R., Falkner, N.: Evolution of Software Development Strategies (2015). https://doi.org/10.1109/ICSE.2015.153
27. Blackwell, A.F.: End-user developers – what are they like? In: Paternò, F., Wulf, V. (eds.) New Perspectives in End-User Development, pp. 121–135. Springer, Cham (2017). https://doi.org/10.1007/978-3-319-60291-2_6
28. Ludwig, T., Pipek, V., Tolmie, P.: Designing for collaborative infrastructuring: supporting resonance activities. Proc. ACM Hum.-Comput. Interact. **2**, 1–29 (2018). https://doi.org/10.1145/3274382
29. Benzi, F., Fogli, D.: The role of gamification in end-user development. In: CoPDA@ IS-EUD, pp. 32–38 (2015)
30. Chou, Y.-K.: Actionable Gamification. Beyond Points, Badges, and Leaderboards (2014)
31. Nielsen, J.: Usability Engineering. Morgan Kaufmann (1994)
32. Wing, J.M.: Computational thinking. Commun. ACM **49**, 33–35 (2006). https://doi.org/10.1145/1118178.1118215
33. Wang, C., Shen, J., Chao, J.: Integrating computational thinking in STEM education: a literature review. Int. J. Sci. Math. Educ. **20**, 1949–1972 (2022). https://doi.org/10.1007/s10763-021-10227-5
34. Román-González, M., Pérez-González, J.-C., Jiménez-Fernández, C.: Which cognitive abilities underlie computational thinking? Criterion validity of the Computational Thinking Test. Comput. Hum. Behav. **72**, 678–691 (2017). https://doi.org/10.1016/j.chb.2016.08.047
35. Tsai, M.-J., Liang, J.-C., Hsu, C.-Y.: The computational thinking scale for computer literacy education. J. Educ. Comput. Res. **59**, 579–602 (2021). https://doi.org/10.1177/0735633120972356
36. Ponce, V., Abdulrazak, B.: Context-aware end-user development review. Appl. Sci. **12**, 479 (2022). https://doi.org/10.3390/app12010479
37. Kimbell, L.: Rethinking design thinking: part I. Des. Cult. **3**, 285–306 (2011). https://doi.org/10.2752/175470811X13071166525216
38. Thienen, J.P.A. von, Clancey, W.J., Meinel, C.: Theoretical foundations of design thinking. In: Meinel, C., Leifer, L. (eds.) Design Thinking Research. Understanding Innovation, pp. 13–38. Springer, Cham (2019). https://doi.org/10.1007/978-3-319-97082-0_2
39. Dorst, K.: The core of 'design thinking' and its application. Des. Stud. **32**, 521–532 (2011). https://doi.org/10.1016/j.destud.2011.07.006
40. Cross, N.: Design thinking: understanding how designers think and work. Berg 2011. Published in 2011 in Oxford New York by Berg (2011)
41. Gero, J.S.: Design prototypes: a knowledge representation schema for design. AI Mag. **11**, 26 (1990)
42. Schön, D.A.: The Reflective Practitioner: How Professionals Think in Action. Routledge, Abingdon (2017)
43. Schwartz, H.S.: The reflective practitioner: how professionals think in action. JSTOR (1987)
44. Dorst, K.: Frame Innovation: Create New Thinking by Design. MIT Press, Cambridge (2015)
45. Beckman, S.L.: To frame or reframe: where might design thinking research go next? Calif. Manag. Rev. **62**, 144–162 (2020)
46. Kelly, N., Gero, J.S.: Design thinking and computational thinking: a dual process model for addressing design problems. Des. Sci. **7** (2021). https://doi.org/10.1017/dsj.2021.7
47. Bryan, L.: How Designers Think: The Design Process Demystified. Architectural Preee and Elsevier (2005)

48. Cross, N.: Designerly ways of knowing: design discipline versus design science. Des. Issues **17**, 49–55 (2001)
49. Johansson-Sköldberg, U., Woodilla, J., Çetinkaya, M.: Design thinking: past, present and possible futures. Creat. Innov. Manag. **22**, 121–146 (2013). https://doi.org/10.1111/caim.12023
50. Clancey, W.J.: Situated Cognition: On Human Knowledge and Computer Representations. Cambridge University Press, Cambridge (1997)
51. Barsalou, L.W.: Grounded cognition. Ann. Rev. Psychol. **59**, 617–645 (2008)
52. Rittel, H.W.J., Webber, M.M.: Dilemmas in a general theory of planning. Policy Sci. **4**, 155–169 (1973)
53. Buchanan, R.: Wicked problems in design thinking. Des. Issues **8**, 5 (1992). https://doi.org/10.2307/1511637
54. Razzouk, R., Shute, V.: What is design thinking and why is it important? Rev. Educ. Res. **82**, 330–348 (2012). https://doi.org/10.3102/0034654312457429
55. Micheli, P., Wilner, S.J.S., Bhatti, S.H., Mura, M., Beverland, M.B.: Doing design thinking: conceptual review, synthesis, and research agenda. J. Prod. Innov. Manag. **36**, 124–148 (2019). https://doi.org/10.1111/jpim.12466
56. Klapperich, H., et al.: Mind the gap: a social practice approach to wellbeing-driven design. In: Design for Wellbeing, pp. 154–169. Routledge (2019)
57. Ryan, R.M., Deci, E.L.: Self-determination theory: Basic psychological needs in motivation, development, and wellness. Guilford publications (2017)
58. Calvo, R.A., Peters, D.: Positive Computing: Technology for Wellbeing and Human Potential. MIT Press, Cambridge (2014)
59. Giovannella, C.: From simplex to complex: designing for wellbeing at scale. In: IxD&A, pp. 123–138 (2023). https://doi.org/10.55612/s-5002-055-006
60. Kimbell, L.: Designing for service as one way of designing services. Int. J. Des. **5** (2011)
61. Karol, E., Smith, D.: Impact of design on emotional, psychological, or social well-being for people with cognitive impairment. HERD **12**, 220–232 (2019). https://doi.org/10.1177/1937586718813194
62. Peters, D., Ahmadpour, N., Calvo, R.A.: Tools for wellbeing-supportive design: features, characteristics, and prototypes. MTI **4**, 40 (2020). https://doi.org/10.3390/mti4030040
63. Tamura, T.: Technologies for well-being: a grand challenge in connected health. Front. Dig. Health **6**, 1503554 (2024). https://doi.org/10.3389/fdgth.2024.1503554
64. Shove, E., Pantzar, M., Watson, M.: The Dynamics of Social Practice: Everyday Life and How it Changes. SAGE, Thousands Oaks (2012)
65. Balka, E., Wagner, I.: Making things work. In: Proceedings of the 2006 20th Anniversary Conference on Computer Supported Cooperative Work - CSCW '06, p. 229. ACM Press, New York (2006). https://doi.org/10.1145/1180875.1180912
66. Mackay, W.E.: Patterns of sharing customizable software. In: Proceedings of the 1990 ACM Conference on Computer-Supported Cooperative Work - CSCW '90, pp. 209–221. ACM Press, New York (1990). https://doi.org/10.1145/99332.99356
67. Fischer, G.: End-user development: empowering stakeholders with artificial intelligence, meta-design, and cultures of participation. In: Fogli, D., Tetteroo, D., Barricelli, B.R., Borsci, S., Markopoulos, P., Papadopoulos, G.A. (eds.) End-User Development. Lecture Notes in Computer Science, vol. 12724, pp. 3–16. Springer, Cham (2021). https://doi.org/10.1007/978-3-030-79840-6_1
68. Alexander, C.: A Pattern Language: Towns, Buildings, Construction. Oxford University Press, Oxford (1977)
69. Nielsen, J.: Enhancing the explanatory power of usability heuristics. In: Proceedings of the SIGCHI Conference on Human Factors in Computing Systems Celebrating Interdependence - CHI '94, pp. 152–158. ACM Press, New York (1994). https://doi.org/10.1145/191666.191729

70. Díez, D., Díaz, P., Aedo, I.: Meta-design blueprints: principles and guidelines for co-design in virtual environments. In: Costabile, M.F., Dittrich, Y., Fischer, G., Piccinno, A. (eds.) End-User Development, pp. 276–281. Springer, Heidelberg (2011)
71. Repenning, A., Ioannidou, A.: What makes end-user development tick? 13 design guidelines. In: Lieberman, H., Paternò, F., Wulf, V. (eds.) End User Development. Human-Computer Interaction Series, vol. 9, pp. 51–85. Springer, Dordrecht (2006). https://doi.org/10.1007/1-4020-5386-X_4
72. Beyer, H., Holtzblatt, K.: Contextual Design: Defining Customer-Centered Systems. Morgan Kaufmann Publishers Inc., San Francisco (1997)
73. Hassenzahl, M.: The thing and i: understanding the relationship between user and product. In: Karat, J., Vanderdonckt, J., Abowd, G., Calvary, G., Carroll, J., Cockton, G., Czerwinski, M., Feiner, S., Furtado, E., Höök, K. et al. (eds.) Funology. From usability to enjoyment. Human-Computer Interaction Series, vol. 3, pp. 31–42. Kluwer Academic Publishers, Dordrecht (2003). https://doi.org/10.1007/1-4020-2967-5_4
74. Hassenzahl, M., Monk, A.: The Inference of perceived usability from beauty. Hum.-Comput. Interact. **25**, 235–260 (2010). https://doi.org/10.1080/07370024.2010.500139
75. Star, S.L., Ruhleder, K.: Steps toward an ecology of infrastructure: design and access for large information spaces. Inf. Syst. Res. **7**, 111–134 (1996). https://doi.org/10.1287/isre.7.1.111
76. Pipek, V.: From tailoring to appropriation support: negotiating groupware usage. University of Oulu (2005)

AI-Assisted Cognitive Support for Caregivers: A RAG and EUD Framework for Geriatric Care

Stefano Valtolina(✉) and Antonio Pugliese

Department of Computer Science, Università degli Studi di Milano, Milan, Italy
stefano.valtolina@unimi.it, antonio.pugliese2@studenti.unimi.it

Abstract. The increasing prevalence of cognitive decline among the ageing population demands scalable, user-friendly tools that empower healthcare professionals to deliver personalised support. This paper introduces a framework that integrates End-User Development (EUD) principles with Retrieval-Augmented Generation (RAG) techniques to enable geriatric caregivers to design, deploy, and adapt customised cognitive intervention plans. Through a web-based platform, caregivers can profile patients, administer screening questionnaires, and automatically generate tailored cognitive exercises delivered via a mobile application featuring a conversational agent. The agent guides patients through daily cognitive tasks while adapting to individual profiles and progress. A preliminary usability evaluation with healthcare professionals assessed the system's learnability, usefulness, and integration potential. Results suggest that the proposed approach can support caregivers in delivering adaptive cognitive care while lowering their technical and operational burden. This work offers promising insights into using AI-assisted, caregiver-driven tools in geriatric healthcare settings.

Keywords: End-User Development (EUD) · Cognitive Support · Geriatric Care · Artificial Intelligence for Aging · Caregiver Support Tools · Human-AI Interaction · Usability in Healthcare AI

1 Introduction

The rising incidence of dementia and other cognitive disorders among older adults has increased the need for long-term, non-pharmacological interventions aimed at preserving cognitive function and quality of life. Recent studies highlight the growing emphasis on such interventions, including structured cognitive stimulation programs within healthcare institutions, which are recognised for their ability to complement pharmacological treatments and slow cognitive decline [1–3]. Early diagnosis of cognitive impairments now allows for more timely and personalised interventions, which can significantly improve outcomes and reduce the progression of decline [4, 5].

However, delivering these personalised cognitive support programs remains resource-intensive. Healthcare professionals—including geriatricians, nurses, and caregivers—must manually design individualised intervention plans, administer cognitive exercises, and continuously monitor patient progress. These tasks, while critical, can

C. Santoro et al. (Eds.): IS-EUD 2025, LNCS 15713, pp. 205–220, 2025.
https://doi.org/10.1007/978-3-031-95452-8_13

add to the already high workload of healthcare providers and limit the scalability of cognitive care.

To address these challenges, we propose an integrated framework that combines End-User Development (EUD) principles [6–16] with Retrieval-Augmented Generation (RAG) techniques [17], enabling non-technical healthcare professionals to configure and adapt intelligent digital tools for elderly cognitive care. EUD empowers caregivers to participate in the creation of digital services—such as configuring conversational agents and scheduling interventions—without relying on software engineers. This is particularly relevant in healthcare settings, where timely support customisation is essential but technical resources are limited.

At the core of our framework is the integration of RAG, a generative AI technique that leverages large language models and structured knowledge retrieval to generate context-aware, dynamic responses [17]. By incorporating patient-specific data—such as cognitive assessments, lifestyle information, and medical history—into the generation process, our system produces personalised intervention plans and chatbot interactions that adapt to each patient's needs over time.

The framework consists of a web-based application that allows caregivers to screen patients using standard tools (e.g. as explain later, GPCOG, SDS, MoCA), generate personalised exercise schedules, and configure a mobile cognitive assistant (CA) to engage patients in daily cognitive tasks. The CA, delivered via a mobile app, interacts with patients through a chatbot that guides them through their personalised training plan.

In collaboration with Dr. Luca Alfredo Grossi, a geriatrics specialist at Crema Hospital, we conducted a preliminary usability study with healthcare professionals (doctors, nurses, and caregivers) to evaluate the system. The study assessed usability, perceived usefulness, and potential for clinical integration using quantitative measures (such as explaine later: SUS, UTAUT, CTS, NASA-TLX) and qualitative feedback, focusing on interaction quality and caregiver acceptance.

This paper aims to contribute to human-AI interaction in healthcare by demonstrating how RAG and EUD can be combined to enable personalised cognitive support tools while reducing the technical burden on caregivers. Our findings highlight the potential for AI-assisted, end-user-configurable systems to enhance the personalisation, accessibility, and scalability of digital health interventions for older adults.

The remainder of the paper is structured as follows. Section 2 reviews digital tools for cognitive deterioration screening and the role of AI solutions in geriatric care. Section 3 details the design and functionalities of the EUD-based web platform. Section 4 describes the generation of personalised cognitive interventions and mobile deployment via conversational agents. Section 5 reports on the usability evaluation and discusses insights from caregiver testing. Section 6 concludes the paper and outlines future research directions.

2 Related Work: Digital Tools and AI Support in Cognitive Care

This section reviews the state of the art in digital solutions for cognitive screening and the role of End-User Development (EUD) and conversational agents in geriatric care.

While advancements in diagnostic tools and AI-driven systems have improved the detection of cognitive impairments, support tools that empower caregivers to personalise interventions remain underexplored. Our work aims to fill this gap by integrating EUD principles and RAG-based personalisation into caregiver workflows.

2.1 Cognitive Screening Tools and Monitoring Systems

Digital screening tools have become efficient alternatives to traditional paper-based methods, facilitating faster and more accessible cognitive assessments across healthcare settings [3, 18]. Widely used tools such as the Mini-Mental State Examination (MMSE) [4, 5] have been instrumental in screening for dementia, yet they are limited by their inability to detect mild cognitive impairments and their standardised nature, which overlooks individual differences.

Recent alternatives offer more sensitive and nuanced assessments. For instance:

- The General Practitioner Assessment of Cognition (GPCOG) [19] provides a brief and clinically validated assessment combining direct testing with informant reports, which is particularly useful in primary care settings constrained by time.
- The Symptoms of Dementia Screener (SDS) [20] gathers qualitative input from caregivers and relatives, offering complementary context when direct assessment is difficult.
- The Montreal Cognitive Assessment (MoCA) [21] detects early-stage cognitive impairments by assessing attention, executive function, and visuospatial abilities.

These tools support earlier diagnosis and personalised care planning. However, current systems often stop at assessment and offer limited support for customising interventions or integrating follow-up activities. This leaves a critical gap in post-diagnostic support—particularly in tools designed for caregiver use.

Our framework builds on this foundation by embedding these validated screening instruments into a caregiver-facing platform that collects data and uses it to drive personalised interventions.

2.2 From Assessment to Action: Limitations of Existing Digital Tools

Although many digital platforms exist for dementia care—including AI-enhanced diagnostics and wearable-based monitoring systems [1, 2]—few provide interactive tools for caregivers to manage, personalise, and automate cognitive interventions.

Most platforms focus on passive monitoring or generalised training content without offering adaptable workflows that reflect each patient's specific needs.

Caregivers often remain responsible for interpreting data, selecting exercises, and engaging patients manually. This contributes to increased workload and restricts the practical adoption of digital tools in everyday care routines.

Some solutions incorporate conversational agents (CAs) that assist with reminders or deliver exercises, such as Ada, Florence, and Woebot [22–24]. However, these agents are typically pre-configured and lack meaningful customisation, particularly regarding exercise difficulty, language, or interaction style. Additionally, many of these tools have not undergone rigorous validation with older adults or professional caregivers [25–28].

This lack of personalisation, coupled with low configurability, limits the relevance of these systems in clinical geriatric care, where both patient heterogeneity and caregiver constraints must be considered.

2.3 Empowering Caregivers Through End-User Development (EUD)

End-User development (EUD) [6–16] refers to methodologies allowing non-technical users to tailor or create digital solutions. In healthcare, EUD is increasingly seen as a way to bridge the gap between the flexibility needed in clinical settings and the rigidity of traditional software development lifecycles.

In geriatric care, EUD approaches can empower healthcare professionals to:

- Configure personalised exercise plans;
- Design patient-specific chatbot interactions;
- Modify intervention schedules based on real-time data.

Despite these benefits, few systems offer usable EUD interfaces tailored to healthcare workflows. Barriers include technological resistance, regulatory constraints, and the complexity of configuring AI-based tools [29–32].

Our approach directly addresses these limitations. Integrating EUD principles into a caregiver-facing web application enables healthcare professionals to generate and deploy patient-specific cognitive interventions without programming knowledge. The system includes intuitive tools for scheduling, chatbot behaviour customisation, and automatic content generation through Retrieval-Augmented Generation (RAG).

2.4 The Role of Conversational Agents in Elderly Cognitive Support

Conversational agents hold strong potential for enhancing elderly engagement, adherence, and motivation in digital health interventions. Unlike traditional UIs, CAs offer natural language interactions that can simulate coaching, companionship, or reminders [33]. Studies show that older adults are increasingly open to using such tools, particularly when they are user-friendly and context-aware [4, 29, 32–34].

Yet, challenges persist. Most current CAs are not designed for personalisation and fail to adapt their behaviour to patient-specific cognitive profiles or goals. Moreover, few provide caregivers with control over agent behaviour or conversation flow.

Our framework integrates RAG-based CAs to fill this gap. These agents dynamically tailor interactions using patient data (e.g., diagnosis, habits, preferences), enabling geriatric professionals to deliver adaptive, emotionally supportive, and clinically relevant cognitive training. Modifying engagement rules, tone, and scheduling through a simple prompt interface allows caregivers to fine-tune the patient experience.

3 The EUD-Based Platform for Geriatric Professionals

The proposed system is designed as a web-based platform that allows geriatric professionals to profile patients, administer validated cognitive assessments, define personalised cognitive intervention plans, and generate customised conversational agents (CAs) to support elderly users in their daily routines. The development of the platform followed an iterative, user-centred methodology, informed by collaborations with both healthcare institutions and academic partners, in particular personnel from ASST (Azienda Socio Sanitaria Territoriale - Territorial Social Health Company) of Crema, Italy and students and faculty from the University of Brescia, specifically from the degree course for Healthcare Assistants.

We used user stories as a design tool to gather concrete requirements and ensure usability in real-world settings [35]. These narratives reflected the perspectives of multiple stakeholders—doctors, nurses, caregivers, and patients—and helped structure the functional priorities of the platform. Everyday use cases included the need to profile patients through standardised screening tools, monitor their cognitive status over time, and plan daily cognitive stimulation activities that could be followed at home through a simple, guided interface.

According to the results of this formative study, we designed a platform to provide healthcare professionals with the ability to administer three validated screening questionnaires—the GPCOG [19], SDS [20], and MoCA [21]—directly within the system. These tools support the early detection of cognitive decline and serve as the basis for patient profiling. The interface displays both questionnaire results and preliminary diagnoses, enabling a streamlined and repeatable process for cognitive assessment.

Figure 1 illustrates an example of the patient list screen, which allows geriatric professionals to administer and modify diagnostic questionnaires. The profiling section collects essential information, including personal data, lifestyle habits, and medical history, forming the basis for tailored interventions.

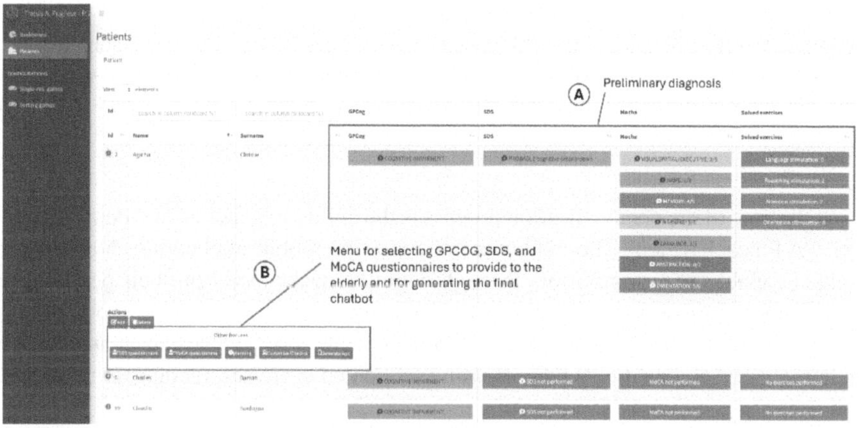

Fig. 1. The screenshot depicts a list of patients translated into English and anonymised. Section A shows the preliminary diagnosis results for each patient based on the respective questionnaire results. Section B presents a menu for selecting questionnaires (GPCOG, SDS, and MoCA) to administer to older adults and for generating the final chatbot.

Beyond diagnosis, the platform facilitates the creation of individualised plans consisting of cognitive exercises tailored to each patient's profile. These exercises are organised across multiple cognitive domains, including memory, orientation, reasoning, and language, and are scheduled over a weekly timeline. Figure 2 shows the diagnostic interface with a preliminary summary of patient results and access to assessment tools, while Fig. 3 provides an overview of exercise monitoring, which visualises the frequency and outcomes of specific activity categories.

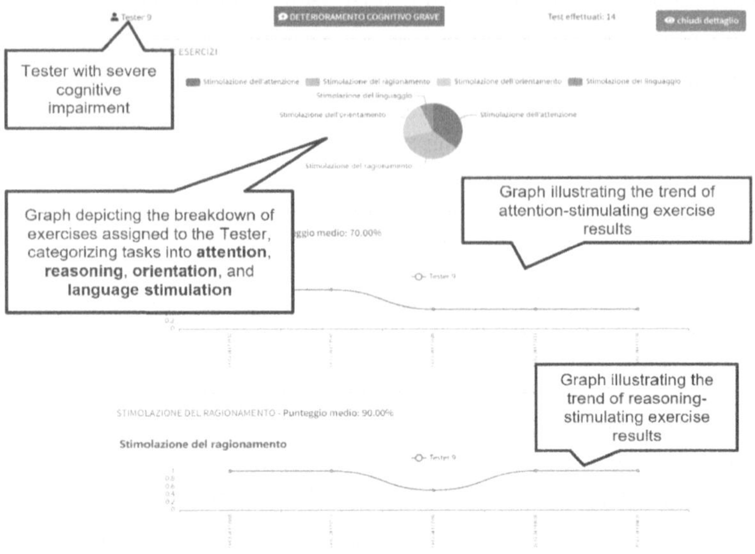

Fig. 2. The screenshot (not translated into English due to graphs) showcases a monitoring page to visualise information for a tester with severe cognitive impairment. The first graph provides a breakdown of exercises assigned to the tester, categorising tasks into attention, reasoning, orientation, and language stimulation. The second graph illustrates the trend of attention-stimulating exercise results, while the final graph portrays the reasoning-stimulating exercise results.

At the core of the personalisation process is the ability to generate and deploy a dedicated CA for each patient. The chatbot is embedded in a mobile application and is a digital assistant capable of guiding users through cognitive tasks based on their personalised plans. Caregivers can define the chatbot's behaviour using structured prompt engineering, setting the assistant's tone, rules for engagement, and feedback mechanisms. The chatbot interacts with patients by presenting scheduled exercises, recognising correct or incorrect responses, and adapting the interaction accordingly.

The platform is designed with flexibility in mind: caregivers can manually customise the scheduling of activities, modify exercises as needed, and regenerate the chatbot with updated configurations. This model aligns with EUD principles, allowing healthcare professionals to iteratively adjust their digital interventions without relying on technical staff. At the same time, the interface remains accessible and easy to use, requiring only minimal training for operation.

In addition to activity assignment, the platform enables real-time monitoring of patient progress. Healthcare professionals can visualise trends in task performance, allowing for early detection of deteriorating cognitive functions or the adjustment of exercise plans. Integrating personalisation, plan generation, and monitoring within a single platform ensures that cognitive care can be efficiently managed while reducing administrative burdens on staff.

Fig. 3. Page for planning cognitive exercises for a patient.

4 Automated Generation of Personalised Exercise Plans and Mobile Applications

The platform integrates a series of automated processes to assist healthcare professionals in generating personalised cognitive intervention plans and deploying them within a mobile application for elderly patients. These processes rely on a combination of web technologies, AI frameworks, and mobile development tools seamlessly connected to deliver an end-to-end cognitive support system.

Once the patient profile has been established through screening and background data collection, the system prompts the caregiver to generate a weekly cognitive exercise plan (see Fig. 3). The caregiver inputs key variables such as cognitive assessment results, patient preferences, and scheduling constraints. This data is processed through a pipeline that combines several technologies, including VueJS[1] for the front-end interface, Symfony[2] for the back-end logic, LangChain[3] for AI orchestration, and Flutter[4] for mobile app compilation.

The exercise plan is generated using a RAG approach, where LangChain connects the system to a Gemini 1.5-Flash model [36] optimised for real-time interaction. Structured patient data—including test scores and health indicators—is serialised in JSON format and transmitted to the LangChain middleware, which queries a corpus of cognitive tasks and constructs a tailored weekly schedule. The final plan is organised into a table, with

[1] https://vuejs.org/.
[2] https://symfony.com/.
[3] https://www.langchain.com/.
[4] https://flutter.dev/.

days of the week as columns and cognitive domains as rows. Each task is contextually selected to match the patient's cognitive level and therapeutic goals.

The generated plan remains editable within the platform. Caregivers can adjust the number of exercises daily, select different task types, or reallocate time slots to match the patient's routine. This flexibility is critical for ensuring the intervention remains feasible and personalised as the patient's condition evolves. Once finalised, the plan is stored in the database and becomes the basis for configuring the mobile application.

The system allows caregivers to generate a fully functioning mobile application that includes the scheduled exercises and an embedded conversational agent to facilitate the deployment. The deployment workflow begins with constructing a JSON package containing the plan, chatbot parameters, and system metadata. This package is passed to a Flutter Docker container, which compiles the Android APK. The mobile app includes all necessary assets, such as the conversational agent logic, interface components, and configuration settings (see Fig. 4 for some examples).

The CA is configured through structured prompt engineering, allowing caregivers to define interaction style, feedback strategies, and behavioural rules. For example, a prompt may specify how the chatbot should introduce an exercise when it should offer encouragement, or how it should handle incorrect answers. This configuration is embedded into the chatbot logic via LangChain, which manages two main APIs: one for retrieving randomly selected exercises and one for handling caregiver-defined tasks.

The chatbot's interaction model is enhanced by integrating Google AI Embeddings[5] and vectorised search capabilities. User interactions are contextualised through semantic embeddings and matched with relevant response patterns, enabling the chatbot to sustain a coherent dialogue with the user while minimising cognitive load. Streamed responses further enhance the experience, reducing latency and creating a more natural interaction flow.

The mobile application includes standard accessibility features, such as high-contrast themes, adjustable text size, and audio playback. A unique identifier is generated for each patient, and data is stored locally using SQLite[6], with optional synchronisation with the caregiver dashboard. Notifications are managed through the FlutterLocalNotificationsPlugin, allowing the system to remind users about upcoming tasks without external dependencies.

By integrating cognitive assessment, personalised planning, conversational support, and mobile deployment into a single pipeline, the platform offers a scalable and replicable solution for cognitive care. Automating this process reduces the time and effort required by healthcare professionals while ensuring that interventions remain tailored to the evolving needs of each patient.

[5] https://js.langchain.com/v0.1/docs/integrations/text_embedding/.

[6] https://www.sqlite.org/.

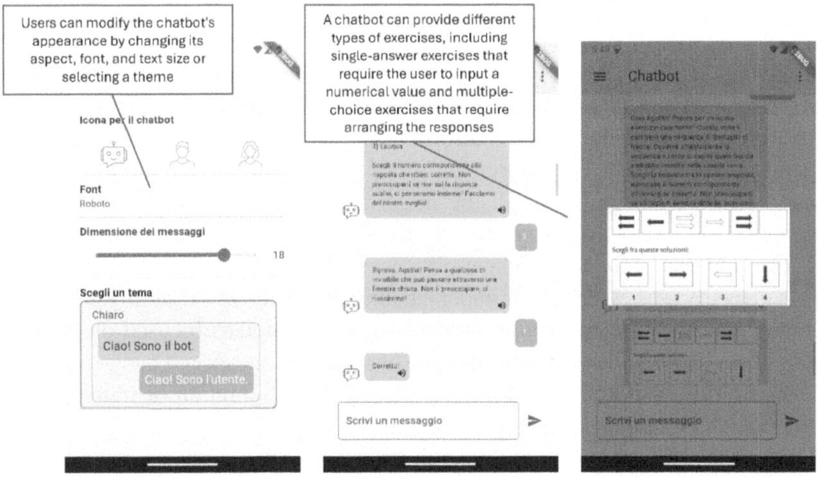

Fig. 4. The figure presents 3 screenshots of the chatbot. Following an initial greeting, users can customise the chatbot's appearance by modifying its aspect, font, and text size or selecting a theme. Then, the chatbot can provide various exercise types, including single-answer exercises that require numerical input and multiple-choice exercises that require arranging responses

5 Usability and User Experience Evaluation

A preliminary evaluation was conducted with healthcare professionals representing the platform's primary user group to assess its usability, perceived usefulness, and potential for integration into clinical practice.

This assessment focused on the web interface, which enables caregivers to configure patient profiles, conduct cognitive screenings, and generate personalised exercise plans. In line with the framework's EUD orientation, the evaluation examined how intuitively non-technical users could interact with the platform and whether they perceived it as a viable support tool in their daily workflows.

The evaluation protocol included practical scenarios simulating everyday clinical tasks—such as entering a new patient, administering a cognitive questionnaire, and configuring a training plan through the calendar interface. These interactions were designed to reflect actual use cases and provided a realistic basis for evaluating learnability, interaction quality, and the system's alignment with professional routines. To ensure comprehensive coverage of the user experience, the protocol combined direct task performance with pre-and post-test questionnaires, enabling both quantitative and qualitative data collection. The use of multiple instruments—specifically the System Usability Scale (SUS) [14], the Unified Theory of Acceptance and Use of Technology (UTAUT) [15–17], the NASA Task Load Index (NASA-TLX) [18], and the Computational Thinking Scale (CTS) [13]—allowed for a multidimensional assessment of usability and user engagement.

The following subsections outline the participant sample and study objectives, describe the evaluation instruments and data collection methodology, present a synthesis of the results, and reflect on the current study's limitations and future directions.

5.1 Sample Selection and Study Objectives

The evaluation included seven geriatric healthcare professionals from two clinical institutions: Crema Hospital and the Don Gnocchi Center in Salice Terme. These professionals were selected to ensure the platform would be tested in contexts consistent with its intended deployment. The participant group was intentionally composed of a mix of roles—three physicians (specialising in geriatrics and neurology), two nurses, and two caregivers—to capture diverse perspectives regarding clinical priorities, technical familiarity, and digital tool acceptance.

This diversity was essential for understanding the platform's usability across different contact points in the caregiving process. While physicians focused on the clinical soundness of cognitive assessments and personalisation, nurses and caregivers concentrated on usability aspects, especially regarding the configuration of training routines and chatbot interactions.

A complementary objective of this evaluation was to investigate how individual differences in computational thinking might affect the ability to engage with the EUD-based features of the system. For this reason, the Computational Thinking Scale (CTS) [13] was included to establish each participant's problem-solving style, which may impact how they perceive and use customisable digital systems. The CTS also helped contextualise other usability indicators by relating them to user predispositions, particularly abstraction and decomposition—skills relevant to creating structured digital workflows.

5.2 Evaluation Tools and Methodology

The methodology followed a multi-instrument protocol combining task-based testing with pre-and post-test questionnaires to evaluate usability and user experience from multiple dimensions. The evaluation was conducted remotely, with each participant receiving individual access credentials, a detailed guide for completing test tasks, and a dedicated feedback form for qualitative impressions.

The Computational Thinking Scale (CTS) was administered before the task-based session to assess problem-solving aptitude across five domains: abstraction, decomposition, algorithmic design, generalisation, and evaluation [37]. This profiling phase allowed a deeper understanding of users' cognitive strategies when engaging with EUD features.

Following the task session, three established instruments were used to assess usability and cognitive workload. The System Usability Scale (SUS) [38] provided a global score for usability perception based on ten items that explore the interface's simplicity, coherence, and efficiency. The Unified Theory of Acceptance and Use of Technology (UTAUT) [39–41] examined factors influencing the likelihood of adoption, such as perceived usefulness, ease of use, social influence, and availability of technical support. Lastly, the NASA Task Load Index (NASA-TLX) [42] offered insight into the mental workload experienced during the interaction, gauging cognitive, temporal, and emotional demands.

Participants also completed a demographic form to contextualise the results regarding age, gender, and prior experience with technology. All data were anonymised and analysed using descriptive statistical methods.

5.3 Results and Interpretation

The analysis of CTS responses revealed varying computational thinking profiles among participants, with differences emerging across roles, as reported in Table 1. Physicians and nurses generally demonstrated higher abstraction and evaluation scores, suggesting greater ease in conceptualising personalised plans and understanding their outcomes. In contrast, caregivers tended to score lower in decomposition and abstraction, reflecting a more concrete, procedural engagement with the system. These results suggest that some aspects of the platform, especially the more open-ended chatbot prompt configuration, may benefit from additional scaffolding or templates for users with limited abstraction capacity.

Table 1. Results of the statistical analysis of the CTS responses.

	Low	Mid	High
Abstractions	2	9	7
Decomposition	6	11	4
Algorithm Design	5	10	13
Generalisation	0	8	20
Evaluation	0	10	18

Usability outcomes were encouraging. The SUS yielded an average score of 81.67, which indicates intense user satisfaction and ease of use. Participants consistently reported that the system was easy to navigate and that tasks such as patient registration and plan generation could be completed without prior training. Several users noted that they became familiar with the interface in less than ten minutes, suggesting practical design affordances.

The UTAUT analysis provided further validation (see Table 2). High scores in *Effort Expectancy* and *Performance Expectancy* demonstrated that users believed the system would improve their work efficiency without imposing significant operational burdens. *Trust* and *User Satisfaction* scores were similarly high, indicating overall confidence in the platform. However, the categories of *Social Influence* and *Facilitating Conditions* revealed important caveats. Specifically, some participants questioned whether their colleagues or institutions would support adopting new tools and whether sufficient technical assistance would be available during onboarding. These concerns are especially relevant in settings where IT support is scarce or resistance to innovation is culturally embedded.

Cognitive workload, measured using the NASA-TLX, returned a low mean score of 32.22, indicating that the interaction did not impose substantial mental strain. This result confirms that the platform's interface and workflows align well with the cognitive demands of its users, a key factor in systems meant to be used under time constraints or in high-responsibility environments.

Table 2. The table contains the average and standard deviation of the answers to the questions of the UTAUT questionnaire.

Variables	*Average*	*Std. Dev*	*Variables*	*Average*	*Std. Dev*	*Variables*	*Average*	*Std. Dev*	*Variables*	*Average*	*Std. Dev*
Effort Expectancy (EE)			**Performance Expectancy (PE)**			**Social Influence (SI)**			**Facilitating Conditions (FC)**		
EE1	4.33	0.58	PE1	4.33	1.15	SI1	4.00	1.00	FC1	3.67	0.58
EE2	3.67	1.15	PE2	4.33	0.58	SI2	4.00	1.00	FC2	4.33	0.58
EE3	4.33	0.58	PE3	4.67	0.58	SI3	2.33	1.53	FC3	2.33	1.15
			PE4	3.33	0.58				FC4	3.33	1.15
			PE5	4.67	0.58						
Trust (T)			**User Satisfaction (US)**			**Behavioural Intention (BI)**					
T1	4.33	1.15	US1	4.67	0.58	BI1		4.00		1.00	
T2	4.67	0.58	US2	4.33	1.15	BI2		4.33		0.58	
T3	4.67	0.58	US3	4.67	0.58						

Qualitative feedback collected from participants further supported these findings. Several users appreciated the structured layout and the clarity of the plan editor. Others emphasised the value of integrating familiar assessment tools, which helped maintain continuity with their current routines. Suggestions for improvement included reducing redundancy in screening questionnaires—particularly when multiple tests overlap in scope—and providing technical support during early system adoption. These insights will guide future refinements of the platform.

5.4 Limitations and Future Directions

While the evaluation produced promising results, several limitations must be acknowledged. The most evident constraint lies in the limited sample size of seven participants, which restricts the generalizability of the results despite offering valuable preliminary insights. While this cohort provided a balanced representation of professional roles, further studies involving a larger and more heterogeneous user base are necessary to validate the platform's usability at scale.

Moreover, the current study focused exclusively on the caregiver-facing interface, which was appropriate for evaluating EUD functionality but did not include testing with elderly mobile applications and chatbot end-users. Since older adults are the ultimate recipients of the cognitive support delivered via the conversational agent, future research must address their interaction patterns, accessibility needs, and user experience. This would also validate the system's full deployment in home or clinical settings.

Lastly, although the RAG-based personalisation features were evaluated regarding caregiver interaction, the clinical efficacy of the generated cognitive interventions was not examined. Longitudinal studies that track cognitive outcomes in patients over time will be essential to determine whether the platform's personalisation engine can deliver meaningful therapeutic benefits.

In sum, the current evaluation confirms the system's usability and relevance for clinical professionals while identifying critical areas—especially related to support infrastructure, institutional integration, and patient-side testing—that require attention in future development phases.

6 Conclusion and Future Work

This work presented a novel platform that combines End-User Development (EUD) methodologies with Retrieval-Augmented Generation (RAG) techniques to support healthcare professionals in delivering personalised cognitive interventions for older adults. Through a web-based interface, the system enables non-technical users to administer validated screening tools, generate individualised training plans, and deploy a mobile application embedded with a conversational agent. The platform lowers the technical barrier to creating adaptive, patient-centered digital interventions in geriatric care by facilitating this process through configurable prompts and automated personalisation.

The system was developed and evaluated in collaboration with clinical professionals specialising in neurology and geriatrics. A preliminary usability study confirmed the platform's ease of use, acceptance, and alignment with professional needs. The integration of RAG technologies into an EUD framework proved effective in supporting task automation without diminishing user control—particularly in creating and personalising cognitive training routines. The findings also highlighted areas requiring further support, such as improving guidance for users with limited computational thinking skills and strengthening the institutional conditions that facilitate system adoption.

Despite these positive results, this study represents an early phase in a broader research effort. Usability testing was limited to the caregiver interface, and the platform's mobile application and patient-facing chatbot remain to be formally evaluated by elderly end-users. This step is crucial for ensuring accessibility and effectiveness among the impacted population. Furthermore, while the system's personalisation capabilities are promising, their long-term clinical impact remains to be demonstrated. Future studies should adopt longitudinal designs to assess how AI-generated cognitive interventions influence cognitive outcomes and engagement over time.

Additional directions for future development include enhancing the proactivity of the chatbot, integrating speech recognition and multimodal interaction for accessibility, and expanding the library of cognitive tasks through automatic generation techniques. On the deployment side, ensuring full cross-platform compatibility—especially on iOS devices—will be essential to maximising reach and inclusivity.

By enabling healthcare professionals to co-design and deliver tailored cognitive support, this platform contributes to a growing field of AI-assisted tools that centre human agency and personalisation. The results encourage continued exploration of hybrid EUD and generative AI systems as a foundation for scalable, adaptive, and ethically grounded solutions in cognitive health care.

References

1. Karimi, L., Mahboub-Ahari, A., Jahangiry, L., Sadeghi-Bazargani, H., Farahbakhsh, M.: A systematic review and meta-analysis of studies on screening for mild cognitive impairment in primary healthcare. BMC Psychiatry **22**(1), 97 (2022)
2. Salmon, D.P., Malkina, A., Johnson, M.L., Gigliotti, C., Little, E.A., Galasko, D.: Effectiveness and utilisation of a cognitive screening program for primary geriatric care. Alzheimers Res. Ther. **17**(1), 23 (2025)
3. Li, A., Li, J., Zhang, D., Wu, W., Zhao, J., Qiang, Y.: Synergy through integration of digital cognitive tests and wearable devices for mild cognitive impairment screening. Front. Hum. Neurosci. **17**, 1183457 (2023). https://doi.org/10.3389/fnhum.2023.1183457
4. He, Z., Dieciuc, M., Carr, D., Chakraborty, S., Singh, A., Fowe, I.E., et al.: New opportunities for the early detection and treatment of cognitive decline: adherence challenges and the promise of smart and person-centered technologies. BMC Digit. Health **1**(1), 7 (2023)
5. O'Brien, K.S., Harkins, K., Peifer, M., Kleid, M., Coykendall, C., Shea, J., et al.: Designing an intervention to improve cognitive evaluations in primary care. Implement. Sci. Commun. **6**(1), 9 (2025)
6. Lieberman, H. (ed.): Your Wish is My Command: Programming by Example. Morgan Kaufmann, San Francisco (2001)
7. Bell, B., Lewis, C.: ChemTrains: a language for creating behaving pictures. In: IEEE Workshop on Visual Languages, Bergen, Norway, pp. 188–195 (1993)
8. Cypher, A.: Watch What I Do: Programming by Demonstration. MIT Press, Cambridge (1993)
9. Eisenberg, M., Fischer, G.: Programmable design environments: integrating end-user programming with domain-oriented assistance. In: Proceedings of ACM CHI Conference, Boston, MA, pp. 431–437 (1994)
10. Fischer, G., Girgenson, A.: End-user modifiability in design environments. In: CHI '90 Conference on Human Factors in Computing Systems, Seattle, WA, pp. 183–191 (1990)
11. Ioannidou, A., Repenning, A.: End-user programmable simulations. Dr. Dobb's J. **302**(Aug), 40–48 (1999)
12. Jones, C.: End-user programming. IEEE Comput. **28**(9), 68–70 (1995)
13. Nardi, B.: A Small Matter of Programming. MIT Press, Cambridge (1993)
14. Pane, J.F., Myers, B.A.: Usability issues in the design of novice programming systems. Technical Report. CMU-CS-96–132, Carnegie Mellon Univ., Pittsburgh (1996)
15. Rader, C., Cherry, G., Brand, C., Repenning, A., Lewis, C.: Principles to scaffold mixed textual and iconic end-user programming languages. In: IEEE Symposium Visual Languages, Nova Scotia, Canada, pp. 187–194 (1998)
16. Repenning, A., Sumner, T.: Agentsheets: a medium for creating domain-oriented visual languages. IEEE Comput. **28**(3), 17–25 (1995)
17. Siriwardhana, S., Weerasekera, R., Wen, E., Kaluarachchi, T., Rana, R., Nanayakkara, S.: Improving the domain adaptation of retrieval augmented generation (RAG) models for open domain question answering. Trans. Assoc. Comput. Linguist. **11**, 1–17 (2023)
18. Wolf, A., Tripanpitak, K., Umeda, S., Otake-Matsuura, M.: Eye-tracking paradigms for the assessment of mild cognitive impairment: a systematic review. Front. Psychol. **14**, 1197567 (2023). https://doi.org/10.3389/fpsyg.2023.1197567
19. Seeher, K.M., Brodaty, H.: The general practitioner assessment of cognition (GPCOG). In: Cognitive Screening Instruments: A Practical Approach, pp. 231–239 (2017)
20. Flaherty, L.B., Midden, A., Mast, B.T.: Psychometric evaluation of the symptoms of dementia screener (SDS) in a geriatric primary care population. Clin. Gerontol. **42**(5), 504–511 (2019)
21. Hobson, J.: The montreal cognitive assessment (MoCA). Occup. Med. **65**(9), 764–765 (2015)

22. Bickmore, T.W., Silliman, R.A., Nelson, K., Cheng, D.M., Winter, M., Henault, L., et al.: A randomized controlled trial of an automated exercise coach for older adults. J. Am. Geriatr. Soc. **61**(10), 1676–1683 (2013)
23. Maiden, N., D'Souza, S., Jones, S., Müller, L., Pannese, L., Pitts, K., et al.: Computing technologies for reflective, creative care of people with dementia. Commun. ACM **56**(11), 60–67 (2013)
24. Trofymenko, O., Prokop, Y., Zadereyko, O., Loginova, N.: Classification of chatbots. Syst. Technol. **2**(139), 147–159 (2022)
25. Digital4: La nuova era dei chatbot: la tecnologia oggi è matura (2022). https://www.digital4.biz/marketing/la-nuova-era-dei-robot-chatbot-la-tecnologia-oggi-e-matura/. Accessed Mar 2025
26. Gamberini, L., Fabregat, M., Spagnolli, A., Prontu, L., Seraglia, B., Alcaniz, M., et al.: Eldergames: videogames for empowering, training and monitoring elderly cognitive capabilities. Gerontechnology **7**(2), 111 (2008)
27. i3Lab Polimi: 5A – 5A project presentation website. https://5a.polimi.it/. Accessed Feb 2025
28. Zeiler, M., Dietzel, N., Kammerer, K., Frick, U., Pryss, R., Heuschmann, P., et al.: Digital screening tool for the assessment of cognitive impairment in unsupervised setting—digiDEM-SCREEN: study protocol for a validation study. BMJ Open **15**(1), e087256 (2025)
29. Mankar, R.V., Jha, H., Golakiya, A., Yeole, R.: Systematic review: digital tools in early diagnosis and intervention of Alzheimer's disease. CME J. Geriatr. Med. **17**(1), 97–102 (2025)
30. Zhou, C., et al.: Barriers and facilitators to participation in electronic health interventions in older adults with cognitive impairment: an umbrella review. BMC Geriatr. **24**(1), 1037 (2024)
31. Bayer, T.A., Liu, Y., Vishnepolskiy, I., Baez, D., Sanders, L., Williams, R., et al.: Usability of an at-home tablet-based cognitive test in older adults with and without cognitive impairment. BMC Digit. Health **2**(1), 66 (2024)
32. Wegener, E.K., Bergschöld, J.M., Kramer, T., Schmidt, C.W., Borgnakke, K.: Co-designing a conversational agent with older adults with chronic obstructive pulmonary disease who age in place: qualitative study. JMIR Hum. Factors **11**, e63222 (2024)
33. Igarashi, T., Iijima, K., Nitta, K., Chen, Y.: Estimation of the cognitive functioning of the elderly by AI agents: a comparative analysis of the effects of the psychological burden of intervention. Healthcare **12**(18), 1821 (2024)
34. Abdi, S., Spann, A., Borilovic, J., de Witte, L., Hawley, M.: Understanding the care and support needs of older people: a scoping review and categorisation using the WHO international classification of functioning, disability and health framework (ICF). BMC Geriatr. **19**, 1–15 (2019)
35. Cohn, M.: User Stories Applied: For Agile Software Development. Addison-Wesley, Boston (2004)
36. Independent analysis of AI models and API providers. https://artificialanalysis.ai/. Accessed Mar 2025
37. Ceylan, V.K., Vural, R.A.: Self-assessment of computational thinking skill: a scale development study (2023). https://doi.org/10.5281/zenodo.8217317
38. Peres, S.C., Pham, T., Phillips, R.: Validation of the system usability scale (SUS) in the WILD. In: Proceedings of Human Factors Ergonomics Society Annual Meeting, vol. 57, no. 1, pp.192–196. Sage, Los Angeles (2013)
39. Venkatesh, V., Morris, M.G., Davis, G.B., Davis, F.D.: User acceptance of information technology: toward a unified view. MIS Q. **27**(3), 425–478 (2003)
40. Venkatesh, V., Thong, J.Y., Xu, X.: Consumer acceptance and use of information technology: extending the unified theory of acceptance and use of technology. MIS Q. **36**(1), 157–178 (2012)

41. Valtolina, S., Matamoros, R.A., Epifania, F.: Methods for evaluating conversational agents' communicability, acceptability and accessibility degree. In: IFIP Conference on Human-Computer Interaction, pp. 372–382. Springer, Cham (2023)
42. Hart, S.G.: NASA-task load index (NASA-TLX); 20 years later. In: Proceedings of Human Factors Ergonomics Society Annual Meeting, vol. 50, no. 9, pp. 904–908. Sage, Los Angeles (2006)

From Digital Self-control Apps to iOS Shortcuts: Enabling Privacy-Centric Wellbeing Research Without Code

Aditya Kumar Purohit[1(✉)] and Alberto Monge Roffarello[2]

[1] Center for Advanced Internet Studies, Bochum, Germany
aditya.purohit@cais-research.de
[2] Politecnico di Torino, Turin, Italy
alberto.monge@polito.it

Abstract. Academic research on Digital Self-Control Tools (DSCTs), i.e., mobile applications that enable users to exercise control over technology use, faces technical and privacy-related challenges. This paper lays the foundations for an alternative approach: empowering researchers to use automation tools, e.g., iOS Shortcuts, to create and evaluate interventions without writing code. First, we interrogate the capabilities of iOS Shortcuts in replicating current DSCT functionalities, grounding our exploration in a state-of-the-art taxonomy of intervention strategies. Findings show that iOS Shortcuts is a viable tool for digital-wellbeing research as it can replicate 75% of the features of contemporary DSCTs, potentially overcoming DSCTs' well-known limits, e.g., through multi-device and feature-level interventions. Then, we report on a between-subject study (N = 193) investigating how researchers should distribute interventions to participants in digital wellbeing experiments. Results highlight that iOS Shortcuts can alleviate initial privacy concerns among participants by empowering them to manually re-create the intervention to be tested.

Keywords: Digital wellbeing · Privacy-sensitive design · End-user programming · Trigger-action programming · iOS Shortcuts · Digital Self-Control Interventions · no-code tools

1 Introduction

Recently, there has been a significant and contentious discussion - both across research communities and on mass media - surrounding the potential drawbacks of excessive technology use [21,58], particularly concerning smartphones [2,14,79]. In parallel, the HCI community has recently started to highlight the importance of supporting users' digital wellbeing [7,57], showing a growing interest in the field of Digital Self-Control Tools (DSCTs) [54,60]. On smartphones, mobile DSCTs are dedicated mobile applications that assists users in exercising self-control over their use of other apps, enabling users to monitor

C. Santoro et al. (Eds.): IS-EUD 2025, LNCS 15713, pp. 221–243, 2025.
https://doi.org/10.1007/978-3-031-95452-8_14

their usage patterns and instantiate interventions such as timers and lock-out mechanisms, e.g., to use Instagram no more than 30 min per days [54]. Nevertheless, the same HCI community highlighted that innovating interventions for digital self-control and evaluating their effectiveness in human subject research is challenging for digital-wellbeing researchers [60]. Specifically, developing DSCTs demands advanced programming skills and faces challenges due to operating system limitations [54], thus forcing researchers to exploit "unconventional" methods to develop their interventions, e.g., using Android's Accessibility APIs [9]. Furthermore, users often have privacy concerns when installing third-party DSCTs that make access to sensitive information like time spent on other apps [35,40].

Building upon the evidence from initial research [69,71,72,74,77], this paper investigates the use of iOS Shortcuts [29] – the popular Apple's automation tool – as a viable alternative to enable academic researchers to a) *create* and b) *evaluate* digital self-control interventions at operating system level. Implementing such an approach would circumvent the complexities of traditional programming and address technical and privacy concerns associated with third-party applications, making DSCT research more accessible to researchers without extensive coding skills, such as those in the medical domain.

To assess the feasibility of *creating* digital self-control tools through iOS Shortcuts, we first interrogated the capabilities of the platform in replicating interventions implemented by existing mobile DSCTs, grounding our exploration in the taxonomy of intervention features set forth by Lyngs et al. [54] (Sect. 3). Specifically, a research group composed of 3 researchers and a Reddit user active in the iOS Shortcuts community tried to construct a digital self-control intervention for each of the 24 DSCT features in the taxonomy, operating on Apple's automation tool on an iPhone. Our findings reveal that iOS Shortcuts can accommodate 18 of the 24 interventions outlined in the Lyngs et al. taxonomy (75% coverage) for a smartphone, positioning it as a viable tool for digital-wellbeing research. Additionally, as discussed in the last section of this paper, iOS Shortcuts can overcome well-known limits of contemporary DSCTs, by easily allowing researchers to develop context-aware and feature-level interventions, as well as combining multiple interventions and targeting multi-device ecosystems.

To explore how to *evaluate* digital self-control interventions built with iOS Shortcuts, we then investigated how researchers could take advantage of this tool to start a digital-wellbeing experiment while minimizing privacy concerns among participants (Sect. 4). Addressing these initial issues is crucial for the sustained use and management of these interventions during and beyond their evaluation, as privacy is major barrier to the installation and adoption of digital wellbeing apps [23,70]. To this end, we conducted a between-subjects experiment involving $N = 193$ participants, wherein we critically compared two different modalities for distributing iOS Shortcuts mobile interventions in digital-wellbeing research studies: manual re-creation by end users *vs.* reuse of pre-built interventions (Study 2, Sect. 4). Our findings show that, despite pre-build interventions were available for review and could potentially be modified, participants had more privacy concerns and perceived more privacy risks when reusing a ready-made intervention. This suggests that allowing users to manually inspect a DSCT before using it, seeing all the steps that characterize its intervention strategies, could potentially reduce initial attrition.

To summarize, this work offers two main contributions. First, we provide the digital-wellbeing researchers with a deeper dive into how iOS Shortcuts can play a role in digital wellbeing research experiments and enhance users' digital self-control (Sect. 3). On top of that, we underpin our assertions with empirical evidence, offering optimal strategies to craft and disseminate these interventions and start digital wellbeing experiments in a manner sensitive to participant privacy concerns (Sect. 4). We conclude the paper by discussing opportunities and challenges that may define the path toward the end-user development of digital self-control interventions (Sect. 5), thereby democratizing such an approach to end users beyond researchers.

2 Background and Related Work

2.1 Achieving Digital Wellbeing by Exercising Self-control

Smartphone use is increasingly linked to terms like overuse [48], compulsive use [79], and addiction [45], prompting researchers to develop psychological scales to measure user dependence [43]. While some debates on technology addiction remain speculative [45], extensive evidence suggests that excessive smartphone use disrupts daily tasks [2,44], harms mental health [44], and reduces quality social interactions [80]. Features like infinite scrolling and autoplay further diminish user agency and self-control [52,61]. Many users express a desire to replace negative digital habits with more meaningful activities [48,59,79]. This growing concern has led to an emerging HCI research field on "digital wellbeing," defined by Burr et al. [7] as "the impact of digital technologies on what it means to live a life that is good for a human being in an information society" (p. 2313). In response, various Digital Self-Control Tools (DSCTs) have been developed to help users manage distracting apps and websites. As highlighted in recent reviews [54,60], most DSCTs are mobile apps offering intervention strategies such as self-monitoring [54] and digital nudges [56,70] to encourage healthier smartphone use.

2.2 Innovating DSCTs: Technical and Privacy Barriers

While DSCTs have shown short- to medium-term effectiveness in modifying technology use [60], developing and evaluating them in human-subject research remains challenging [40,54,57]. A key concern is their paradoxical nature—third-party tools that restrict technology use [52,60], raising privacy and manipulation concerns [84]. As DSCTs access sensitive data, privacy safeguards are crucial and widely demanded [35,40,60]. Rooksby et al. [75] highlight that "data about everyday device use can reveal much about someone's life, raising privacy concerns" (p. 293). Ensuring ethical and privacy-conscious study designs remains an open challenge [60]. This paper examines privacy concerns at the installation stage, where researchers introduce DSCTs to participants. Developing DSCTs also presents technical challenges, requiring advanced programming skills and workarounds for OS restrictions [39]. Research on iOS-based DSCTs remains limited due to Apple's strict platform controls on usage data and app blocking [32,54,57]. On Android, DSCTs often rely on accessibility APIs to bypass restrictions [9]. Across platforms, DSCTs are also vulnerable to software aging [76] and OS updates [39], which can disrupt their functionality. To address these challenges, this paper explores iOS Shortcuts as an OS-level automation tool, offering researchers a low-code approach to designing and testing digital self-control interventions.

2.3 Task Automation Tools and Trigger-Action Programming

There has been sustained interest in HCI in enabling users to automate digital tasks, particularly on smartphones [63]. Recently, iOS Shortcuts (Apple) [29] and Android Rules (Google) [1] have expanded automation possibilities through the Trigger-Action Programming (TAP) paradigm, where predefined rules execute actions based on specific triggers. Building on early TAP systems like iCAP [18], prior research has demonstrated its effectiveness across various domains, including smart homes [81] and IoT [11]. iOS Shortcuts, pre-installed on most Apple devices, enables users to automate tasks across their ecosystem, creating custom workflows such as "If I'm home at 10 p.m., remind me to sleep." Shortcuts are composed of sequential actions, which interact with both Apple's apps (e.g., Notes, Calendar) and third-party applications. Automations extend this by allowing tasks to run automatically based on triggers, such as opening Instagram prompting a project reminder. As an OS-integrated tool, iOS Shortcuts bridges system-level data, settings, and sensors with third-party apps, broadening its applicability. Recently, researchers have leveraged iOS Shortcuts for digital self-control interventions. Purohit and Holzer [69] created a shortcut-based Instagram usage timer to reduce mindless scrolling, while Purohit et al. [72] developed strict and self-regulated newsfeed diets for Facebook, tracking users' app usage. This paper extends this exploration, assessing the feasibility of using iOS Shortcuts as a low-code platform for researchers to design and implement digital self-control interventions more effectively.

3 Assessing iOS Shortcuts for Digital Self-control

This section examines the viability of leveraging iOS Shortcuts as a TAP tool empowering digital wellbeing researchers to create and develop digital self-control interventions. Specifically, we used Apple's automation tool to replicate interventions included in state-of-the-art mobile DSCTs, investigating what can be implemented and what cannot, as well as the degree of difficulty of the implementation. To facilitate reproducibility and reuse of our methods, we are sharing videos and QR codes for the basic steps of all reproduced interventions in the following repository: https://shorturl.at/X2qp2. These steps include tracking Instagram's opening and closing times, recording Instagram usage data, storing this data, and displaying usage timers.

3.1 Methodology

Three researchers from different continents—including the two authors—and a Reddit user from the iOS Shortcuts community collaborated to design digital self-control interventions using iOS Shortcuts. To assess the tool's potential, we restricted development to the iOS Shortcuts ecosystem, avoiding third-party apps. For a structured approach, we followed a taxonomy of digital self-control interventions. After reviewing recent efforts to categorize DSCTs, we adopted Lyngs et al.'s taxonomy [54] due to its comprehensive scope and prior use in digital wellbeing research [15,53,60]. The taxonomy was developed by Lyngs et al. [54] through an in-depth analysis of 367 apps across major platforms and is grounded in a dual systems regulation model. It categorizes intervention strategies into 24 design features categorized as blocking/removing, tracking, goal advancement, and rewarding/punishing. The research team, in particular, tried to construct a digital self-control intervention for each of the features included in the taxonomy, taking inspiration from research-based DSCTs, e.g., those reviewed in [60], and selecting Instagram as the target application. Instagram was chosen for its tendency to create digital wellbeing problems [59] and because researchers have paid less attention to it than Facebook [71].

During solution development, step-by-step action flows were first sketched on paper, aligning with computational thinking principles such as decomposition, which involves breaking problems into smaller parts, and abstraction, which focuses on key attributes [16,20,31]. These conceptual solutions were then implemented as trigger-action protocols using iOS Shortcuts. As with most complex tasks, debugging and iterative refinement were necessary to ensure robustness. Each collaborator independently developed their version of the intervention, and the team met three times a week via video calls to discuss design choices and challenges. Solutions were evaluated based on their alignment with Lyngs et al.'s taxonomy [54] and categorized by implementation difficulty. Solutions with five or fewer actions were considered low difficulty, those requiring six to nine actions were labeled medium difficulty, and those with ten or more actions were classified as high difficulty. It is worth noting that collaborators' programming experience may have influenced their perception of difficulty.

3.2 Findings

Table 1 summarizes the results of our investigation, listing all the *DSCT features* of the Lyngs et al. taxonomy [54] and their *category*, the *interventions* that we tried to replicate through iOS Shortcuts, the *reference* work from which we selected the target interventions, and the level of *difficulty* characterizing the implementation in iOS Shortcuts, if feasible. In the following sections, we detail the findings of our analysis, dividing them according to the category of the targeted DSCT features. Overall, we implemented digital self-control interventions in iOS Shortcuts for 18 of the 24 DSCT features included in the Lyngs et al. taxonomy, reaching 75% of coverage.

Table 1. Summary of Study 1 Results. For each *DSCT feature* from Lyngs et al. [54], we attempted to create a self-control intervention using iOS Shortcuts, inspired by research-based DSCTs (*main reference*). *Difficulty* indicates implementation complexity based on the number of required actions.

DSCT Feature	Category	Intervention	Main Reference	Difficulty
Feature minimization	Block/removal	Turn the smartphone into gray-scale when the user opens Instagram.	Holte et al. [27]	Low
Effortful task to override	Block/removal	Lock the smartphone screen when the user opens Instagram, forcing them to enter the smartphone's PIN.	Park et al. [68]	Low
Block	Block/removal	Redirect to the home screen whenever the user opens Instagram.	Kim et al. [33]	Low
Time limit for use	Block/removal	Allow Instagram access only between 9 AM and 6 PM.	Hiniker et al. [25]	Medium
Time lag before launch	Block/removal	Introduce a 10-second delay before launching Instagram.	Kovacs et al. [40]	Low
Uninstallation prevention	Block/removal	✗	N/A	✗
Pay to override	Block/removal	✗	N/A	✗
Record history	Self-tracking	Log how many times Instagram is opened.	Purohit et al. [72]	Medium
Visualize usage	Self-tracking	Display Instagram usage metrics: openings, time spent, and remaining time before limit.	Kovacs et al. [41]	High
Display a timer	Self-tracking	Notify users when they have been on Instagram for 5 minutes.	Monge Roffarello et al. [57]	Medium
Set time/activity goals	Goal advancement	Define a time objective for Instagram use when the app is opened.	Shen et al. [78]	Medium
Goal reminders	Goal advancement	Notify users when they reach their Instagram usage limit.	Okeke et al. [66]	Medium
Motivational quotes	Goal advancement	Show a random motivational quote whenever Instagram is accessed.	Foulonneau et al. [22]	Medium
Compare behavior w/ goal	Goal advancement	Allow users to track time spent on Instagram relative to their goal.	Kim et al. [32]	Medium
Redirect activity	Goal advancement	Redirect users to the reminders app when they attempt to access Instagram.	Inie et al. [30]	Low
Praise/blame/please/annoy	Reward/Punish	Send a notification blaming users who exceed their Instagram usage limit.	Collins et al. [10]	High
Gain points/streaks	Reward/Punish	Grant points when Instagram use stays within the goal limit.	Ko et al. [38]	High
Lose points/streaks	Reward/Punish	Deduct points if Instagram use exceeds the goal limit.	Liu et al. [49]	High
Unlock achievements	Reward/Punish	✗	Zhou et al. [87]	✗
Social sharing leaderboards	Reward/Punish	✗	Ko et al. [37]	✗
Points as life forms	Reward/Punish	✗	Liu et al. [49]	✗
Real-world reward/punishment	Reward/Punish	✗	Park et al. [67]	✗

Blocking/Removing. Humans inherently possess a propensity for distraction. Our brains are naturally inclined to gravitate towards stimuli that are enjoyable, pose a threat, or present novelty [3]. The interventions in the cluster of blocking/removing are characterized by their ability to restrict users' access to the application or remove functionality that tempts users to spend more time than they would have otherwise [54]. Concerning the blocking/removing category, we were able to implement 5 out 7 DSCT features included in the Lyngs et al. taxonomy with iOS Shortcuts:

- *Feature minimisation*: The goal of feature minimisation is to put obstacles in the way of distracting functionality [53]. For example, hiding the newsfeed, hiding notifications, or dimming the screen [23]. For feature minimization, we took inspiration from Holte et al. [27] and Zimmermann et al. [88] based on which we constructed an intervention which turns the smartphone into gray-scale when the user opens Instagram. The gray-scale intervention creates as an obstacle in the way of using Instagram. On iOS Shortcuts, we used the Color Filters action with two automations to detect Instagram's opening and closing (low difficulty, $<=$ 5 actions).
- *Effortful task to override*: The aim of an effortful task to override is to implement a deliberately effortful task that needs to be fulfilled prior to gaining access to the desired application [53]. For example, introducing a lockout task that requires user to input 10-digit number when the target app is opened [34]. In our initiative to develop an intervention characterized by intentional effort, we found inspiration in the study conducted by Park et al. [68]. We devised an intervention that locks the smartphone screen upon opening Instagram, forcing the user to input their smartphone pin upon accessing the application. To achieve this on iOS Shortcuts we used the Lock Screen action, associating it with an automation intercepting the opening of the Instagram app (low difficulty, i.e., $<=$ 5 actions).
- *Block*: The aim of this DSCT feature is to block all access to the target application [53]. For example, blocking certain apps during certain time of the day [35]. In our block intervention approach, we drew inspiration from the works by Ko et al. [35] and Kim et al. [33]. Based on these, we devised an intervention that redirects the user to the smartphone's home screen upon opening Instagram, preventing access to the app. To achieve this on iOS Shortcuts we used the Open action, using the home screen as the target destination whenever the associated automation intercepted the opening of the Instagram app (low difficulty, $<=$ 5 actions).
- *Time limit for use*: The intention behind this DSCT feature is to restrict the frequency and timing of app activations [60]. For example, limiting app usage to 10 min per day [25] or restricting access to specific hours [54]. In our initiative to develop an intervention that limits the use, we took inspiration from the DSCT presented by Hiniker et al. [25]. We designed an intervention restricting Instagram access to 9 AM-6 PM. Attempts to open the app outside this window redirect users to the home screen. In iOS Shortcuts, this was implemented by checking the current time and triggering the previously described "block" shortcut if access was outside the allowed period (medium difficulty, $5 <$ actions < 10).
- *Time lag before launch*: The intention behind time lag before launch is not to fully restrict access to the application or service. Instead, it introduces a delay in loading, aiming to deter persistent usage [54,60]. A few examples

that exist induced delay on the websites [40,41,70,76]. We took inspiration from Kovacs et al. [40] and introduced a 10-s delay before the Instagram app is launched. As directly delaying Instagram when its opening was intercepted was not possible in iOS Shortcuts, we developed a shortcut – with a dedicated icon on the home screen – that launched Instagram after waiting 10 s through a Wait action (medium difficulty, i.e., $5 < \text{actions} < 10$). The goal is to open Instagram via the shortcut instead of its app icon.

In the block/removal category, we could not implement *uninstallation prevention* or *pay to override*. The former aims to prevent users from removing interventions, such as blocking DSCT uninstallation, which requires root access. The latter involves charging users to bypass a blocking session, necessitating third-party service integration. Unsurprisingly, we found no similar interventions in the HCI literature (Monge Roffarello et al. [60], Fig. 3).

Self-tracking. The pursuit of electronically detecting a wide array of phenomena has remained a persistent goal in the domains of engineering and computer science [64]. Interventions grouped in the self-tracking category are characterized by their ability to log user activity history, present visualizations of the gathered data, and incorporate timers or countdown mechanisms [54]. Fundamentally, these interventions are designed to examine user behavior and furnish feedback. Concerning the self-tracking category, we were able to implement all the 3 DSCT features included in the Lyngs et al. taxonomy with iOS Shortcuts:

- *Record history*: The aim of recording history is to allow users with logging facilities. For example, monitoring the frequency of app launches [60], quantifying the duration of app utilization [66], and tracking the remaining allowance before hitting the predetermined daily usage limit [83]. For this intervention we took inspiration from Purohit et al. [71], developing an intervention that logged when how many times Instagram was opened locally on the Notes application of the iOS device. In iOS Shortcuts, we automated Instagram's launch to log the date and increment the opening count in Notes (medium difficulty, i.e., $5 < \text{actions} < 10$).
- *Visualise usage*: This DSCT feature facilitates users in viewing their past data and potentially enables the reception of real-time feedback [60]. For example, Okeke et al. [66] utilized haptic (vibration) feedback to give users immediate updates on the duration they've spent, as the app simultaneously logged the history. Building on Kovacs et al. [41], we designed an intervention that provides real-time feedback on Instagram usage, displaying the number of accesses, time spent, and remaining time before reaching the usage limit. In iOS Shortcuts, this was implemented using two automations to detect Instagram's opening and closing, along with actions to track and visualize usage data (high difficulty, $\text{actions} >= 10$).
- *Display a timer*: Through this DSCT feature, a timer is leveraged to present the usage data in real-time for immediate insight [60,69]. For example, Monge Roffarello et al. [57] implemented a timer-based intervention in their Socialise

app to notify users when they are using an app for too long. Drawing insights from both Purohit et al. [69] and Monge Roffarello et al. [57], we designed a timer intervention within iOS Shortcuts. The timer notified users once they've been on Instagram for 5 min. If Instagram is closed before 5 min, the timer turns off (medium difficulty: 5–10 actions).

Goal Advancement. The interventions under the goal advancement are components of self-determination and self-management, serving as a meta-cognitive strategy enabling users to control and modulate their behaviour [42,54]. In the goal-advancement cluster, interventions help users to set explicit goals and remind them, as well as to measure, record, and visualize their actions and compare them to their goals. Concerning this category, we were able to implement all the 7 DSCT features included in the Lyngs et al. taxonomy with iOS Shortcuts:

- *Set concrete time goals* and *set activity goals*: These two DSCT feature allow user to choose/set a concrete goal, either in terms of time to be spent on an app or in terms of other activities to be performed online or offline. For example, Shen et al. [78] gave users the option to establish specific time targets to handle smartphone usage addiction. Drawing from Shen et al. [78], we harnessed iOS Shortcuts to craft an intervention prompting users to establish a specific time objective each time they accessed Instagram. To realize this within Shortcuts, we utilized the Menu action, associating it to an automation that intercepted the opening of Instagram. This granted users the option to select a specific time goal, ranging from 30 s to 120 s, to spend on the app (medium difficulty, i.e., 5 $<$ actions $<$ 10).
- *Concrete goal reminder* and *value/general goal reminder*: Reminders about concrete or general goals notify users once they surpass a predetermined time limit, by using haptic or notifications. For instance, Okeke et al. [66] utilized haptic (vibration) feedback to give users a reminder that they have reached the time limit. To build this intervention within iOS Shortcuts we took inspiration from Collins et al. [10] and Okeke et al. [66], devising a timer that notifies users when they have reached their usage limit. We used automations to detect Instagram's opening and closing, Timer actions to manage usage time, and a Show Notification action to display the timer. (medium difficulty, i.e., 5 $<$ actions $<$ 10).
- *Motivational quotes*: The objective of motivational quotes is to bolster confidence, motivation, and foster empowerment [4]. For example, Foulonneau et al. [22] utilized persuasive messages like *"Less time on your smartphone means more time with loved ones, better focus on your work, or simply peace of mind"* Following a similar approach, we developed an intervention within iOS Shortcuts that presented a random quote whenever Instagram was accessed. To implement this intervention, we utilized the Notes action in Shortcuts. When Instagram was accessed, a random quote from the Notes app was selected and presented to the user in the form of a notification (medium difficulty, i.e., 5 $<$ actions $<$ 10).

- *Compare behaviour w/ goal*: This DSCT feature enables users to contrast their actual behavior with their predetermined objectives [60]. For example, Chisler et al. [8] provided users with information about their set goals and their current status in relation to those goals. Similarly, Kim et al. [32] displayed time left in the notification drawer. Inspired by Kim et al. [32], we crafted a shortcut allowing users to track their progress relative to their set goals. This shortcut was engineered to either operate autonomously for status checks or activate upon opening Instagram. Within iOS Shortcuts, our implementation logic is as follows. If Instagram is opened, then log the opening time. Conversely, if Instagram is closed, note the closing time, calculate the session duration by subtracting and subsequently display the time left from the user's goal (medium difficulty, i.e., $5 < \text{actions} < 10$).
- *Redirect activity*: This DSCT feature directs the user to a constructive activity or service before allowing access to a website or app that might be distracting. [60]. For example, Inie et al. [30] crafted a Chrome extension that steered users towards a learning platform when they attempted to visit a site deemed distracting. In a parallel approach, we fashioned a shortcut that redirected users to the reminder application whenever they tried accessing Instagram. To achieve this on iOS Shortcuts, we employed the Open action and linked it to the reminder app, activating it upon the launch of Instagram through a dedicated automation (low difficulty, i.e., $<=$ 5 actions).

Reward/Punish. Diving into reward/Punish, it is essential to acknowledge a principle within the discipline of psychology that posits behaviors are primarily shaped by their ensuing consequences. This foundational theory argues that individual actions can be steered and modified through the dual avenues of rewards and punishments [24,62]. In the Lyngs et al. [54] taxonomy, in particular, the interventions grouped in the cluster of reward/punish aims at influencing the expected value of control, a cost-benefit analysis that weighs the potential gains and losses of exerting self-control, ultimately influencing its strength. In regards to reward/punish category, we successfully implemented 3 of the 7 DSCT features from the taxonomy by Lyngs et al. using iOS Shortcuts:

- *Praise/blame/please/annoy*: The objective of this DSCT feature is to praise or blame users when they achieved a goal or failed to meet a goal [60]. For example, Collins et al. [10] blamed the user for being unproductive on the interface of RescueTime *"17% less productive than usual and you are 31% less focused."* Drawing from the work by Collins et al. [10] and RescueTime interface, we crafted an intervention that sends users a blame-toned alert if they fail to meet their goal. Using iOS Shortcuts, we set up two automations: one triggered when Instagram is opened and another when it is closed. Users set a daily Instagram time limit; if exceeded, they receive a blaming notification the next day (high difficulty, i.e., actions $>=$ 10).
- *Gain points/streaks*: The goal of the gain points/streaks feature is to influence user behavior through gamification. Specifically, users earn points when they

achieve their set goals [60]. For instance, Ko et al. [36] informed how many points they would receive if they met their goals. Inspired by this approach, we developed a shortcut that allowed the user to choose how many points they would like to receive if they met a certain goal. Using iOS Shortcuts, we set up two automations: one activated upon opening Instagram and another upon its closing. The automation logged points in a JSON-formatted dictionary, storing them for future retrieval (high difficulty, actions >= 10).

- *Lose points/streaks*: Building on the principle of behavioral influence through gamification, the objective of the lose points/streaks feature is to deter users from deviating from their set goals by deducting points [60]. Drawing from Liu et al. [49], who instilled a sense of loss when users deviated from their goals, our implementation deducts points if users surpass their daily limits. Utilizing iOS Shortcuts, we crafted two automations: one triggered when Instagram is initiated and another upon its termination. These automations log and store points in a JSON-formatted dictionary on the device for future access(high difficulty, i.e., actions >= 10).

In the reward/punish category, we were not able to implement, *unlock achievements*, *social sharing leader-boards*, *points represented as life forms*, and *real-world reward/punishment*. The aim of the first three DSCT features is to steer and modify the user behaviour through complex gamification strategies. Examples include interventions that gradually become stronger depending on the user's behavior (Zhou et al. [87], *unlock achievements*), rankings comparing user's self-regulation achievements (Ko et al. [37], *social sharing leader-boards*), and virtual flowers that wither if the user does not respect their own limits (Liu et al. [49], *points represented as life forms*). Implementing these features mandates the integration of both graphic capabilities and external APIs. The aim of *real-world reward/punishment*, instead, is to steer user's behavior leveraging real-world incentives or deterrents, e.g., making the user lose money if they spend too much time on the smartphone (Park et al. [67]). These strategies, particularly those suggesting micro-financial incentives, necessitate integration with third-party service providers.

4 iOS Shortcuts in Digital Wellbeing Research

This section examines how digital wellbeing researchers could take advantage of iOS Shortcuts in their digital wellbeing experiments. Specifically, we conducted an online experiment to investigate the approaches that researchers and practitioners should take to distribute a digital self-control intervention and start a digital wellbeing experiment while minimizing users' privacy concerns.

4.1 Methodology

Intervention Design and Distribution Modalities. To run our investigation, we first developed an intervention on iOS Shortcuts implementing a *Time*

Limit For Use (Block/Removal) feature, i.e., Siri providing a voice-based feedback to users when they have spent 2 min on Instagram (Fig. 1). The implementation was informed by two main reasons. First, according Lyngs et al. [54], *Time Limit For Use* feature is among the most used features in their taxonomy. We chose 2 min as the time threshold as users often visit apps intending to check for just a few minutes and are immediately sucked into the addictive social media newsfeed, watching video after video [85]. Second, to minimize bias in the study, we opted for a voice-based delivery method for the timer. Such an approach avoided interventions delivered through traditional notifications, which users might have encountered in commercially available apps, potentially influencing their behavior in our research. Supported by previous works with smart speakers [46], in particular, we considered a voice-based intervention as more privacy intrusive – even just when it comes to its creation – than defining the same intervention in the form of a visual notification or popup. As shown in Fig. 1, the intervention comprises a set of actions to be executed when Instagram is opened (Step 1) and closed (Step 2), respectively, which are then associated to two different automations (Step 3).

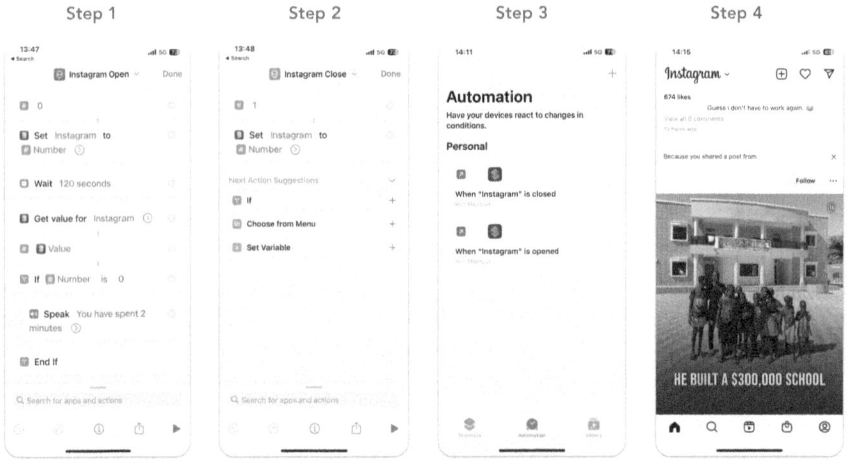

Fig. 1. Voice based Digital self-control intervention via Shortcuts.

Inspired by two of the most popular programming modalities typically adopted in TAP, we considered two alternative strategies for distributing the developed intervention, i.e., *manual re-creation* and *reuse*. Manually operating on trigger-action rules in TAP platforms involves using wizard-based interfaces to link specific triggers with the desired actions [17]. Prior work in the domain of web and IoT personalization demonstrated that manual creation allows users to have fine-grained control over the programmed behavior, at the cost of sometimes being a complicated task for non-technical users [13,28]. Reusing pre-built trigger-action rules in TAP platforms, instead, involves directly activating trigger-action rules suggested by the platform or by other users [13]. In the web and IoT personalization domain, in particular, recommender systems suggesting pre-built trigger-action rules have been used to speed up and simplify the composition process [12,13,55]. In our work, participants in the *manual re-creation* condition were provided with a detailed step-by-step tutorial on how to implement the voice-based Instagram intervention[1]. The tutorial included 15 steps, guiding participants on creating actions and linking them to automation. In the *reuse* condition, participants received a prebuilt intervention, only needing to scan a QR code to import it. However, they were encouraged to review the intervention with the same level of detail as those who manually recreated it.

Procedure, Participants, and Measures. To examine how iOS Shortcuts-based digital self-control interventions influence privacy concerns, we conducted an online experiment with 193 participants using a between-subjects design. Participants were recruited via Prolific and met the following criteria: native English speakers, iPhone users, and Instagram users with at least 10 min of daily usage. The final sample included 164 female participants (85%), 25 male (13%), and 4 non-binary/other (2%). Participants' education ranged from 2 to 24 years (M = 14.5, SD = 3.97), and ages ranged from 18 to 59 years (M = 25.1, SD = 7.89). Participants were randomly assigned to either the manual re-creation or reuse condition. In the manual re-creation condition, participants followed a step-by-step tutorial to build and test the intervention on Instagram for 10 min. To ensure accurate implementation, we conducted a manipulation check, requiring participants to describe their Instagram session. In the reuse condition, participants received a prebuilt intervention and tested it under the same conditions.

Following the intervention, participants completed a survey measuring perceived privacy concerns (PCON) and perceived privacy risks (RISK), adapted from Xu et al. [86] using a seven-point Likert scale (1 - Strongly disagree to 7 - Strongly agree). Sample items include *"I am concerned that the information I submit to this intervention could be misused"* (PCON1) and *"In general, it would be risky to give personal information to this intervention"* (RISK1). Both scales demonstrated excellent reliability (PCON: α = .96, RISK: α = .95). To ensure consistency, negatively worded items were reverse coded, enhancing the reliability and validity of the data.[2].

4.2 Results

Before analyzing perceived privacy concerns and risks, we conducted a Levene's test for equality of variance, which indicated that homogeneity assumptions did

[1] The tutorial is available at https://osf.io/yu5m8/?view_only=c71e492d663248128767842679d3d074.

[2] The complete survey scales are available at https://osf.io/yu5m8/?view_only=c71e492d663248128767842679d3d074.

not hold for both metrics ($p = .014$ for privacy concerns, $p = .018$ for privacy risks). Consequently, we performed Welch T-tests to compare differences between the two study conditions. Regarding perceived privacy concerns (PCON), participants in the manual re-creation condition reported lower concerns ($M = 3.871$, $SD = 1.808$) compared to those in the reuse condition ($M = 4.664$, $SD = 1.604$). The Welch T-test confirmed a statistically significant difference ($t(169.27) = -3.181$, $p < .001$), with a medium effect size (Cohen's $d = 0.465$). This suggests that manually recreating digital self-control interventions in iOS Shortcuts reduces perceived privacy concerns at installation time.

Similarly, perceived privacy risks (RISK) were lower in the manual re-creation condition ($M = 4.338$, $SD = 1.671$) compared to the reuse condition ($M = 4.782$, $SD = 1.451$). The Welch T-test revealed a significant difference ($t(167.13) = -1.941$, $p = .027$), though with a smaller effect size (Cohen's $d = 0.284$). This further indicates that manually recreating interventions mitigates perceived privacy risks at installation time. Overall, these findings align with prior research on digital nudges. While pre-built nudges are often perceived as intrusive or manipulative [5,47,82], self-constructed interventions—termed self-nudging [73]—can empower users to take control of their digital environments [50,73] and reinforce their sense of agency [82].

5 Discussion and Conclusion

5.1 Implications for Digital-Wellbeing Researchers

Developing Digital Self-Control Tools (DSCTs) is challenging, particularly in mobile ecosystems where programming expertise is often required. Researchers must navigate technical barriers, such as OS restrictions that limit third-party applications, forcing them to adopt complex and time-consuming strategies [9,51]. Our work demonstrates that iOS Shortcuts, an integrated OS automation tool, can provide an accessible, ethical, and effective alternative for creating (Sect. 3) and evaluating (Sect. 4) digital self-control interventions. By leveraging OS-level integration, iOS Shortcuts grants researchers access to data and settings typically unavailable to third-party apps while offering a user-friendly interface that eliminates the need for extensive coding.

One key advantage of this approach is the democratization of DSCT development. The accessibility of iOS Shortcuts allows researchers from non-technical backgrounds to participate in designing and studying digital wellbeing interventions, fostering interdisciplinary collaboration. Additionally, our findings suggest that involving participants in manually re-creating DSCTs can reduce initial privacy concerns by making intervention strategies more transparent. Unlike third-party applications, which obscure implementation details, iOS Shortcuts naturally supports intervention decomposition through its end-user programming interface. While privacy concerns may evolve over time, minimizing them at installation could help reduce the high attrition rates commonly observed in DSCT research trials [19,40,76]. Privacy concerns have historically been a major factor in user resistance to digital wellbeing apps [23,70], and our results align with prior evidence suggesting that TAP-based tools like iOS Shortcuts offer greater privacy control than traditional third-party DSCTs [69,72,74].

Beyond replicating existing DSCTs, TAP-based interventions can address well-known DSCT limitations. Since iOS Shortcuts operates across Apple devices, it enables interventions that extend beyond smartphones, reaching iPads and MacBooks. This integration helps overcome the single-device focus of many DSCTs [54,58,60]. Additionally, iOS Shortcuts allows the combination of multiple intervention strategies, creating a bundle of interventions rather than a single, isolated measure. Research suggests that rotating intervention strategies can improve user retention [40]. Furthermore, TAP enables context-aware interventions, linking digital self-control strategies to triggers such as time of day or location [26,59,60]. Finally, our approach supports feature-level interventions, which target app mechanisms directly. For instance, detecting user interactions via smartphone gestures could be used to mitigate attention-capture design patterns like infinite scrolling [61,72]. Overall, leveraging iOS Shortcuts not only simplifies DSCT development but also enhances intervention flexibility, privacy control, and contextual adaptability, opening new opportunities for digital wellbeing research.

5.2 End-User Development of Digital Self-control Interventions

This study examined the feasibility of iOS Shortcuts for designing and distributing digital self-control interventions in digital wellbeing experiments. Findings from our second study suggest a promising direction: empowering end users—beyond researchers—to create personalized interventions. By shifting from passive consumers to active creators, users can enhance intervention effectiveness through customization, integrating multiple actions and contextual triggers to tailor interventions to their specific needs.

However, broader adoption of end-user development (EUD) for DSCTs requires further research. While participants in our study followed a structured tutorial, Trigger-Action Programming (TAP) usability challenges remain, particularly in uncontrolled settings. Prior research shows that users frequently misinterpret TAP behavior [28] and encounter common programming errors [6]. These challenges are especially relevant when creating complex interventions requiring multiple automations, such as tracking app openings and closures. In the short term, community-driven platforms like RoutineHub could help mitigate the learning curve by enabling collaborative DSCT development. However, long-term TAP adoption for digital wellbeing requires further simplification of intervention creation. Two key design improvements could enhance future TAP platforms for DSCTs: First, native support for DSCT mechanisms would reduce the need for workarounds. iOS Shortcuts lacks direct support for common intervention strategies, requiring manual solutions such as storing usage thresholds in local JSON files. Future TAP platforms could model high-level triggers and actions, such as event-based usage statistics, automated timers, and lockout mechanisms, aligning with IoT-based high-level TAP models [11,17]. Second, better third-party app integration would expand intervention capabilities. The effectiveness of iOS Shortcuts depends on its built-in features and the extent to which external apps expose custom actions. Future TAP platforms should facilitate deeper app integration to streamline intervention design. For example, Lukoff et al. [51] had to rebuild a video-streaming app from scratch to counteract YouTube's recommendation system. Instead of requiring full app reconstruction, community-driven modification frameworks like GreaseDroid [39], which allow non-expert users to disable dark patterns, could offer researchers feature-level intervention tools rather than app-level solutions. By improving TAP-based platforms to better support digital wellbeing interventions, both researchers and end users could develop, share, and refine self-control strategies more effectively, fostering a more inclusive and adaptable approach to digital wellbeing.

5.3 Limitations and Future Works

This study has several limitations that offer directions for future research. First, it focuses solely on iOS Shortcuts, limiting its applicability to other task automation tools and operating systems. While Android Rules [1] provides similar functionality, future research should explore whether our findings generalize across platforms. Second, our study assessed the feasibility of iOS Shortcuts for digital wellbeing experiments, focusing on intervention creation and distribution rather than their long-term impact. Future work could examine whether these interventions produce sustained behavioral change, for instance, through longitudinal studies tracking users' digital wellbeing over time. Third, intervention effectiveness is constrained by iOS Shortcuts' capabilities. Blocking strategies such as usage timers depend on friction to prevent bypassing [53,57], but users can easily disable shortcuts, as they would with third-party DSCTs. Future research should explore ways to enhance intervention persistence and user commitment. Further, integrating third-party apps could enable richer interventions, such as gamification and features targeting internal app mechanisms like recommendations and newsfeeds. Lastly, our study examined privacy concerns only at installation, but perceptions may evolve during continued use. Future research should investigate how privacy concerns change over time and whether transparency in intervention creation influences trust. Additionally, our sample was skewed toward female participants, potentially limiting generalizability. However, as previous DSCT research has been male-dominated [65], our findings help balance prior perspectives. Furthermore, this study highlight its versatility in replicating digital self-control interventions and suggest that empowering users to manually re-create interventions can help reduce privacy concerns in research studies. Overall, this work underscores the role of OS-level automation tools in digital wellbeing research, offering a scalable, accessible, and customizable approach to DSCT development for both researchers and end users.

References

1. 9to5Google: How to create rules on pixel (2022). https://9to5google.com/2022/03/23/how-to-create-rules-on-pixel/

2. Ames, M.G.: Managing mobile multitasking: the culture of iphones on Stanford campus. In: Proceedings of the 2013 Conference on Computer Supported Cooperative Work, CSCW 2013, pp. 1487–1498. Association for Computing Machinery, New York (2013). https://doi.org/10.1145/2441776.2441945
3. Bailey, C.: Hyperfocus: How to Manage Your Attention in a World of Distraction. Penguin (2018)
4. Bedrov, A., Bulaj, G.: Improving self-esteem with motivational quotes: opportunities for digital health technologies for people with chronic disorders. Front. Psychol. (2018). https://doi.org/10.3389/fpsyg.2018.02126
5. Bongard-Blanchy, K., Rossi, A., Rivas, S., Doublet, S., Koenig, V., Lenzini, G.: "i am definitely manipulated, even when i am aware of it. it's ridiculous!" - dark patterns from the end-user perspective. In: Proceedings of the 2021 ACM Designing Interactive Systems Conference, DIS 2021, pp. 763–776. Association for Computing Machinery, New York (2021). https://doi.org/10.1145/3461778.3462086
6. Brackenbury, W., et al.: How users interpret bugs in trigger-action programming. In: Proceedings of the 2019 CHI Conference on Human Factors in Computing Systems, CHI 2019, pp. 1–12. Association for Computing Machinery, New York (2019). https://doi.org/10.1145/3290605.3300782
7. Burr, C., Taddeo, M., Floridi, L.: The ethics of digital well-being: a thematic review. Sci. Eng. Ethics **26**(4), 2313–2343 (2020). https://doi.org/10.1007/s11948-020-00175-8
8. Chisler, A., Volkova, Y., Pyshkin, E.: Handle with it addiction: a browser extension for overcoming excessive tv-series streaming. In: Proceedings of the 12th Central and Eastern European Software Engineering Conference in Russia. CEE-SECR 2016. Association for Computing Machinery, New York (2016). https://doi.org/10.1145/3022211.3022213
9. Cho, H., Choi, D., Kim, D., Kang, W.J., Choe, E.K., Lee, S.J.: Reflect, not regret: understanding regretful smartphone use with app feature-level analysis. Proc. ACM Hum.-Comput. Interact. **5**(CSCW2) (2021). https://doi.org/10.1145/3479600
10. Collins, E.I.M., Cox, A.L., Bird, J., Cornish-Tresstail, C.: Barriers to engagement with a personal informatics productivity tool. In: Proceedings of the 26th Australian Computer-Human Interaction Conference on Designing Futures: The Future of Design, OzCHI 2014, pp. 370–379. Association for Computing Machinery, New York (2014). https://doi.org/10.1145/2686612.2686668
11. Corno, F., De Russis, L., Monge Roffarello, A.: A high-level semantic approach to end-user development in the internet of things. Int. J. Hum. Comput. Stud. **125**, 41–54 (2019). https://doi.org/10.1016/j.ijhcs.2018.12.008
12. Corno, F., De Russis, L., Monge Roffarello, A.: Heytap: bridging the gaps between users' needs and technology in if-then rules via conversation. In: Proceedings of the International Conference on Advanced Visual Interfaces, AVI 2020. Association for Computing Machinery, New York (2020). https://doi.org/10.1145/3399715.3399905
13. Corno, F., De Russis, L., Monge Roffarello, A.: Taprec: supporting the composition of trigger-action rules through dynamic recommendations. In: Proceedings of the 25th International Conference on Intelligent User Interfaces, IUI 2020, pp. 579–588. Association for Computing Machinery, New York (2020). https://doi.org/10.1145/3377325.3377499
14. Coughlan, S.: Smartphone 'addiction': young people 'panicky' when denied mobiles (2019). https://www.example.com/smartphone-addiction-panicky-youth. Accessed 1 Aug 2023

15. Davis, K., et al.: Supporting teens' intentional social media use through interaction design: an exploratory proof-of-concept study. In: Proceedings of the 22nd Annual ACM Interaction Design and Children Conference, IDC 2023, pp. 322–334. Association for Computing Machinery, New York (2023). https://doi.org/10.1145/3585088.3589387
16. De Santo, A., et al.: Promoting computational thinking skills in non-computer-science students: gamifying computational notebooks to increase student engagement. IEEE Trans. Learn. Technol. **15**(3), 392–405 (2022). https://doi.org/10.1109/TLT.2022.3180588
17. Desolda, G., Ardito, C., Matera, M.: Empowering end users to customize their smart environments: model, composition paradigms, and domain-specific tools. ACM Trans. Comput.-Hum. Interact. **24**(2), 12:1–12:52 (2017). https://doi.org/10.1145/3057859
18. Dey, A.K., Sohn, T., Streng, S., Kodama, J.: ICAP: interactive prototyping of context-aware applications. In: Proceedings of the 4th International Conference on Pervasive Computing, PERVASIVE 2006, pp. 254–271. Springer, Heidelberg (2006). https://doi.org/10.1007/11748625_16
19. Eysenbach, G.: The law of attrition. J. Med. Internet Res. **7**(1), e11 (2005). https://doi.org/10.2196/jmir.7.1.e11
20. Farah, J.C., Moro, A., Bergram, K., Purohit, A.K., Gillet, D., Holzer, A.: Bringing computational thinking to non-stem undergraduates through an integrated notebook application, p. 14 (2020). http://infoscience.epfl.ch/record/278325
21. Foer, J.S.: Technology is diminishing us (2016). https://www.theguardian.com/books/2016/dec/03/jonathan-safran-foer-technology-diminishing-us. Accessed 15 July 2021
22. Foulonneau, A., Calvary, G., Villain, E.: Stop procrastinating: tilt, time is life time, a persuasive application. In: Proceedings of the 28th Australian Conference on Computer-Human Interaction, OzCHI 2016, pp. 508–516. Association for Computing Machinery, New York (2016). https://doi.org/10.1145/3010915.3010947
23. Geza, K.: Habitlab: in-the-wild behavior change experiments at scale (2019)
24. Gordan, M., Krishanan, I.A.: A review of bf skinner's 'reinforcement theory of motivation'. Int. J. Res. Educ. Methodol. **5**(3), 680–688 (2014)
25. Hiniker, A., Heung, S.S., Hong, S.R., Kientz, J.A.: Coco's videos: an empirical investigation of video-player design features and children's media use. In: Proceedings of the 2018 CHI Conference on Human Factors in Computing Systems, CHI 2018, pp. 1–13. Association for Computing Machinery, New York (2018). https://doi.org/10.1145/3173574.3173828
26. Hiniker, A., Sobel, K., Suh, H., Sung, Y.C., Lee, C.P., Kientz, J.A.: Texting while parenting: how adults use mobile phones while caring for children at the playground. In: Proceedings of the 33rd Annual ACM Conference on Human Factors in Computing Systems, CHI 2015, pp. 727–736. Association for Computing Machinery, New York (2015). https://doi.org/10.1145/2702123.2702199
27. Holte, A.J., Giesen, D.T., Ferraro, F.R.: Color me calm: grayscale phone setting reduces anxiety and problematic smartphone use. Curr. Psychol. **42**(8), 6778–6790 (2023). https://doi.org/10.1007/s12144-021-02020-y
28. Huang, J., Cakmak, M.: Supporting mental model accuracy in trigger-action programming. In: Proceedings of the 2015 ACM International Joint Conference on Pervasive and Ubiquitous Computing, UbiComp 2015, pp. 215–225. Association for Computing Machinery, New York (2015). https://doi.org/10.1145/2750858.2805830

29. Apple Inc.: Welcome to shortcuts on IOS. Apple Support (2023). https://support.apple.com/guide/shortcuts/welcome/ios
30. Inie, N., Lungu, M.F.: Aiki - turning online procrastination into microlearning. In: Proceedings of the 2021 CHI Conference on Human Factors in Computing Systems. CHI 2021. Association for Computing Machinery, New York (2021). https://doi.org/10.1145/3411764.3445202
31. Kelly, N., Gero, J.S.: Design thinking and computational thinking: a dual process model for addressing design problems. Des. Sci. **7**, e8 (2021). https://doi.org/10.1017/dsj.2021.7
32. Kim, I., Jung, G., Jung, H., Ko, M., Lee, U.: Let's focus: mitigating mobile phone use in college classrooms. Proc. ACM Interact. Mob. Wearable Ubiquitous Technol. **1**(3) (2017). https://doi.org/10.1145/3130928
33. Kim, J., Jung, H., Ko, M., Lee, U.: Goalkeeper: Exploring interaction lockout mechanisms for regulating smartphone use. Proc. ACM Interact. Mob. Wearable Ubiquitous Technol. **3**(1) (2019). https://doi.org/10.1145/3314403
34. Kim, J., Park, J., Lee, H., Ko, M., Lee, U.: Lockntype: lockout task intervention for discouraging smartphone app use. In: Proceedings of the 2019 CHI Conference on Human Factors in Computing Systems, CHI 2019, pp. 1–12. Association for Computing Machinery, New York (2019). https://doi.org/10.1145/3290605.3300927
35. Ko, M., Choi, S., Yang, S., Lee, J., Lee, U.: Familync: facilitating participatory parental mediation of adolescents' smartphone use. In: Proceedings of the 2015 ACM International Joint Conference on Pervasive and Ubiquitous Computing, UbiComp 2015, pp. 867–878. Association for Computing Machinery, New York (2015). https://doi.org/10.1145/2750858.2804283
36. Ko, M., Choi, S., Yang, S., Lee, J., Lee, U.: Familync: facilitating participatory parental mediation of adolescents' smartphone use. In: Proceedings of the 2015 ACM International Joint Conference on Pervasive and Ubiquitous Computing, pp. 867–878 (2015)
37. Ko, M., Choi, S., Yatani, K., Lee, U.: Lock n' lol: group-based limiting assistance app to mitigate smartphone distractions in group activities. In: Proceedings of the 2016 CHI Conference on Human Factors in Computing Systems, CHI 2016, pp. 998–1010. Association for Computing Machinery, New York (2016). https://doi.org/10.1145/2858036.2858568
38. Ko, M., et al.: Nugu: a group-based intervention app for improving self-regulation of limiting smartphone use. In: Proceedings of the 18th ACM Conference on Computer Supported Cooperative Work & Social Computing, CSCW 2015, pp. 1235–1245. Association for Computing Machinery, New York (2015). https://doi.org/10.1145/2675133.2675244
39. Kollnig, K., Datta, S., Van Kleek, M.: I want my app that way: reclaiming sovereignty over personal devices. In: Extended Abstracts of the 2021 CHI Conference on Human Factors in Computing Systems, CHI EA 2021. Association for Computing Machinery, New York (2021). https://doi.org/10.1145/3411763.3451632
40. Kovacs, G., Wu, Z., Bernstein, M.S.: Rotating online behavior change interventions increases effectiveness but also increases attrition. Proc. ACM Hum.-Comput. Interact. **2**(CSCW) (2018). https://doi.org/10.1145/3274364
41. Kovacs, G., Wu, Z., Bernstein, M.S.: Not now, ask later: users weaken their behavior change regimen over time, but expect to re-strengthen it imminently. In: CHI 2021. Association for Computing Machinery, New York (2021). https://doi.org/10.1145/3411764.3445695

42. Kumm, S., Maggin, D.M.: Intensifying goal-setting interventions for students with emotional and behavioral disorders. Beyond Behav. **30**(1), 14–23 (2021). https://doi.org/10.1177/1074295621996616
43. Kwon, M., Kim, D.J., Cho, H., Yang, S.: The smartphone addiction scale: development and validation of a short version for adolescents. PLOS ONE **8**(12), 1–7 (2014). https://doi.org/10.1371/journal.pone.0083558
44. Lanaj, K., Johnson, R.E., Barnes, C.M.: Beginning the workday yet already depleted? Consequences of late-night smartphone use and sleep. Organ. Behav. Hum. Decis. Process. **124**(1), 11–23 (2014). https://doi.org/10.1016/j.obhdp.2014.01.001
45. Lanette, S., Chua, P.K., Hayes, G., Mazmanian, M.: How much is 'too much'?: the role of a smartphone addiction narrative in individuals' experience of use. Proc. ACM Hum.-Comput. Interact. **2**(CSCW), 101:1–101:22 (2018). https://doi.org/10.1145/3274370
46. Lau, J., Zimmerman, B., Schaub, F.: Alexa, are you listening? Privacy perceptions, concerns and privacy-seeking behaviors with smart speakers. Proc. ACM Hum.-Comput. Interact. **2**(CSCW) (2018). https://doi.org/10.1145/3274371
47. Lavi, M.: Evil nudges. Vand. J. Ent. Tech. L. **21**, 1 (2018)
48. Lee, U., et al.: Hooked on smartphones: an exploratory study on smartphone overuse among college students. In: Proceedings of the SIGCHI Conference on Human Factors in Computing Systems, CHI 2014, pp. 2327–2336. Association for Computing Machinery, New York (2014). https://doi.org/10.1145/2556288.2557366
49. Liu, Y., Jia, Y., Pan, W., Pfaff, M.S.: Supporting task resumption using visual feedback. In: Proceedings of the 17th ACM Conference on Computer Supported Cooperative Work & Social Computing, CSCW 2014, pp. 767–777. Association for Computing Machinery, New York (2014). https://doi.org/10.1145/2531602.2531710
50. Lorenz-Spreen, P., Lewandowsky, S., Sunstein, C.R., Hertwig, R.: How behavioural sciences can promote truth, autonomy and democratic discourse online. Nat. Hum. Behav. **4**(11), 1102–1109 (2020)
51. Lukoff, K., et al.: Switchtube: a proof-of-concept system introducing "adaptable commitment interfaces" as a tool for digital wellbeing. In: Proceedings of the 2023 CHI Conference on Human Factors in Computing Systems, CHI 2023. Association for Computing Machinery, New York (2023). https://doi.org/10.1145/3544548.3580703
52. Lukoff, K., et al.: How the design of youtube influences user sense of agency. In: Proceedings of the 2021 CHI Conference on Human Factors in Computing Systems. CHI 2021. Association for Computing Machinery, New York (2021)
53. Lyngs, U., Lukoff, K., Csuka, L., Slovák, P., Van Kleek, M., Shadbolt, N.: The goldilocks level of support: using user reviews, ratings, and installation numbers to investigate digital self-control tools. Int. J. Hum.-Comput. Stud. **166**, 102869 (2022). https://doi.org/10.1016/j.ijhcs.2022.102869. https://www.sciencedirect.com/science/article/pii/S1071581922000957
54. Lyngs, U., et al.: Self-control in cyberspace: applying dual systems theory to a review of digital self-control tools. In: Proceedings of the 2019 CHI Conference on Human Factors in Computing Systems, CHI 2019, pp. 1–18. Association for Computing Machinery, New York (2019). https://doi.org/10.1145/3290605.3300361
55. Mattioli, A., Paternò, F.: Recommendations for creating trigger-action rules in a block-based environment. Behav. Inf. Technol. **40**(10), 1024–1034 (2021). https://doi.org/10.1080/0144929X.2021.1900396

56. Meinhardt, L.M., et al.: Scrolling in the deep: analysing contextual influences on intervention effectiveness during infinite scrolling on social media (2025). https://doi.org/10.48550/arXiv.2501.11814
57. Monge Roffarello, A., De Russis, L.: The race towards digital wellbeing: issues and opportunities. In: Proceedings of the 2019 CHI Conference on Human Factors in Computing Systems, CHI 2019, pp. 1–14. Association for Computing Machinery, New York (2019). https://doi.org/10.1145/3290605.3300616
58. Monge Roffarello, A., De Russis, L.: Coping with Digital Wellbeing in a Multi-Device World. Association for Computing Machinery, New York (2021). https://doi.org/10.1145/3411764.3445076
59. Monge Roffarello, A., De Russis, L.: Understanding, discovering, and mitigating habitual smartphone use in young adults. ACM Trans. Interact. Intell. Syst. **11**(2) (2021). https://doi.org/10.1145/3447991
60. Monge Roffarello, A., De Russis, L.: Achieving digital wellbeing through digital self-control tools: a systematic review and meta-analysis. ACM Trans. Comput.-Hum. Interact. (2022, just accepted). https://doi.org/10.1145/3571810
61. Monge Roffarello, A., Lukoff, K., De Russis, L.: Defining and identifying attention capture deceptive designs in digital interfaces. In: Proceedings of the 2023 CHI Conference on Human Factors in Computing Systems, CHI 2023. Association for Computing Machinery, New York (2023). https://doi.org/10.1145/3544548.3580729
62. Morse, W., Kelleher, R.: Determinants of reinforcement and punishment. In: Handbook of Operant Behavior, pp. 174–200. Routledge (2022)
63. Namoun, A., Daskalopoulou, A., Mehandjiev, N., Xun, Z.: Exploring mobile end user development: existing use and design factors. IEEE Trans. Software Eng. **42**(10), 960–976 (2016). https://doi.org/10.1109/TSE.2016.2532873
64. Neff, G., Nafus, D.: An introduction to self-tracking. In: Self-Tracking. The MIT Press (2016). https://doi.org/10.7551/mitpress/10421.003.0003
65. Offenwanger, A., Milligan, A.J., Chang, M., Bullard, J., Yoon, D.: Diagnosing bias in the gender representation of HCI research participants: how it happens and where we are. In: Proceedings of the 2021 CHI Conference on Human Factors in Computing Systems, CHI 2021. Association for Computing Machinery, New York (2021). https://doi.org/10.1145/3411764.3445383
66. Okeke, F., Sobolev, M., Dell, N., Estrin, D.: Good vibrations: can a digital nudge reduce digital overload? In: MobileHCI 2018. Association for Computing Machinery, New York (2018). https://doi.org/10.1145/3229434.3229463
67. Park, J., Lee, H., Park, S., Chung, K.M., Lee, U.: Goldentime: exploring system-driven timeboxing and micro-financial incentives for self-regulated phone use. In: Proceedings of the 2021 CHI Conference on Human Factors in Computing Systems, CHI 2021. Association for Computing Machinery, New York (2021). https://doi.org/10.1145/3411764.3445489
68. Park, J., Sim, J.Y., Kim, J., Yi, M.Y., Lee, U.: Interaction restraint: enforcing adaptive cognitive tasks to restrain problematic user interaction. In: Extended Abstracts of the 2018 CHI Conference on Human Factors in Computing Systems, CHI EA 2018, pp. 1–6. Association for Computing Machinery, New York (2018). https://doi.org/10.1145/3170427.3188613
69. Purohit, A.K., Holzer, A.: Unhooked by design: Scrolling mindfully on social media by automating digital nudges. In: Proceedings of the 27th Americas Conference on Information Systems, AMCIS 2021, pp. 1–10. AIS, Virtual Conference (2021)
70. Purohit, A.K., Barclay, L., Holzer, A.: Designing for digital detox: making social media less addictive with digital nudges, CHI EA 2020, pp. 1–9. Association

for Computing Machinery, New York (2020). https://doi.org/10.1145/3334480.3382810

71. Purohit, A.K., Barev, T.J., Schöbel, S., Janson, A., Holzer, A.: Designing for digital wellbeing on a smartphone: co-creation of digital nudges to mitigate instagram overuse. In: Proceedings of the 56th Hawaii International Conference on System Sciences, pp. 4087–4096. HICSS, Hawaii (2023)
72. Purohit, A.K., Bergram, K., Barclay, L., Bezençon, V., Holzer, A.: Starving the newsfeed for social media detox: Effects of strict and self-regulated Facebook newsfeed diets. In: Proceedings of the 2023 CHI Conference on Human Factors in Computing Systems. CHI 2023. Association for Computing Machinery, New York (2023). https://doi.org/10.1145/3544548.3581187
73. Reijula, S., Hertwig, R.: Self-nudging and the citizen choice architect. Behav. Public Policy **6**(1), 119–149 (2022)
74. Roffarello, A.M., Purohit, A.K., Purohit, S.V.: Trigger-action programming for wellbeing: insights from 6590 IOS shortcuts. IEEE Pervasive Comput. **23**(3), 49–56 (2024). https://doi.org/10.1109/MPRV.2024.3416698
75. Rooksby, J., Asadzadeh, P., Rost, M., Morrison, A., Chalmers, M.: Personal tracking of screen time on digital devices. In: Proceedings of the 2016 CHI Conference on Human Factors in Computing Systems, CHI 2016, pp. 284–296. Association for Computing Machinery, New York (2016). https://doi.org/10.1145/2858036.2858055
76. Schwartz, R., Monge Roffarello, A., De Russis, L., Apostolellis, P.: Reducing risk in digital self-control tools: design patterns and prototype. In: Extended Abstracts of the 2021 CHI Conference on Human Factors in Computing Systems, CHI EA 2021. Association for Computing Machinery, New York (2021). https://doi.org/10.1145/3411763.3451843
77. Scott, A.E.: To do or not to do? Managing intentions with technology. In: Extended Abstracts of the 2023 CHI Conference on Human Factors in Computing Systems. CHI EA 2023. Association for Computing Machinery, New York (2023). https://doi.org/10.1145/3544549.3577046
78. Shen, E., Shen, J., Chia, T.L.: Development of an app to support self-monitoring smartphone usage and healthcare behaviors in daily life, BDIOT 2019, pp. 29–34. Association for Computing Machinery, New York (2019). https://doi.org/10.1145/3361758.3361771
79. Tran, J.A., Yang, K.S., Davis, K., Hiniker, A.: Modeling the engagement-disengagement cycle of compulsive phone use. In: Proceedings of the 2019 CHI Conference on Human Factors in Computing Systems, CHI 2019, pp. 1–14. Association for Computing Machinery, New York (2019). https://doi.org/10.1145/3290605.3300542
80. Turkle, S.: Alone Together: Why We Expect More from Technology and Less from Each Other. Basic Books Inc., New York (2011)
81. Ur, B., McManus, E., Pak Yong Ho, M., Littman, M.L.: Practical trigger-action programming in the smart home. In: Proceedings of the SIGCHI Conference on Human Factors in Computing Systems, CHI 2014, pp. 803–812. Association for Computing Machinery, New York (2014). https://doi.org/10.1145/2556288.2557420
82. Vugts, A., Van Den Hoven, M., De Vet, E., Verweij, M.: How autonomy is understood in discussions on the ethics of nudging. Behav. Public Policy **4**(1), 108–123 (2020)

83. Whittaker, S., Kalnikaite, V., Hollis, V., Guydish, A.: 'don't waste my time': use of time information improves focus. In: Proceedings of the 2016 CHI Conference on Human Factors in Computing Systems, CHI 2016, pp. 1729–1738. Association for Computing Machinery, New York (2016). https://doi.org/10.1145/2858036.2858193
84. Widdicks, K.: When the good turns ugly: speculating next steps for digital wellbeing tools. In: Proceedings of the 11th Nordic Conference on Human-Computer Interaction: Shaping Experiences, Shaping Society. NordiCHI 2020. Association for Computing Machinery, New York (2020). https://doi.org/10.1145/3419249.3420117
85. Woolley, K., Sharif, M.A.: The psychology of your scrolling addiction (2022). https://hbr.org/2022/01/the-psychology-of-your-scrolling-addiction
86. Xu, H., Dinev, T., Smith, J., Hart, P.: Information privacy concerns: linking individual perceptions with institutional privacy assurances. J. Assoc. Inf. Syst. **12**(12), 1 (2011)
87. Zhou, X., Rau, P.L.P., Liu, X.: "time to take a break": how heavy adult gamers react to a built-in gaming gradual intervention system. Proc. ACM Hum.-Comput. Interact. **5**(CSCW1) (2021). https://doi.org/10.1145/3449077
88. Zimmermann, L., Sobolev, M.: Digital nudges for screen time reduction: a randomized control trial with performance and wellbeing outcomes (2020)

Empowering End Users to Design for Their Digital Self-control

Alberto Monge Roffarello(✉) and Luigi De Russis

Politecnico di Torino, Corso Duca degli Abruzzi, 24, 10129 Turin, Italy
{alberto.monge,luigi.derussis}@polito.it

Abstract. While smartphones have positively transformed how we live, work, and communicate, concerns about their impact on individual wellbeing have driven research toward solutions that promote more intentional and mindful usage. In this context, Digital Self-Control Tools (DSCTs) aim to help users regulate their technology consumption, but their interventions often remain rigid, offering limited customization and treating users as passive recipients rather than active creators of their own digital wellbeing strategies.

To address these limitations, this work explores the intersection of End-User Development (EUD) and DSCTs, aiming to empower users to design and personalize interventions that suit their individual needs. We first created an Event-Condition-Action (ECA) framework consisting of unique events, conditions, and actions, based on a state-of-the-art taxonomy of DSCT intervention strategies. Then, we developed a mobile application to evaluate the understandability of the framework and the usability of a rule-creation interface built upon it. A usability study with 11 participants revealed that users found the approach understandable and the app highly usable, with an average SUS score of 82.5. These findings underscore the potential of combining EUD with digital self-control interventions to create tailored and user-centered DSCT solutions.

Keywords: Digital self-control · Digital wellbeing · ECA rules

1 Introduction

In recent years, the concept of digital wellbeing—broadly defined by Burr et al. as the ability to lead a fulfilling and meaningful life in today's information-driven society [?]—has gained increasing attention as a response to the challenges posed by the pervasive (over)use of technology, particularly with smartphones [24]. Indeed, while these devices have positively transformed the way we live, work, and communicate, they have also raised concerns about their impact on psychological well-being [18,20] and social interactions [12,33], as many services available on these devices, from social media to video streaming platforms, employ attention-capturing mechanisms that exploit users' psychological vulnerabilities to maximize (often mindless) engagement [31].

C. Santoro et al. (Eds.): IS-EUD 2025, LNCS 15713, pp. 244–263, 2025.
https://doi.org/10.1007/978-3-031-95452-8_15

These issues have prompted the scientific and technological communities to explore effective solutions that promote more mindful and intentional technology use. These solutions, known as Digital Self-Control Tools (DSCTs), seek to mitigate the negative effects of excessive technology use by supporting users' self-monitoring and regulation, providing them with interventions that span from productivity dashboards to usage timers and gamification strategies [26,38]. Despite the progress in this area, existing solutions often remain limited. DSCTs are often rigid, offer little customization, and primarily treat users as passive recipients of predefined intervention strategies rather than active creators of their own digital wellbeing strategies [22]. As a result, they suffer from high attrition rates [17] and low effectiveness in the long term [31].

To address these limitations, this work explores the intersection of End-User Development (EUD) and DSCTs, aiming to empower users to create and personalize flexible and engaging intervention strategies for their digital wellbeing that better accommodate individual differences. Recent studies [4,32] have highlighted the potential of integrating EUD with DSCTs. However, existing research consists of either preliminary investigations [4] or analyses of how existing rule-based platforms, such as iOS Shortcuts, have been repurposed to support digital wellbeing [32], and how to effectively bridge EUD and DSCTs remains largely unexplored: Can Event-Condition-Action (ECA) rules be used to express interventions for digital self-control in a way that enables their management within an EUD solution? Would end users understand and find usable an EUD solution for digital self-control?

To answer these questions, we first created an ECA framework consisting of events, conditions, and actions tailored to the digital self-control domain. ECA rules are a comprehensive implementation of trigger-action programming, an EUD technique that has already been successfully adopted for defining digital interventions for behavior change [41]. It provides an intuitive and powerful model for empowering end users—even those without programming skills—to configure automated behaviors based on an event and a condition that trigger an action. To develop our ECA framework, we built upon Lyngs et al.'s taxonomy of digital self-control intervention strategies [26]. The taxonomy categorizes interventions into four categories: blocking/removal, self-tracking, goal advancement, and reward/punishment. We systematically translated the interventions within these categories into ECA rules by categorizing them into events, conditions, and actions. For example, the *usage limit* intervention in blocking/removal could consist of an "app opening" event, a "daily usage limit exceeded" condition, and a "block the application" action. Similarly, a *motivational quote* intervention could be implemented with an event like "screen unlock," a condition related to time of day, and an action that displays a motivational message on the screen.

After developing the ECA framework, we developed a mobile interface for rule composition leveraging the extracted events, conditions, and actions. The interface follows a wizard-based composition paradigm, similar to those used in popular rule-composition systems in other domains, e.g., smart homes and IoT ecosystems. This approach guides users step by step, first defining an event

(Fig. 1) and its associated condition (Fig. 2), then linking it to a corresponding action (Fig. 3). We evaluated the understandability of the proposed ECA framework and the usability of the rule-composition interface in a usability study involving 11 participants. The results show that the ECA framework was understandable to most users and that the interface was highly usable, with an average SUS score of 82.5. Participants appreciated the simplicity of the configuration process, though some encountered difficulties distinguishing between events and conditions, highlighting potential areas for future improvement. Notably, all participants expressed agreement or strong agreement when asked whether they would use the application, indicating a clear interest in personalizing their digital self-control interventions.

Overall, this study highlighted the feasibility of combining DSCTs and EUD, providing users with more customizable and participatory tools for managing their digital interactions. Our ECA framework and composition interface, in particular, pave the way for testing this approach in real-world scenarios to explore whether it can effectively address the well-known challenges of DSCTs, such as high attrition rates and low long-term effectiveness.

2 Related Works

2.1 Digital Interventions to Support Users' Self-control

While mobile devices provide significant benefits to both individuals and society, growing concerns about their overuse have led academic research and public discussions to frame problematic smartphone use with terms like "addiction [19]," "compulsive use [43]," and "rabbit holes [42]." Research indicates that problematic smartphone use can have detrimental effects on psychological well-being [20,39], e.g., in terms of weakened self-regulation [27] and diminished personal agency [22]. Furthermore it can undermine social interactions [12,33] and physical well-being, e.g., by disrupting sleep [18]. According to recent HCI literature, these issues stem largely from how contemporary mobile apps are designed, as many incorporate engaging strategies [29] or attention-capture patterns [31] that exploit users' psychological vulnerabilities to serve corporate interests. Social media, for example, are designed to maximize user engagement by implementing features such as infinite scrolling [28] and recommendations that appeal to users' guilty pleasures [2]. Similarly, video-streaming apps like YouTube and Netflix reinforce passive consumption by automatically queuing and playing the next video [23,40].

Given these challenges, the concept of digital wellbeing has emerged as a growing research focus within the HCI community. To help users manage their time spent on distracting apps, various Digital Self-Control Tools (DSCTs) have been developed. These tools, now available by default on most Android [13] and iOS [1] devices, support users' self-regulation by offering a range of intervention strategies, such as productivity dashboards, usage timers, and gamification techniques [26,38]. Despite significant progress in the development of DSCTs, many existing solutions still exhibit notable limitations [38]. In particular, prior research has highlighted their rigidity as a primary concern, as these tools often follow a one-size-fits-all approach with fixed, predefined intervention strategies that fail to adapt to the diverse and evolving needs of individual users [22]. This lack of flexibility—which is a critical factor in the success of behavior change interventions [46]—undermine DSCTs' effectiveness. Studies have shown that such tools tend to suffer from high attrition rates [17], with users abandoning them after initial use due to their inability to accommodate personal needs or sustain engagement over time. Additionally, the long-term effectiveness of these tools remains limited [30,38], as users may revert to previous digital habits once the imposed restrictions or interventions become frustrating or irrelevant to their changing circumstances [25].

This work explores the possibility of empowering users to become active creators of their own digital wellbeing interventions as a strategy to address the limitations of contemporary DSCTs.

2.2 Trigger-Action Programming Across Domains

EUD empowers non-expert users to create, modify, or tailor software to better suit their individual needs without requiring extensive programming knowledge [21]. One of the most used programming strategies adopted in this field is Trigger-Action Programming (TAP), which allows users to create automation rules composed of an action triggered by an event. Beginning with iCAP [11], a rule-based framework for developing context-aware applications, numerous studies have highlighted the effectiveness of such an approach across various domains, ranging from smart homes [44] to the broader Internet of Things (IoT) [6]. In parallel, commercial platforms such as IFTTT [15], Zapier [47], and iOS Shortcuts [16], are becoming widespread, enabling users to personalize the joint behaviors of their digital devices and online services. ECA rules [35], in particular, are a widely adopted paradigm for defining active systems [3,7], particularly in the IoT domain, where they effectively allow users to specify when and how smart object behaviors should be triggered in response to detected events [9].

Building on the work of Yardley and Spring [46]—which emphasizes that designing effective behavior change interventions requires a user-centered approach to development—researchers have begun exploring ways to empower end users to create and customize their own digital interventions for behavior change using TAP [41]. Monge Roffarello et al. [32], for example, analyzed a dataset of automations shared on iOS Shortcuts and found that a small proportion of rules were designed to support wellbeing, with most wellbeing-related programs focusing on health and physical exercise. Scott et al. [41] developed a TAP model for behavior change which explains how individuals can design their own DIY digital interventions to transition from their current behaviors to their desired ones. In the specific domain of digital wellbeing, recent studies have begun leveraging iOS Shortcuts as a platform for implementing basic digital self-control interventions. For instance, Purohit and Holzer [36] designed a shortcut that functioned as a usage timer for Instagram, while Purohit et al. [37] introduced two Facebook-related interventions. However, these studies do not explore the end-user perspective; instead, they use existing TAP platforms as a workaround to simplify the development of research-based DSCTs. Despite some preliminary investigations [4], how to support end users in designing and developing their own digital self-control interventions remains unclear. This work explores the intersection of EUD and DSCTs to empower users to create ECA rules for their digital wellbeing that better account for individual differences.

3 An ECA Framework for Digital Self-control

To explore the intersection of EUD and DSCTs we first developed a framework specifically tailored to digital self-control. We leveraged ECA rules given the popularity of TAP in EUD and its recent adoption in digital wellbeing research [4,32,37].

3.1 Methodology

The construction of the ECA framework was carried out by three researchers—including the two authors of this paper—who aimed to systematically translate established digital self-control intervention strategies into a flexible, end-user-configurable structure. We based our framework on Lyngs et al.'s [26] taxonomy of DSCTs interventions, recognizing its comprehensive nature and prior application in digital well-being research [8,25,38]. The taxonomy, developed through an extensive analysis of 367 apps across major platforms, is grounded in a dual-systems regulation model and organizes intervention strategies into design features associated to four categories: blocking/removing, tracking, goal advancement, and rewarding/punishing.

To construct the framework, one researcher selected an intervention strategy for each design feature included in the taxonomy. The three researchers then initially worked independently, each developing their own mapping of the selected intervention strategies into corresponding ECA rules. Each researcher systematically deconstructed interventions, for example, by translating a blocking strategy into an event (e.g., "app opening"), a condition (e.g., "daily usage time exceeded"), and an action (e.g., "restrict access"). This translation phase allowed for diverse perspectives and ensured a comprehensive exploration of possible representations.

Following this independent phase, the researchers met to compare their mappings, resolve discrepancies, and align on a unified framework, ultimately abstracting the resulting ECA rules into a set of unique events, conditions, and actions. This iterative process was crucial for debugging inconsistencies, refining the expressiveness of the ECA model, and ensuring that it could comprehensively accommodate a wide range of user-defined interventions. The results of the translation phase and the complete ECA framework are available in the following repository: https://bit.ly/43geKSx.

3.2 Results

Mapping Design Features to ECA Rules. The translation process involved analyzing all 25 design features across the four main categories of intervention strategies. Of these, we successfully translated 19 design features into ECA rules (76%), while 6 features (24%) could not be directly represented within the ECA structure. The distribution of successfully translated interventions varied across categories as follow.

Blocking/Removal. Blocking/removing intervention strategies aim to reduce time spent on applications by restricting user access or removing elements designed to capture their attention [26]. In this category, 9 out of 9 design features (100%) were successfully translated, as these interventions typically involve clear behavioral triggers and restrictive actions. For example, an intervention like "when application is launched on a specific day or time range, the launch is delayed" (*time lag to launch* design feature) was translated as:

Event : Open [Instagram]
Condition : Time is [10:00 AM]
Action : Delay [Instagram] launch of [30 s]

Self-tracking. Self-tracking intervention strategies aim to enhance users' awareness of their digital habits by providing feedback on usage patterns [26]. In this category, 1 out of 3 design features (33.3%) was translated. Specifically, the intervention "when the application is launched, a timer showing usage time is displayed" (*displays a timer* design feature) was translated as:

Event : Open [YouTube]
Action : Show timer

Other features such as logging detailed usage history or visualizing app interactions were not directly translatable as rules.

Goal Advancement. Goal advancement intervention strategies aim to support users in achieving their digital self-control objectives by setting usage limits, providing reminders, suggesting alternative activities, or reinforcing commitments through motivational messages [26]. In this category, 6 out of 7 design features (85.7%) were successfully translated. These interventions often involved time-based reminders or alternative behaviors that fit well into the ECA logic. For example, an intervention like "when application is used and consecutive time threshold has been reached, the application is blocked" (*set activity goal/s* design feature) was translated as:

Event : Daily usage time of [TikTok] becomes greater than [30 min]
Condition : [TikTok] is in use
Action : Block [TikTok]

The only design feature in this category that we could not translate into an ECA rule was *compare behaviour w/ goal*, as interventions leveraging this feature, similarly to most of the self-tracking strategies, are not meant to be automatically triggered, but rather involve information that can be accessed at any time by the user.

Reward/Punishment. Reward/punishment intervention strategies aim to encourage or discourage certain digital behaviors by providing incentives for self-control, displaying praise or warnings, or introducing effortful tasks to access distracting applications [26]. In this category, we were able to translate 3 our of 6 design features (50%). For example, the intervention "show a blame notification when an application is used in a specific location" (*praise/blame/please/annoy* design feature) was translated as:

Event : Open [Facebook]
Condition : Location is [workplace]
Action : Show notification with ["You will not achieve your work goals if you keep getting distracted!"]

While design features that focus on showing blaming messages or that reward users for desirable behaviors (e.g., gaining points) could be represented, interventions requiring social feedback, real-world consequences, or leaderboard comparisons could not be expressed as event-driven rules.

Events, Conditions, and Actions. Table 1, Table 2, and Table 3 summarizes the ECA framework in terms of unique events, conditions, and actions, respectively, which we extracted by abstracting and synthesizing the results of the translation process described in Sect. 3.2. Events (Table 1) define the triggers that initiate a rule execution, encompassing application behaviors (e.g., app openings and notifications), usage statistics (e.g., daily usage time exceeding a threshold), screen interactions (e.g., screen unlocks), and contextual factors (e.g., time-based or location-based triggers).

Conditions (Table 2) introduce additional constraints to refine when an event leads to an action. They include application states (e.g., whether a specific app is currently in use), detailed usage metrics (e.g., the number of app launches in a given period), screen statuses (e.g., whether the device is locked or unlocked), and contextual attributes (e.g., the current time or location).

Finally, actions (Table 3) represent the system's response when a rule is triggered. These include alerts (e.g., displaying pop-ups or notifications), application-related interventions (e.g., blocking or delaying app access), input requests (e.g., requiring a password before proceeding), device modifications (e.g., activating grayscale mode), and gamification elements (e.g., increasing or decreasing points based on behavior). The variety of actions allows for diverse intervention strategies, ranging from soft nudges to more restrictive measures, supporting different self-regulation needs.

Table 1. Events in our ECA framework, encompassing triggers related to application-related behaviors, usage statistics, screen-related behaviors, and changes in context. Elements in square brackets identify event parameters.

Category	Event
Application	New notification from app [x]
	Open app [x]
	Close app [x]
	Uninstall app [x]
Usage stats	Daily usage time of app [x] becomes greater than [amount]
	Daily launches of app [x] becomes greater than [amount]
	Session time of app [x] becomes greater than [amount]
Screen	Unlock screen
	Lock screen
	Number of screen unlocks becomes greater than [amount]
Context	Every day at [hh:mm]
	Every hour at [:mm]
	Every [day of the week] at [hh:mm]
	A calendar event starts
	I enter [location]
	I exit [location]

Table 2. Conditions in our ECA framework, encompassing applications-related statuses, usage statistics, screen statuses, and contextual conditions. Elements in square brackets identify condition parameters.

Category	Condition
Application	Notification from app [x] contains [text]
	App [x] in use
	App [x] is closed
	App [x] is installed
	App [x] is not installed
Usage stats	Daily usage time of app [x] is above [amount]
	Daily usage time of app [x] is below [amount]
	Daily launches of app [x] are above [amount]
	Daily launches of app [x] are below [amount]
	Session usage time of app [x] is above [amount]
	Session usage time of app [x] is below [amount]
Screen	Screen is locked
	Screen is unlocked
Context	Hour is [hh]
	Date is [dd/mm/yyyy]
	Datetime is [dd/mm/yyyy hh]
	Location is [location]

Table 3. Actions in our ECA framework, encompassing alerts, application-related interventions, input requests, device-related interventions, and gamification interventions. Elements in square brackets identify action parameters.

Category	Action
Alert	Show popup with [animation]
	Show popup with [message]
	Show notification with [message]
Application	Open app [x]
	Close app [x]
	Delay app [x] launch of [amount]
Input	Insert [password]
	Insert [text]
Device	Activate grayscale
	Disable grayscale
	Vibrate with [pattern]
Points and payments	Increase points by [amount]
	Decrease points by [amount]
	Request a payment of [amount]

4 Composing ECA Rules for Digital Self-control

After developing the ECA framework presented in Sect. 3, we designed and implemented a mobile interface for rule composition, leveraging the extracted events, conditions, and actions. The app served two primary purposes. First, it allowed us to investigate the understandability of the ECA framework by assessing how users interpret and interact with it. Second, although this work focuses on the rule definition process, the app provides the foundation for implementing a system that executes the defined rules.

4.1 Design and Implementation

To enable end users to define ECA rules, we designed a wizard-based interface. Interfaces adopting such a composition paradigm employ a step-by-step approach, breaking down complex tasks into simpler, sequential steps, accompanied by clear instructions and visual cues. Wizard-based interfaces are widely used in popular TAP platforms across various domains, such as smart homes and the IoT. In particular, Desolda et al. [9] observed that non-technical users are more familiar with wizard-based procedures, as these are commonly used for tasks such as software installation and service configuration. The card-based layout of IFTTT, one of the most popular TAP platforms and the inspiration for our UI, has been extensively used in EUD research [5,10].

In our interface, each ECA component (events, conditions, and actions) is represented as a sequential step, with the UI guiding users through the rule-creation process in a structured three-step procedure. The final application, whose walk-through is detailed in Sect. 4.2, has been implemented in Kotlin, leveraging the Android SDK to ensure compatibility with a wide range of devices. The app combines local and online storage to store users' rules and retrieve the features supported by the ECA framework, respectively. Furthermore, it integrates Google Maps API for geolocation features, allowing users to view interactive maps and manage geofencing areas.

4.2 App Walk-Through

Figure 1, Fig. 2, and Fig. 3 exemplify the usage of the app by illustrating the creation of an ECA rule that prompts the user with a password before opening Facebook, encouraging reflection before further use. The user begins by creating the event (Fig. 1 - A), first selecting the event type "Application" (Fig. 1 - B), then choosing the specific event "Open app" (Fig. 1 - C). Facebook is selected from a list of all installed apps on the smartphone (Fig. 1 - D).

Fig. 1. The steps for associating an event with an ECA rule. Labels and buttons are in Italian and have been translated into English in this paper for readability.

After creating the event, the user associates a condition to the rule (Fig. 2 - A), first selecting the condition type "Usage stats" (Fig. 2 - B), then choosing the specific condition "Launches are above" (Fig. 2 - C). The number of daily Facebook openings is set in a dedicated popup (Fig. 2 - D).

Finally, the user completes the rule by associating an action to the defined event and condition (Fig. 3 - A). The user selects the action type "Input" (Fig. 3 - B) and the specific action "Insert password" (Fig. 3 - C), setting a manual password (Fig. 3 - D).

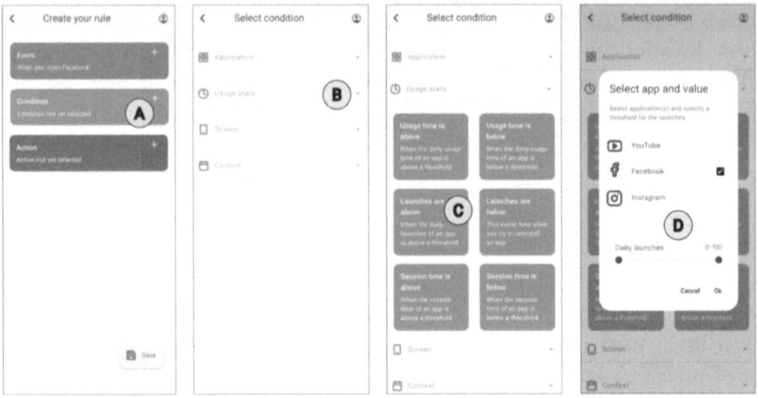

Fig. 2. The steps for associating a condition with an ECA rule. Labels and buttons are in Italian and have been translated into English in this paper for readability.

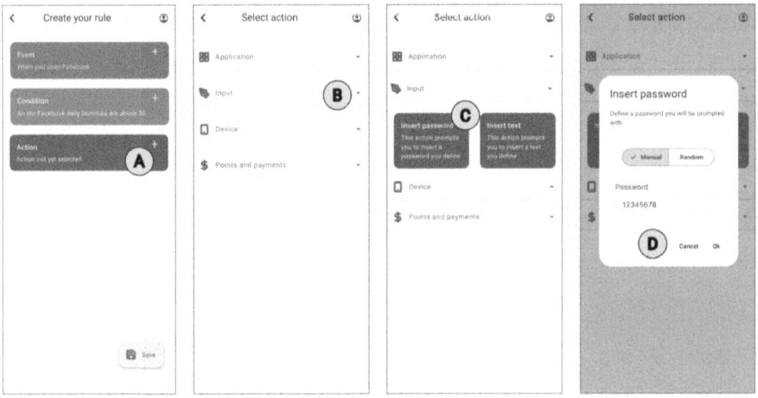

Fig. 3. The steps for associating an action with an ECA rule. Labels and buttons are in Italian and have been translated into English in this paper for readability.

5 Usability Study

We conducted a usability study to evaluate the understandability of the proposed ECA framework and the usability of the rule-composition interface presented in Sect. 4.

5.1 Methodology

Participants. The evaluation involved 11 participants selected through a screening questionnaire designed to identify individuals who frequently use smartphones and are aware of the potential negative effects of excessive use. The participants in the study (three females and eight males) had an average

age of 23.6 years (SD = 3.2 years) and included eight students, six of whom were enrolled in engineering programs, two student-workers, and one full-time worker. Seven participants had prior experience with DSCTs.

Procedure and Metrics. Participants were introduced to the study and signed online an informed consent form. Then, we asked them to complete five tasks designed to assess the understandability of the ECA framework and the usability of the rule-composition interface. These tasks included:

- **Task 1: Limiting app usage during work/lessons.** Create a rule restricting access to specific apps from 9 AM to 6 PM on weekdays.
- **Task 2: Setting a notification for excessive smartphone use.** Create a rule to receive a notification when their total smartphone usage exceeded two hours in a day.
- **Task 3: Encouraging reflection before opening an app.** Create a rule to reflect before launching frequently used apps.
- **Task 4: Modifying an existing rule.** Add a condition to the rule created in Task 3, ensuring it is only activate if the app had been opened more than a certain number of times per day.
- **Task 5: Deleting a rule** Delete the rule created in Task 2.

The study was conducted in person, with participants using a smartphone preloaded with the application. Participants were asked to complete the tasks using the think-aloud method, allowing us to capture their thought process while defining and modifying rules. Sessions were video-recorded following participants' explicit consent. This enabled us to capture both screen activity and verbal feedback, allowing us to collect metrics such as task completion rates and error rates. After completing the tasks, participants filled out the System Usability Scale (SUS) questionnaire and provided additional qualitative feedback. The complete protocol we followed for the study—including detailed descriptions of the tasks and their success criteria, as well as the script and questionnaires used—is available at https://bit.ly/43geKSx. Each study session lasted 28 min on average (SD = 6 min).

5.2 Results

5.2.1 Quantitative Results

Figure 4 summarizes the quantitative results in terms of task success rate (a) and errors made by the participants in completing the tasks (b).

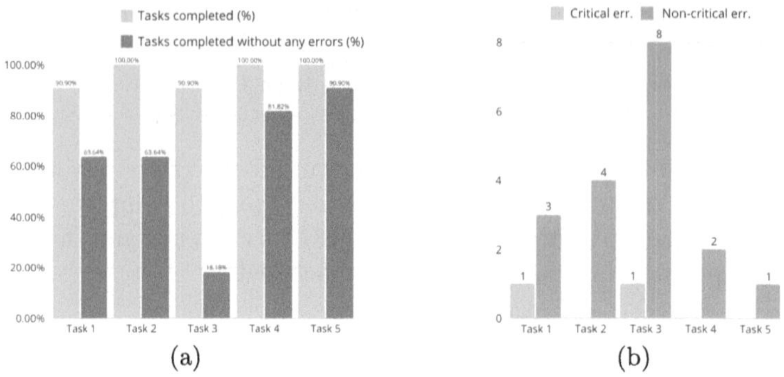

Fig. 4. Quantitative results of the usability test in terms of task success rate (a) and errors made by the participants in completing the tasks (b).

Task 1, which involved restricting app usage during work or study hours, was completed successfully by 10 out of 11 participants (90.90%), with 7 participants (63.63%) completing it without errors. As a result, while almost all users were able to complete the task, some encountered minor difficulties in configuring the correct parameters, making some non-critical errors. Similar to the prior instance, Task 2, which involved setting a notification for excessive smartphone use, resulted in a 100% success rate. Nevertheless, we also noted four non-critical errors among 63.63% of participants. Task 3, which involved creating a self-reflection rule before opening frequently used apps, turned to be the most challenging. Although 10 out of 11 participants (90.90%) eventually completed it, only 2 participants (18.18%) did so without any errors. Many participants, in particular, mistakenly assumed that a condition was mandatory, leading them to introduce unnecessary constraints. In several cases, users applied restrictions that conflicted with their intended behavior, such as requiring multiple app launches before triggering the reflection prompt. By contrast, Task 4, which required modifying an existing rule, was easier to complete, with a 100% success rate and 81.81% error-free completions. The higher accuracy in this task suggests that once users became familiar with the rule composition process, they found modifying existing rules more intuitive than creating them from scratch. Task 5, which involved deleting a rule, was the simplest and most successfully completed, with 100% of participants finishing it and 90.90% doing so without errors.

As shown in Fig. 5, the average SUS score was 82.50, well above the empirical usability threshold of 68, indicating that participants found the system highly usable. Most participants rated the interface positively, with only one scoring below this benchmark.

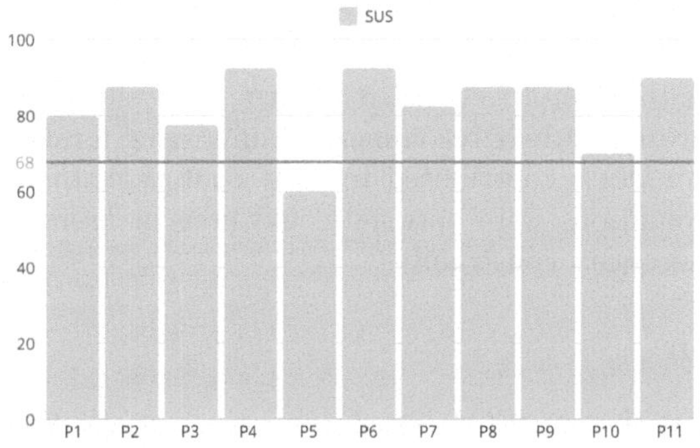

Fig. 5. System Usability Scale scores for each participant. The average SUS is 82.50, well above the empirical usability threshold of 68, indicating a high level of user satisfaction and ease of use.

5.2.2 Qualitative Results

The qualitative analysis of participants' feedback provided insights into how they interacted with the ECA-based rule-composition interface, their understanding of the ECA framework, and their overall experience using the system.

Participants with prior experience using DSCTs found the tasks easier to complete. One of them completed all tasks without errors, while two others made only minor mistakes, such as adding an unnecessary condition in Task 3. This suggests that familiarity with similar tools facilitated comprehension of the rule structure.

When approaching the first task, most participants found the workflow intuitive, but the large number of options initially felt overwhelming. While some appreciated the flexibility, others needed time to understand the distinction between events, conditions, and actions. Across the first three tasks, in particular, some users struggled to correctly identify the event that would trigger the rule. P5, for example, described experiencing a perceived role shift between events and conditions when comparing Task 1 with Task 2, commenting, *"here, the event felt more like what was a condition in the previous task."* The terminology also contributed to some confusion—one participant found labels such as "open app" unclear when associated with an event, whereas the condition "usage time is above" was perceived as more descriptive. However, once users became familiar with the interface, they reported that *"the process became easy and natural"* (P4). Another common mistake was that many participants assumed that a condition was always required, leading them to add unnecessary constraints. P1 admitted: *"I didn't realize I could leave the condition empty; I thought I had to add one."*

In the post-test discussion, participants highlighted both strengths and areas for improvement. The interface was widely praised for being *"intuitive and simple"* (P11), with a clean and minimalist design that *"kept the focus on rule composition"* (P3). Many users reported that *"the logic of rule creation became straightforward after some initial exploration*" (P10) while the "+" button for adding new rules and their elements was described as instinctive. In terms of challenges and areas for improvement, a recurring suggestion was the addition of an onboarding tutorial. Others recommended improving terminology and explanations, as certain labels contributed to early confusion. In particular, clearer indicators that conditions were optional could prevent users from feeling obligated to add unnecessary constraints.

6 Discussion

Our work confirms that an ECA-based approach can effectively support end-user development of digital self-control interventions, allowing users to define customized rules that align with their needs. By translating the taxonomy by Lyngs et al. [26] into ECA rules (Sect. 3), we provided an actionable framework for users to define interventions that fit their self-regulation goals. Using the composition interfaces described in Sect. 4, in particular, participants were able to construct a variety of interventions. Yet, not all intervention categories described in the Lyngs et al. taxonomy could be seamlessly adapted to the ECA framework. One key limitation concerns tracking-based interventions, such as logging and visualizing usage history. These approaches rely on continuous data collection and retrospective analysis, whereas the ECA model is designed for immediate, event-triggered activations. A potential solution could involve integrating a complementary module that automatically collects usage data and presents it in a dashboard format, allowing users to reflect on past behavior in addition to setting proactive intervention rules. Another challenge emerged in translating real-world rewards and penalties, such as financial incentives or tangible prizes. Implementing such mechanisms would require integration with external systems, such as payment platforms or IoT devices, to enforce rewards or penalties based on digital behavior. While technically feasible, these interventions introduce complexities regarding objectivity and personalization, as what constitutes an effective reward or penalty varies significantly between users. Similarly, social sharing mechanisms—which could not be directly translated into ECA rules—could be implemented by allowing users to share rule configurations with peers, fostering a sense of community-driven self-regulation rather than competitive benchmarking.

Findings from the usability study (Sect. 5) align with prior work in TAP [14, 44,45]. In particular, we observed frequent confusion regarding the role of conditions in rule definitions. Some participants, for example, struggled to distinguish between events and conditions, a challenge also observed in prior research on TAP in smart home automation [14,45]. This highlights the need for more intuitive labeling and visual distinctions, along with guided onboarding or training mechanisms to support novice users in understanding the rule structure. Furthermore, the misconception that conditions were mandatory suggests a need for clearer guidance. Techniques proposed in EUD research, e.g., progressive disclosure [34], could be used to develop scaffolded interfaces that guide users in structuring rules correctly.

Overall, our work contributes to behavior change research in HCI, particularly in the digital wellbeing context. While previous research has emphasized static interventions such as pre-configured app restrictions [26], our approach introduces user-configurable interventions, aligning with calls for more flexible and adaptive DSCTs [38]. The ability to define custom interventions suggests that users could actively shape their self-regulation strategies, rather than relying solely on externally imposed limits.

6.1 Limitations and Future Works

While our study demonstrates the feasibility of using ECA rules for digital self-control interventions, two main limitations remain. First, we showed that the event-driven nature of ECA rules does not naturally accommodate all the design features of contemporary DSCTs and that users may encounter difficulties in distinguishing events from conditions. Future work could explore more complex ECA formats, e.g., with compound conditions and multiple actions, hybrid approaches that integrate ECA logic with data aggregation and visualization tools, as well as ways to facilitate onboarding, support TAP learning, and reuse rules created by other users as in commercial platforms such as IFTTT. Second, while our evaluation focused on rule definition, we did not assess the impact of rule execution on actual behavior change. Future studies should investigate how users interact with fully implemented interventions over time and whether ECA-based customization leads to sustained improvements in digital self-control.

7 Conclusions

This work explored the feasibility of using ECA rules to enable end-user development of digital self-control interventions. By systematically mapping intervention strategies from prior research into an ECA framework, we provided a structured approach for users to define customized rules for managing their digital habits. Leveraging the framework, we then designed and implemented a mobile interface for rule composition. Our usability test demonstrated that participants could successfully create and modify rules, highlighting the usability and flexibility of the approach.

Acknowledgments. The authors would like to thank the 11 participants of the study for their availability, as well as Martina Mugnolo, who assisted in the creation of the mobile app and conducted the usability tests as part of her M.S. thesis.

References

1. Apple Inc.: Use screen time on your iphone, ipad, or ipod touch (2025). https://support.apple.com/en-us/108806. Accessed 14 Feb 2025
2. Burr, C., Cristianini, N., Ladyman, J.: An analysis of the interaction between intelligent software agents and human users. Minds Mach. **28**(4), 735–774 (2018). https://doi.org/10.1007/s11023-018-9479-0

3. Ceri, S., Daniel, F., Matera, M., Facca, F.M.: Model-driven development of context-aware web applications. ACM Trans. Internet Technol. **7**(1), 2-es (2007). https://doi.org/10.1145/1189740.1189742
4. Chiarle, M., Monge Roffarello, A., Chattopadhyay, D.: Exploring trigger-action programs for designing self-control tools in mobile devices. In: Adjunct Proceedings of the 26th International Conference on Mobile Human-Computer Interaction. MobileHCI 2024 Adjunct. Association for Computing Machinery, New York (2024). https://doi.org/10.1145/3640471.3680237
5. Corno, F., De Russis, L., Monge Roffarello, A.: Empowering end users in debugging trigger-action rules. In: Proceedings of the 2019 CHI Conference on Human Factors in Computing Systems, CHI 2019, pp. 1–13. Association for Computing Machinery, New York (2019). https://doi.org/10.1145/3290605.3300618
6. Corno, F., De Russis, L., Monge Roffarello, A.: A high-level semantic approach to end-user development in the internet of things. Int. J. Hum. Comput. Stud. **125**, 41–54 (2019). https://doi.org/10.1016/j.ijhcs.2018.12.008
7. Daniel, F., Matera, M., Pozzi, G.: Managing runtime adaptivity through active rules: the bellerofonte framework. J. Web Eng. **7**(3), 179–199 (2008)
8. Davis, K., et al.: Supporting teens' intentional social media use through interaction design: an exploratory proof-of-concept study. In: Proceedings of the 22nd Annual ACM Interaction Design and Children Conference, IDC 2023, pp. 322–334. Association for Computing Machinery, New York (2023). https://doi.org/10.1145/3585088.3589387
9. Desolda, G., Ardito, C., Matera, M.: Empowering end users to customize their smart environments: model, composition paradigms, and domain-specific tools. ACM Trans. Comput.-Hum. Interact. **24**(2) (2017). https://doi.org/10.1145/3057859
10. Desolda, G., Ardito, C., Matera, M.: End-user development for the internet of things: EFESTO and the 5W composition paradigm. In: Daniel, F., Gaedke, M. (eds.) Rapid Mashup Development Tools, pp. 74–93. Springer, Cham (2017)
11. Dey, A.K., Sohn, T., Streng, S., Kodama, J.: ICAP: interactive prototyping of context-aware applications. In: Proceedings of the 4th International Conference on Pervasive Computing, PERVASIVE 2006, pp. 254–271. Springer, Heidelberg (2006). https://doi.org/10.1007/11748625_16
12. Genç, H.U., Coskun, A.: Designing for social interaction in the age of excessive smartphone use. In: Proceedings of the 2020 CHI Conference on Human Factors in Computing Systems, pp. 1–13. Association for Computing Machinery, New York (2020)
13. Google: Digital wellbeing (2025). https://www.android.com/digital-wellbeing/. Accessed 14 Feb 2025
14. Huang, J., Cakmak, M.: Supporting mental model accuracy in trigger-action programming. In: Proceedings of the 2015 ACM International Joint Conference on Pervasive and Ubiquitous Computing, UbiComp 2015, pp. 215–225. Association for Computing Machinery, New York (2015). https://doi.org/10.1145/2750858.2805830
15. IFTTT: IFTTT - automation for business and home (2025). https://ifttt.com/. Accessed 14 Feb 2025
16. Apple Inc.: Welcome to shortcuts on iOS. Apple Support (2023). https://support.apple.com/guide/shortcuts/welcome/ios
17. Kovacs, G., Wu, Z., Bernstein, M.S.: Rotating online behavior change interventions increases effectiveness but also increases attrition. Proc. ACM Hum.-Comput. Interact. **2**(CSCW) (2018). https://doi.org/10.1145/3274364

18. Lanaj, K., Johnson, R.E., Barnes, C.M.: Beginning the workday yet already depleted? Consequences of late-night smartphone use and sleep. Organ. Behav. Hum. Decis. Process. **124**(1), 11–23 (2014). https://doi.org/10.1016/j.obhdp.2014.01.001
19. Lanette, S., Chua, P.K., Hayes, G., Mazmanian, M.: How much is 'too much'?: the role of a smartphone addiction narrative in individuals' experience of use. Proc. ACM Hum.-Comput. Interact. **2**(CSCW), 101:1–101:22 (2018). https://doi.org/10.1145/3274370
20. Lee, U., et al.: Hooked on smartphones: an exploratory study on smartphone overuse among college students. In: Proceedings of the SIGCHI Conference on Human Factors in Computing Systems, CHI 2014, pp. 2327–2336. Association for Computing Machinery, New York (2014). https://doi.org/10.1145/2556288.2557366
21. Lieberman, H., Paternò, F., Klann, M., Wulf, V.: End-user development: an emerging paradigm. In: End User Development, pp. 1–8. Springer, Dordrecht (2006). https://doi.org/10.1007/1-4020-5386-X_1
22. Lukoff, K., et al.: Switchtube: a proof-of-concept system introducing "adaptable commitment interfaces" as a tool for digital wellbeing. In: Proceedings of the 2023 CHI Conference on Human Factors in Computing Systems. CHI 2023. Association for Computing Machinery, New York (2023). https://doi.org/10.1145/3544548.3580703
23. Lukoff, K., et al.: How the design of youtube influences user sense of agency. In: Proceedings of the 2021 CHI Conference on Human Factors in Computing Systems. CHI 2021. Association for Computing Machinery, New York (2021). https://doi.org/10.1145/3411764.3445467
24. Lukoff, K., Yu, C., Kientz, J., Hiniker, A.: What makes smartphone use meaningful or meaningless? Proc. ACM Interact. Mob. Wearable Ubiquitous Technol. **2**(1) (2018). https://doi.org/10.1145/3191754
25. Lyngs, U., Lukoff, K., Csuka, L., Slovák, P., Van Kleek, M., Shadbolt, N.: The goldilocks level of support: using user reviews, ratings, and installation numbers to investigate digital self-control tools. Int. J. Hum. Comput. Stud. **166**, 102869 (2022). https://doi.org/10.1016/j.ijhcs.2022.102869
26. Lyngs, U., et al.: Self-Control in Cyberspace: Applying Dual Systems Theory to a Review of Digital Self-Control Tools, pp. 1–18. Association for Computing Machinery, New York (2019)
27. Lyngs, U., et al.: 'i just want to hack myself to not get distracted': evaluating design interventions for self-control on Facebook. In: Proceedings of the 2020 CHI Conference on Human Factors in Computing Systems, pp. 1–15. Association for Computing Machinery, New York (2020)
28. Mildner, T., Savino, G.L.: Ethical user interfaces: exploring the effects of dark patterns on Facebook. In: Extended Abstracts of the 2021 CHI Conference on Human Factors in Computing Systems. Association for Computing Machinery, New York (2021)
29. Mildner, T., Savino, G.L., Doyle, P.R., Cowan, B.R., Malaka, R.: About engaging and governing strategies: a thematic analysis of dark patterns in social networking services. In: Proceedings of the 2023 CHI Conference on Human Factors in Computing Systems. CHI 2023. Association for Computing Machinery, New York (2023). https://doi.org/10.1145/3544548.3580695

30. Monge Roffarello, A., De Russis, L.: The race towards digital wellbeing: issues and opportunities. In: Proceedings of the 2019 CHI Conference on Human Factors in Computing Systems, CHI 2019, pp. 1–14. Association for Computing Machinery, New York (2019). https://doi.org/10.1145/3290605.3300616
31. Monge Roffarello, A., Lukoff, K., De Russis, L.: Defining and identifying attention capture deceptive designs in digital interfaces. In: Proceedings of the 2023 CHI Conference on Human Factors in Computing Systems. CHI 2023. Association for Computing Machinery, New York (2023). https://doi.org/10.1145/3544548.3580729
32. Monge Roffarello, A., Purohit, A.K., Purohit, S.V.: Trigger-action programming for wellbeing: insights from 6590 iOS shortcuts. IEEE Pervasive Comput. **23**(3), 49–56 (2024). https://doi.org/10.1109/MPRV.2024.3416698
33. Moser, C., Schoenebeck, S.Y., Reinecke, K.: Technology at the table: attitudes about mobile phone use at mealtimes. In: Proceedings of the 2016 CHI Conference on Human Factors in Computing Systems, CHI 2016, pp. 1881–1892. Association for Computing Machinery, New York (2016). https://doi.org/10.1145/2858036.2858357
34. Nielsen, J.: Progressive disclosure: reducing cognitive load by revealing information gradually (2006). https://www.nngroup.com/articles/progressive-disclosure/. Accessed 27 Feb 2025
35. Pane, J.F., Ratanamahatana, C., Myers, B.A.: Studying the language and structure in non-programmers' solutions to programming problems. Int. J. Hum. Comput. Stud. **54**(2), 237–264 (2001). https://doi.org/10.1006/ijhc.2000.0410
36. Purohit, A.K., Holzer, A.: Unhooked by design: scrolling mindfully on social media by automating digital nudges. In: Proceedings of the 27th Americas Conference on Information Systems, AMCIS 2021, pp. 1–10. AIS, Virtual Conference (2021)
37. Purohit, A.K., Bergram, K., Barclay, L., Bezençon, V., Holzer, A.: Starving the newsfeed for social media detox: effects of strict and self-regulated Facebook newsfeed diets. In: Proceedings of the 2023 CHI Conference on Human Factors in Computing Systems. CHI 2023. Association for Computing Machinery, New York (2023). https://doi.org/10.1145/3544548.3581187
38. Roffarello, A.M., De Russis, L.: Achieving digital wellbeing through digital self-control tools: a systematic review and meta-analysis. ACM Trans. Comput.-Hum. Interact. **30**(4) (2023). https://doi.org/10.1145/3571810
39. Samaha, M., Hawi, N.S.: Relationships among smartphone addiction, stress, academic performance, and satisfaction with life. Comput. Hum. Behav. **57**, 321–325 (2016). https://doi.org/10.1016/j.chb.2015.12.045
40. Schaffner, B., et al.: An experimental study of netflix use and the effects of autoplay on watching behaviors (2024). https://arxiv.org/abs/2412.16040
41. Scott, A.E., et al.: DIY digital interventions: behaviour change with trigger-action programming. Proc. ACM Hum.-Comput. Interact. **8**(MHCI) (2024). https://doi.org/10.1145/3676497
42. Terzimehic, N., Bemmann, F., Halsner, M., Mayer, S.: A mixed-method exploration into the mobile phone rabbit hole. Proc. ACM Hum.-Comput. Interact. **7**(MHCI) (2023). https://doi.org/10.1145/3604241
43. Tran, J.A., Yang, K.S., Davis, K., Hiniker, A.: Modeling the engagement-disengagement cycle of compulsive phone use. In: Proceedings of the 2019 CHI Conference on Human Factors in Computing Systems, CHI 2019, pp. 1–14. Association for Computing Machinery, New York (2019). https://doi.org/10.1145/3290605.3300542

44. Ur, B., McManus, E., Pak Yong Ho, M., Littman, M.L.: Practical trigger-action programming in the smart home. In: Proceedings of the SIGCHI Conference on Human Factors in Computing Systems, CHI 2014, pp. 803–812. Association for Computing Machinery, New York (2014). https://doi.org/10.1145/2556288.2557420
45. Ur, B., et al.: Trigger-action programming in the wild: an analysis of 200,000 IFTTT recipes. In: Proceedings of the 2016 CHI Conference on Human Factors in Computing Systems, CHI 2016, pp. 3227–3231. Association for Computing Machinery, New York (2016). https://doi.org/10.1145/2858036.2858556
46. Yardley, L., et al.: Understanding and promoting effective engagement with digital behavior change interventions. Am. J. Prev. Med. **51**(5), 833–842 (2016). https://doi.org/10.1016/j.amepre.2016.06.015
47. Zapier: Zapier - automate without limits (2025). https://zapier.com/. Accessed 14 Feb 2025

Leveraging EUD and Generative AI for Ethical Phishing Campaigns

Bernardo Breve[4], Paolo Buono[1], Loredana Caruccio[2], Federico Maria Cau[3], Gaetano Cimino[2], Giuseppe Desolda[1](✉), Vincenzo Deufemia[2], Rosa Lanzilotti[1], Lucio Davide Spano[3], and Cesare Tucci[1]

[1] University of Bari, Bari, Italy
{paolo.buono,giuseppe.desolda,rosa.lanzilotti,cesare.tucci}@uniba.it
[2] University of Salerno, Fisciano, SA, Italy
{lcaruccio,gcimino,deufemia}@unisa.it
[3] University of Cagliari, Cagliari, Italy
{federicom.cau,davide.spano}@unica.it
[4] University of Naples Federico II, Napoli, Italy
bernardo.breve@unina.it

Abstract. Cyber attacks are increasingly emerging as problems. They are caused not only by technological aspects but also by human factors that are often overlooked during the design of interactive systems. Reports by cybersecurity giants such as IBM and Verizon have shown that up to 95% of security incidents result from human error. This phenomenon is dramatically amplified in contexts such as public administrations, which often lack the financial and human resources to defend themselves against cyber attacks. To address this issue, this paper presents a web platform called DAMOCLES that aims to support the digital defense of Italian public administrations through human factor assessments related to cyber incidents and the mitigation of emerging vulnerabilities. In particular, this paper illustrates the EUD techniques used in DAMOCLES to facilitate the creation of ethical phishing campaigns, which serve as a tool within the platform to assess the vulnerabilities of organization's employees.

Keywords: Cybersecurity · Ethical Phishing Campaigns · Generative AI · Live Programming · Programming by Example

1 Introduction

Public administration (PA) is essential for effective governance, facilitating policy implementation and providing a wide range of services. A critical aspect of PA is the management of public and personal data, which is essential for informed decision-making and maintaining public trust [21,24]. Handling such data requires strict compliance with data protection regulations to safeguard

C. Santoro et al. (Eds.): IS-EUD 2025, LNCS 15713, pp. 264–282, 2025.
https://doi.org/10.1007/978-3-031-95452-8_16

individuals' privacy. However, the effectiveness of these measures is often undermined by human error, which has been identified as a major factor in cybersecurity breaches. In 2024, human error is expected to contribute to 95% of data breaches in 2024, driven by insider threats, credential misuse, and user mistakes[1]. The Catalan Data Protection Agency has recorded 182 data leaks from public institutions in 2024. Of these, only a third resulted from cyber attacks, while nearly 60% were due to employee errors[2].

Phishing emails remain the most common entry point for data breaches, exploiting human error and compromising millions of personal records[3,4]. Therefore, assessing cybersecurity awareness among PA employees is crucial [20,41,44]. Simulated phishing campaigns are among the most widely used methods for identifying vulnerabilities and strengthening defenses against attacks. These simulations are particularly effective for institutions managing sensitive data, as they assess employees' ability to recognize and respond to fraudulent emails. The results provide insights for developing targeted training programs, especially for groups that demonstrate higher susceptibility, such as older employees or those in senior positions [23,44]. Additionally, phishing simulations offer insights into the psychological factors influencing employee responses, enabling organizations to refine training strategies to better equip staff to detect and counteract phishing attempts [20,24].

Despite these advantages, designing effective and ethical phishing emails presents significant challenges at the intersection of cybersecurity and psychology. Modern phishing attacks leverage sophisticated psychological manipulation techniques that exploit human cognitive biases and emotional vulnerabilities, which are elements that must be carefully replicated in ethical simulations. However, security professionals face a critical challenge: creating realistic simulations requires incorporating psychological tactics such as persuasion principles (e.g., reciprocity, authority, scarcity) and emotional triggers (e.g., fear, urgency, curiosity), which are the same factors that make actual attacks effective. The resulting "psychological-technical knowledge gap" represents perhaps the most significant obstacle, as few professionals possess the cross-disciplinary expertise needed to design campaigns that accurately reflect current threats while incorporating the psychological sophistication that makes modern phishing so effective.

To support the assessment of sensitive human factors through effective and ethical phishing campaigns, this paper presents DAMOCLES (Detection And Mitigation Of Cyber attacks that exploit human vuLnerabilitiES), a web-based platform designed to defend Italian PAs from cyber incidents caused by human errors. DAMOCLES provides a suite of tools for assessing and evaluating human

[1] https://www.infosecurity-magazine.com/news/data-breaches-human-error.

[2] https://cadenaser.com/cataluna/2025/03/01/hackers-que-aprovechan-el-error-humano-el-60-de-las-filtraciones-de-datos-publicos-en-cataluna-son-por-culpa-de-un-trabajador-sercat.

[3] https://www.myjournalcourier.com/news/article/illinois-human-services-data-breach-19993603.php.

[4] https://www.theguardian.com/australia-news/2024/sep/29/services-australia-hacks-data-breach-scam.

factors in cybersecurity. For example, the platform includes ethical phishing campaigns designed to assess employees' susceptibility to cyber threats. This assessment tool is enhanced by generative AI, which enables the creation of phishing emails that are as convincing as those crafted by experienced attackers while remaining harmless, as the links included do not lead to any malicious content. The effectiveness of ethical phishing emails is closely tied to the quality of the prompts provided to the generative AI. To enhance this process, the platform employs End-User Development (EUD) techniques based on programming by example and live programming. This approach allows campaign designers to maintain full transparency over the prompt while controlling various aspects of the email, such as its topic, the persuasion principles applied, and the emotional triggers used. Additionally, this paper reports the results of a cognitive walkthrough and heuristic evaluation carried out to assess the usability of the techniques.

The rest of the paper is structured as follows: Sect. 2 reviews related work on techniques used in cybersecurity to assess and mitigate human factors, including cybersecurity simulations, EUD, and generative AI. Section 3 introduces the DAMOCLES platform and its role in ethical phishing campaigns. Section 4 describes the usability evaluation methodology, while Sect. 5 presents and discusses the results. Finally, Sect. 6 concludes the paper and outlines future research directions.

2 Related Work

This section provides a brief overview of the key aspects at the core of this study: the techniques used to assess and mitigate human factors that contribute to cyber incidents; the methods employed to simulate cyber attacks, including the use of generative AI; and the EUD techniques adopted in this research.

2.1 Human Vulnerability Assessment (HVA) and Human Vulnerability Mitigation (HVM)

Mitigating human factors in cyber attacks necessitates a comprehensive understanding of aspects such as users' awareness, skills, and risk perceptions [14]. Corradini and Nardelli emphasized the importance of evaluating users' perception of cyber threats as a critical step in developing effective educational interventions [12]. To assess these perceptions and identify vulnerabilities, various Human Vulnerability Assessment (HVA) techniques have been proposed. Psychometric questionnaires, such as those developed by Alissa et al. [5], are commonly used to evaluate risky behaviors, while interactive methods, including simulated cyber threats and manipulative tactics, are employed to assess user susceptibility to threats [31,39].

These assessments lay the groundwork for Human Vulnerability Mitigation (HVM), which focuses on creating tailored interventions to mitigate identified risks. Research has shown that interactive games are particularly effective in educating users about security-related issues and providing immediate feedback that enhances learning more efficiently than passive methods, such as instructional videos [25,46]. The real-time interaction offered by games increases user engagement and knowledge retention, making them more effective than traditional approaches in various contexts [26,37,43,46]. Another effective yet lightweight strategy is embedding training information within warning messages that alert users to potential risks, such as phishing attempts, when dangerous behaviors occur [11,13,48].

2.2 Simulation and LLMs

Simulations might be very effective assessment and mitigation solutions in cybersecurity by creating dynamic and interactive environments where users can engage with realistic and evolving cyber threats in a controlled setting [47]. These simulations are critical for equipping individuals to recognize and respond effectively to threats they may encounter in real-world scenarios. For instance, phishing simulations replicate authentic phishing attacks, challenging users to differentiate between legitimate and fraudulent communications. By emulating the strategies commonly employed by cybercriminals, phishing simulations help users identify deceptive messages and improve their ability to avoid falling victim to phishing attacks.

Likewise, Digital Twins model user behaviors and interactions with the real world, offering a virtual representation of individual actions, preferences, and vulnerabilities [3,15,16,19]. By simulating these behaviors in response to potential security threats, Digital Twins facilitate the evaluation of user reactions to various attack vectors, thus identifying weak points in both system defenses and user awareness. To favor the design and implementation of these simulations, Large Language Models (LLMs), such as GPT-4, offer powerful capabilities in generating sophisticated, contextually relevant scenarios [35], including phishing content that closely mimics human communication patterns, making it more challenging for users to recognize malicious messages [22]. Additionally, LLMs support the implementation of Digital Twins by creating personalized user profiles based on simulated behaviors [22,42], enabling adaptive and tailored attack scenarios that reflect each user's specific vulnerabilities and actions. Integrating LLMs into these simulations fosters a more dynamic and personalized approach, where scenarios can be continuously refined to align with real-world threat landscapes. The DAMOCLES platform incorporates these advancements by utilizing LLM-driven simulations and Digital Twin modeling, enabling users to engage with personalized cybersecurity scenarios, receive real-time feedback, and enhance their responses to evolving risks. By combining these technologies, DAMOCLES offers an adaptive, comprehensive, and engaging training environment that significantly enhances users' awareness, preparedness, and ability to proactively defend against emerging cybersecurity threats.

2.3 EUD-Based Configuration

No-code development provides another promising avenue for mitigating user vulnerabilities, particularly in the context of cybersecurity. This approach enables individuals without programming expertise to create applications of varying complexity through simplified metaphors that abstract the underlying technicalities, often at the expense of limiting expressiveness [36]. No-code development has garnered considerable attention in the tech industry, with leading companies such as Google, Microsoft, and Amazon at the forefront of its adoption [2]. Academic research on EUD [30] has categorized no-code solutions into three main paradigms: component-based, rule-based, and programming by demonstration. Component-based approaches involve combining visual or tangible elements to construct complex programs, while rule-based methods allow users to define Event-Condition-Action (ECA) rules, which trigger actions based on specified events and conditions, with applications across fields such as home automation, IoT, and Virtual Reality [1,7,8]. Programming by demonstration enables users to create logic by providing examples of desired behaviors, which the system generalizes for broader applications and has been applied in areas like web development and robot programming [4,18,29]. Recent HCI research explores how end-users engage in prompt engineering to customize AI behavior and create content without programming. Zamfirescu-Pereira et al. [49] highlight the challenges non-experts face, such as overgeneralization and reliance on human-to-human communication models. Mahdavi et al. [32] investigate users' iterative processes in crafting prompts for text-to-image generation, revealing strategies like "vibe coding" to achieve desired aesthetics. Arawjo et al. [6] introduce ChainForge, a visual toolkit enabling systematic prompt refinement and evaluation. Masson et al. [33] present DirectGPT, a direct manipulation interface that translates user interactions into prompts, facilitating more intuitive AI customization. Vaithilingam et al. [45] demonstrate Dynavis, which allows users to generate dynamic UI components through natural language. Lee et al. [27] propose ConstitutionMaker, enabling users to iteratively guide chatbot behavior via natural language feedback. DAMOCLES applies these paradigms to cybersecurity education and policy creation. Users can interact with visual components to learn abstract concepts and refine existing policies, define security rules through a top-down approach, and employ programming by demonstration to infer security measures from observed network behavior.

3 The DAMOCLES Platform

DAMOCLES has been developed as an innovative web platform that assists Italian PAs in identifying, analyzing, and mitigating cyber threats stemming from human errors, with a particular emphasis on the underlying human factors contributing to these errors. DAMOCLES is centered around two primary activities: Human Vulnerability Assessment (HVA) and Human Vulnerability Mitigation (HVM). For HVA, DAMOCLES offers three distinct strategies to evaluate the human factors leading to errors: 1) psychometric questionnaires, 2) ethical phishing campaigns, and 3) digital twins. Each assessment technique helps create a user profile defined by a range of pertinent human factors. Regarding HVM, DAMOCLES provides training modules tailored to each user based on their profile. Below, we outline the activities associated with HVA and HVM.

3.1 Human Vulnerability Assessment

Questionnaires. DAMOCLES facilitates the assessment of sensible human factors in relation to cyber threats through three psychometric questionnaires:

- *Susceptibility to Persuasion II* [34]: evaluates an individual's propensity to be influenced by deceptive tactics.
- *Big Five Inventory* [17]: measures personality traits that may correlate with cybersecurity behaviors.
- *Trait Emotional Intelligence* [40]: assesses emotional regulation and decision-making abilities.

These questionnaires have been chosen for their effectiveness in assessing the human factors that influence an individual's susceptibility to cyber threats [14]. Evaluators are assisted in creating a questionnaire campaign by using an intuitive wizard that enables the selection of one or more of these questionnaires.

To illustrate this process, let us consider the following scenario involving Paolo, a cybersecurity expert at a university. Paolo intends to evaluate the human factors that can lead to cyber incidents among employees. He logs into the DAMOCLES platform and goes to the "User Assessment" section to access "Questionnaire Campaigns." Here, he can start a new campaign using a configuration wizard. The setup process begins with specifying the campaign details, including title, description, and expiration date. Paolo then selects all three psychometric questionnaires offered by the platform. Next, he chooses all employees from the Computer Science Department to participate. After confirming the details, he launches the campaign, sending email invitations to the selected employees to complete the assessments. Throughout the campaign, Paolo monitors participation metrics via the platform's dashboard, tracking completion rates and time taken. Once all responses are collected, the platform analyzes the data and provides Paolo with a detailed report.

Ethical Phishing Campaigns. DAMOCLES provides the Ethical Phishing Campaign tool, which allows evaluators to conduct simulated phishing attacks on employees to measure their susceptibility to deceptive emails and their ability to recognize social engineering attempts.

The DAMOCLES platform allows evaluators to design phishing emails that closely resemble real-world attacks, integrating common deceptive techniques such as the use of emotional triggers and persuasion principles. In the original version of the platform, which this study improved by using EUD approaches, evaluators have to customize pre-defined prompts for generative AI models, which are used for the generation of ethical phishing emails. After the emails are drafted and the campaign is deployed, the platform collects valuable behavioral data, including:

- Whether users opened the phishing email.
- Whether they clicked on the embedded malicious link or attempted to enter credentials.
- How much time elapsed between receiving the email and taking action.

To show how DAMOCLES supports this activity, let's consider a scenario with Paolo. He decides to enhance user profiles from the questionnaire by conducting an Ethical Phishing Campaign to gauge real user reactions to phishing emails. In the "User Assessment" section, Paolo selects "Ethical Phishing Campaigns" and accesses a dashboard of past campaigns with an option to create a new one. A wizard procedure helps him create the campaign by prompting for a title, description, and expiration date. Then, the platform guides him in drafting ethical phishing emails using a customizable generative AI prompt, which Paolo refines by editing and selecting, from a list of options, emotional triggers and persuasion principles. Once the prompt is ready, the emails can be generated by the AI model. Paolo targets the same users as in a previous campaign. Upon launch, DAMOCLES collects real-time data on key metrics: the open rate, the number of users who clicked the phishing link, and interaction time. At the campaign's end, Paolo receives a report summarizing findings and identifying high-risk users needing further cybersecurity training.

Digital Twins. The Digital Twins tool in DAMOCLES enables data-driven cybersecurity risk assessment by simulating user behavior through virtual replicas. Drawing on employee traits collected through questionnaires and ethical phishing campaigns, these digital twins let evaluators to identify vulnerabilities without involving real users. Unlike traditional methods, they enable organizations to simulate phishing attacks and other cybersecurity threats against virtual copies of real users, which are created by using generative AI.

Once digital twins are created, evaluators can simulate phishing attacks by sending phishing emails to these digital replicas instead of real users. Generative AI helps craft these attacks against digital twins. DAMOCLES tracks responses, offering insights into whether the digital twin opened the email or clicked on a malicious link, along with the reasoning based on psychological attributes.

To detail this feature, let us consider the following scenario. To enhance cybersecurity, Paolo initiates a Digital Twin Campaign using DAMOCLES . He selects the "Digital Twin Campaigns" option in the "User Assessment" section, providing an overview of existing campaigns and the option to create a new one. The setup wizard prompts him for the campaign title, description, and threat category such as phishing or ransomware. After customizing inputs for creating digital twins, Paolo selects the employees to test and launches the campaign. By clicking on the "Detailed Analysis" button, he accesses real-time feedback on each digital twin's responses, including whether the email was opened, if a malicious link was clicked, and a behavioral analysis of the decisions made.

3.2 Human Vulnerability Mitigation

Currently, the DAMOCLES platform mitigates vulnerabilities found via HVA assessments by generating personalized training programs. Instead of generic content, it delivers *targeted educational content* aligned with each user's risk profile, enhancing cybersecurity awareness.

Paolo, after completing the three HVA activities from DAMOCLES , decides to launch a training campaign to address human vulnerabilities. He logs into the platform and selects "Training Campaigns" from the "User Mitigation" drop-down menu to access the campaign dashboard. Then, to create a new campaign, he clicks on "Create New Campaign" and enters the campaign title, description, expiration date, and selects phishing as the threat category. He chooses a text-based training format, with prompts for AI models visible for customization. After that, Paolo selects the real users for training. Once the participants are confirmed, the campaign is created and added to the dashboard. Selected employees receive notifications to complete their training and Paolo tracks the campaign's progress on the dashboard, which provides real-time updates on participant engagement and training completion.

3.3 Ethical Concerns

In recognition of the sensitive nature of simulated phishing attacks, we also address the ethical implications associated with these practices. For example, balancing the need to conduct realistic phishing simulations with the imperative to protect user privacy is central to our approach. We introduce measures such as data anonymization, informed consent, and strict adherence to applicable data protection regulations (e.g., GDPR) to ensure that the platform's activities remain both ethical and legally compliant. By embedding these safeguards directly into the design of the DAMOCLES platform, our work not only enhances cybersecurity awareness but also demonstrates a commitment to ethical research practices and user protection. This discussion sets the stage for our deeper examination of the trade-offs between simulation realism and privacy preservation, which we detail in subsequent sections

4 An End-User Development Approach for Prompt Engineering in Phishing Campaigns

Generative AI in cybersecurity offers opportunities and challenges, especially for ethical phishing campaigns. AI can generate realistic phishing emails for security assessments, but refining prompts is complex, particularly for non-technical users. Ethical phishing emails must mimic the psychological tactics used in real phishing scams, such as persuasion principles and emotional triggers. As a result, configuring phishing simulations often requires expertise in both cybersecurity and psychology, which makes the process difficult for many professionals.

To address this issue, DAMOCLES uses EUD techniques to simplify prompt design for creating ethical phishing emails with advanced psychological tactics.

This makes the creation of AI-driven phishing emails more transparent and flexible while also lowering the barriers to user entry.

EUD, which has been already beneficial in cybersecurity (e.g., see [10]), is particularly relevant in this context as phishing simulations must balance realism, ethics, and adaptability. Security professionals need to craft emails that closely resemble real phishing attempts while maintaining ethical guidelines and ensuring the effectiveness of awareness training. Standard prompt-based AI interactions are often opaque, requiring trial-and-error adjustments with little guidance on how changes affect outputs. By applying EUD principles, DAMOCLES provides an interactive and iterative design process, empowering evaluators to efficiently refine pre-defined prompts and phishing email content.

To achieve this, DAMOCLES employs two key EUD techniques: *example-based programming* and *live programming*. Example-based programming allows evaluators to define ethical phishing emails by providing examples of email content and scam strategies without delving into the underlying prompts. When creating a phishing campaign, DAMOCLES allows the user to first define the general information related to the study. After that, the evaluator is supported by the example-based technique to design the ethical phishing email(s) by:

1. Selecting an email topic from a list of predefined options, or by providing an email to infer a topic, and then choosing an email from the options proposed by DAMOCLES on that topic (See Fig. 1).
2. Choosing the persuasion strategy and emotional triggers to be used in the email (See Fig. 2 and Fig. 3).
3. If needed, revising the generated email by highlighting a portion of the text and requesting the AI to change it (See Fig. 4).

The example-based approach behind these activities aims to reduce the cognitive load required for decision-making by focusing on strategy effects rather than understanding how it works or predicting outcomes. Additionally, it enhances transparency by letting users compare phishing email variations, showing the impact of modifications. Moreover, highlighting AI-generated changes in the emails ensures that evaluators remain fully aware of automated adjustments, reinforcing user control over the final phishing simulation.

The live programming approach enables real-time preview and iterative refinement of AI-generated content. When users adjust parts of the email text by prompting the LLM, DAMOCLES dynamically updates the email output, providing immediate feedback. This technique ensures that users can observe the direct effect of their choices without waiting for multiple AI interactions, significantly improving usability. Moreover, in the last step, a panel on the right side explains if and how the email is exploiting psychological strategies, allowing the designers to understand and evaluate the potential effectiveness of the emails.

The integration of these EUD techniques makes DAMOCLES a novel approach to AI-assisted phishing campaign configuration. Unlike traditional platforms that rely on fixed templates or manual content creation, DAMOCLES provides an interactive, AI-driven process, enabling users to explore, modify, and refine phishing simulations while maintaining control.

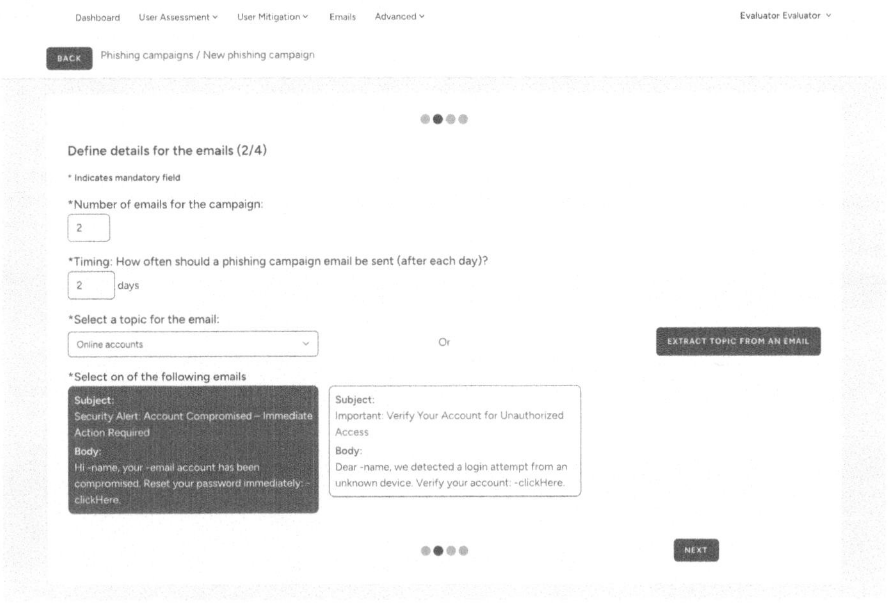

Fig. 1. Topic selection and email selection.

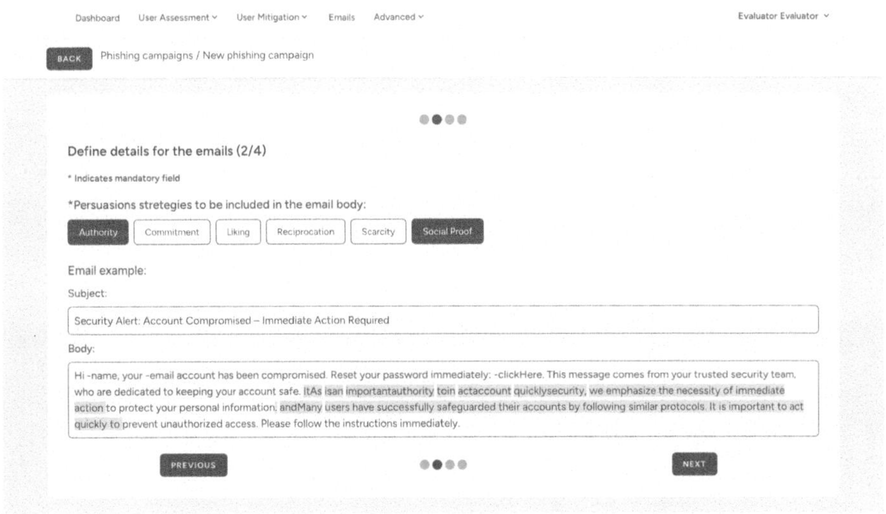

Fig. 2. Persuasion strategies selection.

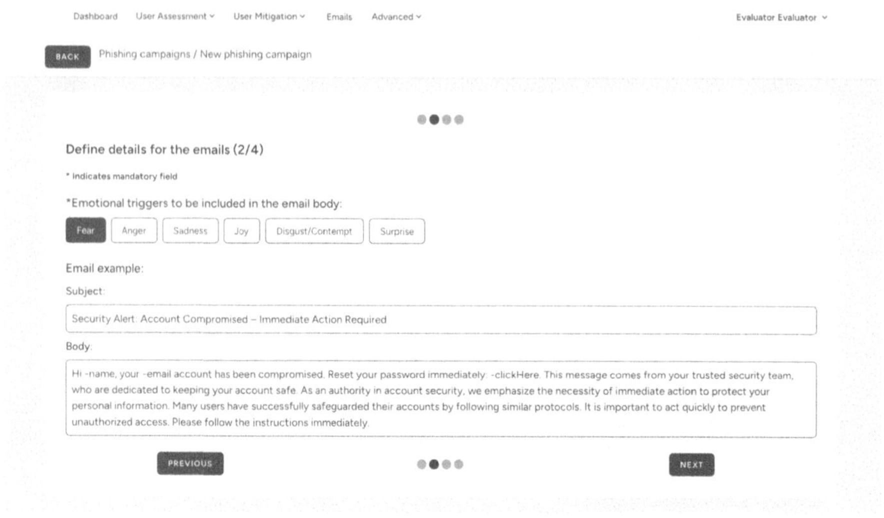

Fig. 3. Emotional trigger selection.

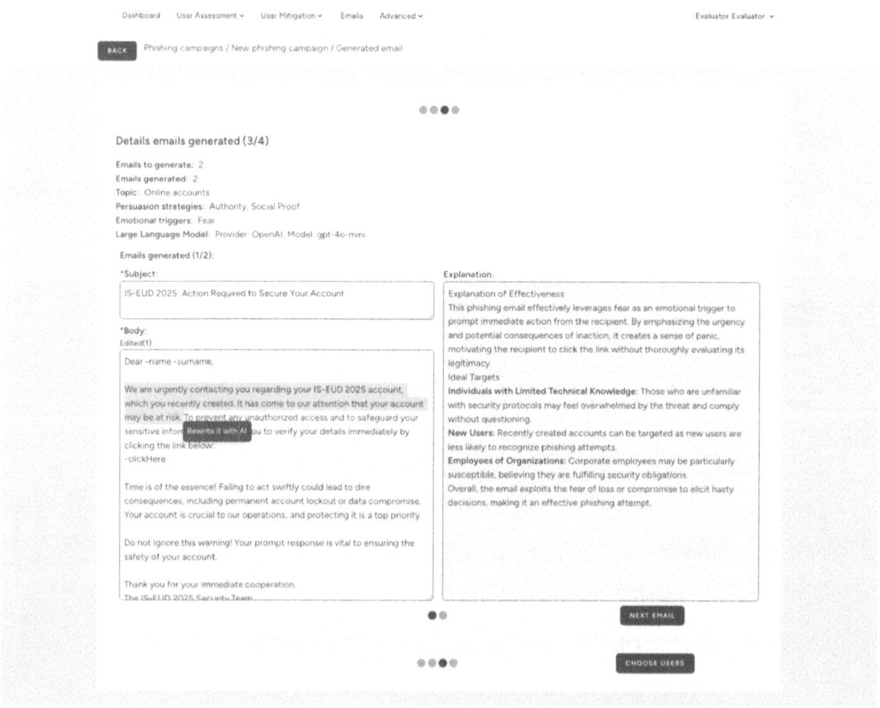

Fig. 4. The box on the left side allows for email text refinement by highlighting a section of the text and requesting changes to AI. The box on the right side explains whether and how the email is using psychological strategies.

5 Expert Based Evaluation

In order to assess the proposed information for managing the phishing campaigns in DAMOCLES , we conducted two types of expert-based evaluations: heuristic evaluation and the cognitive walkthrough [9,28].

5.1 Cognitive Walkthrough

The cognitive walkthrough method [28] is a usability evaluation technique that focuses on understanding how users interact with a system when performing specific tasks. It examines each step using four key questions: (Q1) Will the user know what to do at this step? (Q2) Will the user see that the correct action is available? (Q3) Will the user understand what happens after performing the action? (Q4) Will the system provide appropriate feedback?

For the DAMOCLES platform, the cognitive walkthrough was conducted using a hierarchical task structure, analyzing the process of creating a phishing training campaign. Below, we discuss the identified usability issues, linking them to the respective tasks where they arise.

Identified Tasks.

1. **Start a new phishing campaign**
2. **Enter the campaign metadata**
3. **Enter topic and timing**
   3.1 Enter topic from list
   3.2 Enter topic from example
   3.3 Enter campaign timing
4. **Selecting the persuasion strategy**
   4.1 Pick a persuasion strategy
   4.2 Assess the persuasion strategy effect
5. **Generate the emails**
   5.1 Select LLM
6. **Authoring generated emails**
   6.1 Direct input
   6.2 Authoring with AI
7. **Select the target users**
8. **Start the campaign**

Identified Issues and Discussion. The first issue concerns task discoverability (Task 1). While the platform provides a clear way to manage training campaigns, the placement of this feature under the *User Assessment* menu may not be intuitive for users unfamiliar with cybersecurity terminology (Q2). It could lead to difficulties in initially locating the correct functionality.

In the campaign metadata entry phase (Task 2), the system performs well, as it clearly presents the required fields and offers proper feedback. However, in the topic selection process (Task 3), there is potential for confusion when selecting a topic from an example (Task 3.2). While the system displays example emails, the presence of an *Extract Topic from an Email* button may divert users' attention, making them uncertain about the differences between manually selecting an example and extracting a topic automatically (Q1, Q3).

Another usability concern arises in the LLM selection process (Task 5.1). While the interface provides a dropdown menu to choose the language model, it does not offer contextual information about the available models. Non-technical users may struggle to understand the implications of their choice, which can impact the effectiveness of generated phishing emails (Q3).

A similar issue is observed in the AI-assisted email authoring feature (Task 6.2). When users enter a prompt for AI-generated content, the system does not retain the input visibly after the request is processed. While the result appears, its connection to the user's input is not explicitly reinforced (Q4). This lack of visibility could hinder users from iterating effectively on their prompts.

Finally, the campaign launch process (Task 8) is hindered by the placement of the *Start Campaign* option within a dropdown button. This design choice reduces its visibility, making it less obvious to users attempting to finalize their campaign (Q1). A better approach would be to place the primary action in a more prominent position, with secondary options in the dropdown.

Despite these areas for improvement, the DAMOCLES platform benefits from an example-based approach that aids users in understanding, inspecting, and controlling the phishing campaign setup. The presence of editable AI-generated content, structured input fields, and clear step-by-step progression supports user engagement and learning. Enhancing the visibility of key actions and improving guidance for critical decisions would further strengthen the platform's usability.

5.2 Heuristic Evaluation

Heuristic evaluation is a method for identifying usability issues in an interface by comparing it to established usability principles. This evaluation applies Jakob Nielsen's ten usability heuristics [38] to the DAMOCLES platform, examining how well the system adheres to these principles.

Visibility of System Status. The DAMOCLES platform effectively enhances visibility of system status during phishing campaign creation, providing users with clear feedback on their actions. However, the AI-based email authoring feature could be improved. When users submit a prompt for AI-generated content, the original prompt disappears, making it hard to see the connection to the output. Keeping the prompt visible alongside the generated content would enhance transparency and user control.

Match Between the System and the Real World. The platform generally follows familiar terminology, particularly in cybersecurity. However, some terms may be unclear to non-technical users. Providing inline explanations or tooltips could help bridge potential gaps in understanding.

User Control and Freedom. The DAMOCLES platform provides users control and flexibility in tasks, allowing them to modify inputs and adjust settings as needed. Its combination of pre-defined options and direct text authoring enables effective campaign fine-tuning while maintaining user empowerment. The system also highlights changes from LLM-based editing, ensuring transparency in AI-assisted modifications. However, the navigation structure requires users to move through the interface sequentially using "Previous" and "Next" buttons, limiting flexibility. Incorporating a task overview panel or direct access to specific steps would enhance user autonomy and streamline interactions.

Consistency and Standards. The platform maintains a consistent design, ensuring an positive user experience across its interface. Uniform button placements and menu structures reduce cognitive load, while adherence to common UI conventions makes it user-friendly for those familiar with similar systems.

Error Prevention. The platform reduces errors in form-filling by clearly labeling required fields and using input validation mechanisms. It helps users provide accurate information, reducing mistakes in data entry. Conversely, the example-based sections encourage a trial-and-error approach, allowing users to refine their inputs and explore different suggestions. This method promotes iterative discovery in the phishing email authoring task. Users can revert to a previous state if unsatisfied with an AI-generated text, striking a balance between exploration and control while minimizing unintended changes.

Recognition Rather than Recall. This heuristic is partially supported. While most information is presented through text, visual aids like colors and icons help users understand the impact of their choices. However, improvements could enhance interaction by incorporating more graphical elements, tooltips, or contextual previews in place of some textual explanations.

Flexibility and Efficiency of Use. The DAMOCLES platform offers strong flexibility by supporting various campaign types, enabling users to tailor phishing simulations to different threat scenarios. It allows for both predefined templates and manual content creation, which are useful for both novices and experts. Currently, the focus is on learnability and effectiveness, guiding users through the campaign creation process with an emphasis on clarity over speed. Future enhancements could improve efficiency through streamlined workflows and automation, all while maintaining robust flexibility.

Aesthetic and Minimalist Design. The platform UI design uses a clean and easy-to-read interface. The styling is simple yet effective, avoiding unnecessary visual clutter while ensuring clarity in navigation and interaction. Basic design principles, such as ample spacing and consistent typography, enhance readability and usability. This minimalistic approach supports user focus and reduces cognitive load, making the system accessible without overwhelming the user with excessive visual elements.

Help Users Recognize, Diagnose and Recover from Errors. LLMs' probabilistic nature leads to unpredictable results that are hard to diagnose. Although users can refine prompts, the lack of clear explanations makes error recovery a matter of trial and error. Enhancing transparency with features like revision history or structured editing suggestions could help users understand and address undesired outputs, which might complicate the interface.

Help and Documentation. Currently, support is provided through inline guidance, offering basic help without interrupting workflow. However, a more structured, task-based help system would be beneficial for users to access relevant instructions based on their actions. Integrating a dedicated chatbot could enhance support by providing context-aware assistance, answering common questions, and guiding users through complex interactions, allowing them to resolve uncertainties quickly and maximize the platform's effectiveness.

6 Discussion

Effectiveness in Supporting Ethical Phishing Campaigns. The DAMOCLES platform helps Public Administrations mitigate cybersecurity risks from human errors with its Ethical Phishing Campaign functionality. This feature allows evaluators to design and assess phishing simulations to measure user susceptibility. It provides step-by-step guidance for creating realistic phishing emails ethically. The evaluations confirm that the platform's structured design and email crafting flexibility effectively enhance cybersecurity awareness in a controlled environment.

Positive Assessment of the Usability Heuristics. The heuristic evaluation shows that DAMOCLES effectively supports ethical phishing campaigns. Its visibility of system status provides clear feedback, while user control and freedom allow evaluators to customize phishing emails through predefined options and direct text editing. The highlighting of changes in AI-generated content enhances transparency, enabling oversight of the editing process and promoting ethical practices. The platform ensures consistency, error prevention with structured input fields and clearly labeled options. This iterative AI-based authoring helps evaluators refine emails, ensuring systematic and reproducible campaigns.

Challenges and Areas for Improvement. The usability evaluation of DAMOCLES highlights improvements needed for ethical phishing campaigns. A key issue is the rigid navigation due to "Previous" and "Next" buttons, which limits users' ability to navigate freely. Adding a task overview panel could enhance usability. Additionally, the AI email authoring feature lacks visible retention of user prompts after processing, making it difficult for users to refine content. Displaying prompts alongside generated text would increase transparency. Lastly, expanding help and documentation is essential. While current inline help is basic, a task-based support system with a chatbot would better assist users in executing campaigns effectively.

Balancing Learnability, Flexibility, and Efficiency. The usability evaluation highlighted that DAMOCLES prioritizes *learnability and effectiveness* over efficiency, ensuring evaluators systematically create phishing campaigns without skipping critical steps. As the platform evolves, enhancing efficiency through template-based automation, bulk processing, and faster navigation would benefit expert users managing multiple campaigns. The trial-and-error nature of AI-assisted phishing email creation is an intentional design choice, that promotes exploration. Unlike traditional form inputs, AI-generated content requires iterative refinement, and DAMOCLES supports this flexibility while ensuring evaluators retain control over the final output.

Control over the AI-Assisted Content. A key consideration in the design of DAMOCLES is ensuring that ethical phishing campaigns remain transparent, explainable, and controlled. The heuristic evaluation confirms strong error prevention in structured form inputs, but AI-based interactions present challenges in error recognition and recovery. Because AI-generated content is probabilistic, users may sometimes receive unexpected results that are difficult to diagnose and correct. While users can modify prompts and retry text generation, additional features such as revision history or structured AI editing suggestions could improve transparency and help users understand the reasoning behind certain AI outputs. Furthermore, to ensure that AI-generated phishing e-mails do not contain malicious content in practical applications, solutions such as Retrieval-Augmented Generation (RAG) will be explored. RAG optimizes LLM output by referring to an authoritative knowledge base outside its training data sources before generating a response. In other words, RAG extends the already advanced capabilities of LLMs to specific domains without re-training the model. It is a cost-effective approach to improve LLM output to remain relevant, accurate and useful in various contexts. In our case, an RAG for generating safe phishing emails could be built by training it on non-dangerous phishing examples.

7 Conclusion and Future Work

This paper introduced an EUD approach to simplify prompt engineering in generative AI, applied within the DAMOCLES platform for ethical phishing campaign design. By integrating example-based interactions and live programming techniques, the system enhances transparency and user control over AI-generated phishing emails. The usability evaluation confirmed that DAMOCLES effectively supports cybersecurity training, providing structured guidance and flexibility while ensuring accessibility for non-technical users.

While DAMOCLES proves effective, some areas require improvement. Navigation flexibility is limited due to its sequential workflow, making task navigation cumbersome for experienced users. Implementing a task overview panel or direct navigation options could improve usability. Additionally, AI-generated content transparency should be enhanced by retaining user prompts visibly and offering revision history or structured editing suggestions to clarify AI modifications.

As future work, we planned an update of DAMOCLES considering the emerged usability issues, and then a more formal user study with real users. This will allow us to receive more significant insights on how to improve the interaction paradigm and the user interface.

Acknowledgments. This research is partially funded by the Italian Ministry of University and Research (MUR) and by the European Union - NextGenerationEU, Mission 4, Component 2, Investment 1.1, under grant PRIN 2022 PNRR "DAMOCLES: Detection And Mitigation Of Cyber attacks that exploit human vuLnerabilitiES" (Grant P2022FXP5B) - CUP: H53D23008140001.

References

1. IFTTT. https://ifttt.com/. Accessed 14 Mar 2025
2. The most disruptive trend of 2021: No code/low code. https://www.forbes.com/sites/betsyatkins/2020/11/24/the-most-disruptive-trend-of-2021-no-code--low-code/. Accessed 14 Mar 2025
3. Akbarian, F., Fitzgerald, E., Kihl, M.: Intrusion detection in digital twins for industrial control systems. In: Proceedings of International Conference on Software, Telecommunications and Computer Networks, pp. 1–6 (2020)
4. Alexandrova, S., Cakmak, M., Hsiao, K., Takayama, L.: Robot programming by demonstration with interactive action visualizations. In: Proceedings of Robotics: Science and Systems (2014)
5. Alissa, K.A., et al.: An instrument to measure human behavior toward cyber security policies. In: Proceedings of 21st Saudi Computer Society National Computer Conference (NCC), pp. 1–6 (2018)
6. Arawjo, I., et al.: Chainforge: a visual toolkit for prompt engineering and LLM evaluation. In: Proceedings of the 2024 CHI Conference on Human Factors in Computing Systems. ACM (2024). https://doi.org/10.1145/3613904.3642016
7. Ardito, C., et al.: User-defined semantics for the design of IoT systems enabling smart interactive experiences. Pers. Ubiquit. Comput. **24**(6), 781–796 (2020)
8. Artizzu, V., et al.: Defining configurable virtual reality templates for end users. Proc. ACM Hum.-Comput. Interact. **6** (2022)
9. Blackmon, M.H., Polson, P.G., Kitajima, M., Lewis, C.: Cognitive walkthrough for the web. In: Proceedings of the SIGCHI Conference on Human Factors in Computing Systems, pp. 463–470 (2002)
10. Breve, B., Desolda, G., Deufemia, V., Greco, F., Matera, M.: An end-user development approach to secure smart environments. In: Proceedings of 8th International Symposium on End-User Development. Lecture Notes in Computer Science, vol. 12724, pp. 36–52. Springer (2021)
11. Buono, P., Desolda, G., Greco, F., Piccinno, A.: Let warnings interrupt the interaction and explain: designing and evaluating phishing email warnings. In: Extended Abstracts of the 2023 CHI Conference on Human Factors in Computing Systems, pp. 1–6 (2023)
12. Corradini, I., Nardelli, E.: Building organizational risk culture in cyber security: the role of human factors. In: Ahram, T.Z., Nicholson, D. (eds.) Advances in Human Factors in Cybersecurity, pp. 193–202. Springer, Cham (2019)
13. Desolda, G., Aneke, J., Ardito, C., Lanzilotti, R., Costabile, M.F.: Explanations in warning dialogs to help users defend against phishing attacks. Int. J. Hum. Comput. Stud. **176**, 103056 (2023)
14. Desolda, G., Ferro, L.S., Marrella, A., Catarci, T., Costabile, M.F.: Human factors in phishing attacks: a systematic literature review. ACM Comput. Surv. (CSUR) **54**(8), 1–35 (2021)

15. Eckhart, M., Ekelhart, A.: Towards security-aware virtual environments for digital twins. In: Proceedings of the 4th ACM Workshop on Cyber-Physical System Security, CPSS 2018, pp. 61–72 (2018)
16. Faleiro, R., Pan, L., Pokhrel, S.R., Doss, R.: Digital twin for cybersecurity: towards enhancing cyber resilience. In: Xiang, W., Han, F., Phan, T.K. (eds.) Broadband Communications, Networks, and Systems, pp. 57–76. Springer, Cham (2022)
17. Fossati, A., Borroni, S., Marchione, D., Maffei, C.: The big five inventory (BFI). Eur. J. Psychol. Assess. (2011)
18. Ghiani, G., Paternò, F., Spano, L.D., Pintori, G.: An environment for end-user development of web mashups. Int. J. Hum. Comput. Stud. **87**, 38–64 (2016)
19. Glaessgen, E., Stargel, D.: The Digital Twin Paradigm for Future NASA and U.S. Air Force Vehicles. AIAA (2012)
20. Greco, F., Buono, P., Desiato, D., Desolda, G., Lanzilotti, R., Ragone, G., et al.: Unlocking the potential of simulated phishing campaigns: measuring the impact of interaction among different human factors. In: DAMOCLES: Detection and Mitigarion of Cyber Attacks that Exploit Human vuLnerabilitiES Workshop, co-located with AVI'24, p. 10 (2024)
21. Guenduez, A.A., Mettler, T., Schedler, K.: Technological frames in public administration: what do public managers think of big data? Gov. Inf. Q. **37**(1), 101406 (2020)
22. Gupta, M., Akiri, C., Aryal, K., Parker, E., Praharaj, L.: From ChatGPT to ThreatGPT: impact of generative AI in cybersecurity and privacy. IEEE Access **11**, 80218–80245 (2023)
23. Kim, B., Lee, D.Y., Kim, B.: Deterrent effects of punishment and training on insider security threats: a field experiment on phishing attacks. Behav. Inf. Technol. **39**(11), 1156–1175 (2020)
24. Koddebusch, M.: Exposing the phish: the effect of persuasion techniques in phishing e-mails. In: Proceedings of the 23rd Annual International Conference on Digital Government Research, pp. 78–87 (2022)
25. Kumaraguru, P., et al.: School of phish: a real-world evaluation of anti-phishing training. In: Proceedings of the 5th Symposium on Usable Privacy and Security (2009)
26. Kumaraguru, P., Sheng, S., Acquisti, A., Cranor, L.F., Hong, J.: Teaching Johnny not to fall for phish. ACM Trans. Internet Technol. **10**(2) (2010)
27. Lee, H., et al.: Constitutionmaker: supporting end-user alignment of chatbots via natural language feedback. In: Proceedings of the 2024 ACM Conference on Intelligent User Interfaces. ACM (2024). https://doi.org/10.1145/3640543.3645200
28. Lewis, C., Wharton, C.: Cognitive walkthroughs. In: Handbook of Human-Computer Interaction, pp. 717–732. Elsevier (1997)
29. Li, T.J.J., et al.: Appinite: a multi-modal interface for specifying data descriptions in programming by demonstration using natural language instructions. In: Proceedings of IEEE Symposium on Visual Languages and Human-Centric Computing, pp. 105–114 (2018)
30. Lieberman, H., Paternò, F., Wulf, V.: End User Development (Human-Computer Interaction Series). Springer, Heidelberg (2006)
31. Lim, I.k., Park, Y.G., Lee, J.K.: Design of security training system for individual users. Wirel. Pers. Commun. **90**(3), 1105–1120 (2016)
32. Mahdavi, F., et al.: Is it AI or is it me? Understanding users' prompt journey with text-to-image AI. In: Proceedings of the 2024 CHI Conference on Human Factors in Computing Systems. ACM (2024). https://doi.org/10.1145/3613904.3642861

33. Masson, P., et al.: Directgpt: a direct manipulation interface to interact with large language models. In: Proceedings of the 2024 CHI Conference on Human Factors in Computing Systems. ACM (2024). https://doi.org/10.1145/3613904.3642462
34. Modic, D., Anderson, R., Palomäki, J.: We will make you like our research: the development of a susceptibility-to-persuasion scale. PLoS ONE **13**(3), e0194119 (2018)
35. Mudassar Yamin, M., Hashmi, E., Ullah, M., Katt, B.: Applications of LLMs for generating cyber security exercise scenarios. IEEE Access **12**, 143806–143822 (2024)
36. Myers, B., Hudson, S.E., Pausch, R.: Past, present, and future of user interface software tools. ACM Trans. Comput.-Hum. Interact. **7**(1), 3–28 (2000)
37. Ndibwile, J.D., Kadobayashi, Y., Fall, D.: Unphishme: phishing attack detection by deceptive login simulation through an Android mobile app. In: 2017 12th Asia Joint Conference on Information Security (AsiaJCIS), pp. 38–47 (2017)
38. Nielsen, J.: 10 usability heuristics for user interface design (1994). https://www.nngroup.com/articles/ten-usability-heuristics/. Accessed 12 Mar 2025
39. Ovelgönne, M., Dumitraş, T., Prakash, B.A., Subrahmanian, V.S., Wang, B.: Understanding the relationship between human behavior and susceptibility to cyber attacks: a data-driven approach. ACM Trans. Intell. Syst. Technol. **8**(4) (2017)
40. Petrides, K.V., Furnham, A.: Trait emotional intelligence: behavioural validation in two studies of emotion recognition and reactivity to mood induction. Eur. J. Pers. **17**(1), 39–57 (2003)
41. Rizzoni, F., Magalini, S., Casaroli, A., Mari, P., Dixon, M., Coventry, L.: Phishing simulation exercise in a large hospital: a case study. Digit. Health **8**, 20552076221081716 (2022)
42. Rossetti, G., et al.: Y social: an LLM-powered social media digital twin. arXiv preprint arXiv:2408.00818 (2024)
43. Sheng, S., et al.: Anti-phishing phil: the design and evaluation of a game that teaches people not to fall for phish. In: Proceedings of the 3rd Symposium on Usable Privacy and Security, pp. 88–99 (2007)
44. Spithoven, R., Drenth, A.: Who will take the bait? Using an embedded, experimental study to chart organization-specific phishing risk profiles and the effect of a voluntary microlearning among employees of a Dutch municipality. J. Cybersecur. **10**(1), tyae010 (2024)
45. Vaithilingam, P., et al.: Dynavis: dynamically synthesized UI widgets for visualization editing. In: Proceedings of the 2024 CHI Conference on Human Factors in Computing Systems. ACM (2024). https://doi.org/10.1145/3613904.3642639
46. Wen, Z.A., Lin, Z., Chen, R., Andersen, E.: What.hack: engaging anti-phishing training through a role-playing phishing simulation game. In: Proceedings of the CHI Conference on Human Factors in Computing Systems, pp. 1–12 (2019)
47. Workman, M.D., Luévanos, J.A., Mai, B.: A study of cybersecurity education using a present-test-practice-assess model. IEEE Trans. Educ. **65**(1), 40–45 (2022)
48. Xiong, A., Proctor, R.W., Yang, W., Li, N.: Embedding training within warnings improves skills of identifying phishing webpages. Hum. Factors **61**(4), 577–595 (2019)
49. Zamfirescu-Pereira, A., et al.: Why johnny can't prompt: how non-AI experts try (and fail) to design LLM prompts. In: Proceedings of the 2023 CHI Conference on Human Factors in Computing Systems. ACM (2023). https://doi.org/10.1145/3544548.3581388

Classifying User Motivation in Interactions

Giacomo Vaiani(✉) and Stefano Chessa

Computer Science Department, University of Pisa,
Largo Pontcorvo 3, 56127 Pisa, Italy
giacomo.vaiani@phd.unipi.it

Abstract. The absence of standardised criteria for designing and evaluating End-User Development tools limits their adoption, as categorising situational usage contexts remains challenging. This study introduces a novel method for classifying users by motivation, using real-time interaction metrics based on the Transtheoretical Model of Change. By replacing traditional demographic and arbitrary categorisations, this approach enables dynamic and objective user segmentation. A hypothetical case study in caregiving validates its feasibility, comparing usage data with self-assessments to assess effectiveness. The model provides an objective framework for analysing familiarity, motivation, and challenges in using tools for non-experts, facilitating the development of adaptive interfaces that support users through learning and behavioural change.

Keywords: Adaptive Interfaces · Classification Model · End-User Development · Transtheoretical Model of Change

1 Introduction

The field of End-User Development (EUD) enables users to modify or develop software without advanced programming skills. However, the lack of standardised design and evaluation criteria for EUD tools limits their dissemination, adoption, and improvement. Existing categorisation models, based on demographic or arbitrary factors, are non-generalisable, further hindering progress.

This study bridges this gap by proposing a novel approach that categorises users motivationally through real-time interaction metrics. Based on the Transtheoretical Model of Change (TTM), a psychological framework on behavioural change, this method enables dynamic user classification, addressing the limitations of traditional models. Through this approach, the study aims to answer the central research question: **How can users be categorised from a motivational perspective during the use of EUD interfaces?**

By integrating motivation and learning, the study aims to develop a comprehensive framework. A theoretical case study in the caregiving context demonstrates the feasibility of this approach. The methodology involves collecting and analysing real-world data on EUD tool usage and comparing it with users' self-assessments to evaluate the proposed categorisation. This method provides

C. Santoro et al. (Eds.): IS-EUD 2025, LNCS 15713, pp. 283–293, 2025.
https://doi.org/10.1007/978-3-031-95452-8_17

an objective assessment of familiarity, motivation, and challenges in EUD use within a theoretical framework. Future work will include tracking engagement to develop adaptive EUD tools that sustain motivation.

2 Background and State of the Art

The **absence of standardisation** in EUD system design and evaluation remains a significant challenge, worsened by emerging technologies redefining reference parameters [3,11]. The diversity in EUD paradigms, scenarios, and architectural needs complicates the establishment of common evaluation metrics, as highly contextualised interactions limit uniform standards' applicability [27]. Research suggests **adaptive solutions** with modular components could reconcile standardisation with contextual adaptation [4]. However, **inadequate categorisation** of EUD aspects remains a challenge. Existing models rely on static demographic and contextual data, neglecting real user experiences and psychological factors. This results in fragmented criteria, undermining comparability, security, and maintainability. In this context, **motivation** plays a key role in EUD adoption, shaping users' willingness to engage with complex tools [11].

This study examines user motivation through the **Transtheoretical Model of Change**, a psychological theory describing behavioural change as progression through stages of awareness and motivation [24]. In *Precontemplation*, individuals lack intention to change. *Contemplation* involves recognising the need for change. *Preparation* entails clear intentions, while *Action* marks the initiation of change. *Maintenance* consolidates new behaviours over time[1]. The literature recognises the TTM as an iterative and non-linear process, where individuals may progress or regress between stages. Thus, the model is applied flexibly to interpret motivation levels in EUD tool usage without imposing a rigid path. Motivation is pivotal in the TTM's change process, as higher motivation reduces cognitive load, facilitating progression through stages, whereas excessive mental effort impedes advancement. TTM integrates principles from various counselling and behavioural change theories [24] and has been applied in diverse fields, including smoking cessation [30], addiction management [20], and physical activity promotion [12]. In computing, it informs the design of interactive systems aligned with users' motivational states. In education, it supports adaptive learning pathways to enhance engagement and outcomes [32], while in digital health, it personalises notifications to promote healthy behaviours [26]. Motivation critically influences TTM's change process, as higher motivation reduces cognitive load, facilitating stage progression, whereas excessive mental effort hinders advancement. TTM integrates counselling and behavioural change theories, applied broadly in smoking cessation [30], addiction management [20], and physical activity promotion [12]. In computing, TTM guides interactive system designs aligned with user

[1] The *Termination* stage is excluded, as EUD adoption is not definitive; users may develop expertise without sustained motivation or continued use.

motivation. In education, it supports adaptive learning pathways [32], and in digital health, tailors support for healthy behaviours [26].

To our knowledge, no established literature directly links EUD interface actions with qualitative or quantitative assessments of cognitive or emotional states. However, existing research identifies recurring behavioural and motivational data categories relevant to TTM stages, linkable to interface interactions. **Usage time** is critical for assessing cognitive load and operational competence [19]. **Pause analysis** is particularly relevant, as Cognitive Load Theory [29] emphasises alternating between action and reflection. Miller [21] highlights information processing in chunks, alternating between activity and cognitive consolidation. The Pomodoro technique [9], validated for complex tasks [2], recommends 25 min of work followed by 5-min breaks. Pause duration provides additional insights. Interruptions under 30 s indicate active interaction, whereas those exceeding 60 s suggest attention loss [31]. Intensive reading typically occurs within the first 5–30 s of pauses, with longer breaks indicating reduced focus [15]. Another key parameter, **error frequency**, inversely correlates with progression through TTM stages [13]. Analysis of **temporal variations between actions** reveals cognitive load and motivation levels. According to Sweller [29], stable rhythms reflect clear mental planning, while fluctuations indicate uncertainty or difficulty. Norman confirms that unpredictable rhythm changes signal user struggles, particularly during repeated or hesitant actions [23]. Human-Computer Interaction studies show expert users maintain consistent timings, whereas novices exhibit greater variability due to learning [7]. Similarly, **frequency of help requests** objectively measures user difficulty and independence, correlating reliably with informational interactions and support tool usage [5]. Additionally, **abandonment and re-access frequency** predicts user engagement patterns effectively [8]. Finally, the number of **completed tasks** quantifies user performance and TTM stages progression [18].

The review of **related work** highlights studies applying TTM across digital and non-digital behaviours, confirming usability and interaction data support psychology-based user classifications despite limitations. However, critical issues remain. A lack of long-term data hinders assessments of persistent behavioural change and intervention effectiveness, as studies often prioritise intervention development over sustained adoption [16]. Reliance on self-reported questionnaires introduces response bias [10], while limited active interaction monitoring restricts evaluations of motivational interventions [17]. Limited generalisability further reduces the effectiveness of tailored strategies across diverse contexts, underscoring the need for standardised approaches. Existing systems inadequately support early-stage TTM users, often marked by ambivalence [1]. In non-digital contexts, user classification typically involves retrospective questionnaires or threshold-based metrics [19]. Researchers recommend incorporating objective data, such as sensor-based tracking or interaction logs, to more accurately distinguish user motivations and behavioural patterns [22].

3 Classification Model

This study introduces a **conceptual classification model** that maps measurable interaction metrics within EUD graphical interfaces to the stages of the TTM. Unlike previous research, where TTM has primarily been used retrospectively, this approach integrates the theory into real-time analysis. By applying TTM principles, it enables dynamic user classification based on motivation, allowing EUD developers to implement automated systems that detect users' TTM stage for precise segmentation and personalised adaptation. Unlike traditional methods relying on self-assessments or demographic data, this approach enhances objectivity, reduces bias, and improves classification accuracy. To our knowledge, **real-time classification** based on psychological theory remains unexplored in the EUD domain. This method addresses the limitations of conventional categorisations by linking concrete interaction data to established motivational processes, offering a **generalisable** model of user behaviour.

To align user behaviour with TTM stages, the study maps interaction **metrics** to different phases of learning and adoption within an EUD tool. These data are assessed against predefined **thresholds** that assign users to specific TTM stages. The indicators follow a generalisation principle, aiming to identify TTM—relevant metrics—described below-that are objectively measurable across interfaces and comparable through relative threshold values.

Weighted Usage Time. The literature identifies usage time as a key criterion for interaction analysis, requiring a precise metric. However, its definition is challenged by ambiguity and generalisability issues. Measuring usage time is complex, as users may pause, reflect, or engage in parallel activities rather than continuously interact with the interface. The EUD literature highlights the situational nature of activities, making interaction types and standard time-frames difficult to define. To resolve these ambiguities, the measurement paradigm has been reversed: instead of treating usage time as an absolute variable, this metric is based on inactivity time, where pauses indicate the user's cognitive state. Not all pauses hold equal significance. Some are psychological and aid reflection[2], while others signal disengagement or difficulty. This distinction refines time measurement by recognising the cognitive value of pauses, enhancing the metric's generalisability. *Weighted Usage Time* is defined as $(\text{ActiveTime} + K \times \text{PauseTime})/\text{AbsoluteTime}$ where $ActiveTime$ represents user interaction, such as typing, clicking, or selecting options, and $PauseTime$ denotes intervals without detected input. Their sum determines $AbsoluteTime$, the session's total duration. The coefficient K balances pauses, preventing prolonged inactivity from disproportionately influencing results.

Selecting an appropriate K value is essential for ensuring *Weighted Usage Time* accurately reflects user behaviour. A possible value is 0.2, aligning with literature suggesting an optimal work-to-pause ratio of 80:20 in terms of cognitive

[2] Psychological pauses occur when users stop interacting with the system to reflect, or process information, signalling mental engagement. They are significant as they reflect cognitive activity that supports decision-making, reflection, or understanding.

load. This parameter assigns importance to brief pauses essential for processing while preventing extended pauses from being weighted equally to direct actions. This measurement applies to any interface, requiring only active and total time measurements without advanced tracking. It does not assume users are fully inactive during pauses; instead, the K coefficient balances their impact. The metric remains effective in complex EUD environments, where users alternate between action and reflection without direct interface interaction.

Interactive Disorder. A key parameter for assessing a user's operational ability is error analysis. However, this metric poses challenges, as it requires universal criteria to distinguish correct actions from errors. Execution time alone is unreliable, as speed variations may stem from factors unrelated to user difficulty. To address these limitations, this study introduces a metric that estimates error frequency by analysing behavioural variability during interaction. *Interactive Disorder* quantifies time intervals between actions and their temporal distribution, offering an objective and generalisable measure. It is calculated as $\sigma events/(\mu events + \varepsilon)$, where $\sigma events$ is the standard deviation of time intervals, indicating behavioural stability or irregularity. $\mu events$ denotes the mean interval, normalising the measure relative to overall speed. The ε parameter is a small constant preventing division by zero and ensuring computational stability.

This metric aligns with TTM, as research suggests interaction rhythm reflects user experience, highlighting difficulties or learning processes. It eliminates subjective interpretations, removing the need to define errors, tasks, or action categories, ensuring broad applicability. *Interactive Disorder* remains independent of the number of available functionalities, making it suitable for both complex systems with extensive options and simpler interfaces with limited interactions.

Help Requests. Unlike previous metrics, internal help requests provide an unambiguous measure of user difficulty. Users who find an interface complex or unintuitive rely more on support tools, signalling learning challenges. Conversely, fluid and autonomous interaction suggests familiarity and behavioural stability. This metric quantifies accesses to assistance functions, such as tooltips, tutorials, FAQs, or chatbots, offering a direct and objective indication of user competence and autonomy. Its universal applicability ensures easy implementation, as digital environments either integrate support systems or allow help request tracking.

Interruption and Re-access. Analysing the frequency of user interruptions and subsequent resumptions offers valuable insights into motivation. Frequent, prolonged interruptions may indicate learning difficulties or low motivation, whereas resumption suggests exploration or skill consolidation. This metric quantifies both the number of abandoned sessions and the frequency of resumed sessions, revealing patterns of uncertainty, difficulty, or increasing familiarity with the system. Differentiating between abandonment and resumption enhances understanding of user behaviour over time, providing a concrete measure of usage stabilisation. Its applicability is reinforced by the widespread tracking of user access and session data in digital systems. Most software automatically logs interruptions and resumptions, allowing this measurement without extra tools.

Completed Tasks. The percentage of completed to initiated tasks reflects motivation and progression within the TTM. Persistence and the ability to overcome challenges are essential for sustaining EUD tool usage. Frequent task initiation without completion may indicate cognitive obstacles, interface difficulties, or low motivation, while an increase in completed tasks suggests growing autonomy and confidence. This metric calculates the ratio of completed activities relative to initiated ones, offering a measure of task management and completion ability. Its generalisability is ensured, as many EUD systems incorporate structured tasks or workflows, allowing task completion monitoring. Even in less structured environments, this ratio remains a key indicator, provided that *completion* is redefined based on evolving user behaviour rather than a fixed sequence.

Each metric identified in this study has specific thresholds that determine the user's TTM stage. Through a rigorous method, these thresholds produce a single TTM stage as the final classification output. To enhance rigour, a systematic approach will be developed to assign each metric a **confidence value**, representing the system's certainty in its reliability. The output will then be computed using a **weighted average** based on these confidence values. Each TTM stage is represented by an ordinal numerical value, with each metric assigning users a score from 1 to 5. The final classification is obtained through a weighted average of these scores, where weights reflect each metric's confidence-the more confident the measure, the greater its influence in the weighted measure.

Model Significance. The defined metrics represent **high-level** interactions recognised by the literature as objectively extractable from any EUD tool or user interface. These metrics serve two main purposes: overcoming standardisation constraints by ensuring applicability across diverse contexts without rigid conditions, and maintaining theoretical coherence by aligning closely with existing literature, as outlined in the background section. This balance provides a flexible yet consistent framework adaptable to various EUD contexts. A key feature of the conceptual classification model is its **low granularity**, enabling application across diverse software and interactive environments without significant structural changes. This characteristic facilitates flexible implementation of classification technologies, preserving model coherence while accommodating specific interface requirements. Furthermore, the literature recommends the **combined use of multiple metrics** to reduce ambiguity in single-variable analyses and uncertainty in ambiguous TTM stages. An additional element is the use of **relative thresholds**, independent of absolute data. This approach enhances model generalisability by avoiding thresholds tied to specific conditions. Thresholds are derived from established evidence linking user interactions to TTM stages, supplemented by behavioural data from digital environments. The definition of these thresholds could constitute an original contribution of this study, providing initial reference points grounded in scientific evidence and open to further refinement.

4 Methodology

A hypothetical use case demonstrates the methodology's applicability in caregiving for elderly and cognitively impaired individuals, where technology supports rehabilitation, optimises caregivers' time, and fosters autonomy [14]. Current caregiving practices require significant human and material resources, often constrained by limited time per patient [28]. In this context, EUD provides user-friendly tools for caregivers. The scenario involves developing a system that enables caregivers to **create and modify cognitive exercises**. For instance, a caregiver with limited motivation or skills can access a simplified interface based on predefined templates, avoiding cognitive overload and facilitating the creation of basic cognitive exercises. Conversely, more motivated or experienced users would have advanced personalisation and programming features. Such motivational classification enables a dynamic approach, discouraging dropouts among less prepared caregivers and maximising the EUD tool's positive impact.

Interviews with healthcare professionals (not reported due to space limitations) indicated that caregivers require simple, customisable exercises with adjustable content and parameters tailored to individual patient needs. Although full customisation is preferred, caregivers also desire greater control over the system. Managing complexity, especially in visualising and organising activities, remains a significant challenge. The proposed solution addresses this by introducing a categorisation model that dynamically adapts the system, **balancing** personalisation and control based on user motivation and technical skills.

Thresholds Validation. The classification model includes a validation and threshold refinement phase in which users complete progressively complex tasks and a self-alignment survey, enabling comparison between model measurements and user perception. This phase must involve participants without specific experience, while expert users should be assessed separately to avoid bias and ensure valid results, as noted in a prior review [33]. An effective strategy could involve **5–7 tasks of increasing complexity**, structured according to the TTM, with difficulty increasing as motivation develops. Early tasks focus on awareness and reflection, while later stages assess commitment through progressively complex challenges. Initially, users could create a basic cognitive game using a declarative EUD paradigm via a guided procedure (e.g., wizard-mode) requiring minimal input. As tasks progress, complexity increases, transitioning from visual representations to structured models and culminating in an imperative or meta-programming approach for full game customisation.

Following the practical phase, interviews and standardised questionnaires, particularly **URICA** and **SWAT**, can be administered. These tools assess user motivation and engagement within the TTM framework. URICA evaluates attitudes and intentions towards change and is widely used as a self-assessment tool for TTM [6], while SWAT measures perceived workload, identifying obstacles to smooth progression [25]. The data collected could enable a **comparison** between the assigned phase and users' perceived difficulty, motivation, and readiness for learning. Strong alignment would support the model's validity, while discrepancies would require threshold adjustments. This validation process also refines confidence levels for the thresholds described earlier. Finally, an iterative design cycle will re-evaluate classification metrics based on user feedback, progressively enhancing the system's adaptability to users' evolving needs.

5 Conclusion

Lack of standardisation in personalised assistance stems from the difficulty of rigidly classifying users and situations. This contribution outlines a conceptual framework for classifying user motivation in EUD tools, illustrated through a hypothetical caregiving scenario that demonstrates how users' TTM stage can be identified via real-time interaction analysis against predefined thresholds. The proposed approach monitors motivational and cognitive states—two universally applicable parameters—shifting focus from static categories (*who are the users?*) to measurable behaviours (*what do they do, and how?*). Eliminating dependence on demographic, social, or contextual data enhances generalisability and provides a more objective foundation for EUD standardisation. An abstract formulation ensures flexibility and broad applicability across EUD contexts. In the absence of comprehensive empirical validation, the aim is to introduce the theoretical perspective and lay the groundwork for further investigation. The next phase involves empirical validation and a pilot implementation in a caregiving scenario to assess whether users progress through TTM stages when adopting EUD tools, and whether the proposed metrics can reliably predict motivation and improve engagement. Accurate classification would enable interfaces to adapt dynamically to users' cognitive and motivational needs—offering increased support in early stages and reducing it as users advance. Integrating psychological theory into real-time classification represents an original contribution to HCI, fostering EUD adoption and informing adaptive interface design to support learning and behavioural change.

Future research will address current limitations, including threshold validation biases from self-assessment, the need for a larger user sample, periodic updates to reflect technological and behavioural changes, and limited adaptability to highly specialised EUD interfaces. The overarching objective is integration into broader EUD design frameworks. Beyond user classification, establishing rigorous **guidelines for interface adaptation** based on motivational categorisation is essential to ensure consistency and effectiveness. Another priority is **relapse**, wherein users regress after reaching advanced TTM stages. A formal definition is required to enable systems to anticipate and mitigate such regressions. Further refinement includes incorporating **specific metrics** aligned with visual programming paradigms— such as block-based, component-based, and flow-based—to improve classification and adaptation in specialised contexts. The literature underscores the need for tools that evolve with users and offer sustained support. **Machine learning-based solutions** show promise in this context. Due to the absence of dedicated EUD datasets, unsupervised learning appears particularly appropriate, enabling dynamic adaptation to real-world usage without manual labelling. This approach allows for autonomous refinement of thresholds and confidence levels, gradually improving classification accuracy. A potential advancement involves a *hints* system, wherein the interface, by **predicting** user transitions, proactively delivers stimuli to support progression across TTM phases and prevent relapse.

References

1. Bak, M., Chin, J.: The potential and limitations of large language models in identification of the states of motivations for facilitating health behavior change. J. Am. Med. Inform. Assoc. **31**(9), 2047–2053 (2024). https://doi.org/10.1093/jamia/ocae057
2. Balci, R., Aghazadeh, F.: Effects of exercise breaks on performance, muscular load, and perceived discomfort in data entry and cognitive tasks. Comput. Ind. Eng. **46**, 399–411 (2004). https://doi.org/10.1016/j.cie.2004.01.003
3. Barricelli, B., Cassano, F., Fogli, D., Piccinno, A.: End-user development, end-user programming and end-user software engineering: a systematic mapping study. J. Syst. Softw. **149**, 101–137 (2019). https://doi.org/10.1016/J.JSS.2018.11.041
4. Barricelli, B.R., Fogli, D., Locoro, A.: Eudability: a new construct at the intersection of end-user development and computational literacy. SSRN Electron. J. (2022). https://doi.org/10.2139/ssrn.4129683
5. Broekhuis, M., van Velsen, L., Hermens, H.: Assessing usability of eHealth technology: a comparison of usability benchmarking instruments. Int. J. Med. Inform. **128**, 24–31 (2019). https://doi.org/10.1016/j.ijmedinf.2019.05.001
6. Callaghan, R.C., Hathaway, A., Cunningham, J.A., Vettese, L.C., Wyatt, S., Taylor, L.: Does stage-of-change predict dropout in a culturally diverse sample of adolescents admitted to inpatient substance-abuse treatment? A test of the transtheoretical model. Addict. Behav. **30**(9), 1834–1847 (2005). https://doi.org/10.1016/j.addbeh.2005.07.015
7. Card, S.K., Moran, T.P., Newell, A.: The Psychology of Human-Computer Interaction. L. Erlbaum Associates (1983)
8. Chi, Z., Zhang, S., Shi, L.: Analysis and prediction of MOOC learners' dropout behavior. Appl. Sci. **13**(2), 1068 (2023). https://doi.org/10.3390/app13021068
9. Cirillo, F.: The Pomodoro Technique: The Acclaimed Time-Management System That Has Transformed How We Work. Crown (2018)
10. Di Noia, J., Contento, I.R., Prochaska, J.O.: Computer-mediated intervention tailored on transtheoretical model stages and processes of change increases fruit and vegetable consumption among urban African-American adolescents. Am. J. Health Promot. AJHP **22**(5), 336–341 (2008). https://doi.org/10.4278/ajhp.22.5.336
11. Fischer, G., Ostwald, J.: Seeding, Evolutionary Growth, and Reseeding: Enriching Participatory Design with Informed Participation (2002)
12. Han, H., Gabriel, K.P., Iii, H.: Application of the transtheoretical model to sedentary behaviors and its association with physical activity status. PLoS ONE **12**(4), e0176330 (2017). https://doi.org/10.1371/journal.pone.0176330
13. Horwath, C.: Applying the transtheoretical model to eating behaviour change: challenges and opportunities. Nutr. Res. Rev. **12**, 281–317 (1999). https://doi.org/10.1079/095442299108728965

14. Irazoki, E., Contreras-Somoza, L.M., Toribio-Guzmán, J.M., Jenaro-Río, C., Roest, H.G.V.D., Franco-Martin, M.: Technologies for cognitive training and cognitive rehabilitation for people with mild cognitive impairment and dementia. A systematic review. Front. Psychol. **11** (2020). https://doi.org/10.3389/fpsyg.2020.00648
15. Jacob, R.J.K., Karn, K.S.: Commentary on section 4 - eye tracking in human-computer interaction and usability research: ready to deliver the promises. In: Hyönä, J., Radach, R., Deubel, H. (eds.) The Mind's Eye, pp. 573–605. North-Holland, Amsterdam (2003). https://doi.org/10.1016/B978-044451020-4/50031-1
16. Lee, J.E., et al.: Development of tailored nutrition information messages based on the transtheoretical model for smartphone application of an obesity prevention and management program for elementary-school students. Nurs. Res. Pract. **11**(3), 247 (2017). https://doi.org/10.4162/nrp.2017.11.3.247
17. Levit, T., Cismaru, M., Zederayko, A.: Application of the transtheoretical model and social marketing to antidepression campaign websites. Soc. Mark. Q. **22**(1), 54–77 (2016). https://doi.org/10.1177/1524500415620138
18. Longo, L.: Experienced mental workload, perception of usability, their interaction and impact on task performance. PLoS ONE **13**(8), e0199661 (2018). https://doi.org/10.1371/journal.pone.0199661
19. Marshall, S.J., Biddle, S.J.H.: The transtheoretical model of behavior change: a meta-analysis of applications to physical activity and exercise. Ann. Behav. Med. **23**(4), 229–246 (2001). https://doi.org/10.1207/S15324796ABM2304_2
20. Migneault, J.P., Adams, T.B., Read, J.P.: Application of the transtheoretical model to substance abuse: historical development and future directions. Drug Alcohol Rev. **24**(5), 437–448 (2005). https://doi.org/10.1080/09595230500290866
21. Miller, G.A.: The magical number seven, plus or minus two: some limits on our capacity for processing information. Psychol. Rev. **63**(2), 81–97 (1956). https://doi.org/10.1037/h0043158
22. Nigg, C.R., Harmon, B., Jiang, Y., Martin Ginis, K.A., Motl, R.W., Dishman, R.K.: Temporal sequencing of physical activity change constructs within the transtheoretical model. Psychol. Sport Exerc. **45**, 101557 (2019). https://doi.org/10.1016/j.psychsport.2019.101557
23. Norman, D.: The Design of Everyday Things: Revised and Expanded Edition. Basic Books (2013)
24. Prochaska, J.O., Velicer, W.F.: The transtheoretical model of health behavior change. Am. J. Health Promot. AJHP **12**(1), 38–48 (1997). https://doi.org/10.4278/0890-1171-12.1.38
25. Rubio, S., Díaz, E., Martín, J., Puente, J.M.: Evaluation of subjective mental workload: a comparison of SWAT, NASA-TLX, and workload profile methods. Appl. Psychol. **53**(1), 61–86 (2004). https://doi.org/10.1111/j.1464-0597.2004.00161.x
26. Schweitzer, R., Schlögl, S., Schweitzer, M.: Technology-supported behavior change-applying design thinking to mHealth application development. Eur. J. Invest. Health Psychol. Educ. **14**(3), 584–608 (2024). https://doi.org/10.3390/ejihpe14030039
27. Stegner, L., Mutlu, B.: Designing for caregiving: integrating robotic assistance in senior living communities. In: Designing Interactive Systems Conference, pp. 1934–1947. ACM, Virtual Event Australia (2022). https://doi.org/10.1145/3532106.3533536
28. Stegner, L., Senft, E., Mutlu, B.: Situated participatory design: a method for in situ design of robotic interaction with older adults. In: Proceedings of the 2023 CHI Conference on Human Factors in Computing Systems, pp. 1–15. ACM, Hamburg, Germany (2023). https://doi.org/10.1145/3544548.3580893

29. Sweller, J.: Cognitive load during problem solving: effects on learning. Cogn. Sci. **12**(2), 257–285 (1988). https://doi.org/10.1207/s15516709cog1202_4
30. Tseng, M.F., et al.: Promotion of smoking cessation using the transtheoretical model: short-term and long-term effectiveness for workers in coastal central taiwan. Tobacco Use Insights **15**, 1179173X221104410 (2022). https://doi.org/10.1177/1179173X221104410
31. Tullis, T., Albert, W.: Measuring the User Experience: Collecting, Analyzing, and Presenting Usability Metrics: Second Edition (2008)
32. Udoudom, U., George, K., Igiri, A.: Impact of digital learning platforms on behaviour change communication in public health education. Pancasila Int. J. Appl. Soc. Sci. **2**(01), 110–125 (2023). https://doi.org/10.59653/pancasila.v2i01.512
33. Vaiani, G., Paternò, F.: End-user development for human-robot interaction: results and trends in an emerging field. Proc. ACM Hum.-Comput. Interact. **8**(EICS), 1–40 (2024). https://doi.org/10.1145/3661146

EUD Principles, Methodologies, and Participatory Cultures

Mindsets, Cultures, and Technologies in Support of End-User Development

Gerhard Fischer(✉)

Center for LifeLong Learning & Design (L3D), Department of Computer Science and Institute of Cognitive Science, University of Colorado, Boulder, USA
gerhard@colorado.edu

Abstract. *End-User Development (EUD)* represents a fundamental shift in how individuals engage with technology, enabling them to transition from passive consumers to active co-creators and designers of their digital environments.

While much of the existing research focuses on the technological aspects of EUD, this paper argues that its success depends equally on cultivating the right *mindsets* and *participatory cultures* that foster sustained engagement and innovation. By taking an interdisciplinary approach (drawing from software development, learning sciences, and socio-technical system design), our research has examined *key enablers* of EUD, including meta-design principles, cultures of participation, and distributed cognition. Of equal importance is the analysis of critical *challenges* that hinder the broader adoption of EUD, such as overcoming passive mindsets, reducing the learning effort required for meaningful participation, mitigating participation overload, and striking a balance between user autonomy and structured guidance.

Grounded in long-term research activities and diverse perspectives on the desirability of EUD, we propose a framework that integrates mindsets, cultures, and technologies to guide future design directions, including (1) expanding EUD across *diverse domains* to foster broader adoption and impact; (2) examining the mutual influences between AI and EUD; and (3) deriving design guidelines for *leveraging ChatGPT* tools to augment rather than replace human creativity and learning.

Keywords: End-User Development (EUD) · Mindsets · Cultures of Participation · Meta-Design · EUD in Software Development · EUD in Education · Challenges and Barriers · Artificial Intelligence (AI) · Intelligence Augmentation (IA) · ChatGPT

1 Introduction

The empowerment of users with EUD has been a fundamental and desirable objective in technology design [29], learning and education [10, 36], democratizing innovation [47], empowering citizens [45], and intelligence augmentation [18]). The EUD conferences (started about 20 years ago [31]) have created a community and forum to advance the understanding and identify the challenges and pitfalls of EUD.

C. Santoro et al. (Eds.): IS-EUD 2025, LNCS 15713, pp. 297–311, 2025.
https://doi.org/10.1007/978-3-031-95452-8_18

The terminology used to characterize EUD has a significant impact on how users are perceived, involved, and supported in design activities. The different terms used, including *non-expert users* [31], *domain-experts* [8], *professional amateurs* [5], *users-as-designers* [47], *co-designers* [17], *active learners* [36], and *engaged citizens* [25] emphasize different aspects of the users' role, abilities, and engagement. Each term offers different advantages and limitations. Choosing the most descriptive term depends on the specific goals of the EUD system and the cultural and technological context in which it is applied.

Based on our research over several decades [15], this article identifies the need, opportunities, and challenges for EUD to address fundamental problems (Sect. 2) and describes frameworks and technologies enabling and supporting EUD (Sect. 3). It provides evidence (grounded in our empirical findings) for the *core argument that in addition to technologies, there is a need to understand and promote mindsets and cultures to make EUD successful* (Sect. 4 and 5). Pursuing this expanded framework for EUD creates new challenges and barriers for EUD (Sect. 6). Section 7 identifies future research directions for EUD by (1) applying it to the domain of the learning sciences and education, (2) exploring the mutual impact between AI and EUD, and (3) analyzing the desirable promises and undesirable pitfalls associated with different uses of ChatGPT.

2 Why is EUD a Necessity Rather Than a Luxury

Major problems our societies are facing today include [46]:

- P-1: problems being *wicked, poorly understood,* and *ill-defined* that cannot be delegated and require the involvement of the owners of problems in cycles of improvement and refinement over time [37];
- P-2: problems modeling *changing and unique worlds* being dependent on open, living information repositories and tools [30];
- P-3: problems of a *magnitude* that individuals cannot solve [43]:
- P-4: problems of a *systemic nature* requiring the collaboration of many different minds from a variety of backgrounds [5].

EUD, by fostering mindsets and cultures focused on autonomy, creativity, and innovation, can support and engage stakeholders to cope and address these problems. With the support of socio-technical environments [17], the owners of the problems can directly experiment and refine solutions without needing intermediaries to address these problems.

3 Frameworks and Technologies Enabling and Supporting EUD in Software Design

This section describes how *meta-design* and *human problem-domain interaction* can enable and support EUD. Comparing different design methodologies [3] provides a framework for identifying the unique contribution of EUD.

Professional Design. Traditional software development often assumes a developer-centric model where users are passive recipients of pre-designed solutions, limiting their ability to shape or adapt systems. It was the dominant and appropriate methodology in the early days of computing. The designers and the users were both people who were interested and knowledgeable in "computer topics," and they shared the same knowledge background (as indicated in Fig. 1).

Participatory Design. As computational systems increasingly were developed for a

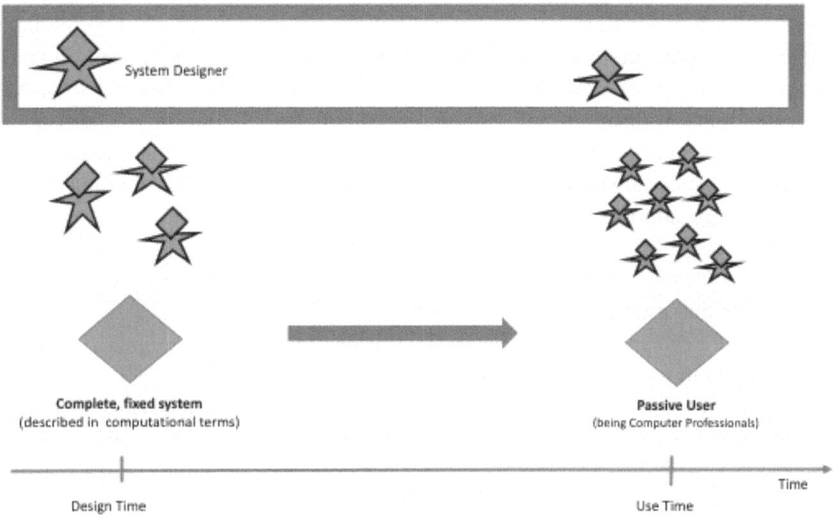

Fig. 1. Professional Design

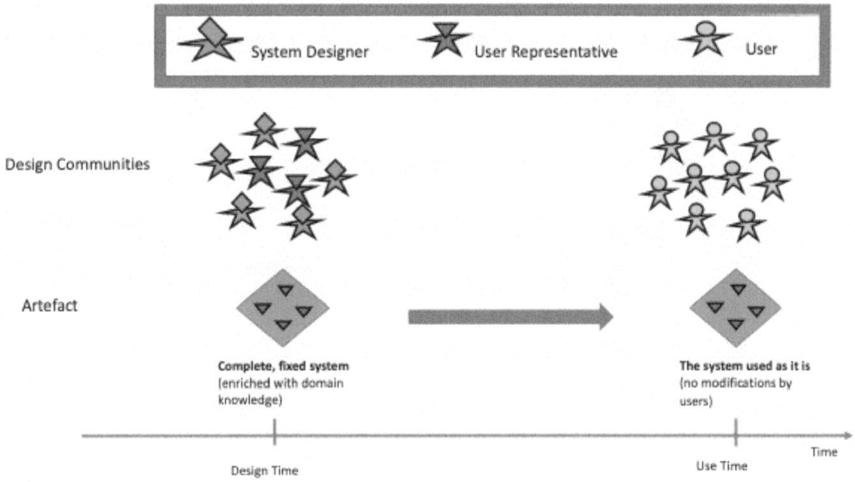

Fig. 2. Participatory Design

great variety of domains, application knowledge complemented computational knowledge and became critically important. To cope with the "thin spread of application knowledge" [9] and the different knowledge backgrounds of the users of the systems, participatory design emerged as a new design methodology [3]. As illustrated by Fig. 2, user representatives participated in the system design and design time to include representations suited for the different knowledge backgrounds of the users.

Meta-design. Participatory design focuses on the initial design phase and provides little or no support for users as active contributors at use time and an ongoing dialogue throughout the lifetime of systems. Meta-design (Fig. 3) complements and transcends participatory design by extending design time indefinitely. Meta-designers (being part of a design team at design time) can create contexts and design tools, and users (e.g., domain experts, engaged citizens) can act as co-creators, ensuring that the solutions are tailored to the specific situated needs and considerations [44]. The defining criteria of meta-design that support EUD can be summarized as follows [15]:

- *creating a framework for change:* design is an ongoing, participatory process rather than a finished product;
- *empowering end-users as co-designers:* shifting control from designers to end-users, allowing them to adapt systems according to evolving needs;
- *sustainability and adaptability*: recognizing the need for long-term adaptability in design and creating open-ended frameworks that grow over time rather than static, pre-defined solutions.

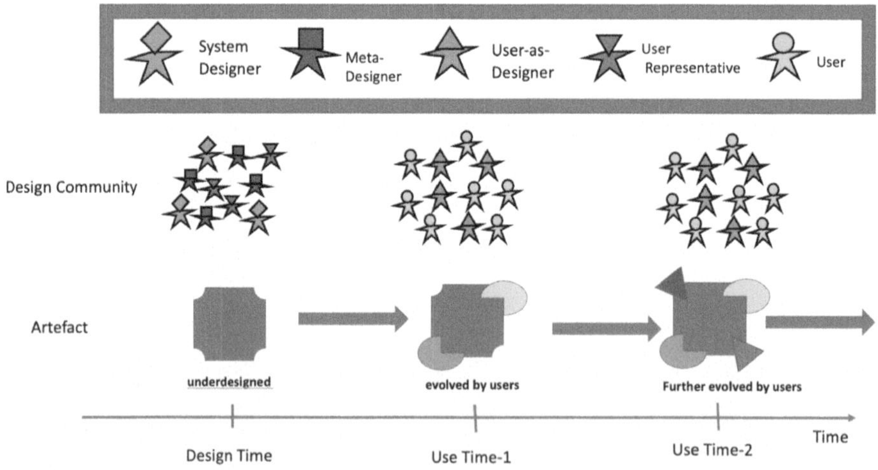

Fig. 3. Meta-Design

To support EUD, combining participatory design and meta-design can be highly effective by leveraging the strengths as follows:

- *initial engagement via participatory design:* using participatory design to co-create initial designs with stakeholders, ensuring inclusivity and context-specific solutions;
- *sustained dialogue via meta-design:* integrating meta-design principles to enable ongoing user participation, allowing systems to evolve and remain relevant.

Empowering Domain Experts by Supporting Human Problem Domain Interaction. Historically designers programming in "high-level" languages (such as Mathematicians using Fortran) were considered "end-users" and the "real" programmers created code in assembly language.

Computational artifacts in today's world exist in almost all domains. The thin spread of application knowledge has been identified as a critical factor [9] for system design in semantically rich domains. A fundamental challenge for empowering domain experts to interact with systems and to engage in EUD, is to advance human-computer interaction to *human problem-domain interaction*, which has been addressed by our long-term research efforts in developing *domain-oriented design environments* [13].

4 Mindsets for End-User Development

As described in the previous sections, EUD is a participatory, evolutionary, and open-ended approach that requires and favors collaborative, creative, and adaptable mindsets. It supports co-creation while challenging fixed, passive, and rigid mentalities [1], thereby favoring and supporting specific mindsets while hindering others. This section documents two examples of mindsets stemming from our empirical work with (1) domain experts engaged in programming and (2) students participating in university courses.

4.1 Example 1: A Geo-Scientist Developing Software

The first example (based on our empirical research to explore the digital literacy of domain experts) documents an interview with a geo-scientist [19].

This geo-scientist's mindset aligns with that of interdisciplinary professionals who prioritize utility over mastery and view tools as a means to achieve domain-specific goals. He sees himself primarily as a scientist, with software development as a supplementary skillset that enhances his research. His focus on autonomy, problem-solving, and scientific rigor empowers him in addressing immediate challenges but may limit his ability to scale solutions or collaborate with domain experts in software development.

Table 1 documents in the left column the statements made by the domain expert, and the right column interprets his underlying mindset and the implications for enriching the understanding of EUD. The example illustrates in a specific context the problems P-1 and P-2 mentioned in Sect. 2.

Table 1. The Mindset of a Domain Expert Acting as an End-User

Statements by the Geo-Scientist	Relevance for Deepening the Concept of 'End User'
I spend in average an hour every day developing software for myself to analyze the data I collected because there is not any available software	No software exists (despite 1.5 Mio Apps) or a potentially useful app is unknown to the user
Even if there is a software developer sitting next to me, it would not be of much help because my needs vary as my research progresses	Change is a constant and software needs to evolve
I cannot clearly explain what I want to do at any moment	Poorly understood, ill-defined problems cannot be delegated, and the owners of problems must have the "authority" to change the problem
If the software developer can manage to write a program for me, I will not know if he or she has done it right without looking at the code	Externalizations need to "talk back" to the owners of the problems
I spent three months to gain enough programming knowledge to get by	Personally meaningful activities will encourage interest-driven learning
Software development has now become an essential task of my research, but I do not consider myself a software developer and I don't know many other things about software development	End-users engage in programming because they want to get their work done and programming is a mean rather than an end for them

4.2 Example 2: Mindsets of Students Appreciating Different Kinds of Courses

The second example contrasts two fundamentally different mindsets of students in educational environments. Some students' mindsets (as exemplified by Student-1) are formed by paradigms of education grounded in settings in which *"a single, all-knowing teacher tells or shows presumably unknowing learners something they presumably know nothing about"* [6]. This traditional education model is still practiced in many educational institutions, leading critics such as Illich [28] to claim that our schools and universities are the *"reproductive organs of a consumer society"*.

In contrast to this paradigm of education, we taught courses for advanced undergraduate and graduate students at our university for many years framed by the following ideas: (1) the teacher should serve as a "guide on the side" and not as "sage on the stage" [38]; and (2) the teacher provides a seed for the course that should be enriched by the interests and participation of the students [20]. This approach is analogous to the EUD approach supported by meta-design, with the students being the active contributors and co-designers.

Table 2. Fundamentally Different Reactions of Students to a University Course

Student-1 —— a negative comment to our course indicating a passive, consumer-oriented mindset	Student-2— a positive comment to our course indicating an active EUD mindset
"I will not ever take a course of this nature again in my undergraduate career, and I hope to find a more structured graduate program with an adviser that is more forthcoming. ***I will reinforce my strengths by continuing to study in the method that I have developed over the past 15 years,*** *I will redirect my weaknesses by avoiding unstructured class environments. I believe that the type of self-directed learning that this class wished to promote is better done during independent studies and thesis work."*	*"When I signed up for this class, I had no idea what it was going to be about. Once I started understanding the material, however, I was extremely thrilled and interested to be a part of one of the most progressive courses on campus. I'm not sure what specifically to say except that I rank this class in the top three that I've taken at CU Boulder.* ***The self-directed nature of the work ensured that I wouldn't be bored or unchallenged, and the interplay between all of us was a lot of fun.*** *After four and a half years in college, I can honestly say that this is one of the first courses where I was treated as an adult, a fact which means more to me than I can describe."*

The students' course assessments for our course resulted in bipolar distributions indicating fundamentally different mindsets among students: students were either enthusiastically positive (rating it with A's on the faculty course questionnaire), or totally negative (rating it with F's).

Table 2 documents two very different reactions. The two students exhibit *fundamentally different mindsets* toward learning: one driven by a preference for structure, control, and external guidance, and the other by curiosity, autonomy, and growth. Student-1 expects the teacher to act as a "sage on the stage", and Student-2 appreciates the chosen design rationale of embracing self-directed learning as a major objective of the course.

By understanding these contrasting mindsets, educators can create more inclusive learning environments that support a spectrum of learner preferences and help students grow beyond their initial comfort zones. For students like Student-1, introducing gradual autonomy (see Section Fig. 5) with clear guidelines and support can help bridge their transition to self-directed learning.

5 Cultures Supporting End-User Development

Cultures of participation [2, 14, 23] focus on how technology can give all humans the means to participate in *personally meaningful activities*. In such a culture, all stakeholders can migrate from being passive consumers to active producers and back, creating an ecology of participation with different users taking on different roles. The rise of cultures of participation across different domains has been facilitated by new technological innovations. Cultures of participation have a unique ability to cope with major problems (see Sect. 2) that society is facing, and that would be hard or impossible to solve with traditional consumer cultures where only a select few become active.

Aspects of cultures supporting EUD have been explored by.

- Illich [29] with his book "Tools for Conviviality" provided a philosophical foundation for EUD by advocating user empowerment, decentralization, transparency, adaptability, and participatory learning;
- Papert [34] rejected the computer-aided instruction approach in which "the computer is being used to program the child" and argued for an EUD perspective in which "the child programs the computer";
- Nardi [33] explored the cognitive and cultural barriers to EUD and proposed strategies to address them;
- von Hippel [47] emphasized the role of user-centered innovation in driving technological and cultural change; and
- Shirky [39] offered a cultural perspective on how technologies can harness user creativity and collaboration.

A fundamental challenge for cultures of participation is to conceptualize, create, and evolve socio-technical environments that not only enable and support users' participation, but also successfully encourage it. Participation is often determined by an individual's assessment of *"value/effort"*. The effort can be reduced by providing the right kind of tools with meta-design, and the value can be increased by contributing to framing and solving a personally meaningful problem and sharing the results with others.

EUD developments will erode monopoly positions held by professions, educational institutions, experts, and high-tech scribes and will situate computation in new cultural and material contexts focusing on enhancing quality of life, not ignoring or diminishing it.

6 Challenges, Drawbacks, and Barriers to End-User Development

The development of an EUD mindset is a dynamic process that emerges from both *internal experiences* [6] and *external encouragement and support* [2]. While internal factors like curiosity, challenges, and lived experiences drive engagement and growth in personally meaningful activities, external sources such as role models, teachers, and intuitive technologies play a pivotal role in initiating, guiding, and reinforcing this mindset. Ultimately, the most effective development comes from a synergy between self-driven exploration and supportive technological environments that provide the tools, inspiration, and encouragement needed to unlock an individual's potential as an active contributor and problem-solver.

In design, there are no *"optimal solutions—only design trade-offs"* [41]. While EUD opens up unique new opportunities, as described in the previous sections, it is not without *drawbacks*. To differentiate between desirable and undesirable developments, it is insufficient to look at EUD as a technology —a more important aspect is *how it is used*. The movie *"October Sky"* (https://en.wikipedia.org/wiki/October_Sky) represents and illustrates a story (based on real events) that the successful exploitation of EUD mindsets and participatory cultures is facing numerous challenges and barriers. This section describes two examples of barriers and strategies on how to overcome them.

6.1 Avoiding the Fallacy of the "Big Switch"

New technologies accompanied by changes in mindsets and culture represent exciting possibilities to support EUD and to rethink learning and teaching. Attempts to instill new values cannot be conceived in isolation but instead must take the changes in mindsets very seriously. Being exposed to a consumer mindset for many years, research has shown that humans are likely to be strongly influenced by the values they have learned from and practiced in their previous experiences [36]. If learners in educational environments are exposed to a consumer mindset (one indication being the response of Student-1 in Table 2), it will require a "big switch" to eventually acquire an EUD mindset to cope with the problems of the digital age (see problems mentioned in Sect. 2).

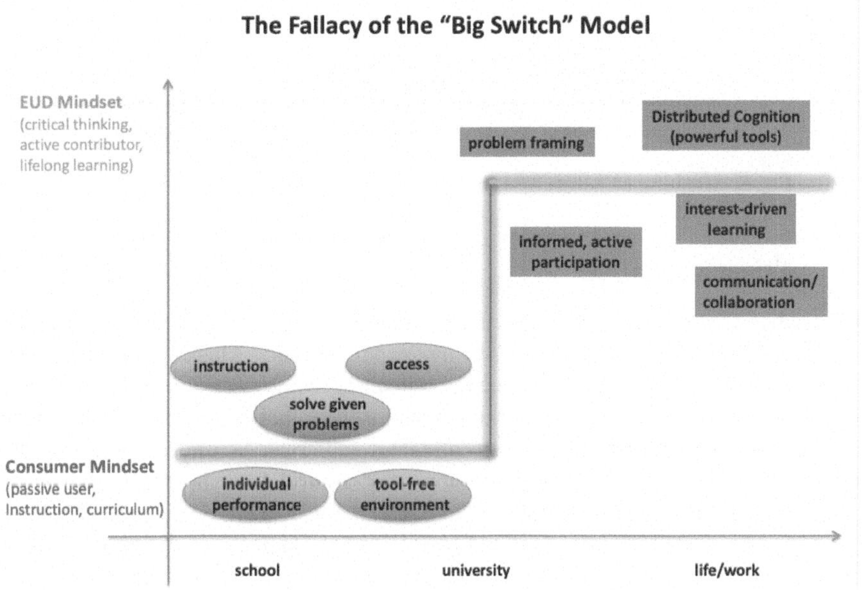

Fig. 4. The Fallacy of the "Big Switch"

To avoid the fallacy that stakeholders will be able to master the "big switch" mindset change (Fig. 4), learners and users should be exposed from an early age to artifacts and participatory cultures [1, 22, 36]. The green bubbles in Fig. 5 are specific approaches and developments supporting the green curve, leading to a *gradual acquisition* of an EUD mindset, thereby avoiding the big switch.

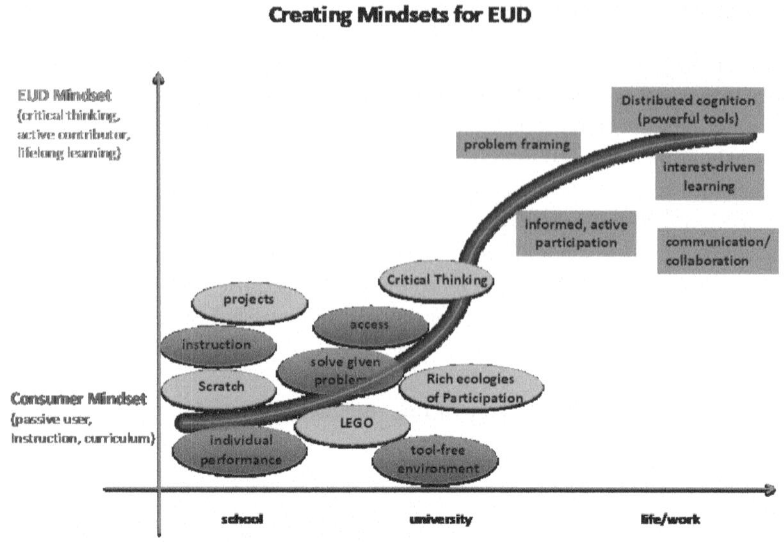

Fig. 5. Creating Mindsets for Lifelong Learning and End-User Development

6.2 Participatory Overload

One drawback associated with EUD is that humans may be forced to cope with the burden of being active contributors in *personally irrelevant activities.* This can be illustrated by "do-it-yourself societies" (e.g., companies offloading work to customers [5]) in which humans are forced to perform many tasks themselves that were done previously by skilled domain workers serving as agents and intermediaries. As argued in the preceding sections, this shift provides power, freedom, and control to stakeholders, but it also can require people to act as contributors in contexts for which they lack the *experience* (which professionals have acquired and maintained through the daily use of systems) and the *broad background knowledge* to do these tasks efficiently and effectively. More experiences and assessments are required to determine the *design trade-offs* for specific contexts and application domains in which the *advantages* of EUD will outweigh the *disadvantages.*

7 Future Directions for Mindsets, Cultures, and Technologies in EUD

The 2021 edition of IS-EUD focused on EUD for AI-based systems, where end users are called on to become end-user developers of intelligent agents, digital twins, and collaborative and social robots. The 2025 edition of IS-EUD is focused on discussing the adoption of EUD in new fields (Sect. 7.1), the proposal of novel EUD paradigms (Sect. 7.2), and the impact of AI-based EUD in terms of user acceptability and appropriation (Sect. 7.3).

7.1 Learning Sciences and Education: Exploring EUD in Different Domains

Educational settings where teachers act as meta-designers fundamentally challenge the traditional "sage on the stage" model by shifting from a "teacher-centered instructionist" to a "learner-centered constructionist" approach [30]. While the traditional model emphasizes content delivery and standardization, the EUD model prioritizes creativity, collaboration, and adaptability, better preparing learners for real-world challenges and lifelong learning (as briefly described in Sect. 2).

Conventional educational environments will lead to mindsets as indicated by Student-1 in Table 2 and create the "fallacy of the big switch" (see Fig. 4). EUD-inspired educational environments provide the seeds and foundations for *rich ecologies of participation* [35] in which learners at an early age are provided with opportunities (see Fig. 5) to become self-directed, interest-driven, and active participants in their education [36].

7.2 AI-Based EUD and EUD-Based AI

EUD as a research strategy is focused on complementing and augmenting human abilities with socio-technical systems for supporting more inclusive societies instead of increasing the digital divide [21].

In the Age of AI (not just in the last few years but more or less from the very beginning), two distinct approaches originated and emerged with separate traditions, values, priorities, and visions in the computing world [18, 24, 32]:

- one being *(strong) Artificial Intelligence (AI)* [4, 27] to *replace* human beings, automating the human experience, and duplicating human behavior with computing systems;
- the other being *Intelligence Augmentation (IA)* [12, 40] to *expand and complement* human abilities with sociotechnical environments.

The mutually beneficial relationship between EUD and IA should be further explored. EUD is a key enabler for IA by giving stakeholders the power to design, adapt, and evolve AI systems.

Future EUD research and support can be grounded and guided by frameworks and design objectives from IA, including.

- keeping *"humans in the loop"* for decision-making (an example being "libertarian paternalism" in politics [45]);
- supporting *"co-creation with meta-design"* (see Fig. 3) and [19]);
- empowering domain experts by supporting *"human problem-domain interaction"* with domain-oriented design environments [13];
- *"making AI more helpful for everyone"* (an example is Google's commitment to integrating AI advancements into their products and services to enhance knowledge, learning, creativity, and productivity; https://io.google/2024/).

This differentiation between strong AI and IA can provide the foundations for formulating the most interesting and relevant questions that future AI research should explore [7, 42]. Our IA approach [16] is focused less on *"Will AI replace humans (e.g.: teachers, journalists, radiologists,…)?"*, but explores from an EUD perspective the question

"Will 'humans not using AI' be 'replaced by humans using AI'"? as the more important research direction to pursue.

7.3 ChatGPT

The newest AI developments are *Generative AI Models* and, more specifically, *Large Language Models (LLMs). ChatGPT* is currently the most prominent example of an LLM, and it provides a specific example and a contemporary context for new interpretations of the theme and the particular topics of this article.

Research objectives, design trade-offs, and usage scenarios focused on ChatGPT that need to be critically examined include *promises* such as: will it.

- change our minds about how we think, learn, and work and what *human creativity* really is [11];
- enrich our understanding and increase the support for *"distributed cognition"* frameworks [26].

Equal attention needs to be given to analyzing *pitfalls* and *hindrances* such as.

- its fluency is an illusion that stems from the combination of massive amounts of data, immense computing power, and novel processing techniques;
- its limited support for asking questions and framing problems;
- the difficulty for humans to scrutinize the answer produced;
- the fact that it hallucinates and gives wrong answers;
- its unreflective use leading to an overreliance on technology.

We developed a narrative to illustrate that ChatGPT can be *used* in fundamentally different ways as a "*Personal Speechwriter*". High-level politicians, industry leaders, and other decision-makers are using human speechwriters to assist them in giving presentations. If speechwriters provide a text and the "important persons" deliver the speech by reading the text literally given to an audience, the "important persons" engage in the least demanding activity: all they need to be able to do is read. What the listeners of the speech hope for and expect is that the "important persons" superimpose their own ideas based on the ideas provided by the speech writers.

Most students writing an essay as a homework assignment, or workers writing a job application, cannot afford to have a human as a personal speech writer. They can use ChatGPT as their "personal speech writer" in the following two fundamentally different ways:

- *Behavior-1:* they use the text created by ChatGPT as their final product (governed by a passive consumer mindset);

  or
- *Behavior-2:* they can use ChatGPT to generate a first draft and then rewrite the text to reflect their own voices and experiences (governed by an EUD mindset).

In using ChatGPT as indicated by Behavior-2, the technology can contribute to making learners and workers more creative and acquire critical thinking skills by blending computational power with human intuition and expertise [16].

The *integration* of EUD and ChatGPT opens new possibilities for user empowerment, creativity, and system adaptability: (1) *ChatGPT can support EUD* by generating initial content freeing users to focus on more creative, high-level tasks; offering quick, data-driven insights; and automating routine and repetitive tasks while preserving creativity; and (2) *EUD can shape the evolution of ChatGPT* with frameworks and principles that future iterations of ChatGPT can evolve from general AI assistants to personalized, user-configurable knowledge agents. EUD empowers users to shape AI, rather than AI shaping users [40].

8 Conclusion

EUD represents a transformative shift in how individuals and communities interact with and shape their environments, moving beyond passive consumption toward active creation and co-design to address and cope with the numerous wicked problems defining the digital age. Through an interdisciplinary lens and based on our long-term research activities, we described and analyzed conceptual frameworks and empirical findings, providing the rationale that should be incorporated in future developments:

1. EUD should not be defined and investigated as a technological development but should be conceptualized and explored by emphasizing the interplay of mindsets, cultures, and technologies that foster environments conducive to sustained user empowerment and engagement.
2. EUD while focused on software development and use in the past, provides foundations for rethinking learning and education and democratic societies.

Broadening the understanding of EUD from these perspectives can guide the future development of EUD, ensuring its relevance and impact in the digital age.

Acknowledgments. The author wishes to thank Daniela Fogli, Barbara Rita Barricelli, Anders Morch, Antonio Piccinno, Ben Shneiderman, Volker Wulf, Steffi Haag, and the three reviewers who provided insightful comments that significantly improved earlier versions of this article.

Disclosure of Interests. The authors have no competing interests to declare that are relevant to the content of this article.

References

1. Barricelli, B.R., Fogli, D., Locoro, A.: EUDability: a new construct at the intersection of end-user development and computational thinking. J. Syst. Softw. **195**, 11516 (2023). https://doi.org/10.1016/j.jss.2022.111516
2. Benkler, Y.: The Wealth of Networks: How Social Production Transforms Markets and Freedom. Yale University Press, New Haven (2006)
3. Binder, T., De Michelis, G., Ehn, P., Jacucci, G., Linde, P., Wagner, I.: Design Things, Cambridge. MIT Press, Cambridge (2011)
4. Bostrom, N.: Superintelligence: Paths Strategies. Oxford University Press, Dangers (2014)

5. Brown, J.S., Duguid, P.: The Social Life of Information, Boston. Harvard Business School Press, Massachusetts (2000)
6. Bruner, J.: The Culture of Education, Cambridge. Harvard University Press, Massachusetts (1996)
7. Brynjolfsson, E., McAfee, A.: The Second Machine Age: Work, Progress, and Prosperity in a Time of Brilliant Technologies, W. W. Norton & Company (2014)
8. Costabile, M.F., Fogli, D., Mussio, P., Piccinno, A.: End user development: the software shaping workshop approach. In: Lieberman, H., Paternò, F., Wulf, V. (eds.) End User Development, pp. 183–205. Springer, Dordrecht (2006)
9. Curtis, B., Krasner, H., Iscoe, N.: A field study of the software design process for large systems. Commun. ACM **31**(11), 1268–1287 (1988). https://doi.org/10.1145/50087.50089
10. Dewey, J., Democracy and education: An introduction to the philosophy of education. New York: WLC Books (Original work published 1916) (2009)
11. Eapen, T.T., Finkenstadt, D.J., Folk, J., Venkataswamy, L.: How generative AI can augment human creativity. Harv. Bus. Rev. **101**(4), 56–64 (2023)
12. Engelbart, D.C.: Toward augmenting the human intellect and boosting our collective IQ. Commun. ACM **38**(8), 30–33 (1995). https://doi.org/10.1145/208344.208352
13. Fischer, G.: Domain-oriented design environments. Autom. Softw. Eng. **1**(2), 177–203 (1994)
14. Fischer, G.: Understanding, fostering, and supporting cultures of participation. ACM Interact. **18**(3), 42–53 (2011). https://doi.org/10.1145/1962438.1962450
15. Fischer, G.: End-user development: empowering stakeholders with artificial intelligence, meta-design, and cultures of participation. In: Fogli, D., Tetteroo, D., Barricelli, B.R., Borsci, S., Markopoulos, P., Papadopoulos, G.A. (eds.) End-User Development (IS-EUD 2021), LNCS 12724, pp. 3–16. Springer, Cham (2021)
16. Fischer, G.: A research framework focused on AI and humans instead of AI versus humans. interaction design and architecture(s), IxD&A J. **59**, 17–36 (2024)
17. Fischer, G., Fogli, D., Piccinno, A.: Revisiting and broadening the meta-design framework for end-user development, in new perspectives in end user development. In: Paternò, F., Wulf, V. (eds.) New Perspectives in End-User Development, pp. 61–97. Springer, Cham. (2017)
18. Fischer, G., Nakakoji, K.: Beyond the macho approach of artificial intelligence: empower human designers - do not replace them. Knowl.-Based Syst. **5**(1), 15–30 (1992). https://doi.org/10.1016/0950-7051(92)90021-7
19. Fischer, G., Nakakoji, K., Ye, Y.: Meta-design: guidelines for supporting domain experts in software development. IEEE Softw. **26**(5), 37–44 (2009)
20. Fischer, G., Ostwald, J.: Seeding, evolutionary growth, and reseeding: enriching participatory design with informed participation. In: Proceedings of the Participatory Design Conference (PDC'02), Malmö University, Sweden, CPSR, pp. 135–143 (2002)
21. Fogli, D., Piccinno, A., Carmien, S., Fischer, G.: Exploring design trade-offs for achieving social inclusion in multi-tiered design problems. Behav. Inf. Technol. **39**(1), 27–46 (2020). https://doi.org/10.1080/0144929X.2019.1634153
22. Gauntlett, D., Thomsen, B.S.: Cultures of Creativity (2013). http://www.legofoundation.com/en-us/research-and-learning/foundation-research/cultures-creativity
23. Jenkins, H.: Confronting the Challenges of Participatory Cultures: Media Education for the 21st Century. MIT Press, Cambridge (2009)
24. Harari, Y.N.: Nexus — a Brief History of Information Networks from the Stone Age to AI. Random House, New York (2024)
25. Hetland, P., Mørch, A., Ponti, M.: Researching Citizen Science by Adopting Ideas from End-User Development: On User Roles, Expertise, and Scaffolding (2014). https://homes.di.unimi.it/cslab/copda2014/submissions/submissions/copda2014_submission_09.pdf

26. Hollan, J., Hutchins, E., Kirsch, D.: Distributed cognition: toward a new foundation for human-computer interaction research. ACM Trans. Comput. Hum. Interact. **7**(2), 174–196 (2000). https://doi.org/10.1145/353485.353487
27. Kurzweil, R.: The Singularity is Near. Penguin Books (2006)
28. Illich, I.: Deschooling Society. Harper and Row, New York (1971)
29. Illich, I.: Tools for Conviviality. Harper and Row, New York (1973)
30. Lessig, L.: Remix: Making Art and Commerce thrive in the Hybrid Economy. Penguin Press, New York (2008)
31. Lieberman, H., Paterno, F., Wulf, V.: End User Development. Kluwer Publishers, Dordrecht (2006)
32. Markoff, J.: Machines of Loving Grace: The Quest for Common Ground Between Humans and Robots. HarperCollins Publishers (2016)
33. Nardi, B.A.: A Small Matter of Programming. The MIT Press, Cambridge (1993)
34. Papert, S.: Mindstorms: Children, Computers and Powerful Ideas. Basic Books, New York (1980)
35. Preece, J., Shneiderman, B.: The reader-to-leader framework: motivating technology-mediated social participation. AIS Trans. Hum. Comput. Interact. **1**(1), 13–32 (2009)
36. Resnick, M.: Lifelong Kindergarten — Cultivating Creativity through Projects, Passion, Peers, and Play. MIT Press, Cambridge (2017)
37. Rittel, H.: Planning problems are wicked problems. In: Cross, N. (ed.) Developments in Design Methodology, pp. 135–144. John Wiley & Sons, New York (1984)
38. Rogoff, B., Matsuov, E., White, C.: Models of teaching and learning: participation in a community of learners. In: Olsen, D.R., Torrance, N. (eds.) Handbook of Education and Human Development: New Models of Learning, Teaching and Schooling, pp. 388–414. Blackwell, London (1996)
39. Shirky, C.: Cognitive Surplus — Creativity and Generosity in a Connected Age. Penguin Press, New York (2010)
40. Shneiderman, B.: Human-Centered AI. Oxford University Press (2022)
41. Simon, H.A.: The Sciences of the Artificial. The MIT Press, Cambridge (1996)
42. Susskind, D.: A World Without Work: Technology, Automation, and How We Should Respond. Metropolitan Books/Henry Holt & Company, New York (2020)
43. Sloman, S., Fernbach, P.: The Knowledge Illusion — Why We Never Think Alone. Riverhead Books, New York (2017)
44. Suchman, L.A.: Plans and Situated Actions. Cambridge University Press, Cambridge (1987)
45. Thaler, R.H., Sunstein, C.R.: Nudge — Improving Decisions about Health, Wealth, and Happiness. Penguin Books, London (2009)
46. United-Nations. The Sustainable Development Goals Report 2024 (2024). https://unstats.un.org/sdgs/report/2024/
47. von Hippel, E.: Democratizing Innovation. MIT Press, Cambridge (2005)

Assessing Computational Thinking Skills Through Artefacts: The Case of ModeLLer

Chiara Mannari[1,2(✉)], Tommaso Turchi[1], Caterina Frosali[1], Manlio Bacco[2], Alessio Ferrari[3], Cristina Conati[4], and Alessio Malizia[1,5]

[1] Department of Computer Science, University of Pisa, Pisa, Italy
chiara.mannari@phd.unipi.it, tommaso.turchi@unipi.it, manlio.bacco@isti.cnr.it

[2] Institute of Information Science and Technologies "Alessandro Faedo" - ISTI, CNR, Pisa, Italy
caterina.frosali@studenti.unipi.it, alessio.malizia@unipi.it

[3] School of Computer Science, University College Dublin (UCD), Dublin, Ireland
alessio.ferrari@ucd.ie

[4] Department of Computer Science, University of British Columbia, Vancouver, Canada
conati@cs.ubc.ca

[5] Molde University College, Molde, Norway

Abstract. Computational thinking (CT) skills provide structured approaches to problem-solving that are valuable for navigating the increasing complexity of technological environments. CT skills can be assessed through various methods and perspectives. EUDability provides a framework for evaluating end-user development (EUD) tools, with core dimensions directly aligned to CT skills. This paper explores how CT skills manifest in the creation of visual models, an activity that supports the representation and understanding of socio-technical systems. We propose an evaluation method employing ModeLLer, a block-based EUD modelling tool and a user study. We carry out a structured evaluation integrating the EUDability inspection and process-based CT skills evaluation with the assessment of the artefacts produced by end-users. Results highlight the ability of ModeLLer to support the modelling activity while also providing insights into the EUDability of the tool and end-users' CT skills. Furthermore, although preliminary, our results illustrate the relationship between tool capabilities, user skills, and modelling outcomes.

Keywords: EUDability · visual models · Computational Thinking skills

1 Introduction

In today's increasingly digital world, where Artificial Intelligence (AI) and automation technologies are rapidly transforming work processes, technological

C. Santoro et al. (Eds.): IS-EUD 2025, LNCS 15713, pp. 312–321, 2025.
https://doi.org/10.1007/978-3-031-95452-8_19

literacy has become essential across all sectors of society. Computational Thinking (CT) provides structured approaches to problem-solving that are valuable for navigating complex technological environments [21]. However, many individuals, particularly those already in the workforce, may lack the computational background necessary to adapt to these increasing demands [7]. Although CT has been promoted as a fundamental concept in everyday life [21], much of the existing research concentrates on its application within education [6]. This gap is crucial as work environments evolve toward greater technological complexity, requiring more problem-solving activities and knowledge management [13].

End-User Development (EUD) addresses this challenge by empowering individuals without programming expertise to create and extend digital artefacts [10]. By providing tools that align with users' capabilities, EUD enables them to become active participants in technology development rather than passive consumers. This empowerment is also relevant in co-design contexts where stakeholders with different backgrounds interact to co-create and assess technological solutions. In such contexts, methodologies for supporting effective communication ensure shared understanding and collaborative decision-making.

Our broader research examines visual models as structured representations serving for problem-solving and system design. Among different modelling approaches, visual models are designed to simplify complex information and make it easier to understand, analyse, or communicate [14]. In the context of the Horizon Europe project CODECS (Maximising the CO-benefits of agricultural Digitalisation through conducive digital ECoSystems) [1], we adopt visual models to assess the impacts of agricultural digitalisation in the context of living labs, i.e., networks of researchers, practitioners and policymakers [12].

Building on prior research that emphasises modelling as a fundamental activity related to CT, primarily involving skills such as abstraction and decomposition [21], this study aims to explore whether there is a relationship between end-user development of visual models and Computational Thinking. To address this challenge, we propose an evaluation method leveraging ModeLLer [11], a block-based modelling tool that enables end-users to generate formal models, and a user study based on the EUDability framework [3].

Our contribution is threefold: first, although with preliminary results, we illustrate the relationship between tool capabilities, user skills, and modelling outcomes; second, we provide an EUD tool to model systems and we demonstrate its suitability with a user study obtaining valuable insights for its improvement; third, as a methodological contribution, we extend the EUDability framework by moving beyond traditional inspection and self-assessment techniques.

2 Related Work

Since its initial definition by Wing [20], CT has become recognised as a fundamental skill for problem-solving and innovation, with a growing body of research emphasising its importance in various disciplines [17,18,21].

Selby and Woollard [16] contributed to CT formalisation by proposing a set of five core skills including *abstraction* (focusing on the important information only and ignoring irrelevant details); *decomposition*, (breaking down a complex problem or system into smaller, more manageable parts); *algorithm design*, (developing a step-by-step solution to a problem); *evaluation*, (assessing whether a solution or algorithm works effectively and efficiently); *generalisation*, (extending a solution or approach to a wider range of problems).

TSAI et al. [18] proposed the Computational Thinking scale (CTS), an operationalisation of Selby and Woollard's CT skills that can be measured through a 19-item questionnaire. The scale has been developed for the purpose of self-assessment of an individual's attitude to implement mental strategies taking a process-oriented approach.

Starting from the observation of students learning to code with Scratch, Brennan and Resnick [4] developed the idea that CT is a dynamic concept requiring an evaluation from multiple, integrated perspectives. Consequently, they outlined an assessment framework encompassing project portfolios analysis, interview on artefacts and different design scenarios. Most empirical research on CT skills has concentrated on the education field [9], with many contributions on coding [4,8] and fostering CT skills through student engagement [5,19]. Barricelli et al. proposed EUDability [3], a construct to evaluate how effectively EUD environments support users' CT skills. The framework assesses tools across five dimensions that directly map to corresponding CT skills: *concreteness* (presenting concepts intuitively, supporting abstraction), *modularity* (enabling problem decomposition), *structuredness* (guiding step-by-step solution development), *reusability* (facilitating solution sharing and adaptation), and *testability* (supporting outcome verification). By examining these dimensions, researchers can evaluate how well EUD tools accommodate users with varying levels of CT.

In a recent study [2], the authors carried out an evaluation of EUD tools with domain experts from the healthcare field integrating the assessment of the EUDability of the tools and users' CT skills. While the EUDability framework provides valuable insights into tool capabilities and their alignment with users' CT skills, it does not yet address the assessment of artefacts produced through these tools.

3 Methodology

In this study, we investigate the creation of visual models as an activity that requires the application of CT skills. Thus, we propose an evaluation method based on: 1) ModeLLer, an open source modelling tool designed for end-users, and 2) a user study to identify and assess CT skills under diverse perspectives.

3.1 ModeLLer

ModeLLer is designed to support end-users to model systems without any knowledge of formal notations and without the intervention of expert engineers [11].

The current version of the tool enables users to generate models in UML, BPMN, and iStar notations through a block-based visual editor[1]

3.2 User Study Design

The study procedure is illustrated in Fig. 1, which outlines four main steps. Step 1 entails the *EUDability inspection-based evaluation*, where HCI experts examine the tool and compile a checklist based on the original version proposed by Barricelli et al. [2]. Step 2 focuses on *CTS assessment*, where end-users self-evaluate their CT skills through a 19-item questionnaire proposed in prior work [2,18]. In step 3, end-users participate in a *test session using ModeLLer* and complete the task proposed. Before beginning the session, end-users watch a 10-minute video that explains how to model socio-technical systems with ModeLLer. In a pre-test phase, an assessment of the understandability of formal notations is conducted. During the user interaction with the tool, a log is produced containing detailed records of user actions. After the test session, the users answer a NASA-TLX survey to evaluate the cognitive workload of the tool. At this stage of the research, our method does not consider the results of the assessment of the understandability of formal notations, user interaction logs, and NASA-TLX. However, we plan to incorporate these aspects in future research phases. Finally, step 4 consists of *evaluating the artefacts produced by the end-users.* Software engineers receive a set of UML class diagrams, which they assess using a checklist.

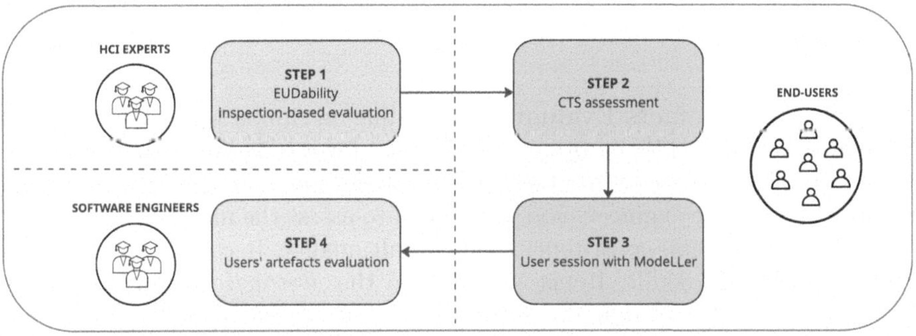

Fig. 1. Study procedure overview.

User Task on ModeLLer. Given the representational nature of the modelling activity, we designed an exploratory task—performed in step 3—in which end-users model a socio-technical system based on a scenario of agricultural digitalisation. The scenario, drawn from a real case within the CODECS project,

[1] The ModeLLer source code, along with a live demo and a video presentation, is available on GitHub: https://github.com/Unipisa/blockly-UML-modeller.

describes the introduction of a sensor-based system for monitoring greenhouse production. The task is divided into two subtasks: the first requires users to read a textual description, create a model from scratch, and export the produced diagrams; the second involves importing a model and extending the representation by adding elements similar to those introduced in the first subtask.

Table 1 outlines the structuring of the task designed by mapping the EUDability dimensions (column 1) to the tool features (column 2), and identifying corresponding actions to be performed by users (column 3). This mapping was intended to ensure that the task would cover all the EUDability dimensions, thereby enabling the observation of the associated CT skills.

Table 1. EUDability dimensions in ModeLLer mapped to user actions

EUDability dimension	ModeLLer feature	User action
Concreteness	Block-based visual language	Interact with blocks
Modularity	multiple blocks and fields within blocks	Use and customise multiple types of blocks
Structuredness	Three-phase model creation	Execute steps: 1) selection; 2) drag and drop; 3) export
Reusability	Import and export	Execute import and export
Testability	Output visualisation and edit	Edit and revise content, extend a previous model

Checklist for Artefacts Evaluation. Building on similar approaches applied in previous research [15], we propose a checklist for a tailored evaluation of the artefacts produced by users interacting with ModeLLer. The checklist is applied in step 4 by software engineers and is designed to assess the models—specifically evaluating correctness, consistency, and overall quality. It consists of 15 items mapped to five CT skills. Items 1–3 refer to the *abstraction* skill and assess the inclusion of relevant domain entities, the informativeness of the model, and the representation of meaningful relationships between the elements within the model. Items 4–6 assess the *decomposition* skill, examining whether the model contains multiple element types, avoids redundancies, and provides adequate detail. Items 7–9 refer to the *algorithm design* skill and evaluate whether the user has completed all necessary steps to finish the task and deliver the output. Items 10–12 assess the *generalisation*, evaluating if the second model produced is an extension of the pre-defined model and maintains consistency with the first model. Items 13–15 assess the *evaluation* skill, focusing on the overall correctness, accuracy and consistency of the model. The checklist is administered as follows: for each case to evaluate, software engineers receive two UML class diagrams, which are the output of the user task, and complete the checklist by assigning *Yes* or *No* response to each item.

4 User Study

To evaluate the proposed method, we carried out a user study involving 21 participants, comprising 15 end-users, which participated in steps 2 and 3, and 6 experts, involved in steps 1 and 4. The end-users had no prior experience with ModeLLer, and most had little to no expertise in formal notations. Among the experts, three had expertise in HCI and five in software engineering and formal languages, with two individuals possessing both areas of expertise. These two experts participated in both steps 1 and 4.

Participants were recruited on a voluntary basis using a snowball sampling technique. The sample of end-users consisted of Italian participants, 60% of whom were male, with an age range of 25 to 34 years. The team of experts included four males and two females, aged between 30 and 50. All data were collected and managed anonymously, in full compliance with data protection regulations and with respect for participant privacy.

During this research phase, we engaged a small number of participants to test our method and minimise the evaluation effort, which resulted in preliminary findings. In the future, we aim to expand the study to include more end-users.

Following the procedure outlined in Sect. 3.2, the study was articulated in four steps. In *step 1*, three HCI experts first explored the tool individually; then, they participated in a debriefing session, answering the EUDability checklist. In *step 2*, end-users completed the CTS questionnaire and provided demographic information. In *step 3*, end-users conducted individual sessions on the tool, supported by a moderator. The moderator introduced the activity, presented the video training, and provided access to a local installation of ModeLLer. The users followed the task proposed and completed the session autonomously, generating multiple models. In this study, UML class diagrams are the only object of analysis, as will be illustrated in Sect. 4.1. *Step 4* involved five software engineers who assessed 30 UML models following the artefacts evaluation checklist. Each expert evaluated six cases, resulting in a double evaluation for each model. The evaluations were then averaged to provide a comprehensive assessment.

4.1 Results

1) EUDability of ModeLLer. The results of step 1 are contained in Table 2, column *Level*. In light of these results, following previous studies [2], column *Min. CT Level* presents the required CT levels for ModeLLer.

2) Users' CT Skills. Table 3 presents the results of the CTS questionnaire administered in step 2. Following the same approach proposed in previous studies [2], the final column *Av. result*, combined with the column *Min. CT Level* in Table 2 suggest that ModeLLer is suitable for end-users participating in the test since they own the minimum CT level required for using the tool.

Table 2. Required CT levels for ModeLLer

EUDability	Level	Min. CT Level	CT skill
Concreteness	mid	mid	Abstraction
Modularity	high	low	Decomposition
Structuredness	mid	mid	Algorithm design
Reusability	high	low	Generalisation
Testability	high	low	Evaluation

Table 3. TSAI responses and average

	Low	Medium	High	Av. result
Abstraction	-	8	7	mid
Decomposition	-	8	7	mid
Algorithm design	-	4	11	high
Generalisation	1	7	7	mid
Evaluation	-	5	10	high

3) Users' Models. Results from step 3 show that all the users completed the task, producing a total of 90 models—30 UML class diagrams, 30 BPMN process diagrams, and 30 iStar goal diagrams. In this study, we focus on the UML class diagrams, using them as the input for step 4.

4) Artefacts Evaluation. Results from the artefact evaluation conducted in step 4 were compared with the CTS scores collected in step 2 to identify possible relationships between users' models and self-assessed CT skills levels. Visual inspection of subplots revealed that *abstraction* and *algorithm design* dimensions showed relatively stable CTS scores across all artefact evaluation levels. *Decomposition* and *generalisation* also spanned all three levels, though *generalisation* had fewer high-score instances, while decomposition had fewer low-score ones. An example of *decomposition* can be seen in Fig. 2. In contrast, the *evaluation* dimension showed generally lower artefact-based scores.

We ran statistical tests to explore these trends. The Shapiro-Wilk test indicated that CTS scores were not normally distributed ($p = 0.0103$), prompting the use of a Kruskal-Wallis test, which suggested a significant difference between at least one pair of groups ($p = 0.0271$). Dunn's post-hoc test revealed a significant difference between low and mid groups ($p = 0.0344$) within *decomposition.*

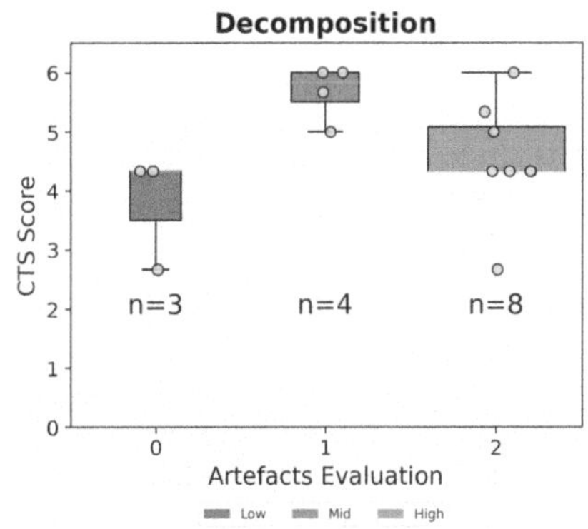

Fig. 2. CTS vs artefacts evaluation bins for decomposition.

5 Discussion and Future Work

Results reveal a misalignment between CTS and artefact-based evaluations. This may suggest that users overestimated their CT levels. Moreover, the variability of results may illustrate the possible role of the EUD tool in supporting individual dimensions. This, in turn, may lead to targeted improvements of ModeLLer. For example, the tool could be enhanced to better support the aspect of *testability*, i.e., the EUDability dimension associated with evaluation.

Although these findings may be affected by the limitations of the current study—namely, the small dataset, which results in preliminary findings with limited statistical significance, and the potential biases in the evaluation method—there is still methodological significance by providing further empirical support to previous research [4], emphasising the importance of evaluating CT skills from multiple, integrated perspectives.

Future work will expand the study to a larger group of end-users, including domain experts and practitioners, and will incorporate process-based evaluation using user interaction logs. This will allow for a deeper analysis of how CT skills manifest during modelling and support the development of adaptive tool features that scaffold end-users according to their varying needs and backgrounds.

6 Limitations

This study has several limitations. First, the small sample size limits generalisability, with the participants not fully representing the diversity of the user population. Second, the artefact-based evaluation is time-consuming, and the checklist, while tailored, is not a standardised instrument. Finally, the proposed evaluation method is context-specific and not generalisable to other EUD tools.

7 Conclusion

This paper investigated the potential of an artefact-based approach to evaluating CT skills within the EUDability framework. We proposed a multi-step evaluation method applied to ModeLLer, a block-based modelling tool for end-users. Building on prior work [2,3,18], our approach combined inspection-based evaluation of ModeLLer using the EUDability checklist and the CTS questionnaire to assess users' CT skills. Then, a user study was conducted, and end-users completed a task designed to elicit five core CT skills—abstraction, decomposition, algorithm design, evaluation, and generalisation. Finally, the resulting models were evaluated using a checklist aligned with these CT dimensions, compiled by expert software engineers. Our findings confirm the complexity of assessing CT and highlight the value of integrating artefact-based evaluation to gain deeper insights into CT and modelling practices. Future work will explore additional perspectives to further refine the evaluation method.

Acknowledgments. Research partly funded by the European Union's Horizon Europe research and innovation programme under grant agreement no. 101060179.

References

1. CODECS. https://www.horizoncodecs.eu/. Accessed 11 Aug 2024
2. Barricelli, B., Fogli, D., Gargioni, L., Locoro, A., Valtolina, S.: Towards the unification of computational thinking and eudability: two cases from healthcare (2024)
3. Barricelli, B., Fogli, D., Locoro, A.: Eudability: a new construct at the intersection of end-user development and computational thinking. J. Syst. Softw. **195**, 111516 (2023). https://doi.org/10.1016/j.jss.2022.111516
4. Brennan, K., Resnick, M.: New frameworks for studying and assessing the development of computational thinking. In: Proceedings of the 2012 Annual Meeting of the American Educational Research Association. Vancouver, Canada, vol. 1, p. 25 (2012)
5. Cheng, Y.P., Lai, C.F., Chen, Y.T., Wang, W.S., Huang, Y.M., Wu, T.T.: Enhancing student's computational thinking skills with student-generated questions strategy in a game-based learning platform. Comput. Educ. **200**, 104794 (2023). https://doi.org/10.1016/j.compedu.2023.104794, https://www.sciencedirect.com/science/article/pii/S0360131523000714
6. Denning, P.J., Tedre, M.: Computational thinking: a disciplinary perspective. Inform. Educ. **20**(3), 361 (2021)
7. DiSessa, A.A.: Computational literacy and "the big picture" concerning computers in mathematics education. Math. Thinking Learn. **20**(1), 3–31 (2018)
8. Fagerlund, J., Häkkinen, P., Vesisenaho, M., Viiri, J.: Computational thinking in programming with scratch in primary schools: a systematic review. Comput. Appl. Eng. Educ. (2020). https://doi.org/10.1002/cae.22255
9. Hsu, T.C., Chang, S.C., Hung, Y.T.: How to learn and how to teach computational thinking: suggestions based on a review of the literature. Comput. Educ. 126, 296–310 (2018). https://doi.org/10.1016/j.compedu.2018.07.004, https://www.sciencedirect.com/science/article/pii/S0360131518301799

10. Lieberman, H., Paternò, F., Klann, M., Wulf, V.: End-user development: an emerging paradigm. In: Lieberman, H., Paternò, F., Wulf, V. (eds.) End User Development. Human-Computer Interaction Series, pp. 1–8. Springer, Cham (2006)
11. Mannari, C., Anichini, E., Bacco, M., Ferrari, A., Turchi, T., Malizia, A.: Modeller - enabling end-users to model systems: a case study in digital agriculture. In: CoPDA@AVI (2024). https://api.semanticscholar.org/CorpusID:270069004
12. Mannari, C., Bacco, M., Spagnolo, G.O., Malizia, A., Ferrari, A.: Towards a method for modelling socio-technical process transformation in digital agriculture. In: REW, pp. 306–315. IEEE (2024)
13. Merisotis, J.: Human work in the age of smart machines. Rosetta Books (2020)
14. Moody, D.L., Heymans, P., Matulevičius, R.: Visual syntax does matter: improving the cognitive effectiveness of the i* visual notation. Requirements Eng. **15**(2), 141–175 (2010). https://doi.org/10.1007/s00766-010-0100-1
15. Moreno-León, J., Román-González, M., Harteveld, C., Robles, G.: On the automatic assessment of computational thinking skills: a comparison with human experts. In: Proceedings of the 2017 CHI Conference Extended Abstracts on Human Factors in Computing Systems. CHI EA 2017, pp. 2788–2795. Association for Computing Machinery, New York (2017). https://doi.org/10.1145/3027063.3053216
16. Selby, C., Woollard, J.: Computational thinking: the developing definition (2013). https://eprints.soton.ac.uk/356481/. conference Paper
17. Tedre, M., Denning, P.J.: The long quest for computational thinking. In: Proceedings of the 16th Koli Calling International Conference on Computing Education Research. Koli Calling 2016, pp. 120–129. Association for Computing Machinery, New York (2016). https://doi.org/10.1145/2999541.2999542
18. Tsai, M.J., Liang, J.C., Hsu, C.Y.: The computational thinking scale for computer literacy education. J. Educ. Comput. Res. **59** (2020). https://doi.org/10.1177/0735633120972356
19. Turchi, T., Fogli, D., Malizia, A.: Fostering computational thinking through collaborative game-based learning. Multimedia Tools Appl. **78**(10), 13649–13673 (2019). https://doi.org/10.1007/s11042-019-7229-9
20. Wing, J.: Computational thinking. Commun. ACM (2006)
21. Wing, J.M.: Research notebook: Computational thinking–what and why? Carnegie Mellon School of Computer Science (2011). https://www.cs.cmu.edu/link/research-notebook-computational-thinking-what-and-why

Scenario-Based Design Tools: From End-User Reflections to Requirements

Benjamin Cham(✉) and Genovefa Kefalidou

University of Leicester, Leicester, UK
{btc10,gk169}@leicester.ac.uk

Abstract. Scenario-Based Design (SBD) processes often struggle with biases, overgeneralization, and limited inclusivity, when designing for complex domains like Autonomous Vehicles (AVs). Through focus groups with non-technical end-users, this study defines requirements for SBD End-User Development (EUD) tools. By thematically analyzing and affinity mapping transcript and note data from 16 participants that engaged with a typical SBD workflow, five core needs for SBD software are identified: (1) context-rich foundations, (2) dynamic persona templates, (2) real-time scenarios reflecting socio-behavioral edge-cases, (3) strong persona-scenario synthesis and natural end-user interaction, (4) explainable and transparent interactions, and (5) data-driven yet interpretable processes and outputs. Findings suggest how EUD design tools can balance human creativity and input with computational rigor, enabling designers to iteratively refine designs while ensuring transparency, inclusivity, and explainability.

Keywords: scenario-based design · automated persona development · user requirements · data-driven design contextualization

1 Introduction

Scenario-Based Design (SBD) provides a narrative framework for envisioning how users interact with emerging technologies by scoping (contextualization), eliciting requirements, prototyping, and evaluating these technologies [1, 2]. By constructing rich, context-based scenarios, designers can uncover both functional, user, and contextual needs [3]. Additional techniques are employed in SBD such as personas [4, 5] and contextual inquiry [3] that allow user motivations, behaviors, and environments to inform these scenarios. Traditionally used HCI methods (e.g., focus groups, ethnographic studies, interviews) have proven effective for improving usability and user experience by encouraging more User-Centered Design (UCD) [6]. However, disruptive technologies, such as Autonomous Vehicles (AVs), AI-driven healthcare, and advanced robotics, demand more adaptive design methods as high-stakes systems require trust and real-time adaptability to all persons [7, 8], exceeding capabilities of static HCI/UCD methods [9, 10], that are vulnerable to biases and homogeneity. This gap underscores the need to integrate data-driven AI solutions into traditional UCD processes to handle complexity, scale, and rapid technological change when designing for diverse user groups, thereby

C. Santoro et al. (Eds.): IS-EUD 2025, LNCS 15713, pp. 322–330, 2025.
https://doi.org/10.1007/978-3-031-95452-8_20

enabling more equitable human-centered design. Current SBD tools focus primarily on scenario visualization [11, 12], and persona generation [13] but do not consider scenario-persona relationships or provide data-driven collaborative ideation or justifications with users. On the other hand, purely data-driven methods risk losing empathic qualities of traditional SBD if not integrated thoughtfully [7]. Therefore, hybrid approaches (i.e., merging human-centered narrative with AI-driven analytics) are needed to capture real-time, context-rich data, maintaining user empathy critical to designing acceptable and trustworthy technologies [8].End-User Development (EUD) lowers barriers for non-technical stakeholders (e.g., designers) to adapt or extend software like generation of design artifacts [14, 15]. In domains like AVs, EUD principles can make early HCD more equitable, transparent, and trustworthy by using AI [9, 16]. Therefore, there is need to understand how non-technical end-users expect to engage with design software to overcome UCD limitations with AI-supported EUD tools.

In this study, we elicit design requirements for data-driven EUD-based tools to support SBD for disruptive technologies by conducting a deductive thematic analysis and affinity mapping of participants' reflections and feature suggestions given an engaged typical SBD workflow. This contributes to EUD literature by establishing how non-technical end-users expect software to support them in designing for complex HCD-requiring technologies in the future.

2 Methodology

2.1 Participants

A total of 16 participants (10 male, 6 female) were recruited using word-of-mouth and snowball sampling methods. Participants were between 18 and 65 years old (M = 31.1, SD = 13.5), and none had professional experience or education in technology design. Sessions included between three and five participants per group. Ethical approval was granted by the institutional review board, and participants received online vouchers for compensation.

2.2 Procedure and Data Collection

This study reports findings from a subset of data collected during four separate 75-min focus group sessions where a conventional SBD workflow for AVs was completed. Each session followed a structured three-phase workflow whereby SBD contextualization was completed by 1) discussing perceived key AV acceptance factors, and 2) AV PACT (People, Activities, Context, Technologies) brainstorming [17], where participants discuss and brainstorm people doing activities in contexts using technologies. Beginning with discussion of AV acceptance factors and then the PACT brainstorming provided a wide scoping discussion about AVs, sufficiently enabling contextual inquiry. Then, participants were introduced to typical next steps in where personas and scenarios are typically defined using contextualized data, before 3) reflecting on stages 1 and 2, and recommending how software could support the SBD contextualization and requirements elicitation using personas and scenarios. Data presented in this paper relates entirely to stage 3 in which reflections and recommendations are made by participants as verbatim (for reflections) or in written form (recommendations). Deductive thematic analysis was chosen because in the previous stages (i.e. trust and acceptance discussion and PACT brainstorming) specific themes had already emerged and during the reflective activities a deductive method allowed for a "deep dive" into the pre-determined categories. Affinity mapping was then chosen to facilitate a grouping technique for the outputs of the deductive thematic analysis.

2.3 Data Analysis

Figure 1 presents the mixed-methods analysis in which a deductive thematic analysis [18] presents a thematic overview of SBD reflections and recommendations from all data artifacts (n = 63).

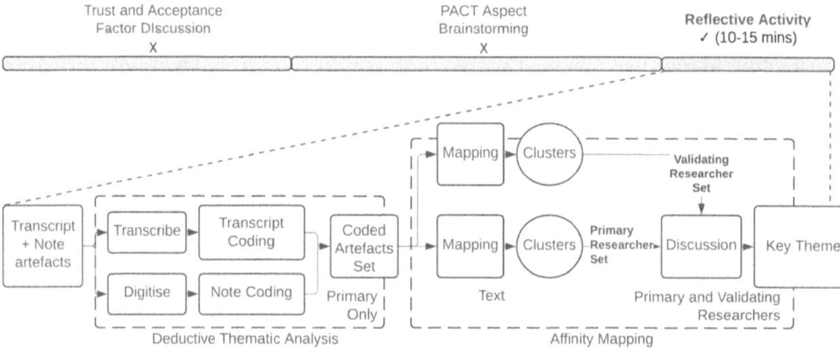

Fig. 1. Overview of study; showing where data is sourced (i.e., the end of an SBD workflow), how data is first transcribed and thematically coded by primary, followed by being affinity mapped and validated; in the end, a set of requirements were elicited based on the generated clustered themes.

An additional benefit brought by the deductive thematic analysis was in contextually grounding data artifacts between the primary and validating researcher, given SBD knowledge variability between primary/validating researchers, when completing affinity mapping [19]. Here, final clusters, representative of SBD reflections and EUD recommendations, were defined by both primary/validating researchers independently clustering the whole dataset before resolving conflicting artifact assignments through discussion in which similar clusters as determined by artifact co-occurrence and independently named themes were merged over a period of 1h 30 min, passing over clusters until primary/validating researcher agreement was made. This approach was chosen to triangulate qualitative insights, providing both breadth and depth to clustered sets [20], whilst limiting biases through deductive contextual coding (see Table 1) for deductively coded artifact example).

Table 1. Example of Deductively Analyzed Artifact in which potential codes are provided by primary researcher prior to affinity mapping.

Session	ID	Data	Potential Codes
04	P0	"Reaction time info from different personas"	Persona Reaction Time, Safety Factors

3 Results and Discussion

This study aimed to identify EUD requirements for SBD tools through deductive thematic analysis and affinity mapping reflections and recommendations from a completed conventional SBD process.

3.1 Deductive Thematic Overview

The deductive thematic analysis shows key conventional SBD reflections and future tool considerations from codes, summarized in Table 2.

Table 2. Overview of Deductive Thematic Analysis with reflections in quotations and SBD suggestions in italics only.

Themes	Key Codes (Deductive)	Example Artifact
Biased Consensus (T1)	Bias/Homogeneity, Participant Profile, Missing Contrasting Opinions	*"We are all from the University so this would be making us biased." (P3); "People are educated people who might think similarly about acceptance."* (P2)
Designers' Conceptual Model Bias (T2)	Overgeneralization, Lack of Nuance, Missing Contrasting Opinions	*"Generalizations about defined personas"* (P7) and *Include Thought Processes - Why someone would be accepting?* (P2),
Mental Model Variations as Constraints (T3)	Varying Knowledge Levels, Contextual Variation	*"Basically, half automated... could be perceived differently depending on knowledge"* (P5)
Persona-Centric Design (T4)	Persona-First Approach, Persona-Linking, Persona Motivation	*"It would make sense to make personas first, then attach these to design considerations"* (P3)
Scenario Multimodality (T5)	Scenario Visualization, Multimedia Representation, Diagrammatic Output	*"Some sort of visual/diagram representation of results"* (P7)
Examples for Realistic Problem-Solving (T6)	Realistic Scenario Outcomes, Problem-Solving Logic, Concrete Vehicle Examples	*"Show realistic outcomes"* (P16); *"Specific examples of a vehicle and how it would work"* (P12)
Context Awareness (T7)	Usability, Tool Adaptability, Concise UI	*"Straight to the point and does not create pages of stuff to read"* (P7)
Trustworthiness (T8)	Transparency, Explainability, Accuracy	Emphasis on clear communication of assumptions, data sources, and safety (P10); "Explainability" (P5)

8 key coded themes were identified. T1 (Bias and Homogeneity) highlights how a narrow participant pool can skew the SBD process, exemplified by remarks on shared

university backgrounds. T2 (Designers' Conceptual Model Bias) underscores the danger of overgeneralizing user needs and missing contrasting viewpoints in SBD. T3 (Mental Model Variations) points to differing expertise and contexts, making uniform assumptions problematic. For SDB tool recommendations, T4 (Persona-Centric Design) emphasizes starting with user personas for authenticity and empathy. T5 (Scenario Multimodality) calls for visual or multimedia outputs to clarify and engage. T6 (Examples for Realistic Problem-Solving) stresses the need for concrete, context-specific scenarios, while T7 (Context Awareness) suggests concise and adaptable UIs. Finally, T8 (Trustworthiness) emphasizes transparency, explainability, and clear communication of underlying assumptions to foster user confidence.

3.2 Themes to Requirements

Now, to establishing succinct yet actionable requirements for EUD-supporting SBD tools primary/validating researchers independently affinity mapped the dataset before comparing and merging similar clusters. Six major clusters emerged from discussion. Each cluster translated directly into actionable requirements (R) described in Table 3.

Table 3. Affinity Mapped Requirements

Requirement Description	Example Artifacts
Data Contextualization as Foundation (R1). Focuses on minimizing bias and overgeneralization by integrating rich contextual data (e.g., user behavior, environment, operational constraints). Ensures realism in scenario design, especially important for safety-critical contexts like AVs	*"We are all from the University so this would be making us biased."* (P3), *"We are possibly all more on the acceptor side because we all work in sciences... But those not from university have different thoughts."* (P6) *"Similar ages as well..."* (P5). *"Scenarios and personas should be adaptability/Moldable from the data"* (P7)
Diverse, Adaptive, and Reactive Personas (R2). Emphasizes creating nuanced, representative personas (including vulnerable or stressed users) that adapt to diverse real-world scenarios. Ensures that differing backgrounds, motivations, and stress levels are accounted for, reflecting the full breadth of user experiences	*The stresses the persona is under should be understandable and realistic* (P14), *Reaction times from different personas should be different* (P14), *"should have varied metrics like level of Persona security"* (P1), *Regarding information: the positives/negatives, and safety are important* (P10)
Intuitive Persona-Scenario Interaction (R3). Highlights the need for visual or multimedia presentations (e.g., diagrams, videos) to illuminate complex persona–scenario relationships. Encourages interactive elements that link personas to specific conditions, aligning with low-code or end-user development tools	*"Some sort of visual/diagram representation of results."* (P7), Scenario videos (P4) *"Conversation with acceptor/rejector... challenge views"* (P13), *Ask people if they would use different AVs based on details given about the cars based on testing done* (P9), *Present some specific scenarios to encourage discussion* (P10)
Usability, Transparency, and Explainability (R4). Stresses clear, intuitive interfaces that show why certain outputs occur (e.g., AI-generated personas, recommended design choices). Calls for "low-threshold" usability for non-experts and transparency to avoid a "black box", thereby fostering user trust and enabling easy validation and debugging of system logic	*Accuracy in tool* (P5), *Explainability* (P5), *Tool should show realistic outcomes with realistic problem solving* (P16), *You could have a large margin and have some explanations* (P14) referring to how to see design context information, *Speech-to-text* (P8), *"Straight to the point and does not create pages of stuff to read"* (P7)
Balancing Data Complexity with Interpretability (R5). Advocates combining data-rich insights (e.g., sensor or operational data) with user-friendly presentation. Helps non-technical designers handle complex scenarios without getting overwhelmed. Reflects EUD's challenge of hiding technical depth while still supporting meaningful exploration and decision-making	*Data Management* (P5), *Synonym/thesaurus recognition* (P8), *Come up with personas find and attach to statements* (P6), *Include thought processes (Why someone would be accepting)* (P2), *"More specialized options for PACT individually, one not specified enough)* (P6) when describing ability to modify PACT, "Adaptability/Moldability... (context-specific scenario creation)" (P7)

Data Contextualization as Foundation (R1). Participants noted that homogeneous participants and overgeneralized scenarios risk bias (e.g., *"We are possibly all more on the acceptor side"*; P6). Incorporating rich, contextual data—user behaviors, environmental conditions, operational parameters—can mitigate these issues and enhance realism, critical for AV safety and trust [2, 7]. EUD literature advocates end-user-friendly tools for importing real-world datasets (e.g., sensor logs, online discourse) without programming expertise [21–23]. Fischer's meta-design framework underscores iterative refinement by domain experts, while Automated Persona Generation (APG) systems [24] illustrate automated personas but often lack robust bias mitigation. Embedding ethical guardrails (e.g., bias detection) can enable diverse personas and scenarios, for instance, by flagging missing age groups.

Diverse, Adaptive, and Reactive Personas (R2). Participants stressed the need for nuanced, diverse personas that adapt to varying contexts (e.g., *"need to involve vulnerable personas"*; P16) and that exhibit realistic stress responses (e.g., *"the stresses the persona is under should be understandable and realistic"*; P14). Building on R1's data foundation, SBD literature cautions that static or homogeneous personas can overlook critical differences, advocating "reactive personas" that respond dynamically within scenarios (e.g., tech-savvy vs. tech-averse in an AV-equipped city). In line with EUD principles [22, 25], tools should let domain experts iteratively refine personas with real-time data, rules, or triggers (e.g., lower interaction complexity if persona is elderly) [26]. However, many SBD tools still treat personas as fixed artifacts, limiting their ability to evolve and remain representative of shifting user behaviors.

Intuitive Persona-Scenario Interaction (R3). Participants requested visual and multimedia scenario presentations to clarify complex interactions (e.g., *"scenario videos"*; P4). This resonates with EUD's focus on low-code, visual interfaces where effective scenario design should directly link personas to conditions, employing interactive visualizations to enhance understanding and engagement [2]. Blackwell's Cognitive Dimen sions (2000) [27] stress that tools should minimize cognitive load through metaphors like storyboards or flowcharts, critical for non-programmers mapping personas to scenarios and in a modern sense, Large Language Models (LLMs) could now illustrate persona-scenario relevance through natural interactions. However, LLMs as a means of enabling SBD interpretations, have yet to be explored but have potential to be well suited for disruptive technologies in which persona-scenario relationships are complex [28].

Usability, Transparency, and Explainability (R4). Participants prioritized clear, intuitive, and trustworthy interfaces. Explainability has become especially prominent with the rise of AI-driven systems [16]. In HCI and AI literature, it's well documented that users (and designers) need visibility into how and why the system produces certain results. Ko et al. (2011) [25] argue that end-user tools must provide "why?" explanations for system outputs (e.g., AI-generated persona suggestions). Usability is paramount because the target users are non-technical. End-user programming, and development, environments must have "low thresholds" to entry (so novices can start using them quickly) [23]. Transparency also involves showing what the tool is doing behind the scenes as a lack of transparency (the "black box") can alienate end users and by providing feedback and explanations to users so they can validate and debug their work

[25]. For any SBD tool advanced features (like AI-generated persona suggestions or simulation of outcomes) the system must be transparent for user trust by explaining *why* it suggested a particular persona behavior, *how* it derived a trend from data and *show* data sources and functions to allow self-validation.

Balancing Data Complexity with Interpretability (R5). Participants highlighted the importance of balancing robust, data-rich insights with clear human interpretability (e.g., simplified interactions like "speech-to-text"; P8). Scenario-based EUD tools should present sensor-rich data clearly and intuitively, empowering non-technical domain experts to confidently explore scenarios. This dual emphasis, integrating detailed data into user-friendly interfaces, is crucial in enabling informed decision-making in complex scenarios, reflects EUD's core challenge: hiding technical complexity without sacrificing depth [23].

Requirements establish a basis for EUD-supportive SBD tools that could benefit the design of disruptive technologies with each requirement relating to at least 1 deductive theme (see Table 4).

Table 4. Affinity mapped cluster requirements relation to general deductive themes.

Requirement	Mapping to Thematic Analysis Outputs
Data Contextualization as Foundation (R1)	Directly responds to themes of Biased Consensus (T1) and Designers' Conceptual Model Bias (T2) by addressing participant/scenario homogeneity generalization through inclusive data context
Diverse, Adaptive, and Reactive Personas (R2)	Corresponds to Persona-Centric Design (T4), emphasizing the creation of diverse and contextually responsive personas
Intuitive Persona-Scenario Interaction (R3)	Links clearly with Scenario Multimodality (T5)), recommending multimedia scenario presentations for enhanced clarity and
Usability, Transparency, and Explainability (R4)	Addresses Context Awareness (T7) and Trustworthiness (T8), and realistic problem solving (T6) emphasizing intuitive interaction and clear, trustworthy interfaces
Balancing Data Complexity with Interpretability (R5)	Responds to Mental Model Variations as Constraints (T3), prioritizing clear interpretation and user-friendly presentations of complex data

These requirements collectively address EUD's central tenet: empowering domain experts (e.g., AV designers) as designers of their own tools. By integrating data contextualization with ethical guardrails (R1) and adaptive personas (R2), future tools can democratize scenario design while mitigating biases. The emphasis on usability (R4) and interpretability (R5) further ensures tools align with EUD's gentle learning curve philosophy [25]. Beyond AVs, this framework applies to healthcare (patient journey scenarios) and smart cities (inclusive urban simulations), advancing EUD's vision of participatory, human-centered design.

4 Limitations

This study acknowledges notably the inherent subjectivity of qualitative participant-based research and sample homogeneity. For example, the use of affinity mapping introduces subjectivity and potential incomplete groupings. Whilst inter-rater reliability was adhered to by affinity mapping and discussion it would be usual to perform a quantitative reliability analysis. However, given the mixed-method it would not be possible for the validator to have coded without being provided the contextual deductive codes. Deductively coding artifact context aimed to narrow this variability whilst preventing biases in affinity mapping; the limitation that introduced however was lack of flexibility in capturing emerging themes, therefore introducing limited capture of data and analyses nuances Furthermore, another limitation is the potential presence of confirmational biases, something which will be addressed in future studies.

5 Conclusion

This study identified five key end-user requirements for next-generation SBD tools, emphasizing adaptive personas, rich contextual grounding, intuitive interactions, explainable AI, and interpretability. Future research should validate these findings through SBD tool development and evaluation and by mobilizing complementary methods to reduce biases.

Interests. The authors have no competing interests to declare that are relevant to the content of this article.

References

1. Carroll, J.M.: Making Use: Scenario-Based Design of Human-Computer Interactions. MIT Press (2003)
2. Rosson, M.B., Carroll, J.M.: Usability Engineering: Scenario-Based Development of Human-Computer Interaction (2002)
3. Beyer, H., Holtzblatt, K.: Contextual design: defining customer-centered systems. San Francisco, Calif.: Morgan Kaufmann (1998)
4. Adlin, T., Pruitt, J.: The Essential Persona Lifecycle: Your Guide to Building and Using Personas. (2010). https://doi.org/10.1016/C2009-0-62475-2
5. Cooper, A., Reimann, R., Cronin. D.: About Face 3: The Essentials of Interaction Design, Third Edition, John Wiley & Sons, Inc. (2007)
6. Gulliksen, J, Göransson, B., Boivie, I., Blomkvist, S., Persson, J., Cajander, Å.: Key principles for user-centred systems design. Behav. Inf. Technol. **22**, 397–409 (2003). https://doi.org/10.1080/01449290310001624329
7. Endsley, M.R.: From here to autonomy: lessons learned from human-automation research. Hum. Factors **59**, 5–27 (2017). https://doi.org/10.1177/0018720816681350

8. Forlizzi, J.: Moving beyond user-centered design. Interactions **25**, 22–23 (2018). https://doi.org/10.1145/3239558
9. Hoff, K.A., Bashir, M.: Trust in automation: integrating empirical evidence on factors that influence trust. Hum. Factors **57**, 407–434 (2015). https://doi.org/10.1177/0018720814547570
10. Lee, J.D., See, K.A.: Trust in automation: Designing for appropriate reliance. Hum. Factors **46**, 50–80 (2004). https://doi.org/10.1518/HFES.46.1.50_30392
11. Dosovitskiy, A., Ros, G., Codevilla, F., Lopez, A., Koltun, V. CARLA: an open urban driving simulator, pp. 1–16 (2017). https://doi.org/10.48550/arXiv.1711.03938
12. Safety Pool Scenario Database. https://www.safetypool.ai/database. Accessed 12 Mar 2025
13. User Persona Creator Tool | Customer Persona Builder. https://uxpressia.com/personas-online-tool. Accessed 12 Mar 2025
14. Lieberman, H., Paternò, F., Wulf, V.: End User Development, vol. 9 (2006). https://doi.org/10.1007/1-4020-5386-X
15. Nardi, B.A.: A Small Matter of Programming: Perspectives on End User Computing, vol. 162 (1993)
16. Shneiderman, B.: HUMAN-CENTERED AI. Human-Centered AI 1–388 (2022). https://doi.org/10.1093/oso/9780192845290.001.0001
17. Benyon, D., Turner, P., Turner, S.: Designing interactive systems: people, activities, contexts, technologies (2005)
18. Braun, V., Clarke, V.: Using thematic analysis in psychology. Qual. Res. Psychol. **3**, 77–101 (2006). https://doi.org/10.1191/1478088706QP063OA
19. Holtzblatt, K., Beyer, H.: Contextual Design: Design for Life. Morgan Kaufmann, Amsterdam (2017)
20. Cresswell, J.W., Plano, C.V.L.: Designing and Conducting Mixed Method Research. 2nd Sage. Thousand Oaks (2017)
21. Fischer, G.: User modeling in human-computer interaction. User Model User-Adapt Interact. **11**, 65–86 (2001)
22. Fischer, G., Fogli, D., Piccinno, A.: Revisiting and broadening the meta-design framework for end-user development. New Perspect. End-User Dev. 61–97 (2017). https://doi.org/10.1007/978-3-319-60291-2_4
23. Myers, B., Hudson, S.E., Pausch, R.: Past, present, and future of user interface software tools. ACM Trans. Comput. Hum. Interact. **7**, 3–28 (2000)
24. Jansen, B., Salminen, J., Jung, S., Guan, K.: Data-Driven Personas. Synthesis Lectures on Human-Centered Informatics, 14:i–317. https://doi.org/10.2200/S01072ED1V01Y202101HCI048 (2021)
25. Ko, A.J., et al.: The state of the art in end-user software engineering. ACM Comput. Surv. (CSUR) **43**, 44 (2011). https://doi.org/10.1145/1922649.1922658
26. Salminen, J., Jansen, B.J., An, J., Kwak, H., Jung, S.: Are personas done? Evaluating their usefulness in the age of digital analytics. Persona Stud. **4**, 47–65 (2018). https://doi.org/10.21153/PSJ2018VOL4NO2ART737
27. Blackwell, A.F., et al.: Cognitive Dimensions of Notations: Design Tools for Cognitive Technology. Lecture Notes in Artificial Intelligence (Subseries of Lecture Notes in Computer Science), vol. 2117, pp. 325–341 (2001). https://doi.org/10.1007/3-540-44617-6_31
28. Koopman, P., Wagner, M.: Autonomous vehicle safety: an interdisciplinary challenge. IEEE Intell. Transp. Syst. Mag. **9**, 90–96 (2017). https://doi.org/10.1109/MITS.2016.2583491

Defining Classes and Semantic Relationships from User Scenarios Through a Heuristic Approach

A. D. Hafiza Aunsa[1], Vita Santa Barletta[2], Paolo Buono[2], C. M. Nadeem Faisal[1,2], Antonio Piccinno[2](✉), Zafar Saeed[2], and Luciana Provenzano[3]

[1] Department of Computer Science, National Textile University, Faisalabad, Pakistan
[2] Department of Computer Science, University of Bari, Bari, Italy
{vita.barlett,paolo.buono,nadeem.faisal,antonio.piccinno, zafar.saeed}@uniba.it
[3] Division of Computer Science and Software Engineering, Mälardalen University, Vasteras, Sweden
luciana.provenzano@mdu.se

Abstract. End-User Development includes approaches, tools, techniques, and environments that empower end users or non-programmers to create and customize software systems as per their needs without requiring technical expertise. The participation of the end user in transforming the user scenarios into a UML diagram is critical to ensure clarity and completeness of the specification by minimizing ambiguities. The current study proposes a heuristics-based approach to extract the classes and relationships from user scenarios using natural language processing by engaging the end user to ensure the correctness of UML modeling. The End-User Development is integrated with proposed techniques that empower the non-technical users to review, create, and specify the input contextual complexity, enabling seamless software modeling. This study collected 120 user scenarios from five systems of different domains with equal distribution over three categories (i.e., low, medium, and high) to extract the classes and relationships. In the evaluation protocol, the proposed approach, experts, and end users are independent of each other for all user scenarios. The results based on the accuracy measure revealed that the proposed approach performs 22% and 13% better than the evaluation performed by the end users and experts, respectively, highlighting the need for the proposed approach to act as a supportive tool to enhance further engagement in EUD.

Keywords: end user development · natural language processing · software requirements · unified modeling language · user scenarios

1 Introduction

Requirement engineering is an integral part of software engineering that helps to extract specifications to build software systems that meet stakeholders' demands

C. Santoro et al. (Eds.): IS-EUD 2025, LNCS 15713, pp. 331–343, 2025.
https://doi.org/10.1007/978-3-031-95452-8_21

and expectations [1,2]. One of the main challenges in engineering is transforming textual requirements, usually expressed in everyday (plain) language, into formalized models for analysis, design, and implementation. A popular standard notation for modeling software systems is UML. It provides a collection of graphical structures for defining system structure and behavior. User scenarios refer to short stories that explain unique system interactions and behavior from the end-users perspective. They are descriptive and valuable sources of requirements in the field of software development. However, translating these user scenarios into UML models, such as class diagrams, is still considered a challenging and effortful activity [3]. Inviting end users to extract, design, and analyze software specifications is crucial to ensure completeness and clarity by minimizing ambiguities. The integration of End-User Development (EUD) will help non-technical individuals view, modify, and refine the input to change the model description and design the software model as per their needs. User scenarios that are usually described in the natural language are primarily incomplete, unclear, and subjective, making it difficult to extract precise specifications [4,5]. Moreover, converting these descriptive and textual scenarios into formal UML models can be time-consuming and error-prone for software developers [6]. A semantic gap exists between natural language descriptions of user scenarios and structured UML models. Bridging this gap is critical to assuring the accuracy and fidelity of the final UML representations [7,8] as extracting semantic relationships from user scenarios is expensive and labor-intensive, especially in large-scale software projects with numerous and complex requirements [9]. Misinterpretation of user scenarios can cause misplaced expectations between stakeholders and software developers, impeding efficient communication and collaboration [10]. Thus, involving end users in the ML system to verify the specification and further validate the output generated from the automated techniques will be a powerful strategy to support the requirements engineering with the integration of EUD methodologies. Because EUD allows end users to alter, modify, and change designs to suit their needs [11]. In this perspective, our work focuses on the principles of End-User Development (EUD) by enabling non-technical users to actively participate in shaping system behavior through scenario-based feedback. End users influence system functionality by categorizing scenario complexity and providing contextual input, which directly informs how the system adapts to different use cases. This reflects the core EUD Goal of empowering end users to adjust and tailor technology to their needs without requiring technical expertise. UML is used as a structured, semi-formal representation that connects user intents with system-level artifacts, even though it is not widely adopted in all software development contexts. In this study, UML is used illustratively rather than prescriptively to show how structured models can be derived from end-user input. An NLP-based model makes it easier to extract UML connections (such as composition and aggregation) from natural language scenarios, decreasing human labor, improving modeling accuracy, productivity, and scalability, and allowing the end user to access the output to adjust with the decision making process of software developer as per their needs. Complete automation of requirement translation can limit user understanding, but we address this concern by proposing a feedback loop where users review and revise auto-generated specifications supporting reflective engagement rather than passive consumption. The contribution of this study is to propose a method to define the classes and semantic relationships from user scenarios seeking design comprehension to improve engagement between end users and automation with the support of EUD. Ultimately, this study could lead to more practical work with less uncertainty and miscommunication by improving software development methods in academia and industry.

2 Background

User scenarios may lack structure or clarity due to the ambiguity in natural language, which is one of the current research concerns. This might result in inaccurate UML relationship extraction [12]. It is also challenging to ensure high accuracy and a broad view since complex sentence structures and domain-specific terminology may be complex for current NLP models to handle. Nasiri et al. developed an automated method to generate UML class diagrams from user stories in Agile methods [13]. They used the computation-independent model to platform-independent model transformation and evaluated it using the NLP tool Stanford Core NLP. The evaluation is based on a case study, and the dataset is qualitative and self-created, focused on a specific domain. They defined extraction rules for actors, classes, and attributes and proposed an algorithm to extract class diagrams with an accuracy of 80%. They suggested that enhancing this approach with artificial intelligence techniques could also help generate cardinalities in class diagrams. Abdelnabi et al. proposed a method to create class models from software specifications using NLP and heuristic rules [14]. They used a five-phase approach, i.e., normalization of natural language text, processing of natural language requirements, applying and mapping heuristic rules to extract UML class elements, clarification of results, generating UML class models, normalizing complex requirements into simple ones using NLP techniques. The qualitative dataset was used with syntactic rules. Moreover, they used UMGAR to generate UML class models by reducing the time and cost of manual design with an accuracy of 75%. They also suggested NLP-based techniques to improve relationship attribute type dependency. A summary of the background studies related to approaches for defining classes and relationships is presented in Table 1. Ibrahim et al. developed a method for extracting class diagrams and requirement analysis from natural language requirements using NLP and domain ontology techniques [15]. They used OpenNLP for annotations, the RACE stemming algorithm for efficiency, and the class extraction engine module for heuristic rules. They specifically used a class identification framework as a dataset. The RACE tool efficiently generates a human-centred UML class model with implicit relationships, which has an accuracy of 83%. They argued that explicit relationships with all dependencies (one to many, one to one, many to many) can be found using advanced NLP techniques, but not with RACE.

Table 1. Relevant studies in literature

Reference	Year	Dataset	Technique
Nasiri [13]	2020	Qualitative (Self-Created)	Standford Core NLP Tool
Abdelnabi [14]	2020	Qualitative (Syntactic Rules)	Heuristic Rule & Umghar Tool
Ibrahim [15]	2010	Theoretical Framework	RACE Stemming Algorithm
Joshi [16]	2012	Theoretical Framework	OpenNLP parser Technique
Robeer [17]	2016	Qualitative (Self-Created)	State of the Art Heuristics & Visual Narrator Tool
Shweta [18]	2018	Qualitative (Use Case Template)	Conversation Rules Method
Bashir [19]	2021	Standardize (Domain Ontologies)	Requirement Engineering Analysis and Design Technique
Gupta [20]	2017	Qualitative (Self-Created)	Transformation Rules and Parts of Speech Method
Rensik [21]	2021	Qualitative (Self-Created)	Graph-based Notions
Chen [22]	2022	Quantitative (Domain Specific)	Customized Design Approach

Joshi et al. developed the requirement analysis and UML diagram extraction (RAUE) methodology for generating UML diagrams from requirement specifications [16]. They used object-oriented analysis, the OpenNLP parser technique, WordNet, and a filtering algorithm to identify and correct parts of speech (POS) tags for each word in requirement sentences. They adopted a theoretical framework, RAUE, as the dataset specification and extracted UML class diagrams using domain ontologies with an accuracy of 82.7% and suggested that enhancing RAUE with artificial intelligence can efficiently find semantic relationships among class entities. Robeer et al. proposed an algorithm incorporating state-of-the-art heuristics and implementing the Visual Narrator Tool (VNT) [17]. Using heuristic rules, they extracted meaningful conceptual models from the natural language requirements. Moreover, they employed heuristics, deriving the models from user stories and natural language requirements. The evaluation was based on heuristic rules, and the dataset is qualitative and self-created, focused on a specific domain. The authors evaluated user stories and developed a conceptual model using the visual narrator tool, which had an accuracy of 85% with high precision and recall. Shweta et al. introduced an intermediate template that transforms the use case description into a UML class diagram by rule extraction procedure [18]. They converted the use case description template into predefined conversation rules. They evaluated the template use case descriptions as a qualitative dataset, applied the class diagram extraction rules, and identified the class diagram elements with an accuracy of 79%. They suggested using human intervention to refine the automated class diagram extraction in this proposed approach. Bashir et al. proposed a system requirement engineering analysis and design technique to generate UML class diagrams using NLP techniques and domain ontologies [19]. They processed the user scenario and split it into sentences and word tokens. Their evaluation is based on analysing the standardized requirements through domain ontologies. They extracted nouns and pronouns and identified the actors and attributes with an accuracy of 88%. Moreover, they suggested that this approach can be enhanced by automatically extracting multicity and semantic relationships from UML class diagrams.

Gupta et al. presented an automated technique for transforming English-documented use case specifications into analysis class diagrams [20]. They evaluated the text specifications of use cases as input and generated parts of speech for each sentence using NLP. The evaluation was based on a use case specifications document, a qualitative approach. They applied the transformation rules to parts of speech and discovered the objects, actors, and relationships between them, with an accuracy of 80.5%, and suggested that this approach can only deal with simple sentences and can extend to compound sentences. Kleppe and Rensink proposed a graph with UML concepts like multiplicity and containment [21]. They used graph notions as a dataset evaluation. In addition, they evaluated graph-based notions and identified dependencies of the UML class diagram with an accuracy of 78%. They further argued that this approach does not provide all the semantics of the UML class diagram between objects. Chen et al. proposed design models for extracting semantics from UML class diagram images [22]. They used a customized design approach (ReSEDI) by embedding images and identifying the relationships from them, which had an accuracy of 85.6%. They suggested that this approach can be extended by evaluating complex multiplicities between attributes and classes.

In addition to automatic UML generation, EUD integration is also critical to strengthening the use of machine learning in software design. Barricelli et al. argue that EUD is a growing field that assists end users, novice designers, and beginners [23]. Costabile et al. emphasized that the involvement of end users in development facilitates them to alter and modify the system as per their needs [24]. Similarly, Weina et al. proposed an end-user-friendly AI framework, categorizing AI decision explanations into feature attributes, instances, and decision trees [25]. These studies highlight the growing potential of end users in making AI-based systems more adaptable and user-driven. Several studies also emphasize the supportive role of EUD and its integration in enhancing the capabilities of AI-based software and environments [26–30]. Barricelli et al. emphasized the need to determine the association between EUD and Computational Thinking to find new practices for the future of workplaces [29]. They further argue that providing appropriate tools and techniques to support EUD is a coping strategy for future changes. Fischer argues that EUD is unique and valuable in coping with problems; hence, determining design trade-offs between EUD and AI with possible integration is required to explore further possibilities [26]. Esposito et al. discussed the potential benefits and challenges of AI and EUD, emphasizing integration in addressing future challenges [27]. They emphasized the use of EUD in the development of AI systems, enabling users to personalize services to meet their needs.

Our work aligns with prior research in requirements engineering and NLP, where heuristics are commonly employed to guide pattern recognition, relationship extraction, and linguistic structuring [14]. In our approach, heuristics are implemented as keyword-driven rules (e.g., detecting ‘contains’ for compositions or ‘part of’ for aggregations), grounded in commonly accepted UML semantics and object-oriented modeling principles. These rules were manually crafted based on recurring patterns in the input scenarios and reflect informed assumptions rather than guaranteed logical deductions, which is why we describe our method as heuristic.

3 Methodology

A rule-based NLP model is employed to automatically identify class relationships (associations, aggregations, and compositions) from textual user scenarios, as shown in Fig. 1. Initially, the acquired data is organized into scenarios. End users engage with the collected user scenarios to provide contextual feedback, which helps to assess and categorize the complexity of each scenario into three distinct levels (i.e., low, medium, and high). For instance, after reviewing a scenario such as "*An employee forgets the login protocol to access restricted data.*", the user may assign it a 'high' complexity rating and add a comment explaining that it involves multiple policy violations. This feedback is then used to refine the scenarios in future iterations. This user input simplifies the scenarios, eliminating any ambiguities that may have been introduced during the data collection and scenario construction phases. A dataset of user scenarios was categorized into three complexity levels: Low, Medium, and High. End users were instructed with clearly defined criteria: 'Low' complexity scenarios contained simple, single-action clauses, 'Medium' scenarios involved two or more related actions or mild ambiguity, and 'High' complexity referred to scenarios with multiple actors, decision-making conditions, or implicit dependencies. Three users independently rated each scenario. In cases where ratings differed, a majority vote was used to assign the final complexity label. If no majority emerged (e.g., 1 Low, 1 Medium, 1 High), a subject matter expert reviewed the scenario to make the final decision. This ensured consistency in labeling and provided a solid foundation for assessing model performance. The primary motivation behind

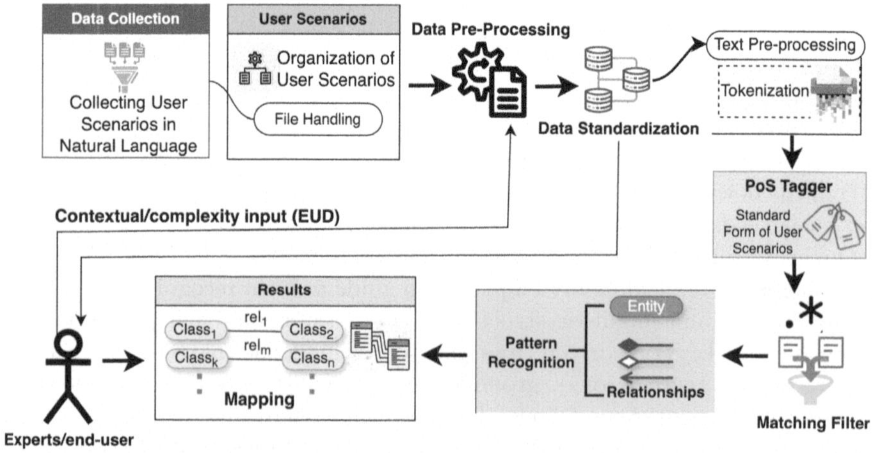

Fig. 1. Flow diagram of the proposed Methodology.

this complexity-based classification is twofold: firstly, it allows for a direct comparison between the accuracy of the proposed methodology and the results provided by experts or end users; secondly, it positions the proposed system as a supportive tool that encourages engagement and interest among end users in the system's design and development process. Next, each scenario is segmented into sentences, and word tokens, and tagged with part-of-speech (PoS). Class names are extracted through a hybrid method that identifies capitalized words, which are then filtered using POS-tagged nouns (NN, NNP, NNPS) to ensure syntactic validity. Relationships are classified using keyword-driven heuristics: compositions are detected with terms such as *"contains"* or *"has,"* aggregations with *"part of"* or *"collection,"*. After processing a scenario data set, which is divided into three categories based on clause complexity: *Low, Medium, and High,* Finally, the system-generated class-relationship triples (Class-A, Relationship, Class-B) were evaluated against a manually curated ground truth using exact-match accuracy, calculated as the true positives divided by the total reference triples. This method automates the generation of UML-like relationships from unstructured text by integrating linguistic rules, syntactic heuristics, and human-informed classification for complexity calibration. The step-by-step execution of methodology is described in Algorithm 1.

Dataset: A diverse user scenario was gathered for five different systems (i.e., Online Product Purchasing, Hotel Booking System, Healthcare Management System, Gym Membership System, and University Enrollment System) to create a well-curated dataset comprised of 100 scenarios distributed over three complexity levels, i.e., low, medium, and high. These scenarios are synthetic but were carefully designed to reflect common real-world user interactions and domain-specific practices. They simulate realistic requirements and behaviors typically observed in practical software development contexts. The use of synthetic scenarios allows for controlled evaluation while maintaining high relevance to actual industry use cases. The scenarios were designed to encompass a diverse range of relationship types, including associations, aggregations, and compositions, based on commonly observed patterns in general object-oriented modeling. Scenario design ensures that each relationship type was well represented across different contexts and complexity levels. This qualitative approach aimed to simulate realistic modeling in practical software development. The ground truth for evaluating the extracted UML relationships was manually constructed

Table 2. Dataset statistics describing class and relationship distribution.

		No. of Classes				No. of Class Relatioships			
No. System	User Scenarios	Low	Medium	High	Unique	Low	Medium	High	Unique
1 Online Product Purchasing	20	23	21	19	18	19	14	6	18
2 Hotel Booking System	20	15	14	17	19	16	11	8	19
3 Healthcare Management System	20	16	16	14	22	12	10	9	18
4 Gym Membership System	20	15	15	16	20	18	8	11	23
5 University Enrollment System	20	24	22	20	20	17	13	12	23
Total	**100**	**93**	**88**	**86**	**99**	**82**	**56**	**46**	**101**

Algorithm 1. Extract classes and relationships

Require: User Scenarios $FILE$ and Ground Truth G as a set (Triples)
Ensure: Class relationships T as a set of triples, and Accuracy A.

```
function PROCESS_DATA(FILE, G)
scenarios = read_data(FILE)
C_r_C ← [ ]
R^co ← {"contain","compose of","part of","has","consist of","own"}
R^ag ← {"belong to","collection of","group of","aggregate","is a member of"}
R^as ← {"associate with","work with","relate to","depend on","link to"}
for each U IN scenarios do
    C_r_C ← EXTRACT-CLASS-RELATIONSHIPS(U, R^co, R^ag, R^as)
    T.Add(U, C_r_C)
end for
Accuracy ← evaluate(T, G)
Return T, Accuracy

function EXTRACT-CLASS-RELATIONSHIPS(U, R^co, R^ag, R^as)
T ← [ ]
S ← sent_tokenize(U)
for each st In S do
    if st Is NULL then
        continue
    end if
    st ← lemmatize_captalization(st)    ▷ retains capitalization while lemmatizing
    tks ← word_tokenize(st)
    tagged_words ← pos_tag(tkn)
    names ← FILTER(tagged_words, tag ∈ {NN, NNP, NNPS})
    C ← capitalized_words(tks) ⋂ names    ▷ candidate classes
    if |C| ≥ 2 then
        s̄t ← st
        for i = 1 to |C| − 1 do
            pos^c1 ← s̄t.loc(C_i)    ▷ Class_1 position in the sentence
            pos^c2 ← s̄t.loc(C_{i+1})    ▷ Class_2 position in the sentence
            phrase = s̄t.substring(pos^c1, pos^c2)
            if R^co match phrase then
                T.add((C_i, "composition", C_{i+1}))
            else if R^ag match phrase then
                T.add((C_i, "aggregation", C_{i+1}))
            else if R^as match phrase OR pattern(C_i, tag ∈ {VB,VBP,VBZ}, C_{i+1})
    then
                T.add((C_i,"association", C_{i+1}))
            end if
            s̄t ← s̄t.substring(pos^c2 + len(C_{i+1}), len(s̄t))
        end for
    end if
end for
remove_redundancy(T)
Return T
```

by the authors based on the original user scenarios. Each scenario was carefully analyzed to identify the intended class relationships (association, aggregation, composition) using standard object-oriented design principles. To ensure accuracy and consistency, these ground truth annotations were cross-validated by two expert researchers in software modeling. In case of disagreements or ambiguities, decisions were made through consensus based on UML design standards. While the ground truth is manually curated, we ensured high internal validity through expert verification. The details of the dataset with the class and relationship distribution concerning three complexity levels are shown in Table 2. Column *Unique* shows the distinct classes and class relationships across all three types of scenarios. *Data Pre-Processing:* In high complexity user scenarios, the

sentences are formed with complex language clauses, therefore, we use spaCy[1] library for effective sentence segmentation due to the rule-based system combined with machine learning models to determine sentence boundaries. Furthermore, a lemmatizer was used to transform words into base form while retaining the capitalization and separating words in tokens. Next, NLTK[2] based part-of-speech (PoS) tagging is used to find noun phrases that are potentially class names. Then, capitalized words are extracted which eliminates unnecessary keywords and leaves just meaningful entity names.

Data Standardization: It is applied to reduce inconsistency in capitalization, spacing, or small lexical differences while standardizing entity names, relationship labels, and structural forms, as shown. To ensure that they conform to the appropriate entries in the ground truth, class names taken from user scenarios are transformed into a uniform case. Primarily, expert contextual and complexity input is used for standardization and simplifying user scenarios.

Evaluation Metric: The evaluation of the proposed model is conducted using accuracy as the primary performance metric, which measures the proportion of correctly identified relationships compared to the total ground truth relationships. Accuracy is calculated by dividing the number of correctly extracted relationships by the total number of relationships in the ground truth dataset. This metric provides a direct and intuitive assessment of the model's effectiveness in identifying associations, aggregations, and compositions between classes within user scenarios.

4 Results and Discussion

For the model's evaluation, 100 user scenarios were selected with three distinct types, categorized as; Low, Medium, and High user scenarios based on clause complexity. In the evaluation protocol, the proposed approach, experts, and end users are independent of each other for all user scenarios for estimating the

[1] spaCy - A Python-based natural language processing library: https://spacy.io/.

[2] NLTK - A Pytha on-based natural language processing library: https://www.nltk.org/.

Table 3. Performance (Accuracy) comparison of the proposed approach with expert and end user based on three scenario types across five systems.

	System	Scenario Complexity Type Low	Medium	High
Experts	Online Product Purchasing	87%	82%	80%
	Hotel Booking System	84%	80%	80%
	Healthcare Management System	85%	81%	79.00%
	Gym Membership System	82.30%	84%	81%
	University Enrollment System	86%	84%	81%
End-user	Online Product Purchasing	79%	76.20%	74%
	Hotel Booking System	78%	74%	74%
	Healthcare Management System	77%	77%	73%
	Gym Membership System	79.60%	74.30%	74%
	University Enrollment System	80%	75%	74%
Proposed	Online Product Purchasing	96%	95%	92%
	Hotel Booking System	97%	94%	92.70%
	Healthcare Management System	96%	94.30%	91%
	Gym Membership System	96%	95%	93%
	University Enrollment System	96%	94.60%	93%

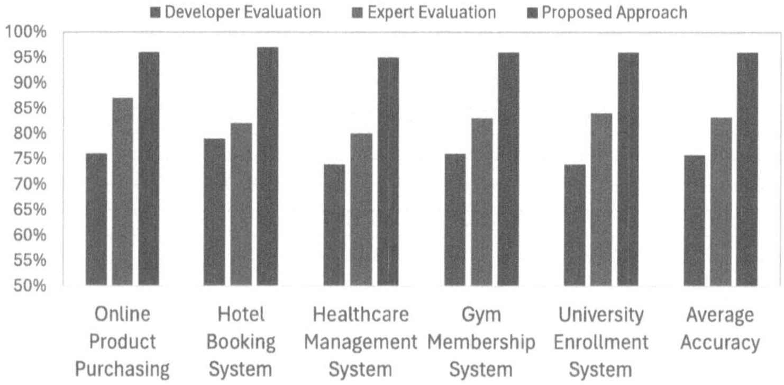

Fig. 2. Comparison of average accuracy of the proposed approach with expert and end user across five systems.

results. The detailed results are shown in Table 3. The results indicate that the proposed system achieved higher average accuracy relative to both expert and end user evaluations across all scenarios and complexity levels, achieving 96% score (see Fig. 2. Experts generally scored higher than end users, with an average accuracy of 83%, while end users scored 76%. This suggests that the proposed method extracted more correct class relationships and can serve as a reliable approach to support decision-making for EUD. The proposed method makes it easier to generate UML class diagrams automatically, by efficiently extracting semantic associations from natural language user scenarios. The method detects associations, aggregations, and compositions. However, its dependence on pre-set linguistic patterns, narration, and contextual complexity makes it less flexible regarding intricate sentence structures and domain-specific terminology. The results based on the accuracy measure revealed that the proposed approach performs 22% and 13% better than the evaluation performed by the end users and experts, respectively, highlighting the need for the proposed approach to act as a helpful tool to enhance further engagement with the support of EUD. Lastly, the method performs well in controlled contexts, managing unclear relationships and context-dependent phrases, but diverse sentence structures can affect the precision of extraction, underscoring the necessity for more sophisticated linguistic processing.

5 Conclusion and Future Work

EUD is useful for empowering novice users with software modeling without requiring technical expertise. The current study proposed a heuristic approach to extract the classes and relationships from user scenarios using NLP by engaging the end user to ensure the correctness of UML modeling. Therefore, the integration of the EUD with the proposed approach was a key objective. This study collected 100 user scenarios from five systems of different domains distributed over three categories (i.e., low, medium, and high) to extract the classes and relationships. The evaluation suggests that the proposed method could be used to support EUD. Accuracy is computed using an exact-match criterion, where all incorrect predictions are treated equally, which is a limitation of the proposed method. In future work, we plan to incorporate transformer-based models, such as BERT, into the NLP pipeline to improve the relationship extraction by identifying more profound semantic dependencies and ranked similarities to distinguish between minor and major mismatches. Lastly, creating an interface having a console or GenAI service that facilitates the end user to input queries & responses will improve the proposed approach's usefulness in software engineering processes and for the creation of well-structured, clear, and accurate UML class diagrams.

References

1. Laplante, P.A., Kassab, M.: Requirements Engineering for Software and Systems. Auerbach Publications (2022)
2. Sanyal, R., Ghoshal, B., et al.: A hybrid approach to extract conceptual diagram from software requirements. Sci. Comput. Program. **239**, 103186 (2025)
3. Anastasakis, K., Bordbar, B., Georg, G., Ray, I.: On challenges of model transformation from UML to alloy. Softw. Syst. Model. **9**(1), 69–86 (2010)
4. Zhao, X., et al.: A comprehensive survey on relation extraction: recent advances and new frontiers. ACM Comput. Surv. **56**(11), 1–39 (2024)
5. Ramzan, M., Sadiqi, G.S., Bashir, M.S., Raza, S., Batool, A.: A rule-based approach for automatic generation of class diagram from functional requirements using natural language processing and machine learning. J. Comput. Biomed. Inform. **7**(02) (2024)

6. Meng, Y., Ban, A.: Automated UML class diagram generation from textual requirements using NLP techniques. JOIV: Int. J. Inform. Vis. **8**(3-2), 1905–1915 (2024)
7. Arora, C., Sabetzadeh, M., Briand, L., Zimmer, F.: Extracting domain models from natural-language requirements: approach and industrial evaluation. In: Proceedings of the ACM/IEEE 19th International Conference on Model Driven Engineering Languages and Systems, pp. 250–260 (2016)
8. Bozyigit, F., Bardakci, T., Khalilipour, A., Challenger, M., Ramackers, G., Babur, Ö., Chaudron, M.R.: Generating domain models from natural language text using NLP: a benchmark dataset and experimental comparison of tools. Softw. Syst. Model. 1–19 (2024)
9. Ambriola, V., Gervasi, V.: Processing natural language requirements. In: Proceedings 12th IEEE International Conference Automated Software Engineering, pp. 36–45. IEEE (1997)
10. Barabás, P., Kovács, L.: Requirement analysis of the internal modules of natural language processing engines. In: 2012 IEEE 10th International Symposium on Applied Machine Intelligence and Informatics (SAMI), pp. 41–46. IEEE (2012)
11. Tzafilkou, A.: Behavioral user modeling for web and cloud end-user development environments (2018). http://dspace.lib.uom.gr/handle/2159/22323
12. Das, S., Deb, N., Cortesi, A., Chaki, N.: Extracting goal models from natural language requirement specifications. J. Syst. Softw. **211**, 111981 (2024)
13. Nasiri, S., Rhazali, Y., Lahmer, M.: Towards a generation of class diagram from user stories in agile methods. In: Advancements in Model-Driven Architecture in Software Engineering, pp. 135–159. IGI Global (2021)
14. Abdelnabi, E.A., Maatuk, A.M., Abdelaziz, T.M., Elakeili, S.M.: Generating UML class diagram using NLP techniques and heuristic rules. In: 2020 20th International Conference on Sciences and Techniques of Automatic Control and Computer Engineering (STA), pp. 277–282. IEEE (2020)
15. Ibrahim, M., Ahmad, R.: Class diagram extraction from textual requirements using natural language processing (NLP) techniques. In: 2010 Second International Conference on Computer Research and Development, pp. 200–204. IEEE (2010)
16. SD Joshi and Dhanraj Deshpande: Textual requirement analysis for UML diagram extraction by using NLP. Int. J. Comput. Appl. **50**(8), 42–46 (2012)
17. Robeer, M., Lucassen, G., Van Der Werf, J.M.E., Dalpiaz, F., Brinkkemper, S.: Automated extraction of conceptual models from user stories via NLP. In: 2016 IEEE 24th international requirements engineering conference (RE), pp. 196–205. IEEE (2016)
18. Shweta, R.S., Ghoshal, B.: Automated class diagram elicitation using intermediate use case template. IET Softw. **15**(1), 25–42 (2021)
19. Bashir, N., Bilal, M., Liaqat, M., Marjani, M., Malik, N., Ali, M.: Modeling class diagram using NLP in object-oriented designing. In: 2021 National Computing Colleges Conference (NCCC), pp. 1–6. IEEE (2021)
20. Thakur, J.S., Gupta, A.: Automatic generation of analysis class diagrams from use case specifications. arXiv preprint arXiv:1708.01796 (2017)
21. Kleppe, A.G., Rensink, A.: A Graph-Based Semantics for UML Class and Object Diagrams. Number TR-CTIT-08-06 in CTIT Technical Report Series. Centre for Telematics and Information Technology (CTIT), Netherlands (2008)
22. Chen, F., Zhang, L., Lian, X., Niu, N.: Automatically recognizing the semantic elements from UML class diagram images. J. Syst. Softw. **193**, 111431 (2022)
23. Barricelli, B.R., Cassano, F., Fogli, D., Piccinno, A.: End-user development, end-user programming and end-user software engineering: a systematic mapping study. J. Syst. Softw. **149**, 101–137 (2019)

24. Costabile, M.F., Fogli, D., Mussio, P., Piccinno, A.: Visual interactive systems for end-user development: a model-based design methodology. IEEE Trans. Syst. Man Cybern. Part a: Syst. Hum. **37**(6), 1029–1046 (2007)
25. Jin, W., Carpendale, S., Hamarneh, G., Gromala, D.: Bridging AI developers and end users: an end-user-centred explainable AI taxonomy and visual vocabularies. In: Proceedings of the IEEE Visualization, Vancouver, BC, Canada, vol. 20, p. 25 (2019)
26. Fischer, G.: Adaptive and adaptable systems: differentiating and integrating AI and EUD. In: Spano, L.D., Schmidt, A., Santoro, C., Stumpf, S., (eds.) End-User Development, pp. 3–18. Springer, Cham (2023)
27. Esposito, A., et al.: End-user development for artificial intelligence: a systematic literature review. In: Spano, L.D., Schmidt, A., Santoro, C., Stumpf, S. (eds.) End-User Development, pp. 19–34. Springer, Cham (2023)
28. Fischer, G.: End-user development: empowering stakeholders with artificial intelligence, meta-design, and cultures of participation. In: Fogli, D., Tetteroo, D., Barricelli, B.R., Borsci, S., Markopoulos, P., Papadopoulos, G.A. (eds.) IS-EUD 2021. LNCS, vol. 12724, pp. 3–16. Springer, Cham (2021). https://doi.org/10.1007/978-3-030-79840-6_1
29. Barricelli, B.R., Fogli, D., Locoro, A.: EUDability: a new construct at the intersection of end-user development and computational thinking. J. Syst. Softw. **195**, 111516 (2023)
30. Stegner, L., Porfirio, D., Hiatt, L.M., Lemaignan, S., Mead, R., Mutlu, B.: End-user development for human-robot interaction. In: Companion of the 2024 ACM/IEEE International Conference on Human-Robot Interaction, HRI 2024, pp. 1355–1357. Association for Computing Machinery New York (2024)

Author Index

C. Santoro et al. (Eds.): IS-EUD 2025, LNCS 15713, pp. 345–346, 2025.
https://doi.org/10.1007/978-3-031-95452-8

The manufacturer's authorised representative in the EU is Springer Nature Customer Service Centre GmbH, Europaplatz 3, 69115 Heidelberg, Germany. If you have any concerns regarding our products, please contact ProductSafety@springernature.com

Printed and bound by CPI Group (UK) Ltd, Croydon, CR0 4YY

30/09/2026

02225585-0004